UTOPIAN EFFECTS, DYSTOPIAN PLEASURES

Ralahine Utopian Studies

Volume 21

PETER LANG
Oxford · Bern · Berlin · Bruxelles · New York · Wien

Peter Fitting

UTOPIAN EFFECTS, DYSTOPIAN PLEASURES

Edited by Brian Greenspan
Introduction by Fredric Jameson

PETER LANG
Oxford · Bern · Berlin · Bruxelles · New York · Wien

Bibliographic information published by Die Deutsche Nationalbibliothek
Die Deutsche Nationalbibliothek lists this publication in the Deutsche Nationalbibliografie; detailed bibliographic data is available on the Internet at http://dnb.d-nb.de.

A catalogue record for this book is available from the British Library.

Library of Congress Cataloging-in-Publication Data

Names: Fitting, Peter, 1940- author. | Greenspan, Brian, 1967- editor. | Jameson, Fredric, writer of introduction.
Title: Utopian effects, dystopian pleasures / Peter Fitting ; edited by Brian Greenspan ; introduction by Fredric Jameson.
Description: Oxford ; New York : Peter Lang, [2021] | Series: Ralahine utopian studies, 1661-5875 ; vol 21 | Includes bibliographical references and index. | Summary: "This collection brings together for the first time Peter Fitting's writings about the utopian impulse as expressed in science fiction, fantasy, cinema, architecture, and cultural theory. These wide-ranging essays trace the constant reconsideration of the utopian project itself over the past four decades, from its mid-twentieth century period of decline to its revival in counter-cultural science fiction of the 1960s and '70s, its second decline with the "dystopian turn" in film, and the rise of feminist pessimism in the 1980s. These pages reveal what popular utopian, dystopian, and science-fiction narratives tell us about today's most pressing political issues, including gender equity, education reform, technological change, capitalist excess, state-sanctioned violence, and the challenges of effecting lasting political change. Through analyses of various popular genres and media, the author demonstrates how utopian visions written from particular political perspectives transcend narrowly partisan concerns to stoke our collective desire for another world and a more adequate human future, teaching us how to become the citizens and subjects that a utopian society demands"– Provided by publisher.
Identifiers: LCCN 2020032836 (print) | LCCN 2020032837 (ebook) | ISBN 9781788743532 (paperback) | ISBN 9781788743549 (ebook) | ISBN 9781788743556 (epub) | ISBN 9781788743563 (mobi)
Subjects: LCSH: Utopias in literature. | Utopias in motion pictures. | Science fiction–History and criticism. | LCGFT: Essays.
Classification: LCC PN56.U8 F58 2021 (print) | LCC PN56.U8 (ebook) | DDC 809/.93372–dc23
LC record available at https://lccn.loc.gov/2020032836
LC ebook record available at https://lccn.loc.gov/2020032837

Cover image: Tai Zimmer

ISSN 1661-5875

ISBN 978-1-78874-353-2 (print) • ISBN 978-1-78874-354-9 (eBook)

ISBN 978-1-78874-355-6 (ePub) • ISBN 978-1-78874-356-3 (mobi)

Published by Peter Lang Ltd, International Academic Publishers,
52 St Giles, Oxford, OX1 3LU, United Kingdom
oxford@peterlang.com, www.peterlang.com

For Lyman

Contents

Figures

Table

Acknowledgments

Like More's *Utopia*, this collection documents an extended dialogue between countless scholars, artists, and friends of the author who have helped to shape the field of Utopian Studies, and not all of whom could ever be acknowledged here. For my own part, I am thankful to Tom Moylan, with whom I first discussed the idea of the "Fitting Reader" some years back over dinner in Belfast, and who, along with Raffaella Baccolini and Michael Kelly of the Ralahine Utopian Series editorial board, ensured it would not remain a merely abstract utopian project. Nor could this volume have been realized without the skilled assistance of Anthony Mason, Christabel Scaife, and Philip Dunshea at Peter Lang. I am also grateful to Fredric Jameson, whose influence is tangible throughout many of these essays, for agreeing to pen the Introduction. Above all, I am indebted to Peter Fitting, who many years ago tracked me down within the cloisters of the University of Toronto, where I was laboring away on my doctorate, in order to discuss the pressing matter of hollow earth utopias. Over countless dinners and bottles of wine shared with he and Barb, Peter offered his friendship and guidance, showing me that I was already a utopian in spirit, and indoctrinating me into the mythical "Peter Fitting group." He also recruited me into the Society for Utopian Studies, where I've met so many brilliant and generous scholars who remain among my strongest influences and closest friends, and who together have guided my editorial judgment in preparing this volume.

The essays collected here were previously presented at many scholarly meetings around the world, or published in journals and collections:

Chapter 1 was originally published in *Science Fiction Studies* 6 (1979), 59–76.

Chapter 2 was presented at the Seventh Annual Conference of the Society for Utopian Studies, Saint John campus, University of New Brunswick, in September, 1982.

Chapter 3 is a revised version of a paper read at an international conference on "Teorie e Prassi Utopiche nell'Età Moderna e Postmoderna" cosponsored by the University of Rome and the University of Reggio Calabria in May 1986; and, in a different form, at the eleventh annual meeting of the Utopia Studies Association in Monterey California (October 1986). It appeared in Sociocriticism 7 (1988): 11–25, and in *Utopia e Modernità: Teorie e prassi utopiche nell'èta moderna e postmoderna*. Ed. Giuseppa Saccaro Del Buffa and Arthur O. Lewis. 2 vols. (Rome: Gangemi editore, 1989), 1: 541–52.

Chapter 4 is a revised version of a talk given at the 1989 meeting of the Society for Utopian Studies at Asilomar, in Monterey, CA, and appeared in *Utopian Studies* 2.1 & 2 (1991): 95–109.

Chapter 5 originally appeared in *Utopian Studies*, 7(2) (1996), 93–112.

Chapter 6 was originally published in *Arena Journal* 25/26 (2006), 37–51.

Chapter 7 was first published in *Science Fiction Studies* 36/1 (March 2009), 121–131.

Chapter 8 appeared in *Caliban* 22 (1985), 43–56, and in *Utopian Studies* 1 (1987), 23–36.

Chapter 9 originally appeared in *Science Fiction Studies* 12/2 (July 1985), 156–183.

Chapter 10 is an expanded and revised version of an article, "The Decline of the Feminist Utopian Novel," written for *Border/Lines* [Toronto] 7/8 (Spring/Summer 1987), 17–19. Earlier versions were presented at the Eaton Conference on Science Fiction and Fantasy held at the University of California at Riverside (April 1987) and at the twelfth annual meeting of the Utopia Studies Association at Media, Pennsylvania (October 1987).

Earlier versions of Chapter 11 were read at the annual meetings of the Society for Utopian Studies (Lexington, KY) and the Modern Language Association (Chicago), and at an international conference on "L'Utopie et ses métamorphoses" in Yverdon-les-Bains, Switzerland. This version was published in *Science-Fiction Studies* 19.1 (56) (March 1992): 32–48.

Chapter 12 is a revised version of a paper read at the 1993 meetings of the Popular Culture Association (New Orleans) and the Society for Utopian Studies (St. Louis), and appeared in *Utopian Studies* 5.2 (1994): 4–15.

Chapter 13 appeared in *Utopian Studies* 11/1 (2000), 91–108.

Chapter 14 is a revised version of a paper read at the annual meeting of the Society for Utopian Studies in Boston in October, 1988. It was published in *Utopian Studies* IV, Ed. Lise Leibacher-Ouvrard and Nicholas D. Smith (Lanham, MD: University Press of America, 1991), 90–96; and appeared in revised form in *Styles of Creation: Aesthetic Technique and the Creation of Fictional Worlds*, Eds. George Slusser and Eric S. Rabkin (Athens: University of Georgia Press, 1992), 153–64.

Chapter 15 is a longer version of a paper read at the sixteenth annual meeting of the Society for Utopian Studies, which appeared in *Utopian Studies* 4.2 (1993): 1–17.

Chapter 16 appeared as part of a Symposium on *Alien* with Jackie Byars, Jeff Gould, Peter Fitting, Judith Newton, Tony Safford, Clayton Lee, Charles Elkins and M.A., published in *Science Fiction Studies* 7/3 (November 1980), 278–304.

Chapter 17 is an expanded and revised version of a paper read at an international conference (July 1986) on "Philip K. Dick et la Science Fiction Moderne," cosponsored by the Université de Paris IV (Sorbonne), Le Centre Franco-Américain Universitaire (Paris), and the University of California at Riverside, and published in *Science-Fiction Studies* 14 (1987): 340–54.

Chapter 18 is a revised and expanded version of an article originally published in *Cineaction* 11 (Winter 1987–1988), pp. 42–51, and reprinted in George Slusser and Eric Rabkin, eds., *Fights of Fancy: Armed Conflict in Science Fiction and Fantasy* (Athens: University of Georgia Press, 1993, pp. 114–131).

Chapter 19 appeared in *Utopian Studies* 13/1 (2002), 69–93. The photographs of Chandigarh appear courtesy of the Fondation Le Corbusier.

Chapter 20 appeared in *Utopia Method Vision: The Use Value of Social Dreaming*, edited by Tom Moylan and Raffaella Baccolini (Oxford: Peter Lang, 2007), pp. 245–266.

Editor's Preface

This collection assembles twenty essays by Peter Fitting, Professor Emeritus of French and Cinema Studies at the University of Toronto, and a leading global expert in Utopian Studies. Written over a span of thirty years (1979–2009), these essays provide an unprecedented glimpse into the changing currents of utopian thought and expression in recent times, as well as the formation of both Utopian and Science Fiction Studies as scholarly fields in their own right, developments in which Fitting has been instrumental.

Throughout his career, Peter Fitting has been at the forefront of ongoing debates and developments in utopian literature, film, and popular culture. An active member of the Society for Utopian Studies since 1976, he served as President from 1994 to 1998, has organized more annual meetings than any other member, and keeps in close contact with the Society's Executive. This long-standing affiliation has brought Fitting into close contact with the field's most influential scholars over the years, including Darko Suvin, Ruth Levitas, Jean Pfaelzer, Fredric Jameson, Lyman Tower Sargent, Hoda Zaki, Kenneth M. Roemer, and Tom Moylan, to name just a few of the voices engaged within this volume. In fact, no matter what areas of Utopian Studies has interested Fitting at any given moment – whether it be eighteenth-century Norwegian literature, colonial architecture, postapocalyptic cinema, or lesbian biker fiction – the Society was for him always the most important experiment of all. He continues to serve as an Editorial Board member of the journal *Utopian Studies* and a Consultant for *Science Fiction Studies*, in which several of the chapters collected here were first published. Other essays were presented at meetings around the world, or have appeared in diverse journals and collections, in both French and English, many of which are currently out-of-print.

Many of these works have already taken on a life of their own as reprints and critical touchstones. Fitting's early work on the science fiction of Philip K. Dick was the subject of a 2001 feature article in *Lingua Franca*, which describes his visit to the famed author's California home in May of 1974. After that cordial afternoon discussing science fiction, the notoriously paranoid Dick wrote to J. Edgar Hoover's successor to warn about the "weird Marxist talk" of "the Peter Fitting group," which he believed was following orders from Stanislaw Lem (Heer 2001). While Fitting in fact never met the Polish author, his understanding of utopia has been informed by his long-standing personal connections with some of the most highly respected authors writing in the genre today, including Margaret Atwood, Peter Watts, Nalo Hopkinson, Carl Schroeder, and Kim Stanley Robinson, as well as many of the formative scholars of science fiction and utopia.

The utopian genre is a motley collection of eclectic projects and designs for living across the eras, and Fitting is at heart a collector – of lesser-known authors, rare books and stamps, industrial thrash albums, foreign films, and French wines. The essays collected here are similarly diverse in their subjects and concerns, yet coalesce around several major themes within Utopian Studies, including gender politics, technology, ideological closure, and the crucial question of how to transform utopian visions into social practice. These essays touch on numerous aspects of utopian and dystopian fiction, cinema, criticism and theory, raising questions about the meaning and value of Utopia in the twentieth and twenty-first centuries. Though written years apart, their concerns and theoretical approaches often overlap and intersect, returning to and reopening earlier debates with a fresh eye, and developing themes in a long theoretical arc that often extends over decades. Together, they weave a compelling account of the origins and development of Utopian Studies as a field over the past four decades.

As the first collection to bring Fitting's writings together in one place, *Dystopian Pleasures* will make his most influential and salient essays about utopian, dystopian, and science-fiction narratives available to a new generation of writers and scholars. The essays collected here are particularly notable for their approaches to twentieth- and twenty-first-century utopian fiction and film, including cyberpunk, space opera, invasion narratives, and feminist utopias. However, Fitting's range of reference is exceptionally broad, extending across the history of utopian literature, from Thomas More's *Utopia*, to eighteenth- and nineteenth-century writers and planners, to modernist and postmodernist SF, all the while making fascinating forays into architecture, popular music, and other media. This long historical view allows him to trace what he calls the constant "reconsideration of the utopian project itself," from its mid-twentieth-century period of decline to its revival and migration to SF in the 1960s and 1970s, followed by its second decline with the "dystopian turn" in film, and the rise of feminist pessimism in fiction of the 1970s and 1980s.

Re-reading these essays today, one cannot help but be struck by their relevance to current popular literature and film, which has for some time been dominated by decidedly pessimistic, dystopian, and anti-utopian visions, as Fitting shows in his chapters on utopian violence and postapocalyptic film. Even when exploring utopias of the 1960s, 1970s and 1980s in his "Short History of Utopian Studies," or discussing the role of men in feminist utopias, his essays have a strikingly contemporary and urgent tone that stems from their unwavering focus on the material effects of utopian expression on the here and now. Likewise, his chapters on the original *Alien* and *Blade Runner* films hold renewed interest following the recent reboots of these franchises, while his previously unpublished essay on "Contemporary Fantasy and the Utopian Impulse" sheds light on the significance of the current boom in fantasy novels, films, and TV shows.

These essays offer endless insights into the history of utopian novels and films, while constantly drawing connections to social and political issues of the day that remain just as relevant to the twenty-first-century reader: from women's rights and gender equity to violence and gun control, capitalist excess, education reform, the state of the publishing industry, Middle Eastern conflict, and the challenges of effecting lasting political change. Such considerations lead him to examine the full spectrum of utopian politics, ideologies, and modes of representation. Whether in his clear-eyed assessment of right-wing utopias as genuinely utopian, rather than merely satiric or anti-utopian in "Utopia Beyond Our Ideals," or in his insistence on comparing feminist and anti-feminist utopias in his "Reconsiderations of the Separatist Paradigm," Fitting never shies away from exploring the less obviously hopeful forms of social dreaming, the cultural surplus that exceeds the immediate mystifications of any given text. This unflinchingly dialectical approach ensures that Fitting's writing is attentive to the rise of new, ambiguous forms of utopian expression that depict "the struggle for utopia rather than the image of a finished and harmonious utopian society." His essays are ever alive to this struggle within utopianism itself, which is manifest in narratives that present only partial solutions, and that feature characters who (unlike the blithely happy mouthpieces of conventional utopias) are fully aware of the contradictions of their own society and subjectivity, yet uncertain of how to improve them.

Part I explores the history and development of utopian literature and film, with an emphasis on utopia both as narrative genre and as method of ideological and cultural critique. Whether discussing the history of "hollow earth" travel narratives (which he explores in his 2004 critical anthology, *Subterranean Worlds*), contemporary fantasy novels, or the disciplinary contours of Utopian Studies itself, these essays coalesce around the critique of capitalism, and an insistence on the urgency of searching for alternatives to the political status quo.

Part II has a dual focus. The central group of essays addresses the role of gender relations in utopian narratives by women, including cyberpunk novels, dystopias, novels about BDSM and violence, and feminist separatist novels that envision worlds by and for women which are largely devoid of male influence. The latter category inevitably raises questions of audience, and of whether or not such narratives need to appeal to readers of all genders. Accordingly, this group of essays is bookended by two chapters theorizing the reception of utopian narratives that challenge their readers' normative expectations. For readers immersed in a contemporary climate of media bubbles and ideological Balkanization, these essays refreshingly consider how utopias written from the perspective of particular social groups or political tendencies (whether radical or conservative) transcend narrowly partisan concerns to stoke our collective desire for another world and a more adequate human future. And for those with little hope of witnessing real social progress, Fitting's focus on gendered violence leads him to an understanding of how such a patently counter-factual genre as the utopia can compel concrete political action in the real world.

The final section examines the utopian role of media and technology, considered as both represented spaces and spaces of representation. It opens with the 1993 essay that first defined the genre of utopian film, followed by chapters about several high-profile SF films of the 1980s and 1990s, and an account of urban planning in Chandigarh that considers modernist utopian spaces from an architectural perspective. All of these essays explore how new narrative media and technologies manage to negotiate the competing demands of utopian wish-fulfillment and ideological containment. The volume closes with the author's account of his progress as a utopian scholar alongside the emergence of the field itself, with a retrospective summary of his own general theoretical and methodological framework, reasserting his understanding that the Utopian Moment arrives only when the text goes "beyond some estranged representation of the present, [...] to give us a glimpse of what an alternative might actually look and feel like." Here, Fitting poses one final time the urgent question of how we might become the citizens and subjects that a utopian society demands.

Introduction

The historical situation in which these essays were written will demonstrate how central Peter Fitting's work has been within the development of science fiction. We cannot call the 1960s (a period that roughly ran from 1953 to 1975) SF's "golden age": that term is already taken, and rightly designates the emergence of a whole SF-Pulp culture in the 1930s and 1940s, organized around scientific gadgets, narrative twists, more credible visions of aliens, space ships, outer galaxies, and the like – a period that produced a generation of remarkable writers of whom Asimov and Heinlein were only the most ambitious. Anthologies old and new can still demonstrate the durability of many of these gems, whose spirit was then prolonged in the television era by the immortal Star Trek series.

In the 1960s, however, something new began to happen in this field, which it would be abusive to characterize in any simple way. Yes, writers appeared of a very different kind than their predecessors – Philip K. Dick and Ursula Le Guin come to mind, the first emerging from unsuccessful mainstream novels expressing the boredom and desperation of the Eisenhower years; the second from a different kind of dissatisfaction, which would gradually become the second feminism (Le Guin's *Left Hand of Darkness* was published in the same year as a book by her college roommate called *Sexual Politics*).

It would not be quite right to see the new generation in terms of a high art/ Mass culture division, although there may be something to that. Nor should one concentrate entirely on the way in which the genre pioneered in the Golden Age was appropriated for what will later on be called social issues; but in retrospect, Dick's preoccupations with drugs and schizophrenia can be seen as the initial trickle of a flood of new and hitherto taboo themes involving sexuality, race, and politics. Yet it is with something of that transition that we tend to think of the 1960s in general: certainly the postwar younger generation had more mature interests than the popular mechanics that absorbs its prewar equivalent.

But the 1960s were also a period of formal innovation; and it sheds a different light on the new SF of the period to remember that it was contemporaneous with the nouvelle vague in film, and that Brian Aldiss, one of the emergent British practitioners, actually wrote something you could call a "nouveau roman." Happenings, abstract expressionism, rock 'n' roll, Black Mountain, Beckett's plays – all those marked the appearance of new forms of SF that were not the least achievements of the new period; and Peter Fitting wrote on all of those, in a catholicity of taste and interest that characterized so many of us at the time, and that prepared the later work collected here.

But I have not yet mentioned the most important innovation in science fiction during this formative new period, which will in our own time today have been overtaken by fantasy and dystopia in yet another unexpected historical reversal. This new event of the 1960s was certainly marked and even motivated by the new SF models I have alluded to, but it involved the emergence of a different kind of discourse, mainly Science Fiction theory, in which Fitting was heavily involved. As the term suggests, the new writing on SF was distinguished from an older criticism by its relationship to and stimulation by that whole wave of literary and cultural theory in general that accompanied all the other innovations I have mentioned and is often (perhaps too narrowly) associated with a French structuralism that took its inspiration from the 1950s anthropological studies of Claude Lévi-Strauss.

But what could be more anthropological than SF, and especially the newer kind, in which all kinds of aliens proved not so alien to us and projected the most complex and interesting social formations, as in Lem, Dick, Le Guin, Delany, Aldiss, Octavia Butler, Joanna Russ, and many others? Meanwhile, the foundational work of Darko Suvin gave SF a new legitimation and a new and literary-philosophical generic status, and led to the publication, in 1973, of the journal *Science Fiction Studies*, around which (as is so often the case with intellectual movements) the new production of SF theory coalesced and in which Fitting was significantly involved.

It has been said that on or around 1980 human nature changed, and the world along with it. Reagan/Thatcher free-market politics, video and the Internet, the emergence of China and the newly industrializing "tigers" along with it, the "era of stagnation" in the USSR, stock market exuberance, and new music and new lifestyles – all of these developments characterized a situation in which all of the older forms, including the SF of the 1960s and 1970s, confronted the challenges of obsolescence and, in particular, the quite unexpected event of the sudden disappearance of the future.

This was not the same kind of development as the ominous premonitions of the 1950s and the imminence of nuclear disaster; or of sputnik and the race to the moon; or the developments of the newer pharmaceuticals, the epidemics like AIDS, and the seemingly endless wars that began with Vietnam in the 1960s and Afghanistan in 1979. Rather, it had the feeling of a Donald Barthelme story: we woke up one day and the future was no longer there.

Political revolution was no longer on the agenda; the rich were securely in possession of 80 percent of the world's wealth; the middle classes (in America at least) securely in possession of that immortal regime of constitutional "freedom and democracy" that was designed to last forever but could be imported nowhere else in the world; the poor now had mass demonstrations and movements, radical religions, irreversible natural degradation and indestructible ghettos and camps, homelessness and incurable life expectancies, which led nowhere politically and seemed designed to last forever. So everyone had the future they deserved, and nothing now awaited anyone in the way of change. The era of stagnation had now extended to the world as a whole (in the form of globalization): accelerationism without growth, special effects without innovation, corporations without individuals.

This is the point then at which Science Fiction mutates into Utopia. The Utopianism of the new century is the response to and the correlative of the disappearance of the future, which it is an attempt to restore and to reinvent, but of whose stubborn absence it is also a symptom. The present collection documents the multiple forms desperately taken by a Utopian politics and a Utopian aesthetics, in a situation in which the old "serious" SF has been replaced by the cheapest and easiest kind of dystopia and an overwhelming flood of the fantasy novels. Theory gnaws in frustration on the barren landscapes of postmodern dystopias, and comes up empty-handed on fantasy in general (even when it is of the quality of *Game of Thrones*). Meanwhile, novel, film, and TV meld into one another, with hosts of unemployed zombies waiting at the door for parts.

Fitting's essays here now grapple with this historical dilemma, scan its past and its origins, and, if they do not attempt prediction or prophecy (what would you have to predict if the future no longer exists?), then at least lay the groundwork for an assessment of that present in which we will continue to exist.

Fredric Jameson

PART I

History and Genre

CHAPTER 1

The Modern Anglo-American SF Novel: Utopian Longing and Capitalist Co-optation

The aim of this paper is to explore the interplay between ideology and utopian longing in the modern SF novel. Western SF is, on the one hand, a form of ideological production, one of the ways in which capitalism speaks itself and determines our ways of perceiving reality, one of the ways through which the real problems and conflicts present in society are transformed into false problems and imaginary resolutions. On the other hand, SF is also an important contemporary manifestation of what Ernst Bloch, for instance, has referred to as "utopian longing," humanity's continued striving for an "adequate future[1]" – a tradition which took on new force and direction in the bourgeois world following the Enlightenment and the French Revolution, which were attended by the belief in the possibility of cognitive progress. Yet this blending of "utopian hopes and fears with the popularizations of the social and natural sciences" (Suvin 1974: 256) was followed, in the mid-nineteenth century, by a sense of failure and gloom. Nonetheless, twentieth-century SF is crucially determined by the combination of these anticipations of liberation with the possibilities of science and technology; SF can be seen as a contemporary focal point for the struggle between, on the one hand, the artistic manifestation of the

1 Cf. among his few works translated into English, Ernst Bloch, *Philosophy of the Future* (New York: Herder & Herder, 1970).

desire for an alternative, emancipated world "in which the free development of each is the condition for the free development of all" (Marx and Engels: 29) and, on the other, capitalism's ability to preempt and co-opt each new eruption of the emancipatory desire. This is the reason why science has been more and more frequently turned against the utopian impulse, and why the positivist tradition has become, in present-day capitalism, a major repressive force. This is how Fredric Jameson describes the phenomenon in his account of Herbert Marcuse's new understanding of utopia:

> Where in the older society (as in Marx's classic analysis) Utopian thought represented a diversion of revolutionary energy into ideal wish-fulfillments and imaginary satisfactions, in our own time the very nature of the Utopian concept has undergone a dialectical reversal. Now it is practical thinking which everywhere represents a capitulation to the system itself, and stands as testimony to the power of that system to transform even its adversaries into its own mirror image [...] For Marcuse, it is the Utopian concept – 'the attempt to draft a theoretical construct of culture beyond the performance principle' which henceforth [...] embodies the newest version of a hermeneutics of freedom.[2] (Jameson 1971: 111)

SF has, of course, been defined in a variety of ways. When it is situated within certain literary traditions for thematic fields, without taking into account its social and historical context, its contemporary significance

2 Jameson is referring specifically to Marcuse's *Eros and Civilization* (Boston, MA: Beacon Press, 1955). Marcuse's position, and my own definition of SF, are grounded in the liberating possibilities of science: "Utopian possibilities are inherent in the technical and technological forces of advanced capitalism and socialism: the rational utilization of these forces on a global scale would terminate poverty and scarcity within a very foreseeable future" (1969: 4). "Is it still necessary to state that not technology, not technique, not the machine are the engineers of repression, but the presence, in them, of the masters who determine their number, their life span, their power, their place in life, and the need for them? Is it still necessary to repeat that science and technology are the great vehicles of liberation, and that it is only their use and restriction in the repressive society which makes them into vehicles of domination?" (1969: 12). For a more pessimistic exposition of the inherent limitations of science from within the same philosophic tradition, see Theodore W. Adorno and Max Horkheimer, *The Dialectic of Enlightenment* (New York: Herder & Herder, 1972).

is obscured. SF has been defined as well as the literature of "cognitive estrangement" (Suvin 1972: 372–383);[3] but this definition, despite its merits, limits SF to a form of knowledge, to an understanding of the present. SF is, certainly, a continuation of various literary traditions; it does use many traditional themes; and, at its best, it is the educational, cognitive literature Darko Suvin defines it to be. But such definitions do not deal with the historical specificity of the SF of the last thirty-five years[4] in its Anglo-American form, nor with its effect upon its readers. As I shall attempt to show in the following paper, the specific characteristics of modern SF lie in its combination of utopian impulse and ideological containment within several distinct thematic configurations of the *future* and of *science*. In the traditional novel, the utopian impulse is manifest in what the Hegelian Lukács described as a yearning for totality, for some lost sense of wholeness which the novelist attempts to restore to a fragmented reality – a longing which is familiar to us in the fictional evocations of a nostalgia for some earlier, lost age. In SF this longing is often associated with the future. But the emancipatory thrust of SF, its ability to imagine alternatives, is often blunted and deformed. Charles Grivel has shown that the predominant ideological functioning of the French novel in the late nineteenth century lay in the mystification of the reader's awareness of his deforming, alienated reality; a reduction, Grivel argues, of *social* antagonisms to *personal* conflicts (Lukács 1971).[5] Ideological recuperation in the SF novel, on the other hand, lies not only in this familiar *reduction* of the social to the personal, but also in the *displacement* of the personal/social dimension to science. Character has traditionally been the central focus of the novel, but SF reverses the usual foreground-background structure of the traditional

3 See also Marc Angenot's definition, "that group of narratives of conjectural imagination that describe a society axiomatically different from the empirical society around the author. The described state of affairs is estranged with a view to liberating the social imagination and promoting a rational criticism […]," "Science Fiction in France before Verne," *Science Fiction Studies* 5 (1978), 58.

4 This chapter was originally published in *Science Fiction Studies* 6/1 (March 1979), 59–76.

5 See also Lucien Goldmann, *Towards a Sociology of the Novel* (London: Tavistock Publications, 1975). Charles Grivel, *Production de l'interet romanesque* (The Hague: Mouton, 1973).

novel: characters are moved into the background, while objects, the products of technical application of the laws of nature, occupy the foreground (Feenberg 1977: 14).

Modern SF begins in 1937, when Campbell assumed the editorship of *Astounding Science Fiction*. Its birth was a part of the changing nature and role of the U.S. scientific community on the eve of World War II (Feenberg 1977: 13–22).[6] SF was at that moment a literary genre which expressed the views of a group without power – scientists and engineers – who felt that science and technology were far more important in shaping history than was generally admitted. Whether in Campbellian SF[7] or in the scientific community itself – as reflected in the *Bulletin of the Atomic Scientists* and particularly in the figure of Robert Oppenheimer – the ideological delusion involved was that science and technology were the privileged solution to the world's ills.

This first period (the 1940s) corresponds to the success of *Astounding* as can be seen in many of the works of the period, beginning with Isaac Asimov's *I, Robot* and his *Foundation* novels. The nine stories of *I, Robot* (1940–1950) relate the different stages in humanity's development and utilization of robots, from the first robot helper to the installation of giant robot computers to manage the Earth's economy. These stories are known primarily for Asimov's formulation of the "Three Laws of Robotics" and the puzzles posed by quirks in robot behavior based on the Three Laws.

6 In such an overview, an initial difficulty lies in the establishment of the corpus. I have based my study on the following selections of long stories and novels: (1) Jack Williamson's composite list of novels from his 1971 brochure "Science Fiction in College"; (2) the 1975 *Locus* poll, "All Time Best Novel" (No. 172, April 15, 1975); (3) the Hugo awards (begun in 1955 and given each year by the vote of fans at the World Science Fiction Convention); (4) the Nebula awards (given each year since 1965 by the Science Fiction Writers of America); (5) the SFWA anthologies, *The Science Fiction Hall of Fame:* I, stories (ed. R. Silverberg, New York: Avon Books, 1971), IIA, novellas, ed. Ben Bova (London: Gollancz, 1973), and IIB, novellas (ed. B. Bova, London: Gollancz, 1973).

7 Campbell's "best" editorials from *Astounding* were selected and published by Harry Harrison as *Collected Editorials from Analog* (New York: Doubleday, 1966); see also Leon Stover's pro-Campbell history of SF, *La Science-fiction américaine* (Paris: Aubier Montaigne, 1972).

But the stories center on human distrust of robots, an obvious metaphor for human fears regarding science and its powers; and two of the stories deal explicitly with the question of technological solutions to human problems, by way of a robot politician ("Evidence") or a future in which the machines ("the vastest conglomeration of calculating circuits ever invented [...] robots within the meaning of the First Law") are "in complete control of [human] economy," an outcome which is shown to be both necessary and good ("The Evitable Conflict").

More significantly, science and technology are also presented as beneficial and critical forces in Asimov's *Foundation* trilogy (which also appeared in *Astounding* between 1942 and 1947). The Foundation uses scientific techniques to map and predict human behavior ("psychohistory": an alloy of psychology, statistics, and theory of history), thus shortening the imminent galactic Dark Ages through strategic interventions in the development of various worlds. Again, this represents an imaginary resolution in which the combination of utopian longing and science has been debased in an inadvertent foreshadowing of the recent political interventions of U.S. imperialism. The world's difficulties are presented as susceptible to scientific solutions while the utopian impulse has been suffocated in the characteristically American abuse of science through subservience to an apparatus of control. Asimov's psychohistory is designed not to bring about a different, better world, but to preserve the already existing society from external threats. The possibility of real change and the reality of history are denied through the Spenglerian cyclical model of history and through the return to a future in which the ethics and economics of capitalism have been maintained. And this colonization of our future is not simply Asimov's response to the threat of Fascism, but also to the threat of alternative social structures the "Communist menace" – insofar as psychohistory can be understood as Asimov's answer to dialectical materialism.[8]

8 For some articles which address the same problems as the present one, see Charles Elkins, "An Approach to the Social Functions of American Science Fiction," *Science Fiction Studies* 4 (1977), 223–227; and Gerard Klein, "Discontent in American SF," *Science Fiction Studies* 4 (1977), 3–13; and specifically on Asimov, Elkins, "Isaac Asimov's *Foundation* Novels," *Science Fiction Studies* 3 (1976), 26–36. All three are rptd. in R.D. Mullen and Darko Suvin, eds., *Science-Fiction Studies: Second*

In the first type of classical Anglo-American SF, then, there is an explicit resolution of human problems through the application of technology, a resolution which displaces those problems from the socioeconomic to the technological sphere. But the optimism that attended this privileging of science, the faith in a specifically scientific resolution of human problems elaborated in the late 1930s and 1940s ended at Hiroshima and with Oppenheimer's disgrace, when the U.S. scientific community realized that their idealistic dreams of political power were illusory. In SF, disillusionment was expressed in the anti-scientific fictions of the 1950s. This category includes many of the best known works of the period, from Ray Bradbury's *Fahrenheit 451* (1951, 1953)[9] and James Blish's *Case of Conscience* (1953, 1958) to Arthur C. Clarke's *Childhood's End* (1950, 1953) and Walter Miller Jr.'s *Canticle for Leibowitz* (1955, 1959).

The modification of my first type of SF had already been taking place in the stories of Clifford Simak published as *City* (1952, which also appeared in *Astounding* from 1944 to 1951). These stories trace the final centuries of human life on Earth and its replacement by alternate forms of intelligent life, including dogs which establish a "peaceable kingdom," Venusian "lepers," and other, more negative forms, from the mysterious, inhuman mutants to the regimented, hierarchical ant society which will dominate the Earth in the year 14,000. While human ideals are shown to be meaningful and life-giving, humans themselves, according to Simak, are flawed because of their manual dexterity, which leads them to seek technical solutions to problems, and because of their innate aggressivity. The dogs genetically improved by humans (with grafted vocal cords and artificial lenses) will take over from a humanity which has lost its raison d'etre; and when these intelligent animals confront some of humanity's old problems they will find new, non-violent and non-technical, solutions. Simak is one of the first writers to link science with "innate aggressivity"; at the same time, he nonetheless advances an emancipatory alternative to the alienating and repressive aspects of contemporary life through a transcendence of what

Series:Selected Articles on Science Fiction 1976–1977 (Boston, MA: Gregg Press, 1978).

9 The first date in parentheses refers to magazine publication, the second to book publication. In many cases, the novel is an expanded version of the original story.

he considers human nature to be. But if Simak's work can be read as the continuation of the utopian impulse, akin to the utopian visions of the English philosopher W. Olaf Stapledon, the rejection of technology will become, in the SF on the 1950s, a rejection of the utopian possibility itself.[10]

A distinction must be made at this point between anti-technological and anti-utopian SF. Anti-technological SF, as exemplified by *City*, rejects the privileging of technological solutions to human problems which was characteristic of the first type of SF outlined above. Anti-utopian SF, on the other hand, couples with that negation of science and technology a denial that it is possible to reconstitute the social and economic order, to eliminate the inequitable distribution of our resources and the domination and exploitation grounded in the class structure of our society. This denial is justified by raising objections such as the flawed character of "human nature," the problem of freedom, and so on.[11]

Ray Bradbury's *Fahrenheit 451* is anti-technological but not anti-utopian. In this near future where firemen find and burn books, the average city dweller alternates between wall-sized television screens and suicide attempts, while the government wages an ever-expanding war. The novel ends with the nuclear destruction of the city – for Bradbury technology itself is the cause of modern alienation – and with the hero's escape and discovery of the nomadic "book people." Bradbury's negation of capitalism and the attendant utopian longing is articulated not in terms of the future, but in

10 Stapledon's most important novels are *Last and First Men* (United Kingdom: Methuen, 1930), the extraordinary *Starmaker* (United Kingdom: Methuen, 1937), and *Sirius* (United Kingdom: Methuen, 1944). For an annotated bibliography of his work, see Curtis C. Smith, "The Books of Olaf Stapledon," *Science Fiction Studies* 1 (1974), 297–299.

11 George Kateb, *Utopia and Its Enemies* (New York: Schocken, 1963), is a good study of the literary, philosophical, and political attacks made on utopianism. Mark Hillegas, *The Future as Nightmare* (New York: Oxford University Press, 1967), is a valuable study of twentieth-century dystopian fiction. The "concern for freedom" as a literary response to the possibility of an alternate social and economic order is best illustrated in two anti-utopias, Y. Zamyatin's *We* (1924) and Aldous Huxley's *Brave New World* (1932). For a powerful critique of Huxley's antiutopianism, see Theodore Adorno's "Aldous Huxley and Utopia," in his *Prisms* (Cambridge, MA: MIT Press, 1976), 97–117.

terms of a return to an earlier pre-industrial world. But in other novels of the 1950s, particularly in Miller's *Canticle for Leibowitz* and Blish's *Case of Conscience* even this nostalgic form of utopian hope is refused, and human suffering and conflict are blamed solely on human nature.

In *Canticle*, Miller uses the theme of a new Dark Ages; but in complete opposition to Asimov's *Foundation*, science is not the means of salvation, but the cause of perdition. As the novel begins, the Earth is recovering from a nuclear holocaust. In the desert, an isolated monastery has set itself the task of preserving the few remaining and now incomprehensible writings from the preholocaust period – for in the immediate aftermath of nuclear destruction, the ravaged population, in a Luddite frenzy, hunted out and destroyed books and scientists. Centuries later, when a new Renaissance dawns, scientific knowledge and morality again part company. And in the novel's final section, the reconstructed nations of the world again attack each other with nuclear missiles. The ending is, nonetheless, ambiguous: some members of the monastery escape in a spaceship with the books, while at the monastery we witness the awakening of an ambiguous new woman, "preternaturally good," "without Original Sin." Here utopian longing is clearly identified with science and is just as clearly condemned by emphasizing flawed human nature. The hope for cognitive progress is explained by reference to the serpent's words in the Book of Genesis account of the original fall: "For God doth know that in what day soever you shall eat thereof, your eyes will be opened, and you shall be as Gods" (Miller 1959: 20). The belief in the possibility of a new Eden of Earth is thus but a temptation of the devil – a familiar religious view which is explicitly demonstrated by the title of a work by the Christian theologian Thomas Molnar: *Utopia: The Perennial Heresy*.

Similarly, Blish's *Case of Conscience* raises and then attempts to repress even more firmly the utopian impulse. In this novel, the misery and frustration of the over-crowded "shelter society" on a future Earth are juxtaposed to the harmonious world of Lithia. But Lithia, in all its alien perfection, is shown to be a Satanic creation; an interpretation which is confirmed by the upheavals caused by a Lithian visitor to Earth – a visit analogous to C.S. Lewis's depiction of the scientific emissary of Satan, Weston, who goes to a new Eden (on Venus) to tempt a new Eve (in *Perelandra*, 1944; U.S. title,

Voyage to Venus). This depiction of the utopian impulse as a temptation of the devil is a specifically religious response to human hopes for a better world "here below." Yet the deferral of hope from this world to a Christian heaven (as in *Canticle*) is in Blish perceived as somehow inadequate: at the end of *Case of Conscience*, the Earth's inhabitants riot, destroying their dehumanizing "shelter society."

In these novels of the 1950s we see, then, the negation of the first, "scientific" type of SF, a condemnation of what is seen as the false and dangerous claims of science; in the last two examples this is accompanied by a repudiation of utopian longing. But the complete rejection of this hope is ideologically unacceptable, for it far too explicitly negates the underlying optimism of "the American Way of Life." In this sense, the Asimovian type of SF was an accurate reflection of the American way of confronting problems – by refusing to see that some problems were caused by the capitalist structure of society itself and by imagining instead that these problems could be resolved through technology. The negation of this type of SF in the 1950s is incomplete, for no new solutions are offered for human suffering and conflict. And in the last two examples discussed, these negative conclusions themselves were already contradicted, however unsatisfactorily, by the ambiguous endings. The 1950s witness the appearance, then, of a third phase where this implicit negation of capitalism is recaptured and defused through a rechanneling of the utopian impulse into another kind of imaginary resolution. For insofar as "human nature" was the illusory obstacle to utopia in the second phase (whether through innate aggressivity or Original Sin), the SF of the late 1950s takes as its central theme the concept of a *changed* human nature. This is effected by depicting various parapsychological possibilities, particularly telepathy.

Within this vision of transcending human nature – already present in Simak's *City* – there are two directions: the possibility of utopia and its denial. Clarke's *Childhood's End* presents human transcendence within a denial of utopia. Significantly, his novel begins with an evocation of the Space Race. But scientific research ends with the arrival of the Overlords who institute a new Golden Age in which humanity turns from competition and drudgery to what is soon perceived by some as an empty kind of leisure. Clarke's vision, however, involves transcendence: the Overlords are not the bringers of utopia, but witnesses to the death of Earth, midwives to the birth of a new telepathic entity. That entity will join in a larger Overmind which roams the universe seeking to join to itself other races ready to forego the physical world and individual identity. Science and cognitive progress are explicitly rejected as steps toward a higher state: the intellectually and scientifically advanced Overlords are repeatedly described as sterile, while human efforts, as embodied in the utopian experiment at New Athens – a device analogous to the Cyprus Experiment in Huxley's *Brave New World* – are cruelly denied. Only the children are capable of transcendence; in the course of their transmutation they forget friends and family, lose their humanity and identity, and finally abandon the material realm itself. This thinly disguised Christian transcendence is only a misanthropic restatement of the anti-utopian, anti-scientific quietism of the preceding novels of Bradbury, Blish, and Miller.

But in two other well-known works of the 1950s, telepathy is the key to a specifically *human* transcendence: in John Wyndham's *The Chrysalids* (1955; U.S. title *Rebirth*) and in Theodore Sturgeon's *More Than Human* (1952, 1953). All of the novels mentioned so far, from *I, Robot* through *Childhood's End*, deal with the themes of science and the future in terms of the larger social context humanity at large is somehow always in question. But in the utopian version of this new type of SF – a permutation of the original scientific model – human problems will be solved and the possibility of human progress reconstituted by improved interpersonal communication. After the original reduction of human problems to technical ones, this is the development of a new false problem that of a "breakdown in communications" and the illusory belief that improved communications would, by itself, lead to understanding and cooperation on a world scale.

In Wyndham's post-cataclysmic world a rigid, hierarchical, agricultural society has slowly emerged from the rubble. Based on the Old Testament accounts of the Flood and of the destruction of Sodom and Gomorrah, the surviving humans on Labrador have developed a religious explanation for the "Tribulation." Mutations – which, according to the alternate, scientific perspective of the novel, form part of a natural process of reclamation of the devastated lands – are seen as sinful, Satanic temptations which must be ruthlessly destroyed, whether in the community's crops or in their children. Yet Wyndham describes the emergence within this static, authoritarian society, of a new and undetected mutation in a few of the children – a telepathic ability which grants the children a more meaningful sense of community, while it also forces them to flee the society which tries to destroy them.

Wyndham's argument for the desirability and necessity of change, where telepathy – improved communications – is the obvious "next step," is made even more explicit in Sturgeon's *More Than Human*, in which children and social outcasts form a new collective entity in the midst of our present society. Sturgeon's *Homo Gestalt* is another variation of the use of telepathy as a symbol for the transcendence of the "human condition." As opposed to Clarke's inhuman suppression of the self and to Wyndham's brutal dismissal of the pretelepaths, Sturgeon's vision of the future development of our species emphasizes human emotions and ideals in a utopian metaphor for new collective alternatives to capitalist bourgeois individualism. And Sturgeon's novel concludes with the invocation of an even larger collectivity of which *Homo Gestalt* was only a "cell among cells": "here was the Guardian of Whom all humans knew – not an exterior force, nor an awesome Watcher in the sky, but a laughing thing with a human heart and a reverence for its human origins" (ch. 3: 20).

The preceding three-part model of the SF of the 1940s and 1950s is no longer appropriate to the changed conditions and writing of the last eighteen years. For this model was intended to explain what I understand to be the dominant currents in SF in its "classical" period, and to illustrate my definition of SF as a specific balancing of ideology and utopian impulse through a study of the configurations that obtain in the use of the themes of science and of the future. To do this, I have tried to follow the SF of the 1940s and 1950s through three stages. In the first, the concept of progress – the utopian impulse – was allied with a conception of science which obscured rather than clarified the concrete dimension of human suffering and conflict. The reaction to this first configuration again obscured the concrete: it blamed science for humanity's "false hopes" while showing that, because of human nature, any real progress was impossible. Even when the utopian impulse reasserted itself, in the novels of telepathy, human problems were shifted to the private sphere. And by the late 1950s, despite the optimism of works like *The Chrysalids* and *More Than Human*, SF seemed to have reached an impasse.

The 1960s were a period of turmoil and change for SF as for American society at large. The boom of the early 1950s had suddenly ended – there had been some forty different SF magazines in 1953 and by the end of 1957 there were only ten – and the reactions to the scientific stance of *Astounding* (as well as the public's own distrust of the optimistic claims for science) were increasing: *science* fiction as such was in decline. The walls of the SF "ghetto" – the closely-knit community of writers and readers – were crumbling as the central importance and popularity of the magazines declined. Until the late 1950s the magazines had been the primary outlet for SF writing and exchanges (through letter columns, editorials, and reviews). But now there was an increasing amount of publishing outside the magazines, and these new outlets were reaching a new and different readership whose interests and literary backgrounds extended beyond the traditional horizons of SF.

The decline and resurgence of SF between 1957 and 1965 has been explained in various ways. The successful launching of the first Soviet satellite (in 1957) triggered a revival of interest in science and science studies in the U.S. while coinciding with (or hastening) the decline in SF. According to some, it was the reality of space flight which rendered SF obsolete. From my perspective, it is also clear that the final phase of the first model – the "spontaneous" development of telepathy – was a dead end, an alternative which took any possibility for change or improvement out of human hands.

The early 1960s were a time of increasing tensions within U.S. society during which the utopian impulse was reinvested in the concrete, in a surge of emancipatory activity – in the collective actions of blacks, women, and other oppressed groups, in the demonstrations against the war in Vietnam, and in the Student Movement and the Counter Culture – which challenged the smooth functioning of U.S. capitalism. This decomposition of America's carefully constructed image of itself has been frequently described in terms of a "breakdown in values." And in the mid-1960s some critics began to write about SF, because it was a genre outside the literary norms and conventions of the Establishment, as the locus for a creative search for viable new myths.[12] In retrospect, the exploration of new value systems in SF writing seems most apparent in the New Wave search for new literary techniques and in the popularity of mystico-religious themes. Robert A. Heinlein's *Stranger in a Strange Land* (1961) is the most famous example of the latter. This novel was to become one of the cult books of the 1960s and did much to attract new readers to SF. The novel begins as a wry critique of the foibles of twentieth-century *homo americanus*, in which the satirical technique of the foreign visitor who naively observes and comments on society is combined with Heinlein's familiar rugged individualism. But the account of the Martian-raised human's rescue and education gives way to escapism as the hero founds a new religion based on the communal sharing of minds, bodies, and money and using the magical properties of the Martian language.

Although this may not be what Judith Merril meant when she began writing about SF and "New Mythologies," Heinlein's interest in new religions is a by now familiar phenomenon which does characterize one response to the contemporary sense of crisis: the belief that the present sorry state of affairs is due exclusively to the bankruptcy of the established *moral and ethical* values of our society, a bankruptcy which can only be resolved on the individual and spiritual level. But the SF of the 1960s which participated in the Counter Culture vogue for alternate value systems and lifestyles was part of a larger mystification of the sociopolitical dimensions of our crisis. Like the Counter Culture itself, this was a negation of the repressive features of capitalism that ultimately had to fail insofar as it diverted emancipatory energies from the public and political spheres to the merely individual and private.

At the same time there was another, similar kind of SF in which the reaction to our crisis took the form of an equally mistaken and unrewarding search, not for new moral and spiritual values, but for a new *aesthetics* – the search for new literary forms and techniques adequate to dealing with what was perceived as the changed reality of the 1960s. SF of this type sought to resolve external conflicts by transforming them into aesthetic subjects and

12 E.g., Judith Merril in the book review columns of the magazine *Fantasy and Science Fiction, 1965–1969.*

problems. The British writer J.G. Ballard is symptomatic for this, and an examination of his work, from the *Drowned World* (1962) and the *Crystal World* (1966) to his "condensed novels" of the late 1960s, when he abandoned SF altogether, may make it possible to understand the importance and interdependence of New Wave and New Mythology in SF.

In Ballard's disaster novels, the sense of crisis and impending catastrophe is transposed from the realm of history to that of nature. The responsibility for the cataclysm, as well as the possibility of doing anything about it, is effectively removed from the domain of human activity. In *Drowned World*, the Earth has lost some of the outer layers of the ionosphere; temperatures have risen, and this in turn has altered plant growth and melted the polar ice caps, flooding much of the planet whose geographical features have reverted to the tropical lagoons of the Triassic Period. While the remaining humans cluster in UN enclaves at the poles, Ballard's hero is drawn to the disaster zone, an inner response to the cataclysm which is explained on several different levels. Biologically, this response is a kind of devolution triggered by the genetically encoded memories of the Triassic; spiritually, it represents the promise of Nirvana contained in this devolution; and aesthetically, it finds its correlative in the author's florid descriptions of the terminal landscape.

These attitudes are even more explicit in the *Crystal World*, where the aesthetic and spiritual significance of the cataclysm lies "in the transfiguration of all living and inanimate forms [...] the gift of immortality a direct consequence of the surrender by each of us of our own physical and temporal identities" (Ballard 1991: 202–203). In *Crystal World*, the Earth – indeed the entire universe – is undergoing a process of crystallization in which time is replaced by space, as beings and objects are metamorphosed into radiant, iridescent jewels. Ballard's hero is again drawn to the disaster area. But here, even more explicitly than in *Drowned World*, human problems will be solved not through resistance, but through an acceptance of the aesthetic and reconciliatory dimensions of the cataclysm. The hero is a doctor who, in the beginning, tries to help the victims of crystallization; but in the end, he suggests that the hospital send all its patients into the crystallizing forest. The novel is set in Africa, but both the hero's emotional problems and the larger racial tensions of the African continent are understood finally as aesthetic problems – as "problems of lighting" – contrasts which will be reconciled and transcended in the transfigured crystal world.

Much of the SF associated with the New Wave belongs to this category; and the "speculative" nature of much of this writing lies not in the exploration of new social and human possibilities, but in the discovery and uses of various modernistic literary techniques (as exemplified in Ballard's acknowledged debt to the Surrealists, or in Judith Merril's frequent inclusion of surrealist writers in her "Best of the Year" SF anthologies of the late 1960s). At the same time, as in Ballard's resolution of racial conflict in *Crystal World*, much New Wave writing moves from the aesthetic resolution of various problems to the literary exploitation of controversial topics, most evident in Harlan Ellison's "revolutionary" anthology, *Dangerous Visions* (1967). The significance of SF's discovery of the avant-garde is perhaps best summed up in the words of Roland Barthes, writing in 1956 on the French avant-garde:

> The avant-garde is always a way of celebrating the death of the bourgeoisie, for its own death still belongs to the bourgeoisie; but further than this the avant-garde cannot go; it cannot conceive the funerary term it expressed as a moment of germination, as the transition from a closed society to an open one; it is impotent by nature to infuse its protest with the hope of a new assent to the world: it wants to die, to say so, and it wants everything to die with it. (1972: 69)[13]

Finally, within this first category of the SF of the 1960s – that of a search for new values – there is a third type of false solution which resembles the earlier scientific model: a revival or continuation of the earlier belief that human problems are above all scientific problems. In the 1960s, this imaginary scientific resolution coincides with the discovery of *ecology*.

13 See also H. Bruce Franklin's assessment of the prevalence of disasters in the SF in the 1950s and 1960s, "Chic Bleak in Fantasy Fiction," *Saturday Review* (July 15,1972), 42–45. For some explanations of the avant-garde's role in the commodification of art in late capitalism which deny the negational or emancipatory function I have been arguing, see R. Estivals, "L'avant-garde culturelle, le gauchisme et la societe de consummation" in *Actes du VIe Congrès de l'Association Internationale de Littérature Comparée* (Stuttgart, 1975); and particularly the concept of "artificial negativity" in *Telos* 35 (Spring 1978) in P. Piccone, "The Crisis of One Dimensionality," 43–54; and Tim Luke, "Culture and Politics in the Age of Artificial Negativity," 55–72.

A first example is Frank Herbert's best-selling *Dune* (1965), which is dedicated to "dry land ecologists." In his portrayal of Paul Atreides and the desert world of Arrakis, Herbert balances a description of the ecology of Dune with an account of the "historical" forces which have led to a galactic crisis. The novel is the story of Paul's revenge for the death of his father as well as an ecological puzzle in which the reader gradually pieces together the reality of Dune. But behind the events lie neither historical forces nor individual will. There is, rather, biological determinism, "the need of their race to renew its scattered inheritance, to cross and mingle and infuse their bloodlines in a great new pooling of genes," which has brought Paul and the Fremen together to bring about that mixing of genes in the only possible way, "the ancient way, the tried and certain way that rolls over everything in its path: jihad" (1965: 22). History and the possibility of human endeavor and change are again reduced to "natural" forces; while ecology is, in this novel, an illusory scientific justification for a kind of wish-fulfillment analogous to that offered by the machines which gave Van Vogt's Gosseyn (in the *Null-A* novels of the 1940s) the ability to transcend time and space and his own death, or by the Martian language which gave Michael Valentine Smith and his followers unlimited powers in *Stranger in a Strange Land*.

Like Heinlein's novel, *Dune* is not the elaboration of some new science, but another instance of fraudulent New Mythology, the contemporary diversion and reinvestment of the utopian impulse in the yearning for false security offered by messiahs and dictators. The real meaning of that type of security is evident in the transformation of Paul's lieutenant, Stilgar: "Paul saw how Stilgar had been transformed from the Fremen naib to a *creature* of the Lisan al-Gaib, a receptacle for awe and obedience. It was a lessening of the man" (1965: 11). *Dune* is, in fact, a denial of the utopian possibilities of science, for the ecologist Kynes had given the Fremen both a dream and a practical means for the gradual transformation of their hostile and barren world, and this utopia is lost when the Fremen accept Paul as their Messiah.

Other, more recent examples of ecological SF can be found in the works of John Brunner, particularly *Stand on Zanzibar* (1968) and *The Sheep Look Up* (1972). These immense novels are skillfully constructed and carefully researched forecasts of the bleak future which awaits us if we continue to ignore the ominous warnings of scientists and futurists about the consequences of our abuses of the biosphere. In *Stand on Zanzibar* Brunner juxtaposes, through a mosaic technique, various characters, countries, and plots to create a depressing vision of a near future in which overpopulation has become the world's major problem. There is one ray of hope (analogous to the "spontaneous" emergence of telepathy in some of the novels of the 1950s) – a "peace gene" which, if successfully synthesized, could counter man's innate aggressivity and allow him to come to terms with the problem of overpopulation. While this ending can scarcely be taken seriously, the basic point of the novel seems to lie in its tour de force quality as the technical solution of an artistic problem: how to encompass and articulate in a single work the diversity and range of the coming catastrophe?

The Sheep Look Up is without even the minimal optimism of *Zanzibar* as it focuses on the USA and the inevitable results of a continued ignoring of ecological imperatives. Again the crisis is situated in the pseudo-scientific context of the pop neo-Malthusianism of the 1960s. Brunner's dire predictions resemble the forecasts of the Club of Rome and the recent discussions of "Lifeboat ethics."[14] In Brunner's account of twelve months in the final collapse of a USA ravaged by pollution, malnutrition, and disease, there is no place for resistance or hope. In the final scene the United States are burning, which provides a solution to the ecological crisis as outlined in the final pages of the novel: "We can just about restore the balance of the ecology, of the biosphere [...] if we exterminate the two hundred million most extravagant and wasteful of our species." Like the destruction of the

14 For an explanation and critique of Garrett Hardin's widely publicized "Lifeboat ethics," see John Vandermeer, "Hardin's Lifeboat adrift," in *Science for the People* 8 (January 1976), 16–19: "Metaphorically, each rich nation amounts to a lifeboat full of comparatively rich people. The poor of the world are in other, much more crowded lifeboats. Continuously, so to speak, the poor fall out of their lifeboats and swim for a while in the water outside, hoping to be admitted to the rich lifeboat, or in some other way to benefit from the 'goodies' on board. What should the passengers on a rich lifeboat do? This is the central problem of 'the ethics of a lifeboat.'" Garrett Hardin, "Lifeboat Ethics," *Bioscience* (October 1974) as quoted in Vandermeer (1975: 16). For an explanation and critique of the Club of Rome's 1972 report, *The Limits to Growth* and its subsequent 1974 report, *Mankind at the Turning Point*, see David Jhirad, Marian Lowe, and Paolo Strigini, "The Limits to Capitalist Growth," in *Science for the People* 7 (May 1975), 14–19, 34–37.

hateful city in *Fahrenheit 451*, the destruction of America would cleanse the world.

There were other writers in the 1960s who used SF to criticize U.S. society by means of a more thorough and explicit identification of the social and political nature of capitalism. This tradition had begun in the pages of *Galaxy* magazine in the 1950s with the masterpiece of Pohl and Kornbluth, "Gravy Train" (1952; published as a novel in 1953 as *The Space Merchants*), a satirical look at a USA under the control of competing advertising empires. In the 1960s the critique of capitalism reappeared in the writing of some of the young U.S. New Wave writers – in works such as Thomas Disch's *Camp Concentration* (1968), Joanna Russ's *Picnic on Paradise* (1968), and Norman Spinrad's *Bug Jack Barron* (1969).

But in a rather different fashion, the most interesting SF of the 1960s is to be found among the nineteen novels written by Philip K. Dick during this period.[15] There is constant reference to the oppressive features of capitalism in his novels, but in a very different vein from the above examples. Rather than satire or critique, each of his novels shows a lived experience of attempted escape through his characters' struggle to maintain and comprehend a fragmented and disintegrating reality. Although the following comments apply, I think, to all his novels, I will mention three of his best known works: *Man in the High Castle* (1962), *The Three Stigmata of Palmer Eldritch* (1966), and *Ubik* (1969). In each of these novels there is, juxtaposed to the given "reality" of fictional world within the novel, at least one other "reality": in *Man in the High Castle*, the alternate reality of a 1950s USA in which Japan and Germany have won World War II is contrasted with the "reality" of an SF novel in which the U.S. won; in *Three Stigmata*, the "reality" of the novel as perceived by various characters is undermined and replaced by drug-induced hallucinations; and in *Ubik*, a group of characters struggles against the "temporal regression" of their "reality" – a struggle

15 Among the most significant of Dick's novels, I would include *Time out of Joint* (1959), *Man in the High Castle* (1962), *Martian Time-Slip* (1963), *Penultimate Truth* (1964), *Dr. Bloodmoney* (1965), *Now Wait for Last Year* (1966), *Three Stigmata of Palmer Eldritch* (1966), *Do Androids Dream of Electric Sheep?* (1968) and *Ubik* (1969). For a complete bibliography of Dick's work, as well as a sampling of critical reactions, see the special number of *Science Fiction Studies* 2 (March 1975).

which apparently takes place in an artificially maintained "half-life" following their deaths in an explosion. Despite the bizarre nature of these condensations of the situation in these novels (which is certainly typical of all of Dick's work), each work is the account of a struggle for understanding and meaning, the narrative of the characters' desperate attempts to distinguish illusion and reality – a search which, in each case, proves futile. The utopian dimension of these novels lies, I think, in Dick's continued rejection of a fictional resolution to the dilemma confronting his characters – which is, in fact, recognition that nothing short of the actual transformation of the world itself could resolve human conflict and alienation. His recurrent depiction of the characters' agonizing experience of an illusory and disintegrating reality is not only the psychological correlative of our everyday experience of alienation, but a powerful representation of the workings of ideology itself. The centering of his novels around the "problem" of reality is an artistic realization that our own "reality" is, in many ways, an imaginary construct: that "reality" is an unconscious, ideologically determined conditioning and shaping of our needs and perceptions which conceals and deforms the real causes of human suffering and conflict while it creates in us "repressive instinctual needs and values," "permeated with the exigencies of profit and exploitation" (Marcuse 1969: 17).[16]

Dick's unending production of imaginary and illusory realities is a monument to the force of "negative thinking," for the alternatives he holds out elude escapism and co-optation because of his characters' continual return to confrontations with the present in the midst of this frustrating search for understanding. His heroes cannot accept the illusory escape offered them. They always seem to return, with varying degrees of hope and despair, to an existentialist commitment to struggle, just as the Martian colonists in *Three Stigmata* return from their drugged fantasies to the reality of life in Chicken Pox Prospects. The "interoffice memo" which serves as the epigraph to the novel sums up that attitude: "I mean after all; you have to consider we're only made out of dust. That's admittedly not much to go on and we shouldn't forget that. But even considering, I mean it's sort of a bad beginning, we're not doing too bad. So I personally have faith that

16 See also his *One-Dimensional Man* (Boston, MA: Beacon Press, 1964).

even in this lousy situation we're faced with we can make it. You get me?" (Dick: 2011)

The central theme of Samuel Delany's *The Einstein Intersection* (1967), in which strange mutated beings roam a post-holocaust Earth, is myth itself – the tenacity of the old myths and the necessity of "working through" them so that new values and meaning appropriate to a changed reality can be created. The novel ends with the destruction of the old myths, but in subsequent novels Delany does not seem to have moved very far toward the elaboration of new "myths." And in the overrated and self-indulgent *Dhalgren* (1975) he seems to have come to resemble Ballard, a young master in the technical appreciation and aesthetic exploration of the rubble of ruined cities. Yet his latest novel, *Triton* (1976), is much more interesting insofar as his ability to experiment with and imagine what might loosely be called different "living arrangements" is gradually being extended from interpersonal to societal dimensions.

Finally, within the context of SF's generic ability to provide a place for imagining utopian alternatives, the critique of capitalism and specifically of sexism has produced some of the most significant SF of the last ten years as exemplified by the work of Ursula K. Le Guin and Joanna Russ.[17] Le Guin's *Left Hand of Darkness* (1969) signaled a return to social speculation in which the imagining of alternate societies grows out of an examination of the social and political structures of the author's own world. Le Guin's story of an emissary from a future federation of intelligent worlds and his mission to the planet Gethen, where he tries to persuade two nations to accept membership in the Ekumen, uses an alien setting to examine human sexuality and sexism. There are serious weaknesses to Le Guin's analysis of

17 I should mention as well the feminist and utopian fictions of Marge Piercy, *Dance the Eagle to Sleep* (1970) and *Woman* on *The Edge of Time* (1977), as well as the anthologies of "SF stories by women and about women" edited by Pamela Sargent, *Women of Wonder* (1974) and *More Women of Wonder* (1977). Among feminist critiques of SF should be mentioned Joanna Russ's reviews over the past few years in *Fantasy and Science Fiction*, and two articles in *Extrapolation:* Beverly Friend, "Virgin Territory: Women and Sex in Science Fiction," 14 (December 1972), 49–58; and Mary Badami, "A Feminist Critique of Science Fiction," 18 (December 1976), 6–19.

human sexual bipolarity, particularly insofar as it "explains" human conflict. As the Ekumen "Investigator" states (ch. 7), the ambisexuality of the Gethenians has resulted in a world in which, "there is no division of humanity into strong and weak, protective/protected, dominant/submissive, owner/chattel, active/passive." Because, as this outside observer explains in her report, ambisexuality has "little or no adaptive value," it seems likely that the Gethenians were an experiment perhaps with the object of eliminating war: "Did the Ancient Hainish postulate that continuous sexual capacity and organized social aggression, neither of which are attributes of any mammal but man, are cause and effect? [...] The fact is that Gethenians, though highly competitive [...] seem not to be very aggressive." As Fredric Jameson has argued "Gethenian physiology *solves* the problem of sex" by an "*excision* of the real," by doing away "with everything that is *problematical* about it" (1975: 226), in much the same way that the description of Gethen's arrested political development is, according to Jameson, "an attempt to imagine something like a West which would never have known capitalism": "It becomes difficult to escape the conclusion that this attempt to rethink Western history without capitalism is of a piece, structurally and in its general spirit, with the attempt to imagine human biology without desire which we have described above; for it is essentially the inner dynamic of the market system which introduces into the chronicle-like and seasonal, cyclical, tempo of precapitalist societies the fever and ferment of what we used to call *progress*. The underlying identification between sex as an intolerable, well-nigh gratuitous complication of existence, and capitalism as a disease of change and meaningless evolutionary momentum, is thus powerfully underscored by the very technique – that of world reduction – whose mission is the utopian exclusion of both phenomena" (1975: 228).[18] Despite these criticisms, *Left Hand of Darkness* is significant because it has expanded the framework for understanding and modifying human behavior; it is important not for its answers, but for the range and imagination with which the questions are posed.

18 The word "utopian" in Jameson's final sentence is used in the older, pejorative sense of "illusory" rather than in the way I have been using it.

In more recent works – Le Guin's *The Dispossessed* (1974) and Russ's *Female Man* (1975) – the authors have elaborated two explicitly utopian worlds. Le Guin's "ambiguous utopia" of Anarres, the moon to which the anarchists have emigrated, is a harsh and inhospitable world where the struggle for survival provides the common purpose holding this society together. And yet, after 170 years of isolation from the mother world of Urras, the anarchist ideals have slowly been undermined by the gradual reemergence of hierarchy and privilege. Russ's world of Whileaway, on the other hand, is a less industrialized future Earth without men, an extremely practical and unsentimental utopia. Both women have reservations about the utopian project itself, and these works are important, not as literal models for the future, but insofar as they use utopian horizons for an analysis of the possibilities and shortcomings of their own society. The transition to the utopian world raises other questions, and in this regard Russ seems more realistic than Le Guin: the latter's Odonians have an available moon on which to construct their utopian society; Russ's Whileaway is finally revealed as having arisen not through reform nor through chance (the Whileawayans' belief that a plague had killed all the men) but through violence in a literal war between the sexes. Each utopia is juxtaposed to a critical portrait of our own society: whereas Russ's recreation a contemporary U.S. is limited by her feminist perspective (which, like Le Guin's explanation in *Left Hand* that human aggressivity is rooted in sexual bipolarity, denies the primacy of social and economic contradictions in the emergence and development of sexual exploitation),[19] Le Guin's Urras is a caricature of the Earth's "three worlds" (US/USSR/Third World).[20]

19 The two opposing views of the emergence and development of human sexuality and sexism are set out in Susan Brownmiller, *Against Our Will: Men, Women and Rape* (New York: Simon & Schuster, 1975), as opposed to Friedrich Engels, *The Origin of The Family, Private Property and The State* (1884) and Wilhelm Reich, *SexPol: Essays, 1929–1934* (New York: Vintage Books, 1972).

20 Joanna Russ has written a very critical and searching review of *The Dispossessed* in *The Magazine of Fantasy and Science Fiction* (March 1975), 41–44; see also her "The Image of Women in Science Fiction," in *Images of Women in Fiction*, ed. Susan Koppelmen Cornillon (Bowling Green, OH: Bowling Green University Press, 1972), 79–94. Given her critique of Le Guin and the promise of *The Female Man*, it must be added that Russ's latest novel, *We Who Are About To …* (1977), was a

My defense of these variants of utopian horizons will raise disagreements in those who disagree with the limited nature of their critique of contemporary society as well as from those who find these utopias too timid and restrictive those for whom utopia lies beyond the hardships of Annarres or the pragmatism of Whileaway. But their importance lies in the revival of utopian thought itself, in the willingness and ability to again envisage emancipatory alternatives.

The thematic configurations of science and the future have developed, as I have tried to show, over two fairly distinct periods. In the first, the optimistic vision of the late 1930s and 1940s – according to which human problems could be solved through technics – was also a repudiation of the desirability of a fundamentally different social order. This faith in science was followed, in the aftermath of Hiroshima, by disillusionment and rejection of science, and then by a denial of even the hope of a world without war or scarcity. This surge of anti-utopianism focused on the essentially flawed character of human nature; like the religious world view of the inhabitants of Labrador in *The Chrysalids*, this was a view grounded in the belief that the very hope for change or an end to suffering in this world was "sinful." Thus the utopian impulse reemerged in the 1950s as a transcending of human nature – but a transcending accomplished not through human design (through science and technology), but accidentally (through mutation) or as part of some "higher plan" (as in *Childhood's End*: compare also the "teaching machines" in Clarke's scenario for the film *2001* [1968]).

In the early 1960s the immediacy of existing social conflicts and the pressure for change broke through the apathy, complacency, and ideological self-deception of U.S. society. This led also to the birth of a new SF in the 1960s. The outbreak of emancipatory activity was matched, in a first phase, by various forms of ideological rechannelings of the utopian impulse, a co-optation with at least three different forms which I discussed under the heading of "New Mythology": (1) the primarily aesthetic preoccupations of the New Wave; (2) the appeal to exotic new religions with their promises of immediate answers and gratification; and (3) the new science

keen disappointment. For some other approaches to the same theme see Pamela J. Annas, "New Worlds, New Words," *Science Fiction Studies* 5 (July 1978), 143–156, and Beverly Friend, "Virgin Territory," *Extrapolation* 14 (December 1972), 49–58.

of ecology. But the 1960s also generated a SF which was, at its best, both critical and utopian – works in which the original recognition of the role of science and reason in human emancipation are reaffirmed. The hero of Le Guin's *The Dispossessed* is a physicist whose theoretical work will lead to the development of an instantaneous communication device which will make possible a league of worlds (the Ekumen of *Left Hand of Darkness*). Although this seems to suggest that problems in communication are at the heart of human conflict and suffering, Le Guin goes beyond the accidental or divine solutions of the 1950s SF: the ansible is a *human invention*, the product of human thought and design and thus an important symbol of humanity's growth and self-liberation.

I will not venture to predict what future developments might take place in SF writing. But it is worth observing, first of all, that SF has traditionally articulated the possibilities which science and technology hold as instruments for transforming the world; and secondly, that books like *The Dispossessed* do promise to supply a new basis for the utopian longing for emancipation that has always been – more or less – a fundamental impulse behind and inside SF.

CHAPTER 2

Contemporary Fantasy and the Utopian Impulse

The basic perspective of this paper is my sense that there is a fundamental contradiction at work in contemporary forms of popular culture – a tension between "utopian" and "ideological" functions.[1] By "utopian" I mean the ways in which a work speaks to and articulates, in however deformed or disguised a fashion, both a refusal of the world as it is presently constituted, and the yearning for a qualitatively different world, a realm of freedom in which repression and alienation are no more. In this context, the "ideological" is then the work's contrary function as a reaffirmation and legitimization of the status quo, the ways in which the work defuses and co-opts the contestatory and as a reaffirmation and legitimization of the status quo, the ways in which the work defuses and co-opts the contestatory and emancipatory tendencies it has aroused.

I began this examination of recent fantasy with some familiar preconceptions shared by many SF fans and critics, namely that fantasy is more shallow and "escapist" than SF; and that the increasing popularity of fantasy – relative to SF – was a regressive and worrying development. Certainly the fantasy with which I was familiar – from Tolkien and Conan through Stephen King and Donaldson – seemed to confirm this opinion. But as I read further, I began to realize that feminism has had an influence on fantasy similar to its effect on SF since the 1960s. In this attempt to present an overview of recent fantasy fiction, I have limited myself to four well-known and representative works. The four works are: Suzy McKee Charnas's *Motherlines*, Elizabeth Lynn's *Dancers of Arun* (Book II of the

1 This paper was presented at the Seventh Annual Conference of the Society for Utopian Studies, Saint John campus, University of New Brunswick (September 1982).

"Chronicles of Tornor"), Patricia McKillip's "Riddle-Master" trilogy and Stephen Donaldson's trilogy, "The Chronicles of Thomas Covenant The Unbeliever." These four works illustrate continuum running from SF to "full" fantasy along an axis of "distance" from the empirical environment of our "world." *Motherlines* is the closest; it is set against the background of a post-cataclysmic Earth in which life continues in the shattered "Holdfast" city – a world in which women are slaves. The alternate world of the novel is that of the "Wild" – the Plains where nomadic groups of women live in the manner of Plains Indians. This novel might be called SF (although the author calls it "science fantasy"), and I have included it inasmuch as, like the other works under consideration, it depicts a world without technology. Indeed, the world and themes of *Motherlines* very much resemble the world of Arun in Lynn's "Chronicles of Tornor" – a small Earth-like pre-industrial land of farming and trade, to which I shall return in a moment.

The worlds of McKillip and Donaldson are, on the other hand, examples of full fantasy worlds far removed from our own Earth. The "High One's Realm" in McKillip's trilogy is, with its kingdoms and cities, a feudal world filled with magic; while the "Land" of Donaldson's trilogy is even further from our own empirical environment, for in addition to magic, it includes a variety of fantastic, non-human creatures (including Giants, Wraiths, Demons, "ur-viles," etc.) The High One's Realm is made up of six kingdoms governed by hereditary rulers whose authority is vested in the "Land-Law" – the ruler's organic awareness of people and things, past and present, which compose that kingdom and those separate awarenesses are in turn bound together in the High One's awareness of his Realm. Donaldson depicts an even simpler society of integrated communities living in complete harmony in the plains and woods of the Land, united under a single, all-embracing world-view whose spiritual and political center lies with the Lords of Revelstone Keep.

Turning briefly to the narratives of these four works, *Motherlines* recounts Alldera's flight from the Holdfast and her integration into the tribal society of the "riding women." Her presence, and her pregnancy, produces tensions in this community. The women resist accepting someone with different ways, from outside the original "motherlines" (that is, the descendants of the original "mothers" from the Holdfast laboratories who developed the techniques of parthenogenesis). Heretofore they have ignored the small community of recently escaped women – the "free fems" – who live on the edge of the Plains, but Alldera becomes the bridge between the two groups as they gradually come to appreciate and understand one another. The novel ends with the possibility of further disruptions as the free fems, with Alldera, plan to invade the Holdfast.

The land of Arun, which we see at 100 year intervals in Lynn's trilogy, is also in flux. *Dancers of Arun* is the furthest of the four works under consideration from a traditional fantasy plot. It is again the story of initiation: that of Kerris, a one-armed boy raised as an outsider in the northern keep of Tornor until his brother comes and takes him away to the South to live in Elath, the "witch-town" – so named because of the psi-powers of many of its inhabitants. In Elath Kerris learns to accept himself – his telepathic ability as well as his physical handicap – and he learns too the importance and function of his brother's way of life in the *chereas*, or group of dancers, which presents in the trilogy, a project for human freedom and development which grows out of and transcends the older, more traditional customs and patterns of life in Arun. The *chereas* are the companies of men and women who, "joined by love and respect and skill," travel the land, "dancing, teaching the weapon's arts, and drawing the hearts of all who watched them [...] into harmony."

In opposition to the minimal narratives of Charnas and Lynn, the fantasies of McKillip and Donaldson are filled with epic battles and extraordinary events. Moreover, unlike the pictures of growth and transformation in the former novels, change is threatening in the works of McKillip and Donaldson where a magical, harmonious land is threatened by elemental, non-human forces. (The *locus classicus* of this type of fantasy is of course Tolkien.)

McKillip's Riddle-master trilogy, like Lynn's *Dancers*, tells of the growth of the hero, Morgon, who only recognizes and accepts the full import of his extraordinary powers in the third book of the series. The basic structure of the trilogy is that of a quest; the solution of each riddle leads to new riddles, and to a continually deepening and expanding situation which becomes a struggle for the survival of the Realm itself. Whereas Kerris's acceptance of his telepathic abilities (in *Dancers*) was a part of the struggle to make Arun a happier and more human society, it was only a small part of an unending process. Morgon on the other hand is a hero. The fate of the High One's Realm depends on him; on his acceptance of his special powers and unique role.

The world is also threatened in the "Chronicles of Thomas Covenant," but both the hero and the threat are different, and the tone of the novels is much more somber and grim. In McKillip, the threat to the Realm was a thirst for power and the tone of the novels is much more somber and grim. In McKillip, the threat to the Realm was a thirst for power and control on the part of some of the prehuman "Earth-Masters." In Donaldson's work, the malevolent Lord Foul seeks to destroy the Land and its inhabitants. As in Tolkien, the struggle has a metaphysical dimension. Lord Foul is an incarnation of absolute evil, while the hero, Thomas Covenant, has been summoned to the Land by the "Creator" to lead the fight against Lord Foul. But the narratives are not my main concern. As is the case with many utopian and SF novels, the narratives in these four works serve, I think, primarily as the occasion to present a fantasy world. Consequently, an important part of my assessment of these works has to do with the worlds themselves; and with the differences between the more "ordinary" worlds of Charnas and Lynn, with their focus on social arrangements and material life, when juxtaposed to the exceptional characters and worlds of McKillip and Donaldson.

To assess these works in terms of their worlds I shall use two criteria, of which the first involves the thematics of change and permanence. It is my contention that in the worlds of Charnas and Lynn the utopian impulse is nourished and encouraged, whereas that same negation of the world as it is and the longing for a disalienated world is defused and co-opted in the fantasies of McKillip and Donaldson. It will be my purpose to set out the reasons for such a judgment, which have to do with the kind of attitudes a work develops or discourages – attitudes toward the desirability and possibility of change, for instance, as well as toward the focus and modalities of change. Certainly, all of these works suggest, through the very creation of other, alternate worlds, a negation of life as-it-presently-exists in the developed capitalist countries in which these works are written and read. Moreover, in their rejection of technology and what they see as the alienating effects of industrialized society, these four works share a yearning for an organic, "ecological" wholeness through an acknowledgment of the importance of the natural environment and its significance for human well-being. But in McKillip and Donaldson, this return to a more ecologically whole life carries with it the implication of a "natural order" which the authors then extend from the physical, external world into the social sphere, and more specifically into social forms which reproduce relations of domination and exploitation. By the depiction of a society which lives according to the patterns and rhythms of nature, these two authors understand not simply a closer, more balanced relationship to the natural environment, but an unchanging hierarchical social order in which everyone knows instinctively and accepts without question his or her place in that society. Such a view thus subtly discourages the propriety of social reform while it conditions the reader to an acceptance of his or her lot in life.

In these two works there is an implicit rejection of change – specifically of social change – under the disguise of a rejection of technology. Moreover, the foundations of technology and technological change – science and the scientific method – are themselves displaced as the principal (and value-free) means of understanding and acting upon external reality. In their place, Donaldson and McKillip put magic; the mastery of secret forces and powers which transcend or supersede the observed "laws" of nature. Just as the validity of the scientific method is denied by the recourse to magic and mysteries in these novels, so too the worlds themselves are no longer "neutral." Instead, these two worlds are "ethically charged," invested with Good and Evil. Human suffering is not explained in terms of specific, historical causes, but as the result of an eternal, transhistorical struggle between Good and Evil (in Donaldson), or in a less metaphysical form (in McKillip) as the result of "pre-human" (i.e., animal) nature – the lust for power. Such an explanation, I would argue, effectively denies the possibility of substantively improving the human condition.

On the other hand, change is not so threatening in the worlds of Charnas and Lynn, although individual characters as well as groups and communities are shown struggling to adjust to change. Although life in these novels is also represented as close to the rhythms and patterns of nature, social structures and practices are not tied to those patterns, and they are not presented as fixed and unchanging, but subject to the ongoing processes of history. At the other end of the spectrum from Donaldson's absolute forces of Good and Evil, Charnas explicitly identifies the "negative" forces at work in her world and ties them to equivalent forces in our own world: the exploitative and oppressive rule of men.

In these four works the utopian impulse manifests itself through the nostalgic evocation of an edenic past. But in the works of McKillip and Donaldson, the collective anxieties and tensions of life under capitalism are explained and resolved as the result of an estrangement from and perversion of the pattern of nature's rhythms. The awakened desire for an end to alienation and want is then defused through the portrayal of a happier, conflict-free world in which social relations of domination and exploitation are legitimized as "natural," while the real causes of human want and alienation are mystified. In these worlds the only hope for the future lies in the willing return and submission to an even more repressive and limited past – unlike the worlds of Charnas and Lynn where, however much they resemble the critique of technology and technological change I have been describing, they nonetheless suggest that hope lies instead in the future, in the transformation and amelioration of their societies.

The second criterion I will use to distinguish between those worlds in which the utopian impulse is fostered and those in which that impulse is co-opted lies in the representation of everyday life. By everyday life I mean, first of all, the daily lives of the characters as well as their function in a social context. And secondly, I understand by everyday life a cluster of issues which feminism has put on the agenda for any serious project of social transformation, most specifically the issues of sexuality and gender roles, as well as questions about the "family."

The consideration of the representation of everyday life suggests a difference between the works of Charnas and Lynn which lift us out of our own lives through the portrayal of an alternative social order in which our daily lives and our work activity could be a vital means of self-realization and the works of McKillip and Donaldson, on the other hand, which lift us out of our lives through the portrayal of the magical, exceptional existence of a hero with whom the reader can identify for a time before returning to his or her own drab and unsatisfying life. The heroes of McKillip and Donaldson are above the duties and tedium of daily life, in stark contrast to the central characters in Charnas and Lynn who are depicted in their daily routines, at work and at play. On reflection, however, the reader may realize that the hero's exceptional existence is sustained through the unquestioning acceptance of a host of characters "behind the scenes" – the farmers and cooks and maids and tailors and soldiers and so on who provide for and make possible the hero's adventurous existence. It is no wonder, then, that the worlds of McKillip and Donaldson are fixed, hierarchical societies in which each character knows and accepts his or her place in that social order. In terms of the reader, the effect is, I think, quite different. Charnas and Lynn give us hope, not by offering us an order. In terms of the reader, the effect is, I think, quite different. Charnas and Lynn give us hope, not by offering us an exceptional existence, but through the promise of a world in which the activities of all are validated, a world in which "the free development of each would be the condition of the free development of all" (Marx and Engels 1959). Donaldson and McKillip merely reaffirm the ideology of individualism. They reinforce the reader's acceptance of the world as it is in exchange for the illusory promise of a private escape – an escapism whose "real life" corollary is the winning lottery ticket rather than any amelioration of the community as a whole.

If life is more "real," more immersed in the quotidian in the novels of Charnas and Lynn, it also contains more moments of happiness and pleasure, of sensuousness and sensuality; and there is an emphasis on physical and emotional well-being. This properly utopian dimension – a world of human self-realization within the context of a community – is particularly evident in the untraditional sexual and "family" arrangements in these works. In McKillip and Donaldson the hierarchical and fixed sociopolitical structures of their societies are reproduced in the basic social unit – the nuclear family. Moreover the almost complete absence of sexuality in fact reaffirms the primacy of the patriarchal family as well as what Marcuse called, "the repressive order of procreative sexuality."

Along with the shift in focus from the magical and heroic dimensions of traditional fantasy to the qualities and textures of everyday life, Charnas and Lynn raise the issues of sexuality and the family. Their societies function in a communal way. In Charnas's society of riding women, the different communities or "camps" resemble the societal organization of the Plains Indians. These camps in turn are made up of different "tents" of five or six women who raise collectively, as "sharemothers," their babies until they are old enough to leave the tent and live on their own with the other children in the "childpack." Within the camps, decisions are made in common, in open debate, although there is a chosen "chief" who deals with administrative questions. Sexual relations among the women are open and non-monogamous, and are depicted as an affirmative and integral part of their lives. In this novel, social forms as well as those of sexuality and child-rearing are, it might be argued, the result of a society without men. However, this suggests not a "perversion" of the natural order, but rather the emergence of new social forms which are no longer based on relations of domination; and it reminds us that our present social organization and family structures are neither "natural" nor immutable.

These ideas are carried even further in Lynn's *Dancers*. In the land of Arun the various towns, keeps and cities are independent, joined together by trade, by a common language and by a tacit (or explicit) recognition of each community's autonomy, although this latter situation is threatened in each of the novels of the trilogy. There are traditional political and familial forms, but this is a society in process, an imperfect world from which a freer and more human world is struggling to emerge. In the town of Elath in *Dancers* we see three generations living and working together with no radical changes in child-rearing itself. But, unlike the traditional social groupings in McKillip and Donaldson, this village functions in a communal way without most of the basic elements of the traditional patriarchal family. There is no sexual division of labor (except in child bearing itself) and there are no taboos or restrictions placed on sexual activities (except against incest between generations). As in *Motherlines*, sexuality is portrayed as an important and satisfying part of the characters' lives. Many of the characters (in both this novel and in *The Northern Girl*, Book III of the series) – and this includes adolescents as well as mature adults – are depicted as sexually active, while homosexual relationships are an accepted and normal part of the characters' sexual lives.

To conclude, then, in the more traditional works of McKillip and Donaldson, everyday life is mystified through the exceptional life and adventures of the hero. Change, whether change in the larger social structures or in the more intimate customs, attitudes and organization of private life, is rejected, while traditional forms and patterns are presented as the reflection of an innate natural order. In the works of Charnas and Lynn, on the other hand, the authors seem convinced that these traditional patterns and customs are neither given nor natural, but an integral part of the existing relations of exploitation and domination at work in our own society. Consequently, much of the fascination and thrill of traditional fantasy has been substantially reinterpreted; the heroic dimension has been replaced with a concern for new forms and patterns of daily life which would allow the emergence of a genuinely human world, beyond the existing forms of social and sexual oppression which the works of McKillip and Donaldson seem to reaffirm.

CHAPTER 3

Ideological Foreclosure and Utopian Discourse

> the incontrovertible point [is] that most 20th century writers who care to speculate about possible societies seem to have lost their utopian dreams.
>
> (Walsh 1962: 17)

> l'hégémonie discursive d'une époque ne sert pas tant à imposer des thèmes obliges et des formes canoniques qu'elle ne semble viser à refouler certaines "choses" dans l'impensable ou l'extravagant.
>
> (Angenot 1984: 29)

My interest in recent utopian fiction has led me back to the 1950s and the recollection that only a short time ago, utopias had been declared obsolete. In this context, the revival of utopian themes in the 1970s raises questions about what can or cannot be written at a given historical moment and about how and why certain themes and genres enter or re-enter public consciousness and discourse.[1] Although there were ostensibly no utopias during the 1950s, this "absence" can be charted and studied in the flourishing of its reverse – the anti-utopia. In this paper, I would like to present the first part of an investigation of the absence of utopias in English during the 1950s: a mapping of the permutations of utopian writing in this period, particularly anti-utopias

1 This is a revised version of a paper read at an international conference on "Teorie e Prassi Utopiche nell'Età Moderna e Postmoderna" cosponsored by the University of Rome and the University of Reggio Calabria in May 1986; and, in a different form, at the eleventh annual meeting of the Utopia Studies Association in Monterey California (October 1986). For a discussion of the revival of utopian themes in the 1970s, see Chapter 8, "Positioning and Closure." For a discussion of the theoretical starting point of this article, see Marc Angenot, "Le discours social: problématique d'ensemble," *Cahiers de recherche sociologique* 2/1 (April 1984), 19–45.

and science fiction.[2] For, according to most critics, the anti-utopia had, by the middle of the twentieth century, become the most important form of modern utopian writing; moreover such anti-utopian writing was now produced primarily within the generic boundaries of science fiction. However, while many critics have discussed this rise in anti-utopian themes, few have attempted to classify its forms or to map the predominantly dystopian permutations of the utopian writing and science fiction of the 1950s.

There are three facets of the inadequacy of existing descriptions of the forms of utopian discourse of the 1950s. There is, not surprisingly, a shortage of criticism limited to the consideration of a single moment like the 1950s (but see Chapman 1975). Critical writing about utopia, even when it has an historical focus, tends to be in much larger sweeps. Manuel's "third period," for instance, covers the entire twentieth century (Manuel 1966: 71); while Berger's study of pessimistic and dystopian science fiction (*Science Fiction and the New Dark Age*) spans the last forty years. I am interested in restricting my investigation to this specific period as a way of trying to understand and explain why utopias could seemingly be written off at a particular moment only to appear with such force a decade later. Secondly, there is the question of the corpus, of the works to be considered. While I will restrict myself to a single decade, I will use a net broad enough to capture all the various manifestations of utopia, including science fiction and anti-utopias. Finally, there has not really been an attempt to set up principles of classification for utopian writing which are historically

2 (A) Anti-utopia as the most important manifestation of modem utopian writing – before the revival of the 1970s: "These pessimistic forecasts of strictly regimented societies must be considered the most important type of modern utopian fiction" (Gerber: 67). "In our time the utopian impulse has been largely replaced by dystopian projections of disastrous current trends" (Scholes and Rabkin: 174). See also Bouchard et al. (1985: 190–204).
(B) Anti-utopia as predominantly science fiction: "the great anti-utopias of the twentieth century constitute […] a single kind of fiction, for which there is no other name than science fiction" (Hillegas: 5). "Strictly and precisely speaking, utopia is not a genre but the sociopolitical subgenre of science fiction" (Suvin 1979: 61). There are several critics who maintain that SF was an optimistic genre until the 1960s, but this is very much a minority view. See Gerard Klein (writing from France [1977]), 3, and Huntington, 140.

specific. Critics have developed abstract models which incorporate all utopian writing; but in dealing with specific socio-historical units, critical analysis has been limited to unsystematic lists of the major developments.[3]

To map the possibilities of utopian discourse during the 1950s, I will use a classificatory system, based on A.J. Greimas's "semantic square," with which I will generate a basic calculus (or *combinatoire*) based on a functional opposition central to contemporary utopian writing: the contrast between change and the fear of change. This method and its results should not be taken as necessarily correct or adequate, but as a heuristic device to help me to discover the permutations of utopian writing at this specific moment.[4]

3 In what is perhaps the most comprehensive and systematic attempt to classify the types of utopian writing, Guy Bouchard proposes a classificatory system for all utopian (and dystopian) writing which contains 192 categories, a system whose complexity and range far exceed my purpose in trying to understand the specificity of the 1950s and the particular absence or "blocking" of utopian writing within a single language at that time (1985: 184–190). On the other hand, in his *Science Fiction and the New Dark Age* (1976), Harold Berger posits three general categories for the "anti-utopias of modem science fiction," under which he elaborates twelve thematic groups: I. *The Threat of Science*: (1) "Hostility to Science," (2) "Man vs. Machine," (3) "The Synthetic Experience," and (4) "Ignoble Utopias"; II. *The New Tyrannies*: (1) "The Totalitarian State of the Future," (2) "The Mind Invasion," (3) "Commerce and Exploitation," and (4) "The Revolt of Youth"; III. *Catastrophes*: (1) "Nuclear War," (2) "The Population Explosion," (3) "Race War in America," and (4) "The Obsessional Catastrophe." Berger's categories, while dealing based on many of the works I will discuss, are primarily labels based on the types and "causes" of the dystopian visions portrayed. Although it identifies many of the major themes of recent dystopian fiction, it is not internally consistent or coherent as a classificatory system; and it is not able to suggest possible utopian (or other) absences within the writing of the period. Raymond Williams (1980: 196–212) does develop an abstract model of the forms of utopian writing which is based on eight categories, four "positive" (utopian), and four negative (dystopian) which negate the previous four types: (1) (+/−) the "heaven" (or "hell"); (2) (+/−) the "externally altered world"; (3) (+/−) the "willed transformation"; and (4) (+/−), the "technological transformation." However, only his third category, "willed transformation," is "characteristic, in the strict sense" of utopia and dystopia (199). See also Greven-Borde (1995).

4 For an application of Greimas to science fiction, see Fredric Jameson, "After Armageddon: Character Systems in *Dr. Bloodmoney*," *Science Fiction Studies* 2 (1975), 31–41. See also Jameson's "Forward" to A.J. Greimas, *On Meaning: Selected*

According to Darko Suvin, whose genealogical clarifications are essential to any serious study of science fiction and utopia, a utopia is:

> the verbal construction of a particular quasi-human community where sociopolitical institutions, norms, and individual relationships are organized according to a more perfect principle than in the author's community, this construction being based on estrangement arising out of an alternative historical hypothesis. (Suvin 1979: 49)

The utopian "verbal construction" of an alternative to one's own community involves a dual operation: at the same time that it sets out a model for a better society, it also, at least implicitly, criticizes the existing society – just as social satire implicitly points to an ideal state of affairs. ("Utopia explicates what satire implicates, and vice versa," Suvin 1979: 54.) The contrast between the "author's community" and the better world implies as well the *desirability of change*, of a movement toward that more perfect society. Anti-utopian fiction, on the other hand, is based on *a fear of change*, and may include both explicit constructions of imaginary worlds which are meant to be worse than the present, and the implicit or explicit critique of utopian ideals.

Using Greimas's "semantic rectangle," the opposition between change and fear of change generates eight types which I will use to map the specific permutations and characteristics of utopian/dystopian writing in the 1950s. CHANGE – more specifically social change, the utopian society toward which the reader is invited to move – generates first of all its opposite, STASIS, the status quo of the "author's community." Moreover, as the opposition utopian *I* dystopian implies, each of these categories has a positive and a negative pole. CHANGE includes both utopian writing (+) and social satire posited in the desirability of change (–), while STASIS is grounded in a fear of change, and includes both works which defend the status quo (+) and works which challenge the desire for change (–). CHANGE also generates two further terms: NOT-CHANGE and NOT-STASIS. NOT-CHANGE signals an impasse, combining fear of change with a rejection of the status quo, whether in works which stress the impossibility of change (–) or which propose an "existentialist" acceptance of the status quo (+). NOT-STASIS, finally, attempts to resolve this impasse. While continuing to reject social change, it introduces the possibility of other forms of change based on/organized around an organic or biological model: evolution (+) and devolution (−). These positions can be schematically represented as follows:

Figure 1 Semantic field of 1950s Utopian/Dystopian Writing

Let us now see how these eight categories account for the various manifestations of utopian and anti-utopian writing in English during the 1950s.

CHANGE

Traditionally, utopias and utopianism – at least since the nineteenth century – have been linked with socialism. Not surprisingly, then, there are no explicitly utopian works from a socialist or communitarian perspective in the 1950s – as opposed to the utopian revival of the 1960s and 1970s.[5] There are however two other types of writing which fall into this category.

Writings in Semiotic Theory (Minneapolis: University of Minnesota Press, 1987). The opposition change/fear of change is basically a subjective one, but it is derived from science fiction's particular ability to mediate our contradictory hopes and fears about the future (see Chapter 1 in this volume, "The Modern Anglo-American SF Novel"; Jameson 1973).

5 Although there were no socialist utopias in English, 1957 was the year of the publication of Yefremov's *Andromeda*. See the chapter "Russian SF and its Utopian Tradition" in Suvin (1979), particularly pp. 265–268.

+ *Utopia* (Focus on change):

Utopias written from a non-socialist and non-communitarian perspective, which are critical of the status quo, as in B.F. Skinner's *Walden II* (1948) and Ayn Rand's *Atlas Shrugged* (1957).

– *Social Satire* (Focus on status quo):

Works which by their criticism of the author's own society also imply the outlines of a more perfect society (e.g., Pohl & Kornbluth, *The Space Merchants*, 1953; Bradbury, *Fahrenheit 451*; Vonnegut, *Player Piano*).

STASIS (Defense of Status Quo/Fear of Change)

Opposed to CHANGE is "fear of change": works which reverse the properties just outlined and warn of the dangers of change, either by portraying the status quo in positive terms (+), or by the portrayal of a dystopian future based on the development or imposition of "foreign" political forms and values (–). The latter category – the political anti-utopia – is defined and illustrated by Orwell's *1984* (published in 1949) which has become synonymous for this type of writing.[6] The explicit defense of the status quo, on the other hand, is a minor form, which is illustrated by some non-fiction works of the period which championed the U.S. (e.g., Morris L. Ernst's *Utopia, 1976* [1955]).[7]

6 *1984* is often considered as the third of a triptych of anti-utopian classics; the others are Zamyatin's *We* (1924) and Huxley's *Brave New World* (1932).

7 Ernst's work is not a novel but, as he puts it, "a dream for our republic in 1976" (3). It is an optimistic projection of what the United States will be twenty years hence, based on the flourishing of the intrinsic qualities and values of the American Way of Life. While the author sees problems and obstacles along the way toward a nation of "Energy, Leisure, Full Rich Life" (1969: 305), he does not propose a change in the essential characteristics of the United States, but the full realization of their potential. For a further discussion of the intellectuals' praise for America during the 1950s, see the chapter "The Celebration of America" in Richard Pells, *The Liberal Mind in a Conservative Age: American Intellectuals in the 1940s & 1950s* (New York: Harper & Row, 1985), 130–147, and the chapter, "The Ideology of the Liberal Consensus,"

– *Anti-Utopia* (focus on change): Orwell, *1984*.

+ *Encomium* (focus on status quo): Morris Ernst, *Utopia, 1976*.

NOT-CHANGE (The Simultaneous Rejection of Utopian Ideals and the Critique of the Status Quo)

The third category is made up of novels which reject utopian aims and ideals even as they acknowledge the flaws of the present system – contradictory themes which are nowhere more evident than in the novels of James Blish, *Case of Conscience* (1958) and Walter Miller Jr. *A Canticle for Leibowitz* (1959). Such a position is based on the critique of the utopian premise of the perfectibility of human beings through the presentation of the flawed character of human nature as in William Golding's *Lord of the Flies* (1954). The positive manifestation of this category includes works which are equally critical of the present and of the possibility of change, but which nonetheless see the possibility of some human hope – a characteristic which is evident in much of the writing of P.K. Dick (e.g., *Eye in The Sky*, 1957).

– *Resignation* (Focus on fallen human nature, impasse): J. Blish, *Case of Conscience*, W. Golding, *Lord of the Flies*, W. Miller, *Canticle for Leibowitz*.

+ *Existentialism* (Attempts to resolve the impasse): P.K. Dick, *Eye in the Sky*.

---

in Godfrey Hodgson, *America in Our Time* (Garden City, NY: Doubleday, 1976), 67–98, as well as his defense of his methods for this chapter, 504–507. See also Miller and Nowak (1977), passim. I have used a non-fictional work as an instance of this category, because the novel works on a dynamic of tension and resolution. Praise is almost by definition descriptive and static. Fiction, according to Charles Grivel, maintains the status quo by representing a threat to the existing order which is resolved at the novel's end. All fiction, thus, might be said to seek to defend the status quo. The status quo is defended, not by directly praising, but by presenting a threat to the system which is subsequently undone. This underlies the problem of the "static" nature of utopian fiction, and, at least on a fictional level, the success of dystopias. Within such a perspective, it might be argued that the most important "utopian" work of the decade was Herbert Marcuse's *Eros and Civilization* (Boston, MA: Beacon Press, 1955).

NOT-STASIS (The Rejection of the Status Quo and of Utopian Ideals Leads to the Imagining of Modes of Change Other Than the Technological or the Political)

Building on the previous three categories, the fourth is made up of fictions which reject the status quo while refusing the utopian possibility of social or technological change; fictions, then, which propose a nonhistorical transformation, outside human agency, and of which the most famous example would be the transcendent ending of Arthur Clarke's *Childhood's End* (1953). This category, in its opposition to the scientific solutions of the traditional utopian answers of earlier science fiction, is perhaps the dominant model of 1950s science fiction, particularly in its positing of a biological model of human evolution, most noticeably through the theme of telepathy as a key to improved human communications (Sturgeon, *More Than Human* [1953]; Wyndham, *The Chrysalids* [1955]). The negative dimension of this final category comprises works which, similar to the impasse portrayed in Blish and Miller in the previous category, use the organic model to show not the emergence of some new or higher form of human being, but its opposite – the gradual return of humanity to some prehuman state; not evolution, but devolution. This latter theme was introduced in Wells's *The Time Machine* (1895), but it is one which U.S. writers, at least until the 1960s (with the full impact of the New Wave,) had difficulty portraying.[8] This development is already apparent, however, by the early 1960s in Britain, in B. Aldiss's *Hothouse* (1962) and in what is perhaps the most remarkable of J.G. Ballard's disaster novels, *The Drowned World* (1962).

8 Traditionally, the destruction of the world has been, in many ways, a taboo theme in popular writing. If the classic narrative portrayed a threat to the social order whose eventual rejection figured the return to normalcy, there is not much room for the portrayal of the destruction of the social order. Science fiction, even at its grimmest, has always found a way to pull back from the edge, at least until the 1960s. The imposition of these norms can best be seen, for instance, in the almost artificial ending of H.G. Wells's *War of the Worlds* (1898) where the seemingly invincible Martians are suddenly thwarted in their conquest of the Earth by their susceptibility to

+ Evolution:

(organic): T. Sturgeon, *More than Human*, J. Wyndham, *The Chrysalids*;

(transcendental): A.C. Clarke, *Childhood's End.*

– Devolution:

(organic): B. Aldiss, *Hothouse*;

(transcendental): J.G. Ballard, *The Drowned World.*

The above schema, while not necessarily complete, is an attempt to map the internal configurations of utopian and anti-utopian writing within a specific field of discourse (English-language writing), at a given historical moment (the 1950s). Moreover, it is not meant to be only an abstract account of the various possibilities inherent in the form, but a way of organizing the actual manifestations of utopian discourse during that period.

Within the basic opposition we saw, first of all, four primary forms: utopia and anti-utopia, encomium and social satire. Most critics see only two forms in this opposition, utopia and anti-utopia: firstly, because the celebration of the status quo (encomium) is usually seen as falling outside the possibility of narrative; and, more importantly, because the critics interested in these questions often do not distinguish between anti-utopia and social satire. There is a useful distinction to be made here, however, based on the attitudes expressed toward the core values of the "author's community." The anti-utopia is a rejection of foreign values which threaten that community's intrinsic organization and beliefs, whether in the fear of political change (i.e., socialism), or in Huxley's critique of both Americanism (the conformity and efficiency of the assembly line, of consumerism, etc.) and of the Soviet system. Social satire, on the other hand, focuses on the flaws and negative developments in one's own system – advertising and the implicit nature of capitalism in *Space Merchants*, or the more ambiguous critiques of the American Way of Life in Bradbury and Vonnegut. While the two may overlap, the anti-utopia usually implies a defense of the values and structures of the author's community which social satire, on the other hand, seems to question. The anti-utopia sometimes ends with the destruction of the dystopian society and the return to the community's original values, while social satire seems to go further and imply the development of a new society. Insofar as they critique the values of their society, both *Fahrenheit 451* and *The Space Merchants*, for instance, end with the brief description of a utopian alternative (although in Bradbury it is a nostalgic evocation of the lost American past).

This description appears to confirm that there are few explicit instances of utopian writing in the 1950s. As compared to thirty-eight dystopias, Sargent (1975) mentions only five novels in his discussion of science fiction utopias published in the 1950s, including three novels by Clarke which I have described as examples of anti-utopias.[9] Indeed, although I did cite two utopias at the beginning of this paper, many critics do not consider *Walden Two* to be a utopia at all. In Berger's study, for instance Skinner's work is used to illustrate the thematic group "Ignoble Utopias." While one

---

terrestrial germs. U.S. SF has often portrayed humanity growing and spreading through the galaxy, colonizing and so on. In *The Time Machine* (1895), he was able to portray the end of humanity in the very distant future. For a discussion of these themes in science fiction, see the various essays in Eric Rabkin, Martin Greenberg, and Joseph Olander, eds., *The End of the World* (Carbondale: Southern Illinois University Press, 1983). British and European writers have often seemed humbler, and more aware of the issue of imperialism. Imperialism has rarely been a theme in U.S. SF, the exception being Le Guin's *The Word for World is Forest* (1973). Olaf Stapledon's *Starmaker* (1937) is perhaps the best known example of a more humble vision of humanity's role in the universe and of the possible extinction of the Earth, along with Clarke, from his *Childhood's End* (1953) to *Rendezvous with Rama* (1973). See also S. Lem's *Solaris* (1961). In U.S. SF this attitude only really changed in the 1960s. Thomas Disch's *The Genocides* (1965) is an early example of this shift in attitudes.

9 Two (of the three) Clarke novels are the same, for *The City and The Stars* is a revised version of *Against the Fall of Night*. For a description of the anti-utopian character of this work see Tom Moylan, "Ideological Contradiction in Clarke's *The City and the Stars*," *Science Fiction Studies* 4 (1977), 150–156. The five novels Sargent (1975) mentions on his list of science fiction utopias published in the 1950s are: Arthur C. Clarke's *Childhood's End*, along with his *Against the Fall of Night* (1953) and the *City and the Stars* (1956); William Walter's *Curve of Snowflake* (1956), and Benjamin Appel's dystopian *Funhouse* (1959). Sargent's complete bibliography of utopian writing (1979) includes perhaps a dozen utopias published during the

must recognize, I think, that in terms of Suvin's definition, *Walden II* is a utopia, this example (and the primarily negative reactions to Skinner's proposals) serves to illustrate and confirm the low fortunes of the utopia at the time.

The positions I have proposed for the first part of this model show the predominance of the fear of change during the 1950s. This fear of social change blocks the imagining of alternatives to the "American Way," except as negative, frightening and ominous prospects. Beyond the opposition CHANGE/FEAR OF CHANGE, the final two categories suggest forms of utopian discourse outside these traditional categories; and ways in which the suppressed utopian impulse works its way through and beyond this "blocking" of utopian writing. The category of NOT-CHANGE described an impasse – a critique of the status quo as well as a rejection of the implicit solution of a willed change in the status quo. In the case of Blish and Miller, this is a familiar theological rejection of the possibility of a "heaven on Earth" which is perhaps best demonstrated in the subtitle of Thomas Molnar's critique of utopianism: *Utopia: The Perennial Heresy* (1967). As opposed to the religious belief in Original Sin and the impossibility of an earthly utopia, Golding's *Lord of the Flies* is a secular rejection of utopianism, based on human "innate aggressivity." In response to this impasse,

---

1950s (including the novels of Rand and Skinner), as opposed to almost eighty dystopian novels (primarily categorized as "authoritarian dystopias"), of which six are referred to as "communist dystopias." Although Sargent's bibliography is an invaluable work, there are always difficulties in distinguishing utopias and anti-utopias, as can be seen in the debates around Skinner's *Walden Two* (see Berger 1976: 53–65), or in my categorizing of Clarke's *Childhood's End* as an anti-utopia. Without being able to discuss at length the issue here, I do not consider works which include utopian societies to be necessarily utopian. *Childhood's End* portrays two utopian societies which are rejected within the context of the novel: the "Golden Age" which follows the Overlords' arrival and which is presented as ultimately boring, and the utopian experiment of New Athens (a community of artists), which is again very deliberately depicted as lacking in some essential quality. The novel depicts these utopian goals and societies in order to critique them, to argue that without some higher transcendental goals and purpose, the human race is doomed to repeat the sterile despair of the Overlords. The other two Clarke titles are versions of the same novel, and again contain, I would argue, a critique of the utopian ideal rather than a defense of it.

I described first of all, "existentialist" solutions – attempts to build a meaningful life from within the system, as at the end of Dick's *Eye in the Sky* where the characters turn to handicrafts manufacture.

The category of NOT-STASIS, finally, is the imagining of modes of transformation which do not involve human agency, but find their impetus and cause in the "natural" world. Given the general negative attitudes toward science at the time and the blocking of explicitly utopian themes, this category becomes the dominant area of science fiction writing in the 1950s (Fitting 1979). As I explained above, this finds its outlet in organic images – evolution (and devolution) – particularly in the widespread portrayal of the "natural" development of telepathy.

As I stated at the outset, this mapping of the possible forms of utopian discourse was a necessary first step in trying to understand the absence of utopias in the 1950s. In a subsequent study I shall discuss the critical explanations for this absence, before attempting to draw my own conclusions.[10]

10 See Chapter 8, "Positioning and Closure."

CHAPTER 4

Utopia Beyond Our Ideals: The Dilemma of the Right-Wing Utopia

> the freedom of writing implies the freedom of the citizen. One does not write for slaves. The art of prose is bound up with the only regime in which prose has meaning, democracy. (Sartre 1983: 47)

> It may well be asked why so many "modern" utopias are socialist – indeed, the two categories almost became coextensive during the nineteenth century. A sociological account would connect the proliferation of socialist theories with the inception and development of capitalism and the visible injustices which resulted. (Goodwin and Taylor 1982: 45)

The Problem: Definitions and Distinctions

As has been pointed out many times, the categories of *utopia* and *socialism*, "almost became coextensive during the nineteenth century." Since the revival of utopianism and utopian scholarship in the 1970s, there has been a growing realization that there are *also* utopias which eschew and even reject socialist ideals; and some critics have begun to argue that the "coextensiveness" of utopianism and socialism might be the result of historical factors rather than evidence of an essential and intrinsic political content of the utopia.[1] The existence of "capitalist"

1 One of the first examinations of this question was Lyman Tower Sargent's 1981 article "Capitalist Eutopias in America," in Kenneth M. Roemer, ed., *America as*

and, more generally, of "right-wing" utopias poses a dilemma for those scholars who, like myself, came to the study of utopia as a continuation of an involvement in socialist and feminist politics. In the following I will probe this dilemma, before examining some typical right-wing utopias.

A reading of the standard definitions of utopia does little to resolve the question of the political "contents" of the imaginary society, as, for instance, in Darko Suvin's formulation, which makes no reference per se to the political features of the utopia:

> Utopia is the verbal construction of a particular quasi-human community where sociopolitical institutions, norms, and individual relationships are organized according to a more perfect principle than in the author's community. (Suvin 1979: 49)

In their study of utopianism and political theory, *The Politics of Utopia*, Barbara Goodwin and Keith Taylor seem, at first, to have found a way of denying utopian status to potential utopias based on the work's contents. Goodwin and Taylor begin with the stipulation "that anything purporting to be a utopia should have universal scope and offer benefits to all those within this frame of reference" (1982: 18). These conditions would in fact eliminate, on the grounds of their elitism and restricted benefits, most of the works I propose to study. Unfortunately, this stipulation of universality is then qualified by the admission that the condition that "all must benefit equally" is itself the imposition "of a particular ideal" (1982: 18). Egalitarianism itself is but one form of the fictional evocation of a better place; the utopia "should aim to benefit everyone, *albeit to differing degrees*" (1982: 18; emphasis added).

Utopia, pp. 192–205. However, in addition to the "capitalist eutopias" he mentions, there are other "right-wing utopias" (like those described by Michael Orth in a paper given to the 1988 meeting of the Society for Utopian Studies), which are not necessarily capitalist. At the same time, there has also been an increasing interest in the "utopian" dimension of fascism. See Alice Kaplan's *Reproductions of Banality: Fascism, Literature, and French Intellectual Life* (Minneapolis: University of Minnesota Press, 1986); as well as Frank Dietz's review of Jost Hermand's *Der alte Traum vom neuen Reich: Volkische Utopien und Nationalsozialismus*, in *Utopian Studies* 1/1 (1990), 137–140.

Despite Goodwin and Taylor's reasoning about egalitarianism, the temptation to rely on some ontological definition of utopia as a way of excluding elitist, sexist, or racist works from the utopian family has played an important role in the establishment of the utopian canon, as can be seen in the critical reaction to B.F. Skinner's *Walden Two*.

I will return to the Skinner controversy in a moment. It is already clear that however satisfying the expulsion of certain works from the utopian family might be, it simply avoids the problem being discussed. Socialists may have little difficulty in acknowledging that the model societies proposed in some older left utopias are no longer adequate or acceptable today, and indeed this critical distance in the name of egalitarianism was at the core of many of the feminist utopias of the 1970s. But insofar as right-wing utopias reject egalitarianism, such works raise a different problem. The coextensiveness of English-language utopias and the socialist tradition was based not only on a mutual commitment to egalitarianism, but on a repudiation of a status quo based on private property. Indeed, the rejection of the status quo may be seen as a fundamental formal characteristic of the utopia insofar as it is the obverse of the utopia's positive imagination of an alternative to the present. "Every utopia, by its very existence, constitutes an ad hoc criticism of existing society" (Goodwin and Taylor 1982: 29). Insofar as the existing society of the author is one based on private property, the right-wing utopia raises the question of how and why the utopian form could be used to promote ideologies which were already, ostensibly at least, hegemonic.

To understand these questions more fully, let us briefly look at the differences between left and right utopias. As Lyman Tower Sargent and others have argued, and as a reading of the feminist utopias of the 1970s quickly shows, there are two major areas of opposition between right and left: private property and equality (Sargent 1981: 199).

This right/left dichotomy is made explicit in the right-wing utopias. For instance, while decrying "the threat of communist domination," and requiring all candidates for office to "renounce their membership in [...] political parties or thought groups," Hunt's "Alpaca constitution" makes a provision for "two worldwide opposing philosophies," "Liberal" and "Constructive," which recapitulate the right/left opposition while making clear where the author's sympathies lie:

> LIBERAL – Stressing privileges for the masses; progress unhampered by tradition; humanitarianism regardless of property rights; paternalistic government; social gains and associated and similar objectives.
>
> CONSTRUCTIVE – Stressing inviolate property rights: individual initiative; the profit motive, free markets; protection against governmental monopoly and associated and similar objectives. (1967: 187)

On the other hand, for the left utopias of the twentieth century, human freedom and equality are not possible under capitalism, a system by which the means of production are in private hands, or in which egotism and the profit motive are the creed.

Nowhere is this opposition more clearly stated than in Neil Smith's deliberate reversal of the meaning of Le Guin's term "propertarian." Early in Smith's novel, *The Probability Broach*, one of his characters explains: "Propertarians believe that all human rights are *property* rights, beginning with absolute ownership of your own life" (12). Smith acknowledges that he has taken the term from Le Guin's *The Dispossessed*; but whereas in Le Guin, "propertarian" was a term of abuse – the grasping egotist – Smith uses it as a positive term, to designate those enlightened men and women who respect the primacy of private property. Le Guin sums up the contrary left utopian belief in the fundamental incompatibility of equality and private property when the central character of *The Dispossessed* explains that on the world of Anarres, "no one eats while another starves."

For the left utopists, human happiness depends on economic equality, or at least on economic security, as summed up in Marx's dictum, "From each according to his abilities, to each according to his needs." Yet real equality also depends on the dismantling of the discriminatory structures built into the innate competitiveness of capitalism. Left utopias (particularly those of the 1970s) are not satisfied with an explicit pledge of equality of opportunity. Instead left utopias attempt to challenge and transform the ways that inequality, as it derives from race and gender, as well as class, functions as a part of our society. Some right utopias do talk about equality of opportunity, but there is an underlying assumption that inequality is not a systemic problem: and in any case, it is *not* the role of the state to attempt to counter inequality. To the contrary, life is usually described in terms of the "survival of the fittest": nothing should be allowed to interfere with these "natural" processes for weeding out the weak and the infirm. More tellingly, the main characters of these utopias are usually white males, while society's "others" are relegated to their traditional roles.[2]

Some Right-Wing Utopias

This contradiction between the utopian form and the inclusion of apparently non-utopian features was at the heart of the debates which followed the publication of B.F. Skinner's *Walden Two* in 1948. Beginning with a brief look at the controversy around Skinner's utopia, I want to discuss seven representative utopian novels which illustrate the parameters of the right-wing utopia. These diverse novels include Ayn Rand's classic *Atlas Shrugged* (1957); three popular science fiction novels: Robert Heinlein's *The Moon is a Harsh Mistress* (1966), Larry Niven and Jerry Pournelle's *Oath of Fealty* (1981), and Neil Smith's *The Probability Broach* (1980); and three examples of utopias published by politically committed small presses: H.L. Hunt's *Alpaca Revisited* (1967), Jill von Konen's *Camp 38* (1984), and Andrew Macdonald's *The Turner Diaries* (1978). Although my examination of these novels will be somewhat abbreviated, I hope nonetheless to give a preliminary description of the principal types of utopian conventions and models they employ, before raising again the question of their place in the utopian classification. (In so doing, I will leave the question of the relative literary merit of these various works aside.)

In his elaboration of "capitalist eutopias," Sargent proposes two basic types of positive capitalist utopia: "works that picture a completely or nearly completely free-enterprise economy," and "works that suggest that although capitalism is the best economic system, it needs reform" (Sargent 1981: 193). But these two categories are not mutually exclusive (Hunt's *Alpaca Revisited* appears in each), and do not really help in trying to establish types of right-wing utopias. In concluding that these works are "similar in form and purpose" to other utopias, however, Sargent returns to the issue with which I began, the puzzle of the capitalist utopia:

2 See Chapter 9, "So We All Became Mothers."

> there is still the problem of why, in comparison to socialist eutopias, they are so rare [...] Utopias are primarily vehicles for criticism. In the United States the defender of capitalism has generally believed that the best possible world already exists. Thus the main criticism implied in the construction of an alternative society would be inappropriate. The prevalence of the antisocialist dystopia in the twentieth century makes the same point; it is designed to show that we are falling away from the good society [...] But the genre was used, and it was used to criticize the failings of the capitalist system and to show that improvements were possible. (Sargent 1981: 202)

In the following I have used a rudimentary classification system based on both positive and negative features; one which takes into account the utopia's critique of and distance from the status quo, as well as considering the contents and form of the alternative society. There are three general headings: capitalist, libertarian and apocalyptic. By "capitalist," I am referring to works which are only marginally, if at all, critical of the status quo and which stress instead the preservation of "The American Way of Life." The difference between it and the libertarian utopia lies not so much in the laissez-faire premise that too much government regulation and interference have brought American free enterprise to its knees, but in the emphasis on the need for drastic changes to confront this crisis. The second characteristic of the libertarian utopia is its abandonment of the Christian heritage, which informs the ideology of the New Right and the so-called Moral Majority today. The "apocalyptic" is marked by the conviction that existing society must be destroyed. However, in contrast to left utopias which also often reject the possibility of reform, apocalyptic utopias differ radically from left utopias (and from capitalist and libertarian utopias) in terms of their explanations of the problems, and in terms of the types of solutions the new society embodies.

Walden Two

Whether we like it or not, *Walden Two* is a utopia. It was clearly intended as a utopia, and it conforms to all of the formal characteristics of the genre, including the familiar narrative of the visit to the experimental community, a detailed exposition of its ideals, and a picture of life in the new society. In fact, there is not one utopian visitor, but two: a skeptical philosopher whose doubts and suspicions grow with each new discovery, and the narrator who ultimately decides that this is indeed the ideal society.

This novel is important, however, not because it typifies the right-wing utopia, but because it illustrates the dilemma with which I began. *Walden Two* is a problematic utopia not because of its form, but because of its content. Its problematic utopianism is evident from the attitudes of critics toward it, as can be seen in the following comments from the closing pages of Negley and Patrick's influential anthology, *The Quest for Utopia:*

> It is ironic to conclude our survey of utopian speculation in the pessimistic mood engendered by *Walden Two*. We have descended from the heights of confidence in man's capacities and noble aspiration for his progressive betterment to a nadir of ignominy in which he is placed on a par with pigeons. (1952: 583)[3]

Skinner's critics argue that, instead of producing a society of free men and women, his reliance on conditioning will simply reproduce the mindless, programmed beings of Huxley's *Brave New World*. Yet, as Krishan Kumar has argued, if we try to read the novel dispassionately, suspending for a moment our awareness of the controversy around behaviorism, Skinner's analysis and suggestions are often reasonable, and in fact overlap with much of the left critique of modern mass society. On the one hand, according to Kumar, Skinner addresses two significant failures of liberal philosophy. "The first is that liberalism has not been able to deal at all adequately with the situation of the 'happy slave' [... The second] has to do with the variety of 'progressive' and 'permissive' techniques currently practiced in many social institutions [which constitute] weak forms of social control" (1987: 370–371). From a positive, utopian perspective, Kumar continues, there is also something to be said for Skinner's proposals:

3 For accounts of the novel and the ensuing debate see: Berger (1976: 51–65); Kateb (1972: 139–216); and Kumar (1987: 347–378). The best-known attack on Skinner's "ignoble utopia" was Joseph Wood Krutch's *The Measure of Man* (New York: Grosset & Dunlap, 1954).

> Given that he chose to include eugenics, collective child-rearing, the destruction of the family, equality of work and rewards, common property and centralized planning, (the attacks on his work were) hardly unexpected. What needs to be emphasized is his considerable success in rescuing these practices from their disfigurement with Nazism and Stalinism. He shows that, given a suitable tentative attitude towards them, they are practices with a real potential for overcoming some of the fundamental discontents of modern society. (1987: 378)

Kumar concludes that *Walden Two* is unlike other utopias insofar as "it is a utopia of means, not ends." "Most utopias have as their main emphasis a vision of ultimate goals [...] To [Skinner] the goals of any perfected society are self-evident [...] What has always flawed utopian schemes, Skinner argues, and destroyed utopian communities, is the lack of a scientific theory of human behavior which would enable those values to be realized" (1987: 349).

The Capitalist Eutopia

H.L. Hunt's *Alpaca Revisited* is the account of a young idealist's decision "to go out into the world centers of thought and culture and seek a cure for [his country's] political plight" (1967: 6). The hero's plan is threefold: "First, to formulate a comprehensive charter, or constitution, for national government. Second, to get it adopted without internal revolution. Third, to make it work, to the people's advantage" (1967: 19).

The novel is composed almost entirely of discussions of the different articles of a new constitution for a small South American country, followed by the text of the constitution, which itself takes up forty pages of the 220-page book. There are several appendices, including one composed of the mostly pro forma replies of various "Heads of Foreign Nations" to whom he had sent copies of his model constitution. A section is also included which explains how "patriots" can act to protect "their liberty and the Nation's independence and sovereignty" against atheism and communism, by actively "promoting Christianity and Freedom" (1967: 221). Another appendix explains that the UN Charter is flawed because of the one nation, one vote principle, which gives too much power to the "international Communist conspiracy" (1967: 206).

This last idea is the key to the Alpaca constitution, which is based on the principle of "selective suffrage"; instead of one citizen, one vote, there is a provision for awarding "responsible citizens" with up to five additional votes, "based on age, experience, active interest and involvement in government, and tax paid" (1967: 191).

As I have said, the novelistic components of *Alpaca Revisited* are minimal. Moreover, the narrative of the drafting of a model constitution is different from most literary utopias which describe instead the already functioning alternative society, although literary utopias often include an explanation of "how the change came about." Hunt's novel ends as the new constitution is voted into place by the citizens of Alpaca. I have included this work because it exemplifies an aspect of my starting point: utopias include a critique of the status quo, something which is almost completely absent here. If it were not for the appendices and concern for protecting the United States against "atheism and Communism," the reader might wonder just what the book's intentions were. In keeping with this theme of defense and the security of American "independence and sovereignty," one could argue that the Alpaca Constitution is not meant for the United States, but for *other* countries, as a way of organizing the rest of the world, in order to best safeguard U.S. Christian capitalism. Thus the novel concludes with the "Freedom Team's 'fervent hope' ":

> that what they had done would not stop with Alpaca; in the many countries similarly situated, or faced with the threat of communist domination, they could watch hopefully for similar plan teams to spring up following their example. [...] [However] they had no way of foreseeing the agitation which led minorities in the USA into demonstrating, a step-up in crime rates, then to riots and finally near-insurrection. [...] Nor could Team Members anticipate that the United States and some other democracies would begin offering and paying a premium for movements so far to the left that they could be called communistic or socialistic, or at least atheistic. (1967: 155–156)

Niven and Pournelle's *Oath of Fealty* begins with that same specter of "agitation" among minorities and stepped-up crime rates, in order to make a more concrete utopian proposal for affluent Americans. Here the agitators' ideology is not communism, but a combination of environmentalism ("The Friends of Man and The Earth" – FROMATES, and their guerilla wing, the "American Ecology Army"), and a festering class resentment at the spectacle of wealth and advantage in the midst of poverty and despair. The novel describes the "arcology" of Todos Santos and its 250,000 inhabitants, built on the ruins of an area of Los Angeles and surrounded by the crumbling city:

> Terrorists had tried to start riots by starting fires in one of the ghetto areas. It had worked fine. They threw so many firebombs that they started a firestorm and burned down square miles of city, leaving a hideous, angry scar, a lot of people homeless, and unemployment soaring. When the consortium that owned Todos Santos offered to rebuild and create a hundred thousand jobs, and solve the fresh-water problem in the bargain, Congress and the state legislature and everybody else had fallen all over themselves to give the money people the incentives they demanded. (1982: 90)

The plot involves the attempts of the American Ecology Army to sabotage and discredit the utopian experiment. The underlying philosophy of Todos Santos, which is owned by a Swiss Corporation and is expected to show a profit, is summed up in the social-Darwinist graffito, "THINK OF IT AS EVOLUTION IN ACTION." This slogan becomes the justification for the residents of Todos Santos to defend their privileged way of life. As a reporter describes it, "an ugly mood has developed lately [...] typified by a phrase which has caught on in Todos Santos" (1982: 177).

Niven and Pournelle are explicit in their linking of "liberal" social ideas and the disintegration of the American Way of Life; they are unable or unwilling, however, to imagine a widespread or national solution. Theirs is a better society within the boundaries of the United States, to which admittance is strictly limited, and in which democracy has been replaced by safety. In exchange for a relatively free, comfortable and above all safe existence, residents have handed over a number of rights and freedoms. Protection is based on an efficient and omnipresent security system which monitors and watches over residents. This is an elitist utopia, restricted to the wealthy few who can afford to live there; it is not a vision of social transformation, but of the ultimate security system.

In some ways, *Oath of Fealty* resembles the libertarian utopias, later to be discussed. Instead of exhorting "patriots" to uphold the American Way of Life, *Oath of Fealty* turns its back on a decaying system in order to imagine an armed and insulated retreat for affluent Americans. However, the libertarian utopias will go further in their rejection of the status quo and in disdain for the Christian "heritage" of values and beliefs. *Oath of Fealty* is a transitional work which does not fully engage with the shortcomings of the United States. Yet there are other utopias which critique much more forcefully what they see as the United States collapsing under the weight of a bloated and restrictive government.

The Libertarian Utopia

Much of the philosophical bases of the libertarian position have been developed from the work of Ayn Rand. Rand's 1957 *Atlas Shrugged* developed many of the same themes by juxtaposing a collapsing America with glimpses of a utopian alternative. The book is an extensive portrait of the devastation of the United States at the hands of "looters" and "wreckers" who, in Rand's account of the decline of the United States, are identified not as men and women motivated by greed and self-interest, but as those who subscribe to the mistaken ideals of altruism. The novel tells of a small group of exceptional men who refuse this "philosophy of guilt":

> We are on strike against martyrdom, [John Galt declares], and against the moral code that demands it. We are on strike against those who believe that one man must exist for the sake of another. We are on strike against the morality of cannibals [...] our terms are a moral code which holds that man is an end in himself and not the means to any end of others. (1957: 740)

From their hidden valley, Galt and his friends watch and wait as the outside society falls apart:

> We did not know whether we'd live to see the liberation of the world or whether we'd have to leave our battle and our secret to the next generations. But now we think that we will see, and soon, the day of our victory and of our return. [...] when they have no pretense of authority left, no remnant of law, no trace of morality, no hope, no food and no way to obtain it – when they collapse and the road is clear – then we'll come back to rebuild the world. (1957: 748)

Although Rand's novel is more than a thousand pages in length, there is little actual description of the utopian society. Unlike the utopias of Heinlein and Smith (which I discuss below), Rand's individualism leads her to reject the possibility of a collective solution: "We are not a state here," Galt says of the hidden valley, "not a society of any kind – we're just a voluntary association of men held together by nothing but every man's self-interest" (1957: 747).

On the other hand, Heinlein and Smith describe, in some detail, the features and working of an alternative society. The plot of Heinlein's *The Moon is a Harsh Mistress* is modeled on the American colonies' breakaway from Britain, and uses the science fiction convention of starting over on an empty and available moon (a convention that is also used in such left utopias as Le Guin's *The Dispossessed* or Samuel Delany's *Triton* [1976]). There is some discussion of the social and economic structures of the lunar economy, and of its underlying libertarian principles ("There ain't no such thing as a free lunch," TANSTAAFL), but the novel's primary focus is on the mechanics of revolution, and the developing personality of a sentient computer. The utopian lunar colony is juxtaposed to an Earth in crisis which is collapsing primarily because of the mistaken "liberal" social and economic policies of various governments.[4]

Neil Smith's *The Probability Broach* makes many of the same points, using a different science fiction convention: that of the parallel or alternative reality in which the history of the United States has unfolded differently (as in P.K. Dick's celebrated *Man in the High Castle*, 1962). Here, Thomas Jefferson's decisive addition of the word "unanimous" to the Declaration of Independence has produced a libertarian "Confederacy." In this alternate

4 For a polemical indictment of liberal social policies toward the third world, see Jean Raspail's novel *The Camp of the Saints* (New York: Scribner, 1975).

United States, the Declaration of Independence reads, "to secure these rights, Governments are instituted among Men, deriving their just powers from the unanimous Consent of the Governed" (1980: 302). Without unanimous consent, the Congress cannot act; consequently, there have been few laws or taxes enacted over the past two hundred years. In our "federalist" United States, the "consent of the governed" is decided by a bogus majority rule, which has led to the proliferation of unnecessary and costly regulations and a vast bureaucracy to enforce them. Like the preceding two novels, *The Probability Broach* juxtaposes a decaying United States, grinding to a halt under the weight of government regulations and bureaucracy, with a healthy, vibrant alternative.

The novels of Heinlein and Smith were written as science fiction and as such, particularly in the case of Heinlein (who has often been ranked as "the most popular SF writer of all time"[5]), this has meant a wider readership for their works than for the other utopias under consideration. Following Rand's own loathing for altruism and state intervention, the libertarian utopias argue for an economic laissez-faire model which extends to the sphere of personal behavior and freedom; in the championing of absolute individual autonomy, these utopias have abandoned other traditional American values, most importantly the Christian moral values and religious beliefs which are at the core of Hunt's *Alpaca*.

Apocalyptic

Finally, there are those utopias which reject reform. A better society is not possible until the existing one has been levelled, a view already expressed in John Galt's triumphant words previously cited. Similar to Rand's elite, the members of Camp 38, in von Konen's novel of the same name, believe that the outside world is corrupt and doomed. However, while there are references to the impending collapse and its causes, this is not *Camp 38*'s primary focus, for it describes in detail a functioning, self-sufficient

5 *Locus* 319 (August 1987), 1.

community based on specific principles and ideals – a utopia to which I shall return.

There are, of course, more extreme visions of the collapse and its aftermath, visions which appear in a subgenre of popular fiction which shares some themes with utopian fiction: contemporary "survivalist" novels, such as the popular series of Jerry Ahern and William Johnston.[6] However, these survivalist communities are not really utopias since they are so small and fragile, barely more than an extended patriarchal family. Yet, the principles and ideals of self-sufficiency are apparent; if and when the fighting is over, a small but strong and self-reliant community will remain. (It is also interesting to note that one of the archetypes of this proto-utopian, survivalist fiction is Robert Heinlein's 1964 *Farnham's Freehold*.) These novels should be viewed as limit cases, works which mark the boundary of the utopian genre insofar as they express an apocalyptic need to begin over from the ruins of this world.[7]

In addition to economic collapse or the outbreak of nuclear war, there is another possible way of explaining the destruction of the existing society – its violent overthrow. The only solution, explains the protagonist of *The Turner Diaries*, is "to destroy the System, root and branch, and build something radically and fundamentally different in its place" (Macdonald 1987: 51). This idea is a familiar element in some left utopias, of which the best known examples would be Marge Piercy's *Woman on the Edge of Time* (1976) and Joanna Russ's *The Female Man* (1975). From a right perspective, the necessity of change through violence in the United States seems unusual. I have already argued that the libertarians were critical of what the United States had become, but this did not involve a total

6 For a complete listing and description of these novels, see Paul Brians's annotated bibliography of the "Atomic War in Fiction," *Nuclear Holocausts* (Kent, OH: Kent State University Press, 1987).

7 This is not unlike the warnings of various evangelical believers in the coming "Tribulation" (e.g., Hal Lindsey). Such religious views reject, of course, the possibility of an earthly utopia. These questions are also discussed in Coates's *Armed and Dangerous*. See also Kevin Flynn, and Gary Gerhardt, *The Silent Brotherhood: Inside America's Racist Underground* (New York: Free Press, 1989). I should note too that some critics, much to the chagrin of the author, have discussed Le Guin's utopia *Always Coming Home* as an after-the-bomb world.

renunciation; Smith proposed the addition of one word to the Declaration of Independence, while Heinlein modeled his lunar rebellion on the breakaway of the American colonies from Britain. Indeed, it is the left which is usually viewed as attempting to import a "foreign" ideology (socialism and communism) or as rejecting reform.[8]

In *The Turner Diaries* it is no longer a question of returning to pure capitalism or to some original intent of the Constitution. The extent of Turner's rejection is made clear from his reaction to the call for new elections:

> Doesn't the old fool understand that the American people *voted themselves* into the mess they're in now? Doesn't he understand that the Jews have taken over the country fair and square, according to the Constitution? (1987: 173)

There are other narratives of violent upheaval in which American patriots fight back against an invasion – the imposition of a foreign ideology by force – as in the film *Red Dawn* (1984), or in the Larry Niven and Jerry Pournelle science fiction novel *Footfall* (1985). According to Macdonald's racist conspiracy theory, it is no longer the communists, but Jews who have taken over the United States government, although Macdonald also stresses the un-American and foreign by calling it the "Zionist Occupation Government." *The Turner Diaries* is the account of the armed struggle of a dedicated band of guerillas to preserve Christian values and the white race – a book which because of its outline of racist ideology and the mechanics of guerilla warfare in the United States, has been labelled "the bible of the racist right."

There is also a legitimate question whether *The Turner Diaries* is a utopia at all. I have included it by analogy with Jack London's *The Iron Heel* (1907) which is usually classed as a utopia. As London's classic, the body of the novel depicts a violent struggle, while the liminal or framing text reveals that years have passed since the events depicted and that a utopian society has emerged:

8 This is a long-established view. In 1935, Earl Browder, the head of the Communist Party (USA), coined the slogan "Communism is Twentieth Century Americanism" to try and combat this image of a "foreign" ideology (Earl Browder, *What is Communism?* [New York: Vanguard Press, 1936]).

> [Turner] helped greatly to assure that his race would survive and prosper, that the Organization would achieve its worldwide political and military goals, and that the Order would spread its wise and benevolent rule over the earth for all time to come. (Macdonald 1987: 211)

The racist ideal society of *The Turner Diaries* tests the limits of the neutrality of the formal definition of utopia. The other example of an "apocalyptic" utopia, von Konen's *Camp 38*, is quite different. Formally, it is certainly a utopia; it describes a functioning, self-sufficient community held together by a set of common ideals. Nonetheless, these ideals are difficult to describe. The book is subtitled, "Current Model of Northern European Lifestyle Before Christianity"; and there are numerous references to a "pre-theocratic" or "pagan" culture, as well as to the legends which inform Wagner's Ring cycle. It also includes advertisements for other Sovereign Press publications, including Thomas Jefferson's *American Christian Bible* in which Jefferson allegedly "cut away from the words and story of Jesus the mutilating Judaic injections." On the next page, however, anti-Semitism is followed by anti-Catholicism, and an advertisement for a book entitled *The Pagan Bible* (von Konen 1984: 195).

Conclusion

I am trying to suggest that the increasing incidence of right-wing utopias is a complex phenomenon which demands further study. My original reaction, to deny that such works are utopias at all, avoids the larger issue of why visions of an alternative society should be important for those whose ideals might be said to have already triumphed. As my brief examination has shown, most of these works were written as critiques of the present reality of the United States, or at least as critiques of what the authors perceived that reality to be. Leaving aside the "capitalist utopia," which does not really criticize the United States, I have described two rather different groups of right-wing utopias.

There is, first of all, the cooler, more calculating vision of the libertarians (which includes *Oath of Fealty*). Theirs is indeed a recognition and rejection of the "compromises" capitalism has made, insofar as modern capitalist states are mixed economies with developed welfare systems. From another perspective, this was not so much a compromise as it was the price to be paid in order to avert more far-reaching upheaval and change: to some extent, it was the development of the welfare state which served to convert the revolutionary potential of a militant working class into today's more reformist socialist and labor parties.

While libertarianism is often associated with permissive moral standards, and with the conviction that the state has no place in the control of personal morality – whether it be sexual behavior and censorship, or Sunday closing laws and the regulation of alcohol consumption – these libertarian utopias go far beyond the defense of permissiveness and individual freedom. Libertarian utopias insist that the state has no role at all to play in the social or economic sphere. As John Galt explains in *Atlas Shrugged*:

> The only proper functions of a government are: the police, to protect you from criminals; the army, to protect you from foreign invaders; and the courts, to protect your property and contracts from breach or fraud by others, to settle disputes by rational rules. (Rand 1957: 1062–1063)

However, Galt's ideal government is still far too intrusive for Smith and Heinlein:

> A free, unregulated laissez-faire market should, and can, take care of everything government claims to do, only better, cheaper, and without wrecking individual lives in the process. (Smith 1980: 13)

The Turner Diaries and *Camp 38* fall into a very different category, and illustrate an opposite pole to the libertarian rejection of any mandated code of behavior or set of religious beliefs. While I have stated that it is difficult to characterize precisely the ideology of *Camp 38*, it is not libertarianism or individualism. Instead, the novel describes a community held together by a rigorous and harsh, albeit very brief, set of rules. These "items of agreement" are based on the notion of the "sovereign individual" and especially forbid groups from having power over individuals, but all members of the community are bound by these rules, and death is "the invariable penalty for breaking [them]" (von Konen 1984: 52).

Moreover, rituals and culture are designed to reinforce this "Northern European Lifestyle," particularly through a modified performance of Wagner's Ring Cycle which plays an integral role in binding the community together – a rather strange irruption of High Art into the rugged, elemental life of the inhabitants of Camp 38.

The racist "Christian Identity" ideology which informs *The Turner Diaries* is much more coherent, and much more explicit in its rejection of the primacy of individual rights. As demonstrated in Earl Turner's explanation of a decision to execute one of their members who questions the need for violent revolution:

> His were the motivations of a libertarian, the sort of self-centered individual who sees the basic evil in government as a limitation on free enterprise.
>
> Someone asked him whether he had forgotten what the Organization has repeated over and over, namely, that our struggle is to secure the future of our race, and that the issue of individual freedom is subordinate to that one, overwhelming purpose. (Macdonald 1987: 51, 52)

Their struggle is based on "an essentially religious attitude" (1987: 52), for Turner "understood" that he and the others were "truly the instruments of God in the fulfillment of His Grand Design" (1987: 71).

The Turner Diaries and *Camp* 38 are also the most explicitly "intentional" of the works I have discussed; the works were published pseudonymously by small, right-wing presses whose catalogues are comprised of books outlining their respective world views. In addition to my copy of *Camp 38*, for instance, I received an unsolicited and unsigned brochure entitled, "An Evaluation of Our American Heritage" which explains the "publishing policy" of Sovereign Press and its dedication to "Individual Sovereignty."[9]

9 The militant racist and religious views of this segment of the radical right were depicted in Costa-Gavras's film *Betrayed* (1988); and there is a synopsis of *The Turner Diaries* given by the radio talk-show host in Oliver Stone's film *Talk Radio* (1988), which is based on the murder of a Denver talk-show host – an event which is often seen as the "opening shot" in the survivalist right's armed rebellion.

Rather than exclude the extremist rantings of Macdonald (and according to Canadian "hate literature" legislation, the book is probably illegal), I would like to briefly explore the dimensions of the utopian in such a work. While the society and principles outlined are fundamentally abhorrent, to some extent the utopian may also be measured by the strength of a work's refusal of this world. Although *The Turner Diaries* is profoundly mistaken in its understanding of the causes of the current situation, it springs from a rejection of the present system.

In the conclusion of his *The Political Unconscious*, "The Dialectic of Utopia and Ideology," Fredric Jameson asks:

> [H]ow is it possible for a cultural text which fulfills a demonstrably ideological function, as a hegemonic work whose formal categories as well as its content secure the legitimation of this or that form of class domination – how is it possible for such a text to embody a properly Utopian impulse? (1981: 288)

He answers that "all class consciousness is Utopian insofar as it expresses the unity of a collectivity":

> The achieved collectivity or organic group of whatever kind – oppressors as much as oppressed – is Utopian not in itself, but only insofar as all such collectivities are themselves figures for the ultimate concrete collective life of an achieved Utopian or classless society. (1981: 289–290)

In this development of what Jameson calls "Bloch's luminous recovery of the Utopian impulse" (1981: 287), he argues that the utopian may be found in all forms of class consciousness, including fascism and racism, or, I would add, in the extremist convictions of Macdonald and von Konen. Macdonald's is a coherent world-view, a dream which, however perverted and sick, is of a world of like-minded men and women, freed at last from the humiliations and oppression they have had to endure. This is not to justify or exonerate its violent racism; but the contrast between it and the libertarian utopias points to a possible explanation of the dilemma with which I began, when I asked what attractions the utopian form could possibly have for those whose ideas and ideology have ostensibly triumphed. For the libertarians, interest in these recent utopias may be described, to use a metaphor which refers to the social-Darwinist image of "red in tooth and claw," as the "scent of blood": a decade of Reaganism and Thatcherism has given the apostles of greed the hope of an imminent roll-back of the social and political gains of the past fifty years and the prospect of a return to an unregulated market.

The Turner Diaries and *Camp 38*, on the other hand, suggest very different origins, grounded not in Rand's "radiant selfishness of soul," but in the suffering and rage of some victims of the unchecked greed and plunder of American Capitalism.

I have not resolved my original dilemma, but at least I hope to have succeeded in showing that the increase in right-wing utopias is of more than a purely scholarly interest. It is important insofar as it coincides to some degree with the waning of the left and feminist utopias of the 1970s. These works should serve to remind us that even the modest liberal gains that have been made over the past few decades are under attack. Perhaps we should read them as we read the dystopia, as warnings of what the future holds if we fail to resist.

CHAPTER 5

Buried Treasures: Reconsidering Holberg's *Niels Klim in the World Underground*

> Who in this country ever hears of Baron Holberg's Journey of Niels Klim to the World Underground, in spite of the fact that since the book appeared in 1741, it has been translated into thirteen languages and published in more than sixty editions? [...] Even though Klim is one of the best examples of the imaginary voyage – only Cyrano de Bergerac's Histoire Comique de la Lune and Swift's Gulliver's Travels are more famous – the author's name is unfamiliar to most students of eighteenth-century literature. (McNelis 2004: vii)

> I will speak first of Subterraneous Cavities and Waters, because they will be of easier dispatch, and an introduction to the rest. That the inside of the Earth is hollow and broken in many places, and is not a firm and united mass, we have both the Testimony of Sence and of easie observations to prove. (Burnet 1965: 93–94)

In 1836 the United States Congress passed a bill establishing what would become the first and most famous American naval scientific exploration, the "United States Exploring Expedition" which lasted from 1838 to 1842 and which led to the establishment of a national museum of natural history – the Smithsonian Institution – to house the more than 50,000 specimens collected. This expedition began in what the historian William Stanton has called the "fervent foolishness" of one man, John Cleves Symmes, Jr., a self-educated former soldier who in 1818 issued his "Circular Number 1," "sending copies to 'each notable foreign government, reigning prince, legislature, city, college, and philosophical society, quite around the earth' " (Stanton 1975: 8). In it Symmes wrote: "I declare that the earth is hollow and habitable within; containing a number of solid concentric spheres, one within the other, and that it is open at the poles twelve or sixteen degrees. I pledge my life in support of this truth, and am ready to explore the hollow, if the world will support and aid me in the undertaking" (quoted in Stanton 1975: 8).

The fortunes of the idea that the earth was "hollow and habitable within," from classical references to the underworld to esoteric and New Age writers today who continue to defend this notion, have been recounted elsewhere, most notably by Walter Kafton-Minkel in his *Subterranean Worlds: 100,000 Years of Dragons, Dwarfs, the Dead, Lost Races & UFOs from Inside the Earth* (1989). Stanton's study of the first U.S. Exploring Expedition is a fascinating account of one of the more intriguing episodes in that history.[1] In this essay I shall clarify the history of the hollow earth and its relevance to utopianism through a close examination of the first major utopia to use it (and the first significant fictional representation of the hollow earth), Ludvig Holberg's *Nicolai Klimii iter subterraneum, Novam Telluris theoriem ac Historiam Quintae Monarchiae adhuc nobis incognita exhibens* (1741).

Ludvig Holberg (1684–1754) was probably the most European of Scandinavian writers before Ibsen and certainly the best known; he is often referred to as the "father" of Danish and Norwegian literature.[2] Although he is usually remembered today as the "Moliere of the North" for his satirical plays, like so many other eighteenth-century figures, he was also the author of historical and political works, philosophical and legal essays,

1 Briefly the rest of the story: Symmes's most enthusiastic convert was Jeremiah Reynolds who organized Symmes's speaking tours, and then, when Symmes was too sick to continue, took over the campaign to outfit a polar expedition. After Symmes's death, Reynolds increasingly disassociated himself "from the more extravagant reaches of the Theory" (Stanton 1975: 15), focusing instead on the practical advantages of a polar expedition: "When early in 1828 the House Committee on Naval Affairs, softened up by heavy bombardment of memorials during the previous months, requested a statement of Reynold's views, his reply showed how much he had learned about the art of lobbying. He now said less of how Antarctic exploration would further scientific knowledge, and nothing whatever of holes in the poles [... instead he argued that only] exploration could find the whale, the seal, the sandalwood, launch a feather trade, and summon up a fishing industry" (Stanton 1975: 16).

2 He is claimed by both countries, which were united at the time, and although he was born in Bergen (Norway), he spent most of his life in Copenhagen.

"Moral Reflections" and autobiographical "Epistles," and an important subterranean utopia: *The Journey of Niels Klim to the World Underground, with a New Theory of the Earth and the History of the Previously Unknown Fifth Kingdom*. Written in Latin, and quickly translated into a number of European languages, *Klim*, although now neglected, had a wide influence at the time, and stands on its own as an important eighteenth-century utopia.[3]

3 The neglect of *Klim* stems from at least three factors. Firstly, because some critics (e.g., Trousson 2000) have complained that the satirical and utopian aspects of the work are overwhelmed by an excess of imagination. More importantly, *Klim* has often been dismissed as an early imitation of Swift's *Gulliver's Travels*. Finally, there is the problem of national literary studies, for despite the European character of this novel (written in the preeminent European language of the time), most criticism dealing with his work has been carried out by Scandinavian scholars who have tended to focus on Holberg's writing in Danish and his very significant role in the development of Danish and Norwegian literature, particularly in terms of the theater. There are two book length studies of *Klim*, Julius Paludan's *Om Holbergs Niels Klim, med saerligt Hensyn til tidligere Satirer i Form af opdigtede og vidunderlige Reiser* (1878); and Sigrid Peters's *Ludvig Holbergs Menippeische Satire: Das 'Iter subterraneum' und seine Beziehungen zur antiken Literatur* (1987). Paludan's 337-page study concentrates on *Klim* as a satire and on Holberg's sources and originality. (A rough translation of the title is: "On Holberg's *Niels Klim*, with particular attention to earlier satires which used the form of imaginary or marvellous voyages, as well as a contribution to knowledge about foreign influences on eighteenth century Danish literature.") As Philip Gove noted in his 1941 study, *The Imaginary Voyage in Prose Fiction*, Paludan's study is rarely acknowledged by (English language) scholars. Here is part of Gove's summary: "Within its limits this book contains more critical information and a wider outlook on the imaginary voyage and its background than any book written before or since; yet no other literary historian discussed in my book has used it or (so far as I can recollect) even referred to its existence. [...] The first chapter, filling nearly half the book, traces the [imaginary voyage] from antiquity down to the imitators of Swift. Paludan shows a development from the mythical geographic sagas and sea stories through fabulous tales of Alexander to the chivalric romances of the Middle Ages, closely allied to journeys to the Holy Land and to the travels of Marco Polo and Mandeville. [...] After the middle part of the book, covering a detailed examination of *Klimius* with copious references to other works, Paludan gives a brief chapter on imitations in Denmark, Germany and France. All these stages are illustrated by examples, not by definition" (1941: 79–80). My Danish is not good enough to say that I have read the book, but I have worked through it. As Gove's final sentence above indicates, Paludan's

"detailed examination" of *Klim* consists almost entirely in tracing the history of the genre and its influences on and relationships to Holberg's novel. While this is a valuable book which would benefit from a translation, each step in his examination consists of references to other works. Where Paludan saw in *Klim* a type of satire using "the form of imaginary or marvellous voyages," Sigrid Peters argues that as satire, *Klim* should be understood in terms of a much more complex tradition, one which might be seen as analogous to Holberg's ambivalent attitude about the "Querelle des anciens et des modernes" in which his love of classical sources is balanced by his commitment to Enlightenment ideals – "To him antiquity was not the foundation of everything but the precondition" (Hougaard 21). From the classics, then, Holberg takes the form of the "Menippean Satire"; while from More and especially Erasmus, he takes the concept of "spoudogeloion" (itself derived from Menippean satire), of the mixing of serious ideas and jokes ("Ernst and Scherz," Peters 1987: 96). The classical form of Menippean Satire, as codified by Casaubon and Dryden (in his 1693 "Discourse on Satire," which Peters supposes Holberg to have read during his visit to the Bodleian library), is more than just the blend of wisdom and folly. It is as well the mix of prose and different kinds of verse, and it includes – and this is Peters's central point – the frequent and unmarked insertion into the text of citations from previous authors as a parodic and satiric strategy (1987: 65). While Paludan admirably situates *Klim* within the tradition of the imaginary voyage as satire, he overlooks the importance of Menippean Satire, especially in terms of Holberg's frequent citations of classical authors. In addition to pointing out the mix of verse and prose present in the Holberg's original Latin (which disappears in the French and English translations I have consulted), the ability to appreciate this satirical technique has disappeared as well: "Through an analysis of the poetic quotations some of the fundamental structures of Holberg's citational procedure become clear, from which one can deduce the ways in which he was responding to particular authors [...] The 'Iter subterraneum' belongs to the tradition of the *spoudogeloion*, in which seriousness and frivolity are woven into a single unity, while the play presented by the manifold possibilities of citation prohibits any pedantic schematism (Peters 1987: 133). (Bei der Analyse der Verszitate wurden einige Grundstructuren des Zitierverfahrens Holbergs sichtbar, aus denen sich ableiten läßt, in welcher Weise Holberg die einzelnen Autoren rezipiert hat. [...] Das "Iter subterraneum" steht in der Tradition des "spoudogeloion," Ernst und Scherzhaftes sind zu einer Einheit verwoben, und der Spaß mit den vielfältigen Möglichkeiten des Zitierens verbietet jeden penibIen Schematismus.) In the second and longer part of her study, Peters turns (like so many other Holberg critics) to the question of his sources, with chapters on Holberg's citation of Virgil's *Aenead* and Ovid's *Metamorphoses* as well as Juvenal, Horace, Petronius, Plautus, Livy and so on. Earlier studies of Holberg's use of classical sources include A. Kragelund who has written several studies of Holberg's use of classical authors: *Ludvig Holberg*

As I will try to show, *Klim* does merit our attention; for it is not only a significant utopia, but its imaginative qualities are equally worthy of attention. One way of appreciating *Klim* is to look at it in comparison to the work from which it is often seen to be derived, Jonathan Swift's *Travels into Several Remote Nations of the World* (*Gulliver's Travels*, 1726).

Because it was published fifteen years after *Gulliver's Travels*, interest in Holberg's utopia has long been overshadowed by Swift's work. It is usually remembered as one of the many works inspired by Swift's classic, although one of the first major twentieth-century studies of *Gulliver's Travels* raises the possibility that Swift's work may have been based on Holberg's. Although this seems unlikely, manuscript copies of *Niels Klim* had been circulating for at least a decade before its publication. In any case, the two works were certainly contemporaneous, and there are some important similarities, most particularly in the narrative of a voyage to a number of imaginary countries as the vehicle for utopian satire.[4]

Citatkunstneren: Holberg og den yngre Plinius (1962), *Holberg og Petronius' Satyrica* (1977), *Holberg og Cicero* (1978), and *Holberg og Seneca* (1983). McNelis occasionally cites Holberg's original Latin sources in a footnote, but many Latin quotations have been omitted. As McNelis explains, the 1742 edition included a number of Latin quotations "untranslated and unidentified" which were translated into English for the 1828 edition, and then "chiefly absorbed into the text in the 1845 edition. [He has] decided to leave out all those quotations which contribute little or nothing to the story" (2004: 233–234). There are three books on Holberg in English: a very short (35 page) appreciation by Simon C. Hammer (Oxford: Blackwell, 1920); F.J. Billeskov Jansen's survey of his life and works for the Twayne "World Authors" series *Ludvig Holberg* (New York: Twayne, 1974); and Sven Rossel, ed., *Ludvig Holberg: A European Writer* (Amsterdam: Rodopi, 1994), a collection of essays on European influences on Holberg, and on Holberg's influence of different European writers. There is also a translation of Jens Hougaard's *Ludvig Holberg: The Playwright and His Age up to 1730* (Odense: Odense University Press, 1993). Although these books provide useful background information, there are few references to *Klim* (the longest, Jansen 99–102). (Although there are several studies in German, there appear to be none in Italian or French.)

4 The resemblances between the two works suggest that Holberg knew Swift's satire – although there is no mention of Swift in his *Memoirs*. William Eddy suggests that Swift may have read a manuscript version of Holberg's utopia before writing *Gulliver's Travels*. He points out that *Klim* was written some years before it was published and concludes: "The date of the first edition in Danish cannot be far

Holberg's utopia recounts the adventures of Niels Klim after his fall through the earth's crust into the center of the earth where a solitary planet moves about a subterranean sun. The first *utopian* part of his adventures is set in the land of Potu (= utop), which is inhabited by a race of intelligent and mobile trees. Although he is eventually recognized as "a rational animal" (for there are unintelligent apes in Potu and the Potuans's initial reaction is analogous to the Houyhnhnms's assumption that Gulliver is a Yahoo), Klim is never able to attain full Potuan status. In a land in which important statements are repeated three times, his quickness is seen as a flaw, and he is nicknamed "Overhasty" (78).[5] In utopian fashion he is assigned

---

from the time of the publication of *Gulliver* in 1726. There is at least a possibility that the Danish story may have suggested to Swift some of the situations in *Gulliver* which resemble it so closely" (68). It is however much more likely that *Klim* was written after 1726 and that Holberg knew Swift's work, as can be seen by that fact that as far as I have been able to determine, none of Holberg's Scandinavian critics takes seriously the possibility that Swift knew Holberg's work. Because Holberg "had taken [his] farewell of poetry and works of pleasantry, devoting [himself] only to such pursuits as were better suited to (his) years and station," he acknowledges that "For this reason I had endeavoured to suppress altogether [*Klim*] which I had composed some years before" (1970: 166). Eddy's comments are based on this admission and the comment that it was "composed some years before." Gove discusses and dismisses Eddy's argument, concluding: "Though Holberg composed it some years before he was persuaded to publish, Danish critics agree that it is an imitation of *Gulliver*, not a predecessor" (305). This continues to be the consensus. In his *Memoirs*, Holberg discusses the writing of *Klim* (1970: 166–175), explaining that it is the work of a "moral philosopher" and that the many characters "may be said to illustrate a complete system of ethics," while the "story, which is only a vehicle for moral precepts and reflections, is a mere trifle" (1970: 168). For a discussion of *Klim* as a work inspired by Swift, see Welcher (1988: 193 *passim*), who concludes that "Holberg's primary difference from Swift is that he presents far more in the way of positive ideals and views" (1988: 194). Volume IV of *Gulliveriana* reprints in its entirety the 1742 English edition. McNelis develops a lengthy comparison of *Gulliver* and *Klim* (2004: xx–xxx): he too considers Holberg to have been influenced by Swift. One major difference is that "Swift concentrates on man, Holberg on society" (2004: xxix).

5 "The threefold repetition of words was made use of to assist the slowness of their perception, in which the natives of this globe were distinguished from all others; for very few could comprehend what they had only cursorily read, or understand

a task in keeping with his character: because he moves so much faster than the trees he is made the king's chief messenger. Klim is frustrated by this prospect, however, for he has just received his university diploma and he aspires to a position in keeping with his degree. ("I thought it the greatest debasement imaginable for one who was a candidate for holy orders and a Bachelor of Arts in the Upper World, to be changed into a vile Subterranean court messenger" [2004: 44].)

After several years as a messenger, he is commissioned to make a tour of the entire planet of Nazar and to report back to the king. The planet is only 600 miles in circumference, and his trip takes him two months instead of the two years it would take a tree. In this section of the book the author turns from utopia to satire, as Klim visits twenty-seven different provinces. The descriptions of these countries – all inhabited by different species of intelligent trees who speak the same language as the Potuans – are very brief, and most present satirical sketches of alternative societies. For instance, in the province of Quamso everyone is happy, healthy and bored; in Lalac, where there is no need to work, everyone is unhappy and sickly; in Kimal the citizens are wealthy, and spend all their time worrying about thieves; and in the "land of Liberty" everyone is at war.

When Klim returns to Potu, his account of the trip around the planet immediately becomes a best-selling book, and he is again frustrated when he is told that he must nonetheless continue as the king's messenger. In a foolish attempt to improve his status, Klim tries to find a brilliant innovation "that should demonstrate the excellence of my genius and wipe away my present infamy" (2004: 79). But changes come very slowly to Potuan society; its laws and institutions have evolved over centuries and proposed changes are examined and judged at length; and there are severe penalties for rash or injurious proposals.

Foolishly, then, Klim settles on a proposal to "exclude women from the administration of public affairs" (2004: 123). Instead of a promotion,

---

what they had only once heard. Those whose forward capacities took a thing presently were deemed defective in judgment, and therefore it was seldom that such were admitted to any weighty posts of offices; for they had learned by experience that the government had been endangered when in the hands of those who were quick of apprehension" (Holberg 2004: 22).

Klim is banished to the "firmament," the underside of the Earth's crust, to which he is carried by a giant bird. His adventures on the Earth's inner crust begin in the kingdom of Martinia – a country of intelligent apes who, because of their preoccupation with fashion and their changeableness, may be seen as a caricature of the French ("light, frothy, talking creatures that have a smooth, fluent jargon of words without the least mixture of seriousness or gravity" [2004: 135]; "a light babbling race of creatures, and vast admirers of novelty" [2004: 130]). Too late, Klim realizes that he has been "translated from a land of sages to a country of fools" (2004: 135). Now he is thought too slow, but because of his strength he is made one of the Syndic's "body chairmen [… with] the honor of carrying only [the Syndic] or his lady" (2004: 135). In Martinia, however, Klim is able to enhance his status through his wits, and he soon makes a fortune by introducing wigs to the Martinians. His success is short-lived, however, for after he rebuffs the advances of the Syndic's wife, he is accused of trying to seduce her. In exchange for a guilty plea he is sentenced to the galleys.

From social satire the book now becomes almost entirely fantasy. As a galley slave, Klim is taken on a trading voyage to the Mezandorian islands, which lie across a vast sea, constituting, as Klim puts it, "a kind of Indies for the Martinians," (2004: 149). They are inhabited by various fabulous creatures, beginning with a country of jack-daws at war with their neighbors the thrushes, and including a malodorous land of creatures who speak "a posteriori," and a country of string basses who communicate by music. "Their necks were pretty long with little heads upon them; their bodies were slender and covered with a smooth kind of bark or rind in such a manner as that a pretty large vacuity was left between the rind and the body itself. A little above the navel Nature had placed a sort of bridge with four strings […]. One of these hands was employed in holding the bow, as the other was in stopping the strings" (2004: 156–157).

After a shipwreck he finds himself in a remote country inhabited not by intelligent animals or trees, but by primitive humans, who, of all the creatures of the subterranean world, "alone were barbarous and uncivilized." Klim sets out to redress the situation, intending "that this reproach would soon be removed and that [they] would recover that dominion which Nature has given to man over all other animals" (2004: 81). One of the bitterest ironies for Klim lay in the fact that every subterranean race he encountered – plant and animal – with the single exception of the human Quamites, were civilized. Unlike Gulliver's loathing of the Yahoos, Klim takes it upon himself to civilize the Quamites; but this civilizing mission is perhaps the most Swiftian part of the book. Using his knowledge he is able to manufacture gunpowder and to conquer, one by one, all of the countries of the firmament.[6] Klim's many conquests lead him to see himself as the "Alexander of the Subterranean world" (2004: 204), and he becomes a tyrant. When his subjects rebel, he is forced into flight; looking for shelter, he falls into the same hole through which he had previously fallen, thus returning to Norway. There he meets an old friend to whom he tells his story, but the friend convinces him that in this time of religious persecution, he would do well to conceal his adventures. Although he was once an emperor, Klim accepts an appointment as a curate, marries and has children. After his death, his friend publishes the manuscript.

Compared to *Gulliver's Travels*, there is a reversal in the book's order. *Niels Klim* begins with the visit to the utopia and then moves to satire and from there to fantasy, while Gulliver visits the best society last. The order of visits is equally important to the development of the two characters, for it is clear that Gulliver's appreciation of the Houyhnhnms follows from his previous experiences; he would not have had the same reaction had he discovered them earlier. If anything Niels Klim undergoes a contrary transformation, growing only more insensitive and selfish while he is in the underworld. At the beginning Klim is unable to appreciate the utopian society, but there is a dawning realization of its advantages as he travels around Nazar. Yet, when he returns to Potu, he is as determined as ever to improve his standing, an ambition which leads to his banishment. Similarly, upon his arrival in Martinia he thinks that he has been transported from a country of sages to a land of fools, but this insight is quickly forgotten

6 This reminds us of the scene in which Gulliver proposes making gunpowder to the king of the Brobdingnagians: "The king was struck with horror at the description I had given of those terrible engines, and the proposal I had made. He was amazed how so impotent and grovelling an insect as I [...] could entertain such inhuman ideas" (Swift 1970: 108).

when he discovers possibilities for advancement, first by inventing wigs and then by becoming a tyrant. He remains throughout an amusing but sometimes perceptive observer, a comic figure rather than Swift's acerbic and misanthropic commentator.

The major differences between *Gulliver's Travels* and *Niels Klim* derive from the more utopian emphasis of the latter, and from the larger place given to fantasy.[7] Although both works are constructed as imaginary voyages, Klim visits dozens of different countries, only one of which (Potu) is dealt with at length. The six or so countries visited by Gulliver, on the other hand, include some utopian features – particularly in Brobdingnag and the Country of the Houyhnhnms – but Swift's descriptions of alternate societies are more detailed and more satirical; and in fact many critics describe *Gulliver's Travels* as the rejection of utopia (Kumar 105–106). As Robert Elliott writes, "the most perfect utopia Gulliver writes of is England (unless, that is, one happens to be a horse)." (1970: 53). In the case of the Houyhnhnms, as Elliott points out, their society does not form a utopia in the sense of a society which humans could attain: "The Houyhnhnms, who cannot conceive of what is evil in a rational creature, who find it unnecessary to struggle to achieve virtue, have not the human curse to cope with. Their utopia is *given*, like the Golden Age; it is not *created* in terms applicable to the human condition" (1970: 66; emphasis in original).

Holberg is aware of this problem, for in his depiction of the society of Potu, he imagines a utopian society whose laws and customs have evolved through a process of trial and error. To distance his utopia from a naturally good society, he also includes a sketch of a primitive society similar to that of the Houyhnhnms. In "The Country of Innocence," the inhabitants

7 Paludan concludes his history of the satiric voyage with a chapter on *Gulliver's Travels* and its imitators (including *Klim*): "Swift og hans Efterlignere" (1878: 119–164). Potu is discussed in terms of the Land of the Houyhnhnms while Martinia is set in the Rabelaisian tradition (1878: 127–131). Here is McNelis on the difference between the two works: "Holberg himself was probably aware that *Klim*, in spite of its immediate popularity and widespread audience, was not so effective as *Gulliver*. The reason he gives […] (without, of course, mentioning *Gulliver*, but certainly with it in mind) is the greater freedom writers enjoyed in England, not his own choice of a primarily expository method and of less vivid images" (2004: xxix).

are "governed not by laws, but by their own innate virtue and disposition" (104). Although Klim acknowledges them to be happy, it is not without some hesitation: "[For] if they had no vices, they had no politeness, art, or elegance, nor any of those things which, though in reality no virtues, are yet extremely like virtues and render men civilized and social. To say the truth, I seemed here to be rather in a forest of real trees than in a rational society" (104).

This points to a continuing utopian debate about education, passion and "effortless virtue" which we know better through the controversy around B.F. Skinner's *Walden Two* (1948). George Kateb sums up Skinner's position in the latter's "warm approval" of a comment made by T.H. Huxley: "if some great Power would agree to make me always think what is true and do what is right, on condition of being turned into a sort of clock and wound up every morning before I got out of bed, I should instantly close with the other" (as cited in Kateb 1972: 160). After laying out the advantages of a society with "no scope for moral choice," Kateb goes on to list the disadvantages of what he perceives Skinner's solution to be. "Is it not true that choice – moral or otherwise – is the hallmark of the civilized man, and that it is the ever-present necessity to choose that distinguishes humanity from the rest of creation [...]? A society in which moral choices ceased to be made would be a society permeated by sluggishness and indolence, and possessed of a *vegetable* quality; it would be a return to an Edenic state, and as such would be no mere return, but a regression" (1972: 164; emphasis in the original). Kateb's description of the "vegetable quality" of this society of effortless virtue is striking in view of Klim's reaction to the inhabitants of the Country of Innocence, when he stated that he seemed "here to be rather in a forest of real trees than in a rational society."

In traditional terms, then, Potu is a utopia, while the many provinces of Nazar offer frequent opportunities for satire. The description of the Philosophical Region, for instance, constitutes a satire similar to Swift's depiction of the Academy of Lagado. Here the philosophers are eager to dissect Klim, not out of evil intentions or "bad design [... but] for the sole illustration of the science of anatomy" (2004: 97). Instead of Swift's biting satire, Holberg's satire is more comical, and the author focuses on what would be missing in a society whose sole preoccupation was abstract speculation. Instead of a land of beauty and wisdom, he finds a dirty, unkempt city: "Philosophers and swine indifferently walked the streets, nor was the one distinguished from the other but by shape, being otherwise perfectly alike in dirt and nastiness" (2004: 94). He is saved from dissection by a philosopher's wife who then makes advances to him, for in this country "the fate of married ladies was extremely hard, for that their philosophic husbands, immersed in learning, neglected conjugal duties" (2004: 97).

As this example suggests, Holberg has added a third element to the customary two-sided utopian structure, for in addition to the conventional juxtaposition of the author's reality and the ideal society, the many provinces of Nazar provide Holberg with the opportunity to satirize various alternatives which have been imagined as utopian solutions. This rejection of utopian extremes can be seen in the "Land of Reason," a country where the wisdom of its citizens has produced a "republic [which] languished for want of fools" (loo). Klim realizes that even wisdom can exist in excess: "Folly is to society what fermentation is to the stomach; too much, or none at all, are alike injurious" (101). This image sums up very well what might be called Holberg's philosophy of moderation. In various cases, Holberg attacks the expectation that happiness depends on an unlimited supply of something which is lacking, as Klim visits unhappy countries with an abundance of doctors, philosophers, health, wealth or long life. Holberg also addresses the opposite utopian extreme, the belief that the elimination of the source of some present-day evil would bring happiness. Thus Klim visits countries without law, without religion, and without work, where again the inhabitants are dissatisfied and unhappy, in contrast to the citizens of the enlightened monarchy of Potu which is a utopia because of its calm respect for the Golden Mean.

Holberg's own Enlightenment ideas lead to a number of such "reasonable" compromises, the most striking of which lies in his utopian emphasis on social and sexual equality: "for among [the Potuans] there was no difference of sexes observed in the distribution of public posts; but an election being made, the affairs of the republic were committed to the wisest and most worthy" (2004: 23). Discovering that the President of the Senate was a woman, and indeed one whose decrees displayed so much wisdom that they were "deemed so many oracles," Klim exclaims: "Bless me! thought I, what if the wife of our mayor of Bergen were to sit in judgement instead of her husband? What if the daughter of Counsellor Sorensen, that all-accomplished young lady, were to plead at the bar instead of her stupid father? Our laws would never receive the least dishonour from them, nor would justice be so often violated" (2004: 25).

Again we can see the principle of sexual equality in the terms of the judgment against Klim which leads to his banishment: "And as a country may often labour under a want of able persons, we think it a great folly [...] to render one entire half of the nation incapable and unworthy of employment solely upon account of their birth" (124). Like his satire of other "extreme" utopian suggestions, the satirical Nazar section of the book includes a society (Cocklecu) in which gender roles have been reversed, one in which "long and ancient custom had so blinded them [that they] quietly believed it was Nature's appointment that the government should be lodged in female hands, and that it was the business of the other sex to spin, to weave, to clean the house, and upon occasion take a beating from their wives" (2004: 90).[8]

There are three issues in his depiction of the utopian society of Potu which particularly concern Holberg: religion, government, and education.[9] Holberg's concern with the religion of utopia stems from his experience of intolerance, at home and abroad.[10] Holberg juxtaposes the religious practices of the Potuans to two extremes: the excess of religion and its complete absence. Klim describes the utopian religion as follows: "[In Potu it] is

8 Paludan offers a review of the literary antecedents from which Holberg may have derived his view of women (1878: 225–250).

9 James Jones briefly describes five themes which characterize the utopia of Potu: (1) the principle of relativity; (2) tolerance; (3) satire of religious disputes; (4) Enlightened Despotism; and (5) the principle of equality (1980: 195–198). In Paludan's chapter "Potu og Nazar" (1878: 178–249) the principal themes discussed are religion, politics, education and the emancipation of women. These critics are following Holberg's own preoccupations since he entitles the chapters describing Potu as: "The Court of the Potuan Empire," "Of the Nature of the Country and the Manners of the People," "Of the Religion of the Potuan Nation," "Of Their Policy," and "Of the Academy."

10 As Jansen points out, the work's emphasis on religious tolerance stems from the decline of tolerance and the rise of Pietism during Christian the VI's reign, 1730–1746 (1974: 98–105).

prohibited to comment upon the sacred books [or] to dispute about the essence and attributes of God […]. They are unanimous in adoring one Supreme Being by whose almighty power all things were created and by whose providence they subsist. Let but this principle be uncontroverted, and they never molest anyone for entertaining different sentiments concerning a method of worship" (2004: 52).

On the other hand, the book contains several instances satirizing religious intolerance, including a description of European religious practices from the perspective of a subterranean, as recounted in a manuscript Klim discovers entitled *Tanians's Journey to the Superterranean World, or a Description of the Kingdoms and Countries upon Earth*, a brief work along the lines of Montesquieu's *Lettres persanes*: "The religious opinions of the Europeans are very sound and agreeable to right reason. They are under an injunction carefully to study the books in which the rule of faith and practice is contained, in order to discover their true sense and meaning […]. [B]ut if any should chance to understand a thing in a different sense from the majority, he is punished for this defect of judgement by fines, imprisonment, whipping, and even sometimes by dying at a stake" (2004: 188).[11]

The other extreme – the absence of religion – is illustrated by the country of Mikolac where there are laws but no religion. When Klim is robbed and seeks legal redress, he discovers that laws without underlying religious belief are worthless: "From hence it appeared what a weak unsettled society that must be which depends for its security upon human laws alone, and how frail are all political edifices unless cemented together by religion […] no safety can be expected in a country too atheistical to have the least sense of religious obligation" (2004: 109).

11 This brief satire reflects another difference between *Gulliver's Travels* and *Klim*, namely the bitterness of the former's direct comments about Europe when compared to Holberg's more modest criticisms. Following Gulliver's laudatory description of his "dear native Country," the king concludes that "the Bulk of your Natives [are] the most pernicious Race of little odious Vermin that Nature ever suffered to crawl upon the Surface of the Earth" (1970: 108). Following the laughter that follows Holberg's description of how one becomes a Doctor of Philosophy, or the yawns and then anger which follow his explanation to the king of the function and habits of lawyers, Klim's tactic is to keep quiet, "fearing lest the Subterraneans should pass very unfavourable judgements upon mankind" (2004: 31).

Holberg's utopian mean as applied to the role of religion is reiterated through the juxtaposition of utopian ideal and excess in the final two countries Klim visits in his trip around Nazar, Jochtana and Tumbac. Because Jochtana allows the open practice of different religions, Klim assumes that this land must surely be "the seat of disorder, confusion, and insecurity"; instead he finds "agreement and concord" (2004: 117–118). In Tumbac, on the other hand, where there is a single religion, the inhabitants are "extremely devout and extremely censorious" (2004: 119): "The citizens here were all Catos, all censors of manners. They walked up and down the streets with pensive looks and folded arms, declaiming against the vanity of the times and condemning every innocent pleasure" (2004: 121). Because they are so morose and sanctimonious, Klim concludes that their zeal must flow "from some vicious humours, or a predominance of the bilious juices, than from true piety" (2004: 121).

While the description of the religion of the Potuans may be seen as similar to other utopian descriptions of a natural religion (like those to be found in More or among the Australians of Foigny and Veiras), the Potuans are at pains to stress that nature is not enough.

> [These doctrines] must appear like mere natural religion; and so indeed it did at first to me. But they assert that all was divinely revealed to them and that some ages ago they received a book which contained their system of faith and practice. Formerly, they say, our ancestors lived contented with the religion of nature only; but experience taught them that the sole light of nature was insufficient, since all those noble principles through the sloth and carelessness of some were forgot, and through an airy philosophy of others [...] were utterly depraved and corrupted. Hereupon God gave them a written law. Hence it appears how great is their error who obstinately deny the necessity of a revelation. (2004: 57)

As with the Potuan religion, and despite the fascination exercised on him and other utopian writers by the often romanticized – or strictly fictional – accounts of naturally good societies in Australia or the Americas, Holberg continued to believe in the need for laws and institutions. His description of the utopian government – in this case an hereditary monarchy – rejects a fully egalitarian society while insisting that the necessary institutions and customs can only come about through a process of trial and error. Thus, Klim is told of a failed experiment in which the king was replaced with an elected official: "For since right reason seemed to require that rulers should excel their subjects in wisdom and all the endowments of the mind, hence it was thought necessary that virtue should be more regarded than birth and that he should be elected for their sovereign who should be thought the most excellent and worthy among the subjects" (2004: 58). Following this reasoning, a philosopher was elected, but this democratic experiment soon led to disaster: "For since the new sovereign was raised from the meanest fortune to the height of power, his virtues and all his arts of government could not procure or maintain that veneration, that respect, that majesty, which is the great support of a monarch's power" (2004: 58).

This is an "enlightened despotism" (Jones 1980: 198), one in which the monarch has a "paternal [rather] than a regal power" (Holberg 2004: 60). "Among the laws of this kingdom, the most salutary is that by which the princes endeavour to preserve an equality between the subjects, that is, as far as the nature of government will admit. You see here no different ranks and titles of honour. Inferiors obey their superiors, and the younger the elder, and this is all" (2004: 60).[12]

Although the Potuans have tried and rejected democracy, equality, including sexual equality, remains a fundamental principle, for it was Klim's proposal to "exclude women from the administration of public affairs" (2004: 123) which led to his banishment. At the same time, the principle of equality has limits. This is a hereditary monarchy where adolescent trees (and Klim) are tested for their aptitudes and assigned occupations

12 In addition to the discussion of this theme in Paludan (1878: 200–212), see Hougaard who carefully situates Holberg in the Dual Monarchy: "So it is this God-given, innate reason which forms the basis of the legal framework and from which the individual acquires knowledge of what is good and what is evil, unless the reason of the individual concerned has been clouded by 'evil upbringing or habits.' Holberg thus suggests a basis on which a uniform legal structure can be built and from which social institutions can allow the inborn discrimination to come to maturity. As a last resort, an ultimate guarantee of order in human relations, Holberg takes over, via Pufendorf, Hobbes's idea of the strong state that is the incarnation of reason. Thus, for Holberg, the absolute monarchy assumes the role of upholder of order in human relations. *This view of society lies behind the entire body of his work*" (1993: 23; emphasis added).

accordingly: "The natives of this empire are not divided into nobles and commons. Formerly indeed this distinction obtained. But when the sovereigns observed that the seeds of discord spring from hence, they wisely removed all such privileges as were derived from birth, so that virtue alone is now the test of honour [...]. The sole pre-eminence of birth consists of a plurality of branches. The offspring is counted noble or ignoble for this reason, because the greater plenty they have, the fitter they are for all manual operations" (2004: 51).[13]

Holberg does distinguish between nature and culture, recognizing the tendency to try and pass off as natural customs and beliefs which were originally the result of decisions which have now been forgotten. For when Klim argues that men are naturally superior to women, he is told "that [he] confounded custom with nature, since the weakness we impute to the female

13 Holberg's treatment of the value of manual labor is expressed in the importance given by the Potuans to the number of branches each tree has is confused. The number of branches is decisive. The first question asked "immediately after the birth of the infant [... is] how many branches it has brought into the world with it" (2004: 44); while at the beginning of his stay with the Potuans, Klim is fitted with "artificial branches" (2004: 25). Similarly, there are several references to the importance of manual labor; "in these dominions husbandmen were held in the highest esteem on account of the great excellence of the duties they were employed in, [...] no way of life was more honourable than that of agriculture" (2004: 31). Yet the Potuans Klim actually meets are mostly high officials, dignitaries, and members of the court; and despite the apparent correlation between the number of branches and manual dexterity, the highest officials have the most branches – as is the case with the heir to the throne, for instance, to whom "Nature has been so liberal as to adorn [...] with six pair of branches, an uncommon circumstance in that tender age" (2004: 66). Moreover in the description of the training and education of the Prince, there is no reference to any manual activities. In fact, the number of branches a particular tree has is only tied to specific activities and skills on a few occasions, where it seems both comic and contradictory. When Klim dines at court he is served by a tree with nine branches who was thus "judged extremely qualified for the domestic business of the court" (42). After the meal he meets the King's Secretary who "was a most extraordinary person, for he had eleven pairs of branches and could consequently write eleven letters all at the same time, and with the same ease and expedition that we can one. Yet he had a very indifferent judgment, upon which account he never could expect any farther promotion [...]" (2004: 43).

sex is derived solely from education" (2004: 92). At the same time, observation and reason lead Holberg to a number of judgments about what is or is not "natural." Consider the Potuans's reasoning about the advantages of breastfeeding when compared to the Potuan critique of singing hymns to God. When Klim tries to argue – in the case of a high official who has just borne a child – that breastfeeding is "too troublesome and too mean an employment for so great a matron," he is told that all mothers suckle their children: "mothers who disdain to nourish their own issue dissolve one of the finest and strongest ties of nature" (2004: 65–66). In the case of singing hymns, on the other hand, the Potuans hold "it ridiculous to express grief and penitence in musical measures, since the displeasure of the Deity is to be appeased by sighs and tears of real sorrow, not by the artifice of tunes and instruments" (2004: 53). In general, then, Holberg is careful to distance himself from a complete reliance on either nature or reason, as we have seen in the depictions of both religion and government in the utopian society of Potu. For in the first case, reason was tempered by revelation, while in the second there was a need for law and a hereditary monarchy.

Finally, as might be expected from the comment "that [he] confounded custom with nature, since the weakness we impute to the female sex is derived solely from education" (92), education in Potu follows many of the same lines. Here is his description of the utopian curriculum:

> The studies pursued [...] are history, economy, mathematics, and law. As to their divinity, since it is so short and concise as the whole is contained in the compass of a couple of pages importing that we ought to love and adore Almighty God, the Creator and Governor of things, Who in some state of existence hereafter will reward virtue and punish vice [...] so it is no academical study, nor indeed can it be, since it is prohibited by law to have any controversy about the essence or attributes of God. [Medicine] in like manner, is not reckoned among the studies of the university; for since these trees live all sober lives, internal diseases are almost wholly unknown. (2004: 71)

The novel begins with Klim's graduation and he frequently refers to his university diploma, perhaps most preposterously as he is floating around the planet Nazar and is approached by a "grim, huge griffin": "So great was my terror that, unmindful of my starry dignity to which I was newly advanced, in that disorder of my soul I drew out my university testimonial, which I happened to have in my pocket, to signify to this terrible adversary that I had passed my academical examination, that I was a graduate student, and could plead the privilege of my university against anyone that should attack me" (2004: 12–13). Holberg's satire of contemporary educational practices seems strongest in Klirn's indignant discovery that disputation, rather than an essential skill for academic achievement and success, is for the Potuans a form of comic theatrical performance.

> For at set times of the year, wagers being laid, and a reward assigned to the conquerors, the disputants engage like a couple of gladiators, and much upon the same terms that fighting cocks or any such battling animals do among us. Here it was a custom among the great to maintain a set of disputants, as we do a pack of hounds, and to give them a logical education, that they may be fit for engagement at the stated times of the year [...].
>
> I was often present at these entertainments, and that with no small vexation. For it seemed to me a horrid and shameful thing that such noble exercises, which give lustre to our schools, should here be prostituted on the stale. And when I called to mind that I myself with the highest applause had disputed in public, and had obtained the laurel, I could scarce withhold my tears. And not only the dispute, but the method of disputing incensed me. For they hired certain stimulators [...] who, when they observed the ardour of the disputants to flag, just pricked their sides with lancets to rekindle it and to rally their declining spirits. (2004: 28)

Klim's chagrin is deepened when, after explaining that he "had written three dissertations upon the slippers of the ancients," his host bursts out laughing. "His wife, alarmed with the noise, flies to know the cause of it; but I was so much out of humour that I disdained to answer her, for I thought it a burning shame so grave and solid a matter should be treated with that ridicule and contempt. But understanding from her husband the truth of the case, she laughed as violently" (30).[14]

14 For a discussion of Holberg's own educational experience as well as a description of the university at the time, see Hougaard's chapter "Ludvig Holberg and the University" (1993: 11–23). It should be noted that the university at the time was primarily a theological college, and the language of instruction was Latin.

Conclusion

> Lest I should seem to speak too arrogantly here, let it be understood that I allude not to my work, but to the scope and design of my work. I say it is the duty of a moral philosopher to instruct, rather than to declaim with tragical fury against vices which the sinners themselves acknowledge. Such is the object of The Journey to the World Underground; what degree of skill or dexterity the author may have shown in the execution of it, others must decide. (Holberg 1970: 170)

Many critics write as if Holberg should have ended his work with the description of the utopia of Potu, or at most, after the satirical voyage around Nazar. Although Trousson explains that following the "austere and monotonous blueprints of Puritan utopias," the eighteenth-century utopia "attempted to renew itself by means of the extraordinary" (1975: 96),[15] he considers that *Klim* goes too far: "While the critique of customs, of morality and of politics is always implicit, presented indirectly as it were, it is nonetheless drowned in the outpourings of the imagination" (1975: 123).[16] In practical terms, Trousson's criticism of the fantastic elements in *Klim* is not so different from Jones's complete disregard of the non-Potu sections of the book in his otherwise excellent treatment of the novel. After outlining the characteristics of the Potuan utopia, Jones writes: "If this brief sketch of the characteristic aspects of the Potuan utopian [...] were all that might be said for the work, we should be tempted to regard it as a curiosity-piece, another literary attempt to portray a society built upon principles higher than those of societies in the 'real' world [...]. This, we would argue is not the case" (1980: 198).

15 "Au XVIIe siècle, l'utopie cherche de nouvelles voies et une sorte de rajeunissement par l'imagination et l'excentricité qui contraste singulièrement avec les austères et monotones utopies-programmes de la littérature puritaine. Monotone par son contenu descriptif, l'utopie l'est aussi par ses structures: c'est ce qui explique qu'elle tente de se renouveler par l'extraordinaire" (Trousson 1975: 96).

16 "Certes, la critique des mœurs, de la morale, de la politique est toujours présente en filigrane, et, en quelque sorte, par ricochet, mais noyée dans ces débordements de l'imaginaire" (1975: 123).

I would agree that "this is not the case," but not for reasons Jones gives. In the remaining four pages of his essay, Jones does not look at the rest of the book or discuss the satiric and fantastic sections (Nazar, Martinia, etc.). Instead he argues that what is significant in *Klim* is that – like Voltaire's portrayal of El Dorado in *Candide* – the author rejects the static vision of utopia: "the fictional characters cannot in the end withstand the degree of perfection that engulfs them" (199). The other, non-utopian two-thirds of the book are simply ignored.

Both Julius Paludan's 1878 study of *Klim* and its antecedents in satire and the imaginary voyage, and especially Sigrid Peters's 1987 study of *Klim* as Menippean satire explain this work in terms of a classical, satirical tradition (see note 3). Peters argues in particular for the influence of Erasmus's *Praise of Folly*; the mixture of fantasy and utopian satire in *Klim* should be seen as a deliberate strategy and not (as some critics would have it), a confused blend of genres. A similar explanation for the fantastic elements of the work is given by Christopher Robinson who discusses *Klim* as the "point at which the various strands of the imaginary voyage tradition that owe something to Lucian have become totally fused. In his preference for pure fantasy over the semi-realism of *Gulliver*, he returns to Lucian" (1979: 144). In fact, Holberg acknowledged Lucian as his predecessor, saying that *Klim* "is to be considered as a philosophical romance [...] The story, which is only a vehicle for moral precepts and reflections, is a mere trifle" (1970: 168).

This corresponds to Holberg's own defense of his method in his *Memoirs*:

> It is true that this production is a literary trifle, but it is not altogether a useless trifle; since instruction in this way be insinuated into many readers who would shrink from a regular didactic treatise; and as Trimalchio had his epitaph written upon a sun-dial, that every body who consulted it might read his name, so a work of pleasantry may be made the medium of instruction to those who will read nothing but books of amusement. A fisherman must bait his book to the taste of the little fishes, if he expects to catch them; and in like manner philosophers of the greatest note have from time to time conveyed instruction through the medium of apologues and entertaining tales. (1970: 169)

Rather than defend the fantastic elements in *Klim* in these terms, I think that its imaginary dimension contributes as much to its interest and significance as do its utopian features or the author's use of classical sources. If Holberg has had a lasting influence, it is not so much in terms of his Menippean blend of utopia and satire, but because of his depiction of a world inside the earth. To my knowledge the earliest appreciation of Holberg's fantastic subterranean setting is to be found in Casanova's preface to his own subterranean utopia, *L'Icosameron* (1788).[17] The narrator of Edgar Allen Poe's "The Fall of the House of Usher" includes "the 'subterranean Voyage of Nicholas Klimm' [sic] of Holberg" among his readings (Poe 1938: 239).

Klim appears to be the first developed instance of this setting. There are, of course, numerous accounts of "subterraneous voyages" (Krappe 1941) and voyages to the underworld, but this vision of a hollow globe with an inner earth and sun as well as an inhabited underside of the Earth's crust is far more complete and radical than any of the subterranean adventures of previous fictions, or than any of the cosmological speculations of Thomas Burnet or Athanasius Kircher. Yet all we know about where Holberg might have derived such a vision is to be found in his *Memoirs* where he links the subterranean world to familiar accounts of faeries and trolls:

> There are many persons of both sexes in my country who speak confidently of their intercourse with fairies and supernatural beings, and who are ready to take their corporal oaths that they have been carried away by subterranean spirits to hills and mountain-caves. This foolish superstition, which suggested materials for the fiction, is ridiculed in Niels Klim, the hero of the tale. (1970: 168)[18]

17 My thanks to Lise Leibacher for pointing out to me the second dedication of *L'Icosameron*, where Casanova writes: "Platen, Erasme, le chancelier Bacon, Thomas Morus, Campanelle et Nicolas Klimiusaussi sont ceux qui me firent venir envie de publier cette histoire, ou ce roman" (cited in Gove 1941: 386). Holberg's work also attracted the attention of Thomas de Quincy who began a translation of *Klim* sometime in the mid-1820s and then apparently abandoned the project (after translating three chapters) when a new translation appeared in 1828. For the text of De Quincy's translation as well as a careful explanation of the circumstances, see S. Musgrove's edition of the manuscript. *Klim's* popularity in the eighteenth century can be evidenced by the number of editions published. Gove refers to Holger Ehrencron-Mueller's bibliography of Holberg's writing (1933–1935), which lists "59 editions in 11 languages [for *Klim*], 34 of them in the 18th century" (1941: 304).

18 The anonymous *Relation d'un Voyage du Pole Arctique au Pole Antarctique par le centre du monde, Avec la Description de ce périlleux Passage, & des choses merveilleuses*

After his fall into the underground world, Klim does not arrive immediately on the inner planet, but instead begins to circle it. After he throws away some stale bread, it in turn begins to circle him: "And from thence I learned the true laws of motion, by which it comes to pass that all bodies placed in equilibrium naturally affect a circular motion" (2004: 11). This is, however, the end of his astronomical speculation; and there is little development of the underground world or its relationship to its inhabitants. While we should acknowledge *Klim* as the first major representation of the hollow earth, there is little development of the idea beyond the setting.

Holberg's use of this amazing and apparently original idea points to the issue of the book's current oblivion, namely that while for many of his critics the utopian aspects are smothered by the fantastic episodes, for a modern reader more interested in the wonders and delights of fantastic speculation and imaginary flights of fancy, the book is too timid and restrained. In looking at aspects of the fantastic which the author did not develop, he could be said to forget all too often, for instance, that the Potuans are trees. The idea of intelligent and mobile trees yields too quickly to what they are meant to represent; the novelty of the concept is not developed. (Look what Tolkien did with the Ents.) In the firmament section, on the other hand, the author occasionally indulges in pure fantasy, as in the invention of the Ice People and of the creatures who speak a posteriori. But

---

& étonnantes qu'on a découvertes sous le Pole Antarctique (Paris, 1721) tells of a traveler whose ship is caught in a whirlpool at the North Pole, rushed through a tunnel in the earth and ejected at the South Pole. There is no subterranean world. Another earlier work with some subterranean scenes is Fieux de Mouhy's *Lamékis ou les voyages extraordinaires d'un Égyptien dans La terre intérieure; avec la découverte de l'Isle des Sylphides* (Paris and Amsterdam, 1735–1738), but again Mouhy's caverns and secret vaults under the pyramids bear little resemblance to the underground world of *Klim*. For early discussions of the subterranean setting, see Regis Messac, "Voyages modernes au centre de la terre," and Alexander Krappe, "The Subterraneous Voyage." Katherine Collier's *Cosmogonies of Our Fathers: Some Theories of the Seventeenth and the Eighteenth Centuries* provides a good account of the writers like Kircher and Burnet who proposed the existence of subterranean cavities in the Earth. Again, none of the cosmological speculation of the seventeenth and eighteenth centuries seems to include the vision of a hollow earth. (See also Kafton-Minkel.)

these fantastic creatures – who serve no satirical purpose – quickly appear and disappear. We learn little of the Ice People beyond their susceptibility to sunlight and the fact that they are punished by being left in the sun; or in the case of Pyglossia, we learn only that communication is an unpleasant and malodorous affair. While these brief glimpses remind us of the fantastic creatures of earlier travel narratives, from Herodotus and Lucian down through the eighteenth century, they seem slightly out of place here, an indication that the book's original satirical and utopian goals are flagging.

Whatever one's perspective, then, there is some disappointment with the book's final sections. Whether because of too much fantasy or not enough, the last part of the book throws the rest of *Niels Klim* out of balance as the utopian and satirical directions of the earlier chapters are almost completely abandoned. This disappointment is accentuated by the changes to the character of Klim. From an amusing and sometimes perceptive observer, he becomes an opportunist and then a vain and superficial tyrant only too willing to participate in slaughter and world conquest. As I have already mentioned, the development of Gulliver's character proceeds in the opposite direction. In Lilliput, Gulliver takes part in a war, while in Brobdingnag his proposals about developing gunpowder and weapons horrify the king. But Gulliver's bloodthirsty ideas are not put into practice, and by the time he leaves the country of the Houyhnhnms he has undergone a substantial transformation, from an uncritical defender of the British monarchy, to a disillusioned and bitter misanthrope who has been granted an impossible revelation of perfection.

Nonetheless *Klim* should be acknowledged as the first major representation of the hollow earth. Although there is little development of the idea beyond the setting, and it seems to be little more than a pretext for Klim's adventures, the underground world is clearly delineated, unlike some other fictional uses of this setting. Until Symmes's enthusiastic espousal of the idea (or Jules Verne's fictional exploration of the world underground some decades later),[19] following *Klim*, the subterranean world will become

19 Although Messac argues that Verne may have known of Holberg (1929: 85–88), to my knowledge none of Verne's critics endorse this claim. In her introduction to the *Voyage*, Simone Vierne, for instance, discusses more generally the question of influences, without mentioning Holberg, saying only that "The question of the internal

a minor location in the repertory of unexplored and undiscovered places available for imaginary societies and fantastic adventures. At the same time, in both Holberg's utopia of moderation and in his use of satire to ridicule contemporary customs and practices as well as the utopian extremes of other visionaries, *Klim* should be recognized as an important and unjustly neglected utopian work, as well as an enjoyable comic fantasy. In terms of Holberg's comment that "others must decide" about the "degree of skill or dexterity the author may have shown in the execution of" his moral philosophy through the medium of this "literary trifle," I hope to have shown that in many ways this work should be considered a success.

---

composition of our earth was obviously very much discussed at the time" ("La question de la constitution interne de notre globe devait être à l'ordre du jour," Verne 1977: 29.)

CHAPTER 6

Fredric Jameson and Anti-Anti-Utopianism

In the following I want to give an account of Fredric Jameson's theory of Utopia as presented in *Archaeologies of the Future.*[1] Like Thomas More's *Utopia*, this is actually two books, the second written before the first, since the latter is made up of eleven previously published essays on science fiction and Utopia, while the first part, aptly entitled "The Desire Called Utopia," was written as an introduction to those essays.[2] In such an account, of course, I can only begin to address Jameson's theories and will thus limit myself to the 250 pages of the Introduction, "The Desire Called Utopia," calling attention to a few of the highlights of this dense but rewarding text, while leaving the specific readings of the second part and the question of science fiction aside.

As many of his readers know, Jameson has had a long involvement with science fiction and Utopia – stretching back at least to 1971 and *Marxism and Form*, where he proclaimed the importance and timeliness of the utopian impulse:

> For where in the older society [...] Utopian thought represented a diversion of revolutionary energy into idle wish-fulfilments and imaginary satisfactions, in our own time the very nature of the utopian concept has undergone a dialectical reversal. Now it is practical thinking which everywhere represents a capitulation to the system itself, and stands as a testimony to the power of that system to transform even its adversaries into its own mirror image. The Utopian idea, on the contrary, keeps alive the possibility of a world qualitatively distinct from this one and takes the form of a stubborn negation of all that is. (1971: 110–111)

1 F. Jameson, *Archaeologies of the Future: The Desire Called Utopia and Other Science Fictions* (London and New York: Verso, 2005).

2 One of the essays, "History and Salvation in P. K. Dick," has not been published before.

While Jameson's writing on science fiction and Utopia began in the early 1970s (as can be seen from some of the essays reprinted in *Archaeologies of the Future*), the full extent and impact of his rigorously dialectical approach to the genre has taken a while to sink in. The outline of that position can be seen in provocative statements like his warning that the literary Utopia should not be perceived as the representation of an ideal society, but as a reflection on "our own incapacity to conceive [of Utopia] in the first place" (1975: 230); or that our "constitutional inability to imagine Utopia itself [is not due] to any individual failure of imagination but is the result of the systemic, cultural, and ideological closure of which we are all in one way or another prisoners" (1982: 153).

But Jameson's position was only sketched out in these earlier articles, particularly in the essays on Louis Marin's *Utopiques* (1977a, "Of Islands and Trenches") and on Platonov's *Chevegur* (1994, "The Seeds of Time"). It is also interesting to note that the concept of Utopia is rarely mentioned in the many articles and books about his theories and method.[3] Now "The Desire Called Utopia" brings a long-awaited systematic and sustained presentation and elaboration of those earlier thoughts on the literary Utopia.

As the two lapidary statements I just cited make clear, the utopian form presents a dilemma or contradiction for Jameson, which he restates in his Preface as follows:

> All these formal and representational questions lead back to the political one with which we began: but now the latter has been sharpened into the formal dilemma of how works that posit the end of history can offer any usable historical impulses, how works which aim to resolve all political differences can continue to be in any sense political, how texts designed to overcome the needs of the body can remain materialistic, how visions of the "epoch of rest" (Morris) can energize and compel us to action.
>
> There are good reasons for thinking that all these questions are undecidable: which is not necessarily a bad thing provided we continue to try to decide them. (2005: xiv–xv)

3 An earlier attempt to assess Jameson's theory of Utopia was undertaken at a meeting of the Society for Utopian Studies in Memphis in 1997, and some of the results were published in a special issue of *Utopian Studies* 9/2 (1998). It is also apparent that these earlier remarks (1971) did not include a fully worked out theory of Utopia, for in this early formulation he does not distinguish between impulse and project, combining them in the "concept" of Utopia.

Following this outline of some of the contradictions to be addressed and clarified, Jameson lays out the grand lines of the next 250 pages of his argument, beginning with a description of what Utopia is:

> Utopian form is itself a representational meditation on radical difference, radical otherness, and on the systemic nature of the social totality, to the point where one cannot imagine any fundamental change in our social existence which has not first thrown off Utopian visions like so many sparks from a comet. (2005: xii)

The fundamental dynamic of any Utopian politics (or of any political Utopianism) will therefore always lie in the dialectic of Identity and Difference, in the degree to which such a politics aims at imagining, and sometimes even at realizing, a system radically different from this one.

This reference to the dialectic is the key to Jameson's interrogation of the Utopian, as indeed are the traditional definitions of the Utopian to which he refers (Elliott, Suvin)[4] that emphasize the genre's dual nature insofar as they constitute a critique of the author's society as much as they propose an alternative to it. A first step in untangling the dialectic of identity and difference lies in acknowledging the impossibility of imagining radical otherness, an acknowledgment which he grounds here in the "empiricist maxim, nothing in the mind that was not first in the senses" (Jameson 2005: xiii). Despite this apparent impasse, Jameson refuses to abandon the Utopian, and "The Desire Called Utopia" will explore and clarify this dilemma. At the same time, as in his earlier statements, he reminds the reader that "at best Utopia can serve the negative purpose of making us more aware of our mental and ideological imprisonment [...] and that therefore the best Utopias are those that fail the most comprehensively" (2005: xiii).

Consequently, the first and most crucial aspect of the dilemma (at least from the perspective of those critics who, like myself, think and write about the utopian features of this or that imagined society) is Jameson's repeated caution about representation and the "literal," about the dangers of reading utopias as depictions of some new society:

4 See R.C. Elliott, *The Shape of Utopia: Studies in a Literary Genre* (Chicago: University of Chicago Press, 1970); D. Suvin, *Metamorphoses of Science Fiction: On the Poetics and History of a Literary Genre* (New Haven, CT: Yale University Press, 1979).

> [I]t is a mistake to approach Utopias with positive expectations, as though they offered visions of happy worlds, spaces of fulfillment and cooperation, representations which correspond generically to the idyll or the pastoral rather than the Utopia. Indeed, the attempt to establish positive criteria of the desirable society characterizes liberal political theory from Locke to Rawls, rather than the diagnostic interventions of the Utopians, which, like those of the great revolutionaries, always aim at the alleviation and elimination of the sources of exploitation and suffering, rather than at the composition of blueprints for bourgeois comfort. (2005: 12)

Unlike some more traditional and systematic approaches to the genre (as in Darko Suvin's definitional and taxonomic efforts in *Metamorphoses of Science Fiction*), "The Desire Called Utopia" is more of a philosophical reflection on the issues and problems posed by the Utopian genre. And unlike traditional definitions, there will be few final answers here, since Jameson is not so much interested in tracking the various manifestations of the genre as he is in understanding and arguing its relevance at a time when it seems that there is no longer any room for alternatives. Jameson continues (in the passage quoted above), that "The confusion [about the positive, literal dimension of the Utopia] arises from the formal properties of these texts, which also seem to offer blueprints: these are however maps and plans to be read negatively, as what is to be accomplished after the demolitions and the removals" (2005: 12). "Reading negatively" is the crucial term, the key to his dialectical approach, which he sums up (at the end of the Preface) in his call for an "anti-anti-Utopianism" (2005: xvi) – a negation of the negation which points to Hegel and the dialectic, and to A.J. Greimas's semiotic rectangle (of which Jameson will make frequent use) as Jameson refuses to describe Utopianism in terms of a simple opposition between Utopia and anti-Utopia.[5]

5 To get a sense of Jameson's use of the dialectic, here is his description of the dialectical method: "[T]he dialectic is in reality the study of all these types of negation together (along with their contradictions with each other): thus, it includes both contrariety and contradiction (the two negative axes of the Greimas square), but also the logical difference between them (a difference which is at once both contrariety and contradiction, a sublation of both which is at one and the same time their synthesis and their differentiation)" (2005: 142–143). Early in the course of his arguments, Jameson describes Niklas Luhmann's concept of differentiation, which is also useful, not so much because it is significant in terms of understanding

"The Desire Called Utopia," then, will be a series of differentiations and dialectical reversals that range over a number of topics, alternating theoretical discussions with readings of science fiction and Utopian texts. In the Introduction Jameson points out that the problem of representation will shift the examination of Utopia from the familiar terrain of content (what a utopia would consist of) to formal questions; and from there to what he calls a "psychology of Utopian production: a study of Utopian fantasy mechanisms, rather, and one which eschews individual biography in favor of historical and collective wish-fulfillment [... which] will necessarily illuminate its historical conditions of possibility" (2005: xiii–xiv).

The first differentiation is the familiar opposition between Utopia's programmatic status and (following Bloch) the utopian impulse. After

---

Utopia, but insofar as differentiation provides another way of understanding how Jameson's argument advances from chapter to chapter: "Thus, a Luhmann-inspired metaphysic would posit something like an undifferentiated substance which begins internally to differentiate itself into so many related but distinct, semi-autonomous 'systems.' We may think of these systems in any form we like: Kant's witty identification of the faculties of the university with the older tradition of the mental faculties offers a good random starting point, for it projects a comparison between the increasing differentiation of the various bodies of the specialized academic disciplines with the separation from each other of 'parts' of the psyche, such as cognition or the will. That these are ongoing and increasingly complex differentiations is a matter of empirical history: the traditional disciplines begin to hive off new ones, such as sociology or psychology, or in our time molecular biology, while modern literature testifies to the emergence of all kinds of new psychic functions which were not registered in the traditional literary genres. But now the juxtaposition of these two evolving fields (the academic disciplines, the psyche) reminds us of the multiplicity of other such fields contained within the social totality (or 'system'): social classes, for example, which then differentiate into a host of strata, professional specializations and the like; or productive activities, which multiply as industry itself becomes refined into ever more varied technological and scientific processes, while the products thus produced (and the demand for them) are multiplied virtually without limit. Meanwhile the political system itself hives off the jurists, who become a separate profession governed by a distinct field of knowledge in its own right, from its administrators and bureaucrats, elective officials, state, municipal and federal employees, along with the multiplications of the welfare state, the appearance of social workers, and the various branches of public medicine as well as scientific research; and so on and so forth" (2005: 14–15).

elaborating this distinction between program and impulse, Jameson wonders who writes utopias anyway? In a typical dialectical and complicating fashion, Jameson passes from the utopian process to consider the larger social totality in which the utopia was written – the "conditions of possibility" of this or that fantasy:

> But such creation must be motivated: it must respond to specific dilemmas and offer to solve fundamental social problems to which the Utopian believes himself to hold the key. The Utopian vocation can be identified by this certainty, and by the persistent and obsessive search for a simple, a single-shot solution to all our ills. (2005: 11)

Not surprisingly, since this is a book about science fiction and Utopia, Jameson will use science fiction examples to demonstrate some of his explanations of the dilemma posed by the Utopia. Our "constitutional inability to imagine Utopia itself" can of course be explained in more political terms, as in Marx's letter to Ruge, that "The world has long since dreamed of something of which it needs only to become conscious for it to possess it in reality" (cited in Jameson 1996: 75). But here, Jameson offers the reader a fascinating study of the representation of the alien in science fiction as a meditation on why and how the truly different of a "qualitatively distinct" society cannot be imagined or thought. Or to put it in opposite terms, science fiction's aliens are little more than amalgams of the already known – the head of an insect, the body of an animal, or the social system of the bees, and so on – although more recent science fiction aliens have sometimes tried to confront directly this limitation.

But the acknowledgment that we cannot really imagine a truly transformed society does not end Jameson's reflections on the Utopian text. Rather, in typical fashion, this seeming dead end produces new insights, as he assures the reader that

> the debate over Utopia's representability [...] indeed over its imaginability and conceptualization, does not threaten to put an end to Utopian speculation altogether and to return us sagely to the here-and-now and our own empirical and historical limits. Rather such debates find themselves drawn inside the Utopian text, thereby becoming occasions for further Utopian productivity. (2005: 142)

This thread leads to a discussion of Utopian intertextuality and to an analysis of some of the familiar antinomies to be found in utopias, like city and country utopias, or utopias of work versus those of leisure, and so on. More generally, Jameson has moved (as I pointed out earlier) from a focus on the contents of Utopia to its form. Thus, the significance of these oppositions lies not only in their substance, but in the ways in which the Utopian "form itself seems to interiorize differences [... becoming] in the Utopian tradition a Bakhtinian dialogue or argument between positions which claim the status of the absolute but are willing to descend into the field of struggle of representability and desire in order to win their case and convert their readership" (2005: 143).

Another example of how Jameson's dialectical method allows him to turn apparent dead ends into rich new directions of investigation lies in the inevitable acknowledgment that insisting that all utopias are historically situated leads to admitting that they are all constrained by that situation, and in that sense are always ideological. But again, this does not signal the end of Utopia's force or importance:

> Whatever the persistence of the Utopian form, then, its content comes to seem irredeemably tainted, and we come to wonder whether any Utopianism is possible which is not some mere projection of our own situation. Does this mean that there cannot even be a minimum formulation of Utopian demands which might somehow retain effective universality? Can we not envision some zero-degree Utopia, a Utopia in which content was reduced to its most undeniable validity for all societies? It was always Adorno's merit usefully to complicate the simple problems, while brutally simplifying the complicated ones: slashing through antinomies and productively using idealism and materialism against each other in the movement of a thought thereby released from its paralysis. It is thus not surprising that we owe just such a minimalist Utopian proposal to this thinker, a proposal calculated to clarify our own options in the present situation [and he now quotes Adorno]: He who asks what is the goal of an emancipated society is given answers such as the fulfillment of human possibilities or the richness of life. Just as the inevitable question is illegitimate, so inevitable is the repellent assurance of the answer, calling to mind the social-democratic ideal of the personality expounded by the heavily bearded Naturalists of the 1890s, who wanted to live a good life. Genuine feeling is only to be found in the crudest response: that no one shall go hungry any more. Every other answer substitutes, for a condition that should only have been defined by human needs, the habits of a system organized around production as an end in itself. (2005: 172)

Adorno's compelling reply or description of the "positive" dimension is not meant, however, to provide a final answer or organizing political strategy. Indeed, Jameson goes on to further complicate this response by introducing again the concept of critical negativity – so that Adorno's "moment of truth" is thus not a substantive one, not some conceptual nugget we can extract and store away with a view toward using it as a building block of some future system. Rather its function lies not in itself, but in its "capability radically to negate its alternative" (2005: 175).

Another of Jameson's attempts to explain and illustrate the problems and limitations of trying to imagine an alternative is that any change would change everything. This is a crucial reminder that a better society cannot be imagined piecemeal, that it is not a question of "fixing" this or that flaw in the present, but of total social transformation. Again there is a celebrated science fiction example, namely one of Ray Bradbury's most famous stories, "Sound of Thunder" (1952), where a time-traveler crushes a butterfly during a visit to the Paleolithic past, an event that has changed the present beyond recognition when the traveler returns. Jameson then goes on to give his own example of a demand which would transform everything, a utopian change to the present which is both necessary and impossible to fully conceive or realize under capitalism:

> Few Utopian fantasies are quite so practical and potentially revolutionary in their effects as the demand for full employment, for if there is any program that could not be realized without transforming the system beyond recognition and which would at once usher in a society structurally distinct from this one in every conceivable way, from the psychological to the sociological, from the cultural to the political, it would be the demand for universal full employment in all the countries of the globe, full employment at a living wage. (2005: 147)

Another aspect of his reflections on the "unknowability thesis" (which provides the substance of his penultimate chapter, "The Fear of Utopia") is perhaps even more shocking, as the reader is taken from the prospect of a transformed and therefore unrecognizable society, which is the familiar face of Jameson's utopian conundrum, to a transformed human nature, so that we would not even recognize ourselves in this new society:

> This brings us to what is perhaps the fundamental Utopian dispute about subjectivity, namely whether the Utopia in question proposes the kind of radical transformation of subjectivity presupposed by most revolutions, a mutation in human nature and the emergence of whole new beings; or whether the impulse to Utopia is not already grounded in human nature, its persistence readily explained by deeper needs and desires which the present has merely repressed and distorted. As we have implied in some of the preceding chapters, this is a tension which is not merely inescapable; its resolution in either direction would be fatal for the existence of Utopia itself. If absolute difference is achieved, in other words, we find ourselves in a science-fictional world such as those of Stapledon, in which human beings can scarcely even recognize themselves any longer [...]. On the other hand, if Utopia is drawn too close to current everyday realities, and its subject begins too closely to approximate our neighbors and our politically misguided fellow-citizens, then we slowly find ourselves back in a garden-variety reformist or social-democratic politics which may well be Utopian in another sense but which has forfeited its claim to any radical transformation of the system itself. (2005: 168)

The final chapter of "The Desire Called Utopia" begins with a "recapitulation" of Jameson's arguments and the persistence of the dilemmas with which he began:

> We have come laboriously to the conclusion that all ostensible Utopian content was ideological, and that the proper function of its themes lay in critical negativity, that is in their function to demystify their opposite numbers. [...] In addition we have been plagued by the perpetual reversion of difference and otherness into the same, and the discovery that our most energetic imaginative leaps into radical alternatives were little more than the projections of our own social moment and historical or subjective situation: the post-human thereby seeming more distant and impossible than ever! (2005: 211)

Again this seeming impasse (the "ideological impasse of utopian content" [2005: 212]) leads to a new series of questions, beginning with that of the future of Utopia, which he considers both in terms of the literary genre itself and of the political program ("radical social alternatives"). He first refers to some recent developments in Utopian writing since its high point in the 1970s – namely the concept of the critical dystopia, on the one hand, and what might be called the "liminal" features of recent Utopian writing, as well as their internalization of these various dilemmas:

> Yet Kim Stanley Robinson's monumental Mars trilogy (1993–1996) is only one example of a new formal tendency, in which it is not the representation of Utopia, but rather the conflict of all possible Utopias, and the arguments about the nature and desirability of Utopia as such, which move to the center of attention. Here the new form seems to reach back and to incorporate within itself all the oppositions and antinomies we have identified in an earlier chapter; to reorganize itself around the increasingly palpable fact and situation of ideological multiplicity and radical difference in the field of desire. Utopia now begins to include all those bitter disputes around alternative diagnoses of social miseries and the solutions proposed to overcome them; and the formal center of gravity then begins to shift precisely to the question of those differences [...]. (2005: 217)

As for the impasses contained in more practical utopian projects, particularly in the context of globalization, he proposes a different utopian formula – a "pluralism of utopias," that is to say a world made up of numerous and distinct utopias, with only two universal directives, "the right of migration; and the abolition of taxes" (2005: 219–220). This means of course that one could leave a utopia that one did not like, while the abolition of taxes means that

> the moneys normally available from taxation are to be replaced by the public work of the citizens themselves [...] everyone will do some civic and even manual labor.
>
> Finally, it should be noted that both these principles are anti-capitalist (without for all that being necessarily or overtly socialist): the first makes the enlargement and expansion necessary to capital impossible; the second removes the medium whereby capital is accumulated. (2005: 220)

In returning to More's starting point – the abolition of money – Jameson has found an example of what he calls a "dramatic rupture" with the present; and "The Desire Called Utopia" ends with a call for more such "utopian disruptions":

> This is indeed how Utopia recovers its vocation at the very moment where the undesirability of change is everywhere dogmatically affirmed [...]. Disruption is then the name for a new discursive strategy, and Utopia is the form such disruption necessarily takes. And this is now the temporal situation in which the Utopian form proper [...] has its political role to play, and in fact becomes a new kind of content in its own right. For it is the very principle of the radical break as such, its possibility, which is reinforced by the paradoxicality of the Utopian form, which insists that its

> radical difference is possible and that a break is necessary. The Utopian form itself is the answer to the universal ideological conviction that no alternative is possible, that there is no alternative to the system. But it asserts this by forcing us to think the break itself, and not by offering a more traditional picture of what things would be like after the break.[6] [...]
>
> Utopia thus now better expresses our relationship to a genuinely political future than any current program of action, where we are for the moment only at the stage of massive protests and demonstrations, without any conception of how a globalized transformation might then proceed. But at this same time, Utopia also serves a vital political function today which goes well beyond mere ideological expression or replication. The formal flaw – how to articulate the Utopian break in such a way that it is transformed into a practical-political transition – now becomes a rhetorical and political strength – in that it forces us precisely to concentrate on the break itself: a meditation on the impossible, on the unrealizable in its own right. This is very far from a liberal capitulation to the necessity of capitalism, however; it is quite the opposite, a rattling of the bars and an intense spiritual concentration and preparation for another stage which has not yet arrived. (2005: 231–233)

As can be seen by the number of quotations I have included, I am still in the process of understanding and assimilating "The Desire Called Utopia." Like Borges' map ("a Map of the Empire whose size was that of the Empire, and which coincided point for point with it"), my attempt to adequately explain Jameson's arguments risks becoming a restating of the argument in its entirety. From a literary perspective, "The Desire Called Utopia" is a rich, complex account of the genre, particularly in conjunction with the readings of specific twentieth-century texts. But it is clear from the very outset that this is also a political text, as he asks in the Preface "how

6 Is it necessary to add that "disruption" here is not a code word for so-called terrorism? Of course, and it is therefore also necessary to add three points on violence, in order to distinguish it from disruption as Novum, as restructuration and the unexpected blasting open of habits, as that lateral side-door which suddenly opens onto a new world of transformed human beings. The points are these: (1) violence is an ideology, constructed around the structural omission of state power and physical oppression authorized by the "law"; (2) violence is always initiated by the Right and by conservative or counter revolutionary repression, to which left violence is then a response; (3) political violence is self-defeating, and dialectically strengthens its opposite number: thus, U.S. expansionism generates al Qaeda, whose growth then encourages the development of an American police state.

[such] visions [...] can energize and compel us to action" (2005: xiv). This is not simply an intervention in some ongoing literary discussions about the nature of science fiction or the role Utopia plays today – although the book will certainly make important contributions to those discussions. Jameson also intends this book as a continuing interrogation of Marxism and its validity today. In those terms, the political role of the utopian disruption may seem paradoxical, frustrating those readers looking for a solution or a particular strategy, who wonder how utopian disruption is meant to replace or supplement other more traditional forms of political activity.

Yet the suggestion that "The Desire Called Utopia" ends with the dilemmas with which it began is only part of the argument. For while it does finish in an "open" fashion, by citing the call from the future asking Connie to help in the struggle to bring the utopians' world into existence (from the final page of *Woman on the Edge of Time*), Marge Piercy's novel also gives us a detailed portrait of a Utopian future. And so it is with Jameson's "The Desire Called Utopia," for in addition to the many dialectical reversals and negations, there are moments (particularly in Jameson's concluding chapter) where he does resolve or point to some possible resolutions of the dilemmas contained in the question he posed about the future of Utopia. The "end" of the Utopian moment of the 1960s and 1970s is not the end of Utopian writing, but its transformation, as he describes (through the example of Kim Stanley Robinson) the heightened self-awareness of the genre's tradition and limitations. Similarly, in terms of practical utopian projects, even as he admits that "we are for the moment only at the stage of massive protests and demonstrations, without any conception of how a globalized transformation might then proceed," Jameson has also offered the reader a vision of a new global system, a "pluralism of utopias," one that is foreshadowed by current events in the present:

> The possibility of a new union of like-minded Latin American states, or the possibility of a Brazilian leadership of a community of states around the world intent on forging a resistance to US globalization, would be other possible figures of the invention of collective entities beyond either empire or secession. (2005: 225)

Finally, within the context of a radical break with the present, Jameson has reiterated several fundamental principles of any new society, from the right of migration and the abolition of money to Adorno's end to hunger and his own call for full employment. This is my own undialectical interpretation of the meaning of anti-anti-Utopianism, as I begin the "intense spiritual concentration" he calls for as part of the "preparation for another stage which has not yet arrived" (2005: 233).

CHAPTER 7

A Short History of Utopian Studies

> Utopian scholarship is in the state of most sciences in the nineteenth century when better description was the basis of building toward more effective understandings of the phenomena being studied.
>
> – Lyman Tower Sargent (1994: 3)

Introduction

There are evident links between science fiction and utopia, although the former term only came into general usage in the middle of the twentieth century, while "utopia" dates back to More's classic (although as we shall see, the term only came to refer to a genre of literature in the nineteenth century). In the 1950s, such utopian scholars as Glen Negley and J. Max Patrick were dismissive of the role of science fiction in utopian literature, although utopian and dystopian currents have always been important to science fiction.[1] By the 1970s, however, there was a revival of utopian writing in English, particularly in the United States, most of it published as science fiction and much of it written by sf writers.[2]

1 "The once and often suggestive field of utopian fantasy has been exploited, perhaps under the comic-book definition, into a bastard literary device known as 'science fiction.' This product bears about the same resemblance to utopian speculation that the tales of Horatio Alger bore to the economic theories of Adam Smith" (Negley and Patrick 1952: 588).

2 There is not space in this essay to examine the specific relationship of these two genres. Darko Suvin has argued that, "precisely speaking, utopia is not a genre but the *sociopolitical subgenre of science fiction*. Paradoxically, it can be seen as such only now that SF has expanded into its modern phase, 'looking backward' from its

Utopian studies – like utopia itself – found a new life with the revival of utopianism in the 1970s – most obviously following the general social upheaval of the 1960s, which contributed to efforts to understand better radical traditions and alternative visions, particularly in a U.S. in which the Cold War and McCarthyism had nearly silenced a generation of activists.[3] In fact, the revival of utopian writing was in many ways *made possible* by science fiction, for as non-realistic fiction, as a genre of fiction that in many instances was set in or on imagined worlds and futures, science fiction provided a way to imagine and describe alternatives to an inadequate present. Today the utopian project of finding a different way of organizing social reality seems more vital than ever, and to that end I will offer here a brief review of the constitution and development of utopia as a field of study.[4]

As Lucian Hölscher argued in 1990:

> The creation of the literary generic concept "utopia" is a complex process which has until today eluded complete explanation. A reconstruction demands distinguishing between the formation of the literary genre itself and the adaptation of the term "Utopie" to it. (1996: 7)

---

englobing of utopia" (1979: 61; emphasis in original). Lyman Tower Sargent disagrees, admitting that while in "the current situation many utopias are published as science fiction, both historically and with utopianism treated as here, utopias are clearly the primary root" (1994: 11). For more on this debate, see Moylan's *Scraps of the Untainted Sky* (Boulder, CO: Westview, 2000), 77.

3 I will raise the question of the relationship between historical events and literary utopias later in this essay. For a brief overview of this utopian revival, see Chapter 9, "So We All Became Mothers." See also Moylan's *Demand the Impossible* (New York: Methuen, 1986).

4 In defining a field such as Utopian Studies, there is a very useful precedent in the July 1999 special issue of *Science Fiction Studies* on "A History of Science Fiction Criticism," particularly Arthur B. Evans's "The Origins of Science Fiction Criticism: From Kepler to Wells" and Gary Westfahl's "The Popular Tradition of Science Fiction Criticism, 1926–1980." For this essay, I have relied on three important contributions to the history of utopian studies: Lucian Hölscher's "Utopie" (originally published in German in 1990), Tom Moylan's *Scraps of the Untainted Sky* (2000), particularly Chapter 3, and Lyman Tower Sargent's pioneering essay, "The Three Faces of Utopianism" (first published in 1967). See also Peter Stillman's "Recent Studies in the History of Utopian Thought" and Toby Widdicombe's "Early Histories of Utopian Thought (to 1950)."

Hölscher's article "Utopie" is an account of that reconstruction, a tripartite "history of the concept" that includes "the history of the literary genre [...] the history of its use in [...] language and finally the history of theoretical reflection on the concept of utopia" (1996: 1). I am primarily interested in the third of those concerns here.

The first steps in the development of utopia as a field of study emerged long before there was a journal called *Utopian Studies* or conferences on utopia, in those instances in which the object of study itself came to be acknowledged as a specific genre, rather than as simply part of a larger category such as the "Imaginary Voyage" or the philosophical novel. There are numerous studies of More's *Utopia* (1516), for instance, but at what moment did commentators acknowledge it as part of a genre? Similarly, there are numerous studies of the Imaginary Voyage, but at what point were narratives of the discovery and description of a utopian land acknowledged as a specific genre its own right?

Prehistory: The Origins of Utopian Studies

There are some obvious places to look for acknowledgments of utopia as a genre, first of all in introductions and prefaces to works that we now consider utopias. In the thirty-six volumes of the late eighteenth-century anthology of imaginary voyages edited by Charles-Georges-Thomas Garnier – "Les Voyages imaginaires, Songes, Visions, et Romans cabalistiques" (Imaginary Voyages, Dreams, Visions, and Cabalistic Novels, 1787–1789) – the term "utopia" does not appear. Instead, the editor calls Ludvig Holberg's *The Voyage of Niels Klim to the World Underground* an "allegory" (Vol. 19: xv); while in the preface to Denis Veiras's 1681 *Histoire des Sévarambes* (History of the Sevarambes), Garnier labels that work an "imaginary voyage," classing it "among our best philosophical and moral novels" ("Avertissement," Vol. 5: vii). Veiras's own introduction to his utopia, however, begins with an interesting caution:

> Those who have read Plato's *Republic* or the *Utopia* of Thomas More or Chancellor Bacon's *New Atlantis*, which are in fact nothing more than the ingenious inventions ["imaginations"] of these authors, may think perhaps that this account of newly discovered countries, with all their marvels, is of a similar type ["sont de ce genre"]. (Vol. 5: xi; my translation)

Rather than situating his own work in the lineage of these classic predecessors, Veiras attempts to distinguish it from that tradition, insisting that, unlike those "inventions," this account is in fact true, and that it will fill in the general lack of knowledge about the "austral lands" (Vol. 5, xv). Pointing out that it has "all the characteristics of a true story," Veiras then turns to an explanation of how he came by the document. Although such cautions are typical of the period and found in many imaginary voyages, what is notable here is the situation of the manuscript alongside three well-known works which we now consider fundamental instances of the utopian canon – a juxtaposition that certainly suggests an awareness of the similarities of what will come to be called utopias, even as Veiras distinguishes this work from those earlier texts.

Another way of tracking the emergence of the utopian as a discrete object can be found in the existence of studies of utopian writing. Lucian Hölscher considers that in France, "Louis Reybaud was one of the first [in 1849] to point out [the] intellectual relationship of [the socialist movements in France and Germany] to the political novels of Plato, More and others" (1990: 13); Hölscher cites Robert von Mohl's 1845 essay "Die Staats-Romane" (The State Novels) as the beginning in Germany of the "real study of utopias within the history of literature" (1990: 14).[5] In English, on the other hand, John Dunlop's *History of Fiction* (1814) deals with utopias, but "under such traditional terms as 'Romance', 'Voyages imaginaires', etc. and not grouped together as a distinct genre" (Hölscher 1990: 13).[6]

5 Toby Widdicombe gives the "laurels for writing the first history of utopianism [...] to Henricus ab Ahlefeld, who in 1704 wrote a dissertation entitled *Disputatio philosophica de fictis rebuspublicis* as part of his studies at Christian Albrecht University in Kiel, Germany" (1992: 3). This work seems to have had little or no influence and has been dismissed by the few critics who are aware of its existence – until Widdicombe.

6 Widdicombe's account of some "Early Histories of Utopian Thought (to 1950)," which covers some similar ground, refers to some of the same works covered by

In his annotated bibliography *The Imaginary Voyage in Prose Fiction*, Philip Gove discusses a series of articles by James T. Presley in the 1870s that attempt to reply to a request for "information about works similar to More's *Utopia*" (1941: 75).[7] Over a four-year period Presley produced a list of ninety-seven titles, as well as an elementary classification system that is worth quoting in full:

> 1. "Utopias" proper; works which describe an ideal state of society, according to the notions which the author may entertain of what political and social conditions it is probable or desirable that the human race should hereafter attain to.
> 2. Those which satirize, under feigned names, the manners, customs, pursuits, and follies of the age or nation in which the writer lives.
> 3. Those which pretend to give a somewhat reasonable account of the possible or probable future state of society or course of historical events, either near at hand or in remote ages.
> 4. Those which, merely for the sake of amusement, or sometimes for the purpose of travestying the wonderful adventures related by actual travelers in remote regions, profess to recount travels or adventures in imaginary countries or inaccessible worlds, in which generally the most extravagant fancy runs riot. (Presley, "Bibliography of Utopias and Imaginary Travels and Histories," qtd. in Gove 1941: 76)

Early in the twentieth century, one of the first studies of utopia in English that uses the term in its title is Joyce Hertzler's 1923 *The History of Utopian Thought*.[8] Although he considers a number of *literary* utopias,

---

Lucian Hölscher's "Utopie." Widdicombe describes his own account as a "review" (and description) of twenty "early histories of utopianism," rather than a study per se, while Hölscher more explicitly studies the emergence of the concept of utopia as an object of study in the late eighteenth and nineteenth centuries.

7 Philip Gove's *The Imaginary Voyage in Prose Fiction* (1941) includes an "Annotated Checklist of 215 Imaginary Voyages from 1700 to 1800," as well as a 185-page "History of Its Criticism and a Guide for Its Study" which could certainly serve as a model for what I intend to do here in a few pages. Gove's "History" also includes an extended discussion of Garnier's anthology.

8 "To my knowledge [this] is the first book that attempts to give an unprejudiced, systematic treatment of the social Utopia as a whole" (Hertzler 1965: v). Hertzler does not seem to have been aware of Lewis Mumford's *The Story of Utopias*, published in 1922, the year before his own study. Widdicombe (1992: 17–21) gives a lengthy description of Mumford's study, pointing to its weaknesses. I have accordingly focused here on Hertzler's much less well known book.

his Preface makes no mention of literature, continuing the blurring of literary and non-literary genres, a practice that has characterized the study of utopia until recently:

> This book embodies two related and yet distinct types of sociological endeavor. It is a study in the history of social thought [...] and attempts to give an historical cross-section of representative Utopian thought. But it is also a study in social idealism, a study in the origin, selection and potency of those social ideas and ideals that occasionally men conceive, with particular emphasis upon their relation to social progress. (1965: v)

Despite the emphasis on "social thought," Hertzler mixes prophets, social dreamers, and utopian authors and planners rather indiscriminately. He begins his historical review of "social utopias" with the "Ethico-Religious Utopians," from the Prophets through Jesus and Augustine, before turning to more familiar texts such as Plato's *Republic* (c. 380 BCE) and More's *Utopia*, as well as Bacon's *New Atlantis* (1626) and Campanella's *City of the Sun* (1623). Then, after chapters discussing various utopian thinkers, including a chapter on the "utopian socialists" from Morelly to Cabet, Saint-Simon, Fourier, and Owen, as well as a brief look at Bellamy and the Wells of *A Modern Utopia* (1905), he turns to "An Analysis and Critique" of Social Utopias. Here is Hertzler's definition:

> The very essence of the various Utopias [described here] was the delineation of the means whereby the writer's vision of social perfection is to be realized. This spirit of hope expressing itself in definite proposals and stimulating action, we have called "Utopianism," meaning thereby the role of the conscious human will in suggesting a trend of development for society, or the unconscious alignment of society in conformity with some definite ideal. We may also think of it in its working out as the realization in life of ideals that prompts men eventually and yet unconsciously, to make them real; they breathe a spirit which gives hope, and encourages action. (1965: 268)

Another way of tracking the emergence of the utopian as a genre following from the preceding examples lies in the gradual establishment of a utopian canon. In addition to Presley's attempt to find "works similar to More's *Utopia*" or the works studied by Hertzler, this development manifests itself in the publication of anthologies devoted to utopias, of which the first in English is probably Glenn Negley and J. Max Patrick's 1952 *The Quest for Utopia: An Anthology of Imaginary Societies*. Negley and Patrick divide their anthology into two sections. The first, "Modern Utopias: 1850–1950," begins with excerpts from Ignatius Donnelly's *Caesar's Column* (1890) and ends with H.G. Wells's *A Modern Utopia* (1905). After a brief section entitled "Classical Utopias: 900 B.C.–200 B.C.," the editors turn to "Utopias from 1500 to 1850," beginning with More and continuing through most of the classics, and ending with Cabet's *A Voyage to Icaria* (1845). There is finally a short ten-page chapter on "Contemporary Utopian Thought" followed by a "utopian fragment" written by a student in 1947.[9]

9 As well as a number of forgotten utopias published between 1850 and 1950, Negley and Patrick include:

1871: Edward Bulwer-Lytton, *The Coming Race*
1872: Samuel Butler, *Erewhon*
1875: Mark Twain, *The Curious Republic of Gondour*
1887: W.H. Hudson, *A Crystal Age*
1888: Edward Bellamy, *Looking Backward*
1890: Ignatius Donnelly, *Caesar's Column*
Theodore Hertzka, *Freiland*
William Morris, *News From Nowhere*
1895: H.G. Wells, *The Time Machine*
1897: Edward Bellamy, *Equality*
1898: Paul Adam, *Lettres de Malaisie*
1903: Daniel Halevy, *Histoire des Quatre Ans*
1904: Gabriel Tarde, *The Underground Man*
1905: H.G. Wells, *A Modern Utopia*
1907: Jack London, *The Iron Heel*
1908: Anatole France, *Penguin Island*
1909: Mark Twain, *Extract from Capt. Stormfield's Visit to Heaven*
1914: H.G. Wells, *The World Set Free*
1923: H.G. Wells, *Men Like Gods*
1924: Eugene Zamiatin, *We*
1932: Aldous Huxley, *Brave New World*
Stephen Leacock, *Afternoons in Utopia*
1933: James Hilton, *Lost Horizon*
1942: Austin Wright, *Islandia*

The 1960s and After

As I stated at the beginning of this overview, the 1960s – particularly in the English-speaking world – saw a vigorous revival in utopian writing, and concomitantly, in the study of the genre. Today the study of utopianism involves a considerable range of scholarly activities, from articles, books, and bibliographies to the founding of library collections, learned societies, journals, and centers. In 1964, for instance (to cite one of the earliest examples), Glenn Negley (the co-editor of *The Quest for Utopia*) donated the first books of what would become the Glenn Negley Collection of Utopian Literature at the Duke University Library. Lyman Tower Sargent published the first version of his "Three Faces of Utopianism" in 1967 and the first version of his bibliography, *British and American Utopian Literature*, in 1979. The first version of Darko Suvin's influential "Estrangement and Cognition" was published in 1972, and his "Defining the Literary Genre of Utopia" in 1973, while Robert Elliott's influential *The Shape of Utopia* was published in 1970. Finally, Carol Farley Kessler's "Bibliography of Utopian Fiction by United States Women" was first published in 1984; an updated version was published in the inaugural issue of *Utopian Studies* in 1990. The Society for Utopian Studies was founded in 1975, while its European counterpart – the Utopian Studies Society – was founded in 1988. There are also a number of research centers, including the Interdepartmental Center for Utopian Studies at the University of Bologna, the Center for Utopian Studies at the University of Lecce, and the Ralahine Centre for Utopian Studies at the University

1944: C.S. Lewis, *Perelandra*
1946: Franz Werfel, *Star of the Unborn*
1948: Stanton Coblentz, *The Sunken World*
B.F. Skinner, *Walden Two*
1949: Robert Graves, *Watch the North Wind Rise*
George Orwell, *Nineteen Eighty-four*

of Limerick. These are all signs of the emergence of the study of utopia as a full-fledged academic field over the past decades.[10]

As Lyman Tower Sargent has repeatedly pointed out, the study of utopianism has been hindered by the "use of a single dimension to explain a multi-dimensional phenomenon" ("Three Faces," 4). Instead, it is important to distinguish the different uses to which the concept of the utopian is put so that it can be understood and discussed in a more systematic fashion. Sargent stresses that there are three aspects of utopianism that should be distinguished from one another and clearly defined: the literary (to which could be added other artistic representations and imaginings of alternatives), the communitarian, and utopian social theory (1994: 4).

Certainly these different aspects of utopianism seem at times to be linked, and one might summarize that complex interrelationship as the formulation of utopian ideas and projects, as well as their expression in literature and attempts to realize these ideals concretely. Critics have examined, for instance, how much Cabet's or Fourier's utopian schemes were realized in their respective colonies (Nauvoo, La Réunion, etc.); or how much this or that literary utopia is the expression or manifestation of particular utopian ideals or theories. But Sargent's tripartite distinction is an essential step in the renewal and progress of utopian studies, an essential part of the clearing of the underbrush in what Darko Suvin famously called a "genological jungle."

The crucial first step in the modern study of utopia was, of course, the definitional one. Important initial work was undertaken by Darko Suvin and Lyman Tower Sargent in particular, both of whose definitions were based on a careful survey of existing definitions. Darko Suvin's formulation is the most comprehensive in its review of earlier definitions, although he makes no reference *per se* to the political features of the utopia; instead he "confine[s] [his] consideration [to] utopia *as a literary genre*" (1979: 38; emphasis in original). He defends this decision by arguing that "In the last

10 There was, of course, scholarly work in utopian studies before the 1970s. As Kenneth Roemer has pointed out, papers on utopia have been presented almost yearly at the annual meetings of the Modern Language Association. See his "Petition for an MLA Discussion Group in Science Fiction, Utopian, and Fantastic Literature" (internal document, Modern Language Association, February 20, 1997).

twenty years [i.e. since 1953], at least in literary criticism and theory, the premise has become acceptable that utopia is first of all a literary genre or fiction" (1979: 46). Here is Suvin's definition:

> Utopia is the verbal construction of a particular quasi-human community where socio-political institutions, norms, and individual relationships are organized according to a more perfect principle than in the author's community. (1979: 49)

Sargent basically accepts Suvin's definition (with a few small cavils), but his "Three Faces" is addressed to the entire field of utopian studies insofar as it goes beyond the literary to clarify and distinguish two other essential areas of the utopian: communitarianism and utopian social theory. Sargent defines communitarianism in terms of "intentional societies": "A group of five or more adults and their children, if any, who come from more than one nuclear family and who have chosen to live together to enhance their shared values or for some other mutually agreed upon purpose" (1994: 15). This aspect of utopianism is the most straightforward (although it sets the threshold for a utopian community somewhat lower than what we might expect). As Sargent points out, existing definitions of communitarianism have usually been based on the study of a specific community, "but most are too specific to include what we know to be the range of institutions actually established. They generally assume a particular model to be the only model" (1994: 14). Moreover, because such communities almost always have written rules or are based on specific writings, there is usually a connection between them and the literary utopia, as Sargent has argued elsewhere.[11]

Sargent sets the second of his categories – utopian social theory – within the history of the idea of progress. Sargent then looks at what he considers the most important current of early twentieth-century utopian social thought, which he sums up in Hans Vaihinger's "theory of fictions" – that utopian thought "is a form of fictive activity" (1994: 22).[12] Using this

11 See his "Utopian Literature and Communitarian Experiments before Bellamy," *ATQ* 3/1 (1989), 135–146.

12 Hans Vaihinger was a German philosopher who proposed a theory of fiction in terms of the "as if" (from the title of his book originally published in 1911): while fictions are not "true," they are useful because they enable us to cope with what would otherwise be the unmanageable complexity of things.

approach, Sargent argues that we can find a defense of the necessity for utopia in the work of Karl Mannheim and Frederick Polak in their contention that "our images of the future help to shape our actual future" (27). Sargent also points out, however, that there are a number of philosophical and political currents that critique the idea of utopianism (e.g., Karl Popper). Of the three "faces," this seems to be the area that needs the most development.

Sargent's third "face" – the literary utopia – brings us back to the area with which we are most familiar and certainly, since the utopian revival, the area that has attracted the most attention. This is also the most contentious area, since following the work of Ernst Bloch, the utopian impulse can seemingly be found everywhere, including in most literary works. Unfortunately this sometimes leads scholars to move from pointing out the utopian impulse in a particular work to claiming on this basis that the work is a utopia. The overly loose designation of works as utopias is far too common – hence the usefulness, if not the necessity, of clear distinctions and definitions.

Sargent suggests two other areas for study, in the form of some further clarifications and precisions in defining the literary utopia. In the first place, he makes an interesting distinction (one that has been virtually ignored) between what he calls "body" and "city" utopias. The former are sometimes overlooked insofar as they are "achieved without human effort," in contrast to the "city utopia," which is "the utopia of human contrivance" (1994: 10–11). Secondly, he attempts to clarify some terminological confusion by distinguishing between "eutopia," "utopia," "dystopia," and "anti-utopia." The latter two terms in particular are sometimes used synonymously and given a variety of meanings. Here are his definitions:

> *Utopianism* – social dreaming.
>
> *Utopia* – a non-existent society described in considerable detail and normally located in time and space.
>
> *Eutopia or positive utopia* – a non-existent society described in considerable detail and normally located in time and space that the author intended a contemporaneous reader to view as considerably better than the society in which that reader lived.

> *Dystopia or negative utopia* – a non-existent society described in considerable detail and normally located in time and space that the author intended a contemporaneous reader to view as considerably worse than the society in which that reader lived.
>
> *Utopian satire* – a non-existent society described in considerable detail and normally located in time and space that the author intended a contemporaneous reader to view as a criticism of that contemporary society.
>
> *Anti-utopia* – a non-existent society described in considerable detail and normally located in time and space that the author intended a contemporaneous reader to view as a criticism of utopianism or of some particular eutopia.
>
> *Critical utopia* – a non-existent society described in considerable detail and normally located in time and space that the author intended a contemporaneous reader to view as better than contemporary society but with difficult problems that the described society may or may not be able to solve and which takes a critical view of the utopian genre. ("Three Faces," 9)

The Dystopian Turn

While it is the revival of utopian writing in the 1970s that led to an equivalent revival in utopian studies, the first half of the twentieth century was dominated by what Tom Moylan calls the "literary utopia's shadow" (2000: 111) – the dystopia and the anti-utopia. In this context it is important to mention not only the renewal of interest in the dystopia in the 1980s (as the world became increasingly less utopian), but also the awareness, among a number of sf critics writing *before* the resurgence of utopian studies, of a strong pessimistic current in science fiction that reflected a larger resistance to technological advances and the better future implied in some of the genre's inventions and visions (a reaction to the new reality of the Soviet Union as much as – in postwar writing – to the consequences of the use of the atom bomb against Japan). This can be seen in the focus – and the titles – of a number of important studies of science fiction written before the 1970s: Kingsley Amis's *New Maps of Hell* (1960), Chad Walsh's *From Utopia to Nightmare* (1962), and Mark Hillegas's *The Future as Nightmare* (1967).

The reexamination of the dystopia and the concept of the "critical dystopia" has been associated with the work of Raffaella Baccolini and Tom Moylan, who co-edited an important collection, *Dark Horizons: Science Fiction and The Dystopian Imagination* (2003). In his earlier *Scraps of the Untainted Sky: Science Fiction, Utopia, Dystopia* (2000: 186), Moylan writes: "Moving beyond the engaged utopianism of the 1970s and against the fashionable temptation to despair in the early 1980s, several sf writers turned to dystopian strategies as a way to come to terms with the changing, and enclosing, social reality." He cites Baccolini's definition of the critical dystopia "as texts that 'maintain a utopian core' and yet help 'to deconstruct tradition and reconstruct alternatives'" (2000: 188).[13]

Another area of recent research is the exploration and discovery of utopian literature and traditions outside the Christian West (which was the primary focus of utopian studies until the 1970s), in conjunction with attempts to understand utopianism in terms of historical moments and countries. Lyman Tower Sargent's bibliographical work on English-language utopias led him to the discovery that such production was not uniform in the different English-speaking countries; from country-specific bibliographies, he has begun to look into the question of utopianism and national identity.[14]

Another form of questioning and rethinking utopia is to be found in the work of Fredric Jameson. In a sense, the entire history of utopian studies flows from or is built on the link between ideas and their expression in literature as much as upon attempts to put these ideas into practice. Jameson does not question this connection; rather, he questions the assumption – if not the conviction – that the literary utopia is meant to be a representation of what the better society would look like: "at best Utopia can serve the

13 The classic examples would include Margaret Atwood's *The Handmaid's Tale* (Toronto, ON: McClelland and Stewart, 1985) and Marge Piercy's *He, She and It* (New York: Knopf, 1991).

14 This research has been developed in the following articles, all of which have been published in *Utopian Studies* over the past decade: "Australian Utopian Literature: An Annotated, Chronological Bibliography, 1667–1999," "Utopian Literature in English Canada: An Annotated, Chronological Bibliography, 1852–1999," and "Utopianism and the Creation of New Zealand National Identity."

negative purpose of making us more aware of our mental and ideological imprisonment [... and] therefore the best Utopias are those that fail the most comprehensively" (2005: xiii):

> [I]t is a mistake to approach Utopias with positive expectations, as though they offered visions of happy worlds, spaces of fulfillment and cooperation, representations which correspond generically to the idyll or the pastoral rather than the utopia. Indeed, the attempt to establish positive criteria of the desirable society characterizes liberal political theory from Locke to Rawls, rather than the diagnostic interventions of the Utopians, which, like those of the great revolutionaries, always aim at the alleviation and elimination of the sources of exploitation and suffering, rather than at the composition of blueprints for bourgeois comfort. (2005: 12)

As can be seen from this brief sketch, the study of utopia has flourished in the last decades of the twentieth century. It has gone well beyond the question of definitions and the establishment of a canon (or of the study of an author, or new interpretations of More's *Utopia* or Orwell's *Nineteen Eighty-Four*); it also tries to understand utopia's relationships to its more negative cousins – dystopia and anti-utopia – and it asks questions about why they wax and wane, and why they prosper at particular moments and in particular countries.

PART II

Gender and Audience

CHAPTER 8

Positioning and Closure: On the "Reading Effect" of Contemporary Utopian Fiction

Fifteen years ago, the critical consensus seemed to be that there was "something of a paralysis of utopian thought and imagination" (Frye 1966: 29), while SF itself had become a predominantly "pessimistic" genre.[1] Accordingly the recent revival of utopian themes in SF has been a surprising and, for many of us, an important and heartening development. The SF boom which began in the late 1960s – and which continues today – corresponds to the social upheavals in the developed capitalist countries and to the collapse of the dominant social consensus. The appearance of utopian themes within SF at that moment was a logical extension of SF's own inherent possibilities and potential, for, more than any other contemporary genre, it was a literature of alternatives, one which offered the reader and writer alternate times and places in opposition to the dominant forms which seemed bound to our own social reality.[2]

1 This is a widely held view. See, for instance, Hillegas (1967).

2 See, for instance, Judith Merril's use of the term "new mythology" in her reviews for *The Magazine of Fantasy and Science Fiction* in the late 1960s: "The as-yet unformulated contemporary mythology is the map modern man must use in the search for his soul […] An increasingly large part of serious speculative fiction, in and out of 'science fiction,' now concerns itself with the examination and analysis of

Beyond the question of how or why SF became an important vehicle for the utopian imagination in the 1970s, this development raises a number of more political questions, not all of which I can attempt to answer here. The first would be to explain the apparent waning of this utopian moment,[3] although it is perhaps too early to pass a final judgment. Another question would be to analyze the accompanying retreat into fantasy fiction, a development which has its political correlate in the projection of collective hopes and fears onto a president who represents a return to an imaginary lost past.

Here my aims are more modest. I would like to look at the "reading-effect" of some recent utopian SF, namely: Samuel Delany's *Triton* (1976), Ursula K. Le Guin's *The Dispossessed* (1974), Marge Piercy's *Woman on the Edge of Time* (1976), and Joanna Russ's *The Female Man* (1975). In more specifically political terms, I would like to examine the effectiveness of this writing about alternate societies in terms of concrete social change: how to link a poetics of the future with a politics of the future.

Within the Marxist tradition, the major critique of utopia lies with the argument that these writings would divert attention and energy away from concrete political action, a situation which, as Fredric Jameson has written, no longer obtains:

> For where in the older society (as in Marx's classic analysis) Utopian thought represented a diversion of revolutionary energy into idle wish-fulfillments and imaginary satisfactions, in our own time the very nature of the Utopian concept has undergone a dialectical reversal. Now it is practical thinking which everywhere represents a capitulation to the system itself, and stands as a testimony to the power of that system to transform even its adversaries into its own mirror image. The Utopian idea, on

mythology, and a significant, if smaller, segment with the creative search for viable modern myths" (December 1936), 31.

3 The situation is, needless to say, quite different in France where a "Socialist" government has further contributed to the undermining of the utopian ideal. See, for instance, James Petras, "Europe's Counterfeit Reformists," *New Left Review* 146 (July–August 1984). Anti-utopianism, thus, seems stronger in France: see, for instance, the second issue of *Science Fiction* (Paris 1984), and in particular, Roland Lew and Hubert Galle, "Sous les pavés de l'enfer utopique," 50–72.

the contrary, keeps alive the possibility of a world qualitatively distinct from this one and takes the form of a stubborn negation of all that is.[4] (Jameson 1971: 100)

The revival of utopian themes has meant, for most of the writers involved, a reconsideration of the utopian project itself, most evident in some significant modifications in the contents and design of the utopian community; but evident, too, as I will argue in a moment, in some of the strategies employed for influencing the reader. In these newer works, then, the utopian project is often ambiguous. Le Guin, for instance, subtitles her novel, "an ambiguous utopia"; while Delany (1976: 345) calls his a "heterotopia";[5] and all four novels describe societies which are far more open and problematic than earlier utopias. More specifically, each of these works depicts the struggle for utopia rather than the image of a finished and harmonious utopian society.

In Delany's *Triton*, which is set in an enclosed city on one of Neptune's moons, the advanced technology of the twenty-second century has made possible an almost completely free society whose members are guaranteed access to food and shelter. Although this society is threatened from without, by the "inner worlds" of Earth and Mars who wish to maintain their economic dominance over their former colonies – the smaller and sparsely settled "Outer Satellites" – the principal break with traditional utopian writing lies in the portrayal of a hero who is not happy. Whereas Delany problematizes the concept of utopia through an unhappy central character – one who is, moreover, not typical of the inhabitants of Triton, indeed, who is to blame for his unhappiness, Le Guin's reservations about the utopian project[6] go beyond individual failure to question the very

4 This was written in the context of Bloch and Marcuse; but Jameson has also written on SF and utopia. See his "Progress Versus Utopia, or; Can We Imagine the Future?," *Science Fiction Studies* 9/2 (July 1982), 147–158; and his lengthy review of Louis Marin's *Utopiques*: "Of Islands and Trenches: Naturalization and the Production of Utopian Discourse," *Diacritics* 7/2 (June 1977a), 2–21.

5 In a quotation from Michel Foucault, *Les mots et les choses* (Paris: Gallimard, 1966).

6 Unlike the other three writers under consideration, Le Guin has written a number of dystopian works, particularly the stories, "The Ones who walk away from Omelas" (1973) and "The New Atlantis" (1975), and to some extent her novel, *The Lathe of Heaven* (1971).

possibility of a better society. On the world of Annares – juxtaposed in familiar fashion to a flawed world very much like our own – the original anarchist principals of the new community have congealed into a bureaucratic apparatus while many of the utopians themselves have internalized a conformity to the system.

On the other hand, the most striking feature of the utopian society of Whileaway, in Joanna Russ's *The Female Man*, is the absence of men. Formally it is the least conventional of these four novels: it is constructed of short chapters which mix narration and dialogue with polemic and passages addressed directly to the reader. The novel is set in the present (or at least in an alternate present) where Janet, from the Earth 900 years in the future, describes to Joanna and Jeannine how, after a plague had killed all the men, the women of Earth learned to fend for themselves and developed, in the process, a more human and nourishing society. But as we learn late in the novel, the "natural" emergence of the utopian society is a myth. The world without men is instead the result of a choice, for there was, in fact, an interim stage between the present and the future in which our world split into warring camps – men against women – and from which the women emerged victorious.

Finally, Marge Piercy's *Woman on the Edge of Time* depicts an unambiguously utopian world which is, nonetheless, under attack from without. The central character is an impoverished Mexican-American woman in the present who has been institutionalized against her will and who is contacted telepathically from the future which she is then able to visit in the same way. As in *The Female Man*, the utopian society of Pierce's Mattapoisset is set on Earth in a future which can only come about through a struggle in the present: both novels portray characters from the future who have come to enlist help in our present in order to build a utopian future.

Turning then to the effect of these works, it is a mistake to think that attention to the reader or to the effect of literature is new, born with what is new called "reader-response" criticism. There are various esthetic currents in the twentieth century which have been concerned with the reader, of which the most important is that of didactic and committed art, and whose most famous practitioner is the communist playwright Bertolt Brecht. His call for an art which would "arouse [the spectator's] capacity for action" and "force [them] to take decisions" (Brecht 1964: 37) was not simply a slogan, but a concrete political and esthetic project which he developed through the "alienation" or "estrangement" effect. Moreover, the effect is, as you probably know, central to Darko Suvin's definition of SF as "the literature of cognitive estrangement" (1979: 3–15).[7]

In his paper at the 1984 Utopian Studies conference, Kenneth Roemer reviewed some of the categories of external evidence available for studying a work's actual readers. But, as his paper suggested, the most problematic and potentially the most fruitful area for reader-oriented criticism lies in the examination of a work's internal elements – the ways in which a specific literary text constructs its implied reader. Without reviewing here the (various) manifestations and developments of such criticism,[8] I would like to focus on several internal elements of recent utopian writing. My approach arises from the political concerns mentioned earlier – the potential effectiveness of utopian writing – and it originates as well in the recognition that different social activities and practices, beginning with the infant's acquisition of language and including literature and art, construct or "hail" (interpellate) specific individuals as psychological and social subjects. I am interested in the ways that the very form of a novel reproduces in the reader the unacknowledged acceptance of and adherence to the dominant ideology, and how traditional narrative strategies work to produce a subject for that ideology.[9]

7 The book contains an important chapter on utopias, "Defining the Literary Genre of Utopia."

8 For a useful summary of these approaches, see Steven Mailloux, *Interpretive Conventions* (Ithaca, NY: Cornell University Press, 1982). See also Hans Robert Jauss, *Aesthetic Experience and Literary Hermeneutics* (Minneapolis: Minneapolis University Press, 1982). For an empirical treatment of these questions which goes beyond the usual "sociology of literature" approach (Escarpit), see Jacques Leenhardt and Pierre Jozsa, *Lire la lecture: essai de sociologie de la lecture* (Paris: L'Harmattan, 1982). See also Brian Stapleford, "Notes towards a Sociology of Science Fiction," *Foundation* 15 (January 1979), 28–41.

9 This is of course a reference to the work of Louis Althusser, "Idéologie et appareils idéologiques d'État," 4 *La Pensée* (mai-juin 1970), 3–38, reprinted in English in *Lenin and Philosophy and Other Essays* (New York: Monthly Review Press, 2001). Of the many applications and accounts in English, see R. Coward, and J. Ellis, *Language and Materialism* (London: Routledge, 1977); see also my "Reality as

Although the most evident means by which a text constructs its reader is through the "shared reading conventions" of author and reader, it must be remembered that these conventions include not only the esthetic codes and generic expectations of SF and utopia, but the form of the novel itself; and more importantly, they include a number of frequently overlooked extra- or pre-literary conditions – beginning with the English language itself – which affect the interaction of text and reader insofar as they limit and determine what can be written or read at a given historical moment. In the case of utopian themes in SF, some of these conditions would include:

1. the "sexist" dimensions of the English language, an issue to which the most recent wave of feminism has called attention, and which is a specific concern in Russ's *The Female Man* and Piercy's *Woman on the Edge of Time*;[10]
2. the predominance, in the SF of the 1950s and early 1960s, of anti-utopian themes which reflected the larger social consensus of the period – albeit a consensus which had already begun to unravel. According to the dominant view, the ideal society had already been achieved and only minor adjustments and continuing technological improvements remained possible. The imagining of a different society was by definition the evocation of a degraded version of utopia, or the description of an alternative which threatened our own success and stability;
3. and carrying this further, one could say that the utopian imagination was effectively blocked during this period as well because of the historical linking of utopian thought with socialism – an alternative which, during the McCarthy period, it was literally impossible to write about favorably.[11]

Ideological Construct: A Reading of Five Novels by Philip K. Dick," *Science Fiction Studies* 10/2 (July 1983), 219–236.

10 As, for instance, in Piercy's invention of a new possessive pronoun – *per* (from *person*) – to replace *his* and *her*. Language is an issue in *The Dispossessed*, but not around sexism, i.e., the avoidance of the possessive pronoun as a way of defeating "propertarianism."

11 An extreme and amusing treatment of this theme can be found in F. Pohl and C.M. Kornbluth's *The Space Merchants* (New York: Ballantine, 1953), which portrays satirically a future U.S. run by advertising conglomerates which is threatened by an underground organization united around what we would call today "ecological" issues. Insofar as they seek to conserve life on the planet they are called "Conservationists" or "consies" – a thinly disguised allusion to the contemporary paranoia about the "commies" in our own society. In many ways, SF was during the McCarthy period the only vehicle for social criticism.

But the widespread sense of contentment and prosperity was contradicted in the l960s by the increasing militancy and dissatisfaction of various groups to whom the supposedly universal benefits of the American dream were denied, from the "discovery" of poverty in the United States (in Michael Harrington's book, *The Other America*), the Civil Rights movement and the mobilization against the war in Vietnam to the re-invigorated women's movement along with the struggle or recognition of lesbians and gay men. This outburst of contestatory and liberatory demands was the moment of the rebirth of SF, now no longer as the fiction of technological optimism or pessimism, but increasingly as a literature of alternatives.[12]

In the following analysis I will concentrate on two internal aspects of the reading conventions and narrative strategies of utopian writing which are significant in understanding how this recent writing try to break out of the passivity and illusionism of the traditional reading experience in an effort to push the reader to work for change. These aspects are: (1) the "positioning" of the reader within the text: how the reader is addressed by the text as well as the perspective from which he or she views the utopian society; and (2) that of "closure" – how the traditional novel manages social tensions through the return to harmony and stability which mark its ending.[13]

These recent novels differ, in their construction of the reader, from the strategies of the traditional utopian novel. Although More's *Utopia*, for instance, has been described in terms of its dramatic structure, its basic form is that of a philosophic dialogue. Indeed, this rational mode of addressing

12 For an overview of these developments, see Chapter 1, "The Modern Anglo-American SF Novel." On the 1960s, see *The 60s Without Apology*, ed. Sohnya Sayers et al., (Minneapolis: University of Minneapolis Press, 1984).

13 The term "positioning" is borrowed from feminist film theory. See Annette Kuhn, *Women's Pictures: Feminism and Cinema* (London: Routledge & Kegan Paul, 1982). For "closure" see Roland Barthes, *S/Z* (Paris: Editions du Seuil, 1976), Charles Grivel, *Production de l'interet romanesque* (The Hague: Mouton, 1973) and *Tel quel: Theorie d'ensemble* (Paris: Editions du Seuil, 1968). On the management of social contradiction in popular culture, see various works by Fredric Jameson, most noticeably his "Reification and Utopia in Mass Culture" (1979) and his book *The Political Unconscious* (Ithaca, NY: Cornell University Press, 1981).

or constructing the reader as an intelligent person, open to well-reasoned arguments, is the dominant form of utopian writing well into the nineteenth century. Thus, one of the developments apparent in the enormous success of Edward Bellamy's *Looking Backwards* (1888) is precisely the alteration in the techniques of persuasion, for there has been a change in the intended audience (to the wider public of the newly formed middle classes in the United States) as well as a shift from philosophic dialogue to utopian romance. As readers, we are no longer addressed simply as listeners; we have become involved in an experience which goes beyond the discovery and apprehension of a better society, one in which the description of the ideal society forms the background to a sequence, however flimsy, of unfolding events which we follow through the eyes of a hero and in terms of his own changing attitudes and feelings. Thus the "novelization" of utopia involves a significant transformation: from the positioning of the reader as the addressee in a philosophic dialogue who is persuaded through reasoned presentation, to the process of identification with a fictional character where the reader is implicated on an emotional and experimental level as well as on the intellectual one.

A similar shift in utopian writing can be seen in the evolution of another of its narrative conventions. For if the setting of a better society "somewhere else" (or "nowhere") implied, in earlier utopian writing, a permanency to the reader's situation, the impact of the Industrial and French revolutions was to render imaginable the possibility of changing one's own society. While the dominant convention of the first moment of utopian writing was that of the voyage, it became, in the second moment, that of a temporal voyage, most familiarly through the topos (or commonplace) of the awakened sleeper. The figure of the dream, moreover, not only underlines the distance between the real and imagined worlds, but the absence of a connection between them. This is not to say that the works of the second period of utopian writing do not address the transition to utopia – both Bellamy and Morris have chapters explaining "how the change came about" – but they do not attempt to involve the reader in such a transition.

In contrast to such traditional utopias, contemporary utopian SF uses different strategies for the reader which I have called positioning and which include: the perspective from which the utopian society is depicted; the techniques of identification, namely the reader's identification with a character who is emotionally involved with the utopian community; and the "distance" between the reader's empirical reality and the utopia, including the contrasting of the two societies as well as attempts to break the reader's passivity through various "performative" strategies.

In this sense, Piercy and Russ go further than Delany and Le Guin in their attempts to link their alternate worlds with the present. The libertarian city-state in *Triton*, for instance, has apparently emerged "naturally," as a result of the harsh conditions on a frontier world;[14] but there is no explanation of how its social forms or state apparatus have developed, and particularly, no indication of the amount of conscious choice or planning involved – in contrast, I think, to the other three novels. The reader is given a description of what some would consider the institutions and infrastructure of a "better" society, but there are few suggestions of a connection between it and our present day world. In *The Dispossessed*, on the other hand, which is set much further away in space and time, the utopian society of Annares is founded on the basis of a worked-out social philosophy. But the conveniently empty moon to which the followers of Odo emigrate to set up this society again discourages the reader from seriously considering how such a society could be achieved on our own planet.

The Female Man and *Woman on the Edge of Time*, on the other hand, are set in the present and the reader's identification is with characters who – unlike Bellamy's Julian West – remain in the end in the present. Moreover, in each case, this character has been contacted from the future to help bring the utopian society into being. Through these characters the reader is "hailed" as a potential actor in the process of building utopia, unlike the passive role traditionally assigned to the reader, where it suffices to dream and to wait.[15]

14 The locus classicus of the theme of the development of a libertarian society in the context of the harsh environment of a space colony is Robert Heinlein's *The Moon is a Harsh Mistress* (1966). But as opposed to the "welfare" system on Triton (Delany 1976: 178), the rule in Heinlein is "TANSTAAFL": "There ain't no such thing as a free lunch."

15 Professor Kenneth Roemer has pointed out to me that a number of nineteenth-century utopias do end with direct appeals to the reader. The second edition of

The Female Man attempts to subvert a number of novelistic conventions in the recognition that, like language itself, these apparently neutral forms are neither natural nor neutral, but instruments for the maintenance of the status quo. The process of identification, as well as the ideological myth of a rational, unified subject is undermined through the presence of four overlapping characters whose names all begin with "J," including the authorial persons, Joanna: "I said goodbye and went off with Laur, I, Janet; I also watched them go, I, Joanna; moreover I went off to show Jael the city, I, Jeannine, I Jael, I myself" (Russ 1975: 212). Through her fictional practice, Russ reminds us that the positioning of the reader is actually an important feature of how we construct our own identities: we learn our roles and responses from reading novels even as we "know" that they are not real. This points to current debates around "stereotyping" in the novel, as Russ (1975b) argued in her review of *The Dispossessed*. For whatever Le Guin's intentions, the reader was offered characters with whom to identify according to traditional sexist roles.

Under the concept of positioning, then, I have discussed how the reader is produced in these texts, beginning with the character from whose perspective the events and the utopian society are seen and experienced, and including performative strategies which attempt to directly engage the reader, rather than simply reaffirming the solitary and passive nature of the reading experience. Now I would like to argue that the technique of closure is a powerful mechanism for insuring that passivity, insofar as it returns the reader to an original tranquility and order which was disrupted

---

Looking Backwards, for instance, included a post-script addressed to the reader, while King Camp Gillette's *The Human Drift* (1894) included certificates which the reader could mail in to buy stock in Gillette's "people's corporation," and the back cover of Frederick U. Adams's *President John Smith* (1897) had an appeal to the reader to form "majority clubs." These appeals are part of the physical reality of the book and certainly are an attempt to link fiction and reality. Moreover, the total experience or act of "consuming" narrative increasingly – since the advent of television – includes direct appeals which interrupt the actual narrative. Popular novels, too, often include forms of advertising: inserts and coupons, etc. While this is not strictly equivalent to the nineteenth-century novels mentioned above, I am only concerned in this paper with forms of appeals to the reader which are integrated into the narrative itself.

at the beginning of the work. This basic narrative structure can be seen in *Looking Backward*, for instance, which opens with the disruption of the status quo as the hero awakes in the future where his friends and fiancée are long dead. From there the novel moves through moments of tension and disorder – his efforts to adjust – to a final resolution in which he realizes that this is a better society where he has found true happiness. This is the substance of the ideological effect of closure in the traditional novel: the disruption of an established fictional order, followed by an eventual re-establishing of that order. In this way, the reader's anxieties vis-a-vis larger social contradictions are acknowledged and then displaced to the fictional concerns and tensions of the novel where they are resolved through the novel's own resolution of the fictional tensions and the return to harmony and order. Furthermore, in *Looking Backward*, the process of the persuasion of the reader is reproduced in the underlying structure of the novel. More's *Utopia*, written as a philosophic dialogue, ends with the skeptical assent of the addressee, the "stand-in" for the reader:

> In the meantime I cannot agree with everything that he said, for all his undoubted learning and experience. But I freely admit that there are many features of the Utopian Republic which I should like – though I hardly expect – to see adopted in Europe. (More 1965: 132)

Looking Backward, on the other hand, concludes with Julian happily ensconced in the utopian future: his – and the reader's – assent to that alternate society marked not only, or not so much, in intellectual terms, as in emotional ones. For Julian's gradual conversion to the principles of utopia is also a seduction: the novel ends with his love for the utopian "explainer's" daughter, a love which is of course reciprocated and whose promised consummation closes the novel, just as his engagement to be married to a woman of his own time opened it.

Closure is significant in terms of what it does and in terms of what it prevents. In the present historical conjuncture, it is one of the methods through which literature serves the status quo, by reinscribing the reader within the dominant order which represents itself, like the traditional work of art, as whole and meaningful, without flaws or contradiction. The initial disruption which opens the traditional novel is a displaced expression of our collective tears and anxieties which is thus reassuringly dealt with at the novel's end. Thus at the end of *The Dispossessed* we have the figure of the return as the novel ends where it began, at the Annares spaceport. This novel is conclusive in another way, for although it ends with Shevek's commitment to struggle, it also concludes with the invention of the "ansible" – the instantaneous communications device – which becomes then, in typical SF fashion, a technological solution to social conflict insofar as it identifies imperfect communication as the problem.

Closure is also important for what it prevents: writing which in the Brechtian terms I mention earlier, would "arouse the [reader's] capacity for action." It goes without saying that to write utopian fiction today implies a dissatisfaction with the present state of affairs and a desire for change. In this sense closure undermines this will to change through the "imaginary resolution" of its formal return to the implied harmony which is disrupted at the novel's beginning.

The ending of *Triton* is very different from the pacifying effect of the end of *The Dispossessed*; but the tactic of bringing the reader to some sort of critical judgment through the absence of closure in Delany's novel is undermined by the fact that the reader had been turned too much toward one character's confusion and unhappiness, so that the only realization possible for the reader seems focused on the character of Bron himself. Indeed, in contrast to the other three novels, Delany's world lacks one of the central components of most utopian communities – a common ideal or philosophy. The government of Triton attempts to provide the minimal structures for the happiness and well-being of its citizens, but within this libertarian ideal state there is little sense of a collective commitment to those goals. Bron's unhappiness is, the reader feels, Bron's own fault, but at the same time, in the absence of collective ideals, his solitude and isolation do not seem surprising.

The contrast with *The Female Man* and *Woman on the Edge of Time* is striking, not only in terms of their commitment to shared ideals, but in their attempts to break with the traditional novel to directly move the reader. In traditional terms, *Woman on the Edge of Time* might have ended with Connie remaining in Mattapoisett (a la Bellamy), or at least with her successful escape from the hospital. By her desperate attempt to begin to struggle in the present – by poisoning the doctors' coffee – and in the documents relative to her case which close the novel, the reader is refused any such comforting illusions. Connie is still trapped, probably under even more repressive and humiliating circumstances as the involuntary subject of experimental psychosurgery designed to control anti-social behavior. As with the ending of *Triton*, we are left with the pain and suffering of the principal character, but here that suffering has an identifiable cause which the reader is called upon to help end, as Connie has been asked to help: "We must fight to come to exist, to remain in existence, to be the future that happens. That's why we reached you" (Piercy 1976: 190).

Similarly, *The Female Man* ends with a direct address to the reader:

> Remember: we will all be changed. In a moment, in the twinkling of an eye, we will all be free. I swear it on my own head. I swear it on my ten fingers. We will be ourselves. Until then I am silent; I can no more. I am God's typewriter and the ribbon is typed out.
>
> Go, little book, trot through Texas and Vermont and Alaska and Maryland and Washington and Florida and Canada and England and France [...] do not mutter angrily to yourself when young persons read you to hrooch and hrch and guffaw, wondering what the dickens you were all about. Do not get glum when you are no longer understood, little book. Do not curse your fate. Do not reach up from readers' laps and punch the readers' noses.
>
> Rejoice, little book!
>
> For on that day, we will be free. (Russ 1975: 213–214)

In attempting to understand the effectiveness of recent utopian writing I have not looked at the question of the new social subjects who, since the 1960s, have been the audience for the discourses of social transformation; nor have I dealt with the empirical questions of "actual" readers as addressed by the sociology of reading. Instead I've argued that cultural practices such as reading are already socially meaningful, regardless of authorial intentions or even individual responses; and that the forms and meanings of these practices, specifically the novel, have evolved in particular historical circumstances and serve to consolidate and maintain the political and ideological hegemony of the dominant class. I have argued, moreover, that the traditional form of the novel, through its structure of tension and resolution, is a mechanism for managing social anxieties and conflict: these tensions are acknowledged and then displaced onto the events and characters of the story, only to be resolved at the novel's end. Positioning, on the other hand, serves to reinforce the production of individual subjects within the social formations, as gendered and unified subjects who act in specified and comprehensible ways which are repeated over and over again through the stereotypes and patterned popular fiction,

In recent utopian writing there has been, as I've tried to show, a questioning of closure: firstly, in the very design of utopia, for traditional closed and unitary utopias – from More through Bellamy – have been superseded by ambiguous utopias which are still struggling to come to be. Secondly, on a deeper structural level, the novels of Piercy and Russ in particular sought to implement their utopian politics through a break with the isolation and passivity fostered by the reading experience itself, by refusing to the reader the familiar satisfying closure of the traditional novel. The rhetorical strategies of the utopian tradition have evolved, from philosophic dialogue to attempts to seduce the reader into an acceptance of the utopian society through the character's own seduction. These four recent works reject such strategies in favor of involvement with characters who were themselves filled with question and doubts. For those to whom the idea of a better society is of more than academic interest, the better society will not come about as the result of dreaming, nor are its forms already determined: it must be struggled and fought for, as Bee tells Connie: "We must fight to come to exist, to remain in existence, to be the future that happens. That's why we reached you."

CHAPTER 9

"So We All Became Mothers": New Roles for Men in Recent Utopian Fiction

One of the features of the most recent wave of feminism has been a renewed interest in what a world without sexual exploitation and domination would actually look and feel like, and how men and women might live together according to new social and sexual relationships. While many feminists have concentrated on the analysis of the forms and nature of capitalist patriarchy, and many more women (and men) are involved in struggling against the institutions and practices of patriarchy, some writers have set out to imagine non-patriarchal societies.[1] Over the last decade there has been a revival in the literary depiction of alternate societies based on new social and sexual relationships, particularly within the existing popular genres of fantasy and SF. In a recent bibliography, Carol Kessler (1984: 236) shows that from 1830 to 1980 there were 137 book-length utopias written by women in the U.S. alone; and of these, none were published in the 1950s, four in the 1960s, and seventeen in the 1970s (the previous high was six in the 1890s).[2]

In this paper I would like to outline some of these recent works, particularly insofar as they portray non-hierarchical and non-oppressive social and sexual relationships and patterns of behavior, and as they attempt to imagine a society which would be created by these new patterns and structures of behavior as much as it would enable them. Such visions are essential to the struggle for human emancipation because they help us to

1 For an interesting introduction to the question of both real and imaginary alternative communities, see the many in Rohrlich & Baruch.

2 In addition to a selection of utopian stories, this book contains a very useful introduction and an annotated bibliography of 137 book-length utopias by American women through 1980.

articulate what we understand by a qualitatively different society, something we sometimes lose sight of in the midst of our day-to-day lives, and also because these alternate visions reach beyond the restricted public of the already politicized and speak to a wider audience which often seems to no longer believe in the possibility of desirable or feasible alternatives to the fundamental insufficiency of the present.

As a critic, then, I am attempting to assess both the "contents" of these utopias – the transformed social and sexual relations depicted and the imaginary societies constructed around those new relationships – and their rhetorical and "performative" features, their potential effectiveness in awakening and giving shape and direction to emancipatory hopes. It is thus pertinent to acknowledge, first of all, that I am writing this paper from a position of privilege along the several axes of power addressed in these novels: that of a white, heterosexual male with the economic and social advantages of my situation in class society. Nonetheless, these visions of a full human society freed from the deformations of class exploitation and sexual oppression also speak to me, intellectually and emotionally, and I share the commitment to a politics of transformation inscribed in those works. As to the specific issue of a man writing about feminist utopias, and of the criticism that in so doing I am to preempt and neutralize the force of the feminist critique of patriarchal forms, I can only reply that unless we all join in the struggle to transform relations of exploitation and domination we risk losing the future and any possibility of creating a genuine human society here on Earth.[3]

To represent fully the range and features of the recent revival of utopian writing under the impact of feminism, I have chosen to discuss seven novels. Four are utopian SF novels usually considered the "basic texts" of the utopian revival of the 1970s: Samuel Delany's *Triton* (1976), Ursula K. Le Guin's *The Dispossessed* (1974), Marge Piercy's *Woman on the Edge of Time* (1976), and Joanna Russ's *The Female Man* (1975). Along with these, I include a more traditional utopia from the same period, Ernest

3 For a discussion of the objection that for a man to write about feminism is another form of the male exercise of power which feminism sets out to dismantle, see the opening chapter ("The Gendering of Critical Discourse") of K.K. Ruthven's *Feminist Literary Studies: An Introduction* (Cambridge, UK: 1984).

Callenbach's *Ecotopia* (1975), as well as Suzy McKee Charnas's "science fantasy" *Motherlines* (1978), and one important instance of recent feminist utopian fantasy, Sally Gearhart's *The Wanderground* (l979).[4]

SF and fantasy are popular fictional genres with a wide readership and frequently characterized by their sexism and their stereotyping of male and female characters.[5] But in the hands of a newer generation of writers, the generic potential of these forms to describe other worlds and societies – in opposition to the dominant realist paradigm of mainstream popular fiction – has been richly developed. The utopian writing I would like to look at is both critical and constructive. Each novel grows out of the

4 There will always be disagreements about which works to include in such a study. In their respective articles on feminist utopias, Gearhart (1984) and Russ (1981) exclude the two novels written by men, *Ecotopia* and *Triton* (and Gearhart also excludes *The Dispossessed*), while adding some of the stories of Alice Sheldon (James Tiptree), Monique Wittig's *Les Guerilleres* (1969), and a novel or more by Marion Zimmer Bradley (particularly *The Shattered Chain* [1976]). The stories, first of all – e.g., "Houston, Houston, Do You Read?" – are much too short to give the reader more than the briefest of glimpses of the new society, while Wittig's novel (English translation, 1971) was written very much outside the context under consideration. The novels of Bradley have interested feminists primarily because of the "Free Amazons" rather than on the basis of the description of a new society (see Leith). For critics who refer to the SF novels of Delany, Le Guin, Piercy, and Russ as the basic texts of the recent utopian revival, see the articles by Jameson (1982), Lewicki (1984), and Moylan (1982). On the other hand, I have chosen Gearhart's *The Wanderground* as the best of the more anti-technological feminist fantasies, a category which includes Dorothy Bryant's *The Kin of Ata Are Waiting for You* (1976) and Mary Staton's *From the Legend of Biel* (1975) (see Pearson). The abnegation and denial of the former are so extreme that it cannot, in my opinion, be considered by any stretch of the imagination a utopia. A much more interesting feminist fantasy with strong utopian overtones is Elizabeth Lynn's "Towers of Tornor" trilogy (1979–1980), comprising *The Watchtower*, *The Dancers of Arun*, and *The Northern Girl*. Finally, in my use of terms and distinctions – "fantasy," "SF," and "utopia" – I am relying on the pathbreaking work of Darko Suvin, in *Metamorphoses of Science Fiction* (New Haven, CT: Yale University Press, 1979).

5 For a rather limited look at the problem, see Betty King, *Women of the Future: The Female Main Character in Science Fiction* (Metuchen, NJ: Scarecrow Press, 1984). This book is basically a series of plot resumés of a not very representative selection of SF novels. See also the article by Rabkin and Russ's "Amor Vincit Foeminam."

feminist critique of the ideological, psychological, social, and economic forms of gender division and their interlocking with the exploitative and oppressive structures of capitalism; and each novel constructs an alternate society based on egalitarian social and sexual relations.

The first characteristic of this recent utopian writing lies in its differences from older utopias, which include not only the "contents" of the utopia, the changed sexual and social relations, but also its very form and focus. The influence of feminism, as well as the anti-utopianism of the Cold War period (particularly in the linking of utopian thought with socialism) and the present reality of the existing socialist countries, has produced a shift in utopian writing, away from the older, systematic, planned utopias (see, for instance, Edward Bellamy's *Looking Backward* [1888]) to more open and ambiguous imaginary societies which focus instead on the forms and textures of everyday life. These recent works also invent societies which are grounded in the economic and political reorganization of society and which emphasize communitarian goals and ideals. But there is an emphasis on decentralization and cooperation; and unlike traditional utopias, which were often presented as uniform and unchanging, these newer works depict societies in process, straining to come into being and open to change. For the most part, they leave the political and economic structures in the background and concentrate on the lived reality of the characters, who are often themselves caught up in doubts and the need to work for change. Finally, whereas older utopias were often plotted as a kind of guided tour of the new society, recent utopian writing has tried to involve the reader on a different level, by means of the thoughts and feelings of the characters in that new society who are involved in the daily struggle to build a world of human freedom and self-fulfillment.

This emphasis on daily life is an application of the feminist slogan "the personal is political" and a recognition that the purpose of any social transformation is to produce genuine changes in our lived experience of our daily lives. Consequently these novels address as central to the new society such "personal" issues as living arrangements, in opposition to the hegemony of the nuclear family; sexuality, as against the "norms" of heterosexuality and procreative sexuality; and more generally, the ideological, psychological, and economic structures of gender division under capitalism. In calling attention to the centrality of the everyday to any project of human liberation, these works attempt to imagine new societies in which all forms of human behavior are valorized and in which the older dichotomies which inform our lives have been transformed: work versus play, intellectual versus manual labor, creative versus noncreative, the home versus the workplace, productive versus non-productive work, and so on.

Thus the valorization of all forms of human activity begins with a fundamental transformation of work itself, from an "obligation enforced by poverty and external goals" (wage labor) to more rewarding and largely self-determining activities.[6] The availability of work according to individual inclinations marks the end of the sexual division of labor in these novels. Moreover, to ensure that individuals can vary tasks according to ability and inclination, and to balance those inclinations with social needs, these novels propose a variety of work-posting schemes. Disagreeable work is shared more equitably, or in some cases reduced through technology, while in all these worlds there is a reduction in the socially necessary labor each individual must perform.

Although socialists have usually focused on the workplace as the primary site of contestation, this is no longer the case in these utopian novels, which go beyond issues of economic exploitation to show that alienation and domination are embedded in the patriarchal structures of everyday existence – structures which, however, would not of themselves disappear following the collectivization of the means of production. As we shall see, then, these works develop new social forms based on equality of the sexes and on alternative forms of love relationships, living patterns, and parenting. Women are in full control of their reproductive functions, and

6 I have taken many of my ideas about the transformation of work from Herbert Marcuse, *Eros and Civilization* (Boston, MA: Beacon Press, 1955), and from the writings of Andre Gorz, especially his *Farewell to the Working Class* (Boston, MA: South End Press, 1982). Consider, for instance, his call for the "abolition of work" in the latter: "Thus the abolition of work does not mean abolition of the need for effort, the desire for activity, the pleasure of creation, the need to cooperate with others and be of some use to the community. Instead, the abolition of work simply means the progressive, but never total, suppression of the need to purchase the right to live" (Gorz 1982: 2).

there is an acceptance of diverse forms of sexual expression, most particularly of homosexuality.[7]

Finally, the emphasis on everyday life extends to the biosphere as well. These works all reject the earlier utopian commitments to growth and the domination of nature. In varying ways and to varying degrees, they espouse rather the development of an integrative and non-exploitative attitude toward nature. In the attention given to everyday life, then, these works blend the practical description of new social and human relations with the vision of an alternative society and with the images of an emancipated human nature in which playfulness, spontaneity, creativity, and eroticism are no longer sublimated to the demands of capitalism and patriarchy.

Three of these seven instances of recent utopian writing I am considering depict societies without men: Charnas's *Motherlines*, Gearhart's *Wanderground*, and Russ's *Female Man*. *The Wanderground*, first of all, juxtaposes the "natural" lives of the Hill Women in the countryside to the repressive patriarchy of the cities. Although there is not a single plot or main character, the reader learns of the backlash against the women's and gay rights movements which led up to the situation described in the novel, along with the revolt of the Earth herself and the subsequent impotence of men and machines outside the cities. The novel recounts the Hill Women's fragile relationship with a few sympathetic men in the cities as well as the risks faced by those Hill Women who live there disguised as men in order to monitor the situation. But the book's main focus is on the changed lives and developing rituals of the Hill Women themselves. *Motherlines*, on the other hand, tells of Alldera's flight from the collapsing city of Holdfast and of her integration into the tribal society of the Riding Women, where her presence – and especially her pregnancy – creates problems. The women resist accepting someone with different ways, someone from outside the handful of genetic lines from which they are descended and which reach

7 The term homosexuality is itself the subject of debate insofar as it connotes, for some feminists, male homosexuals (see Adrienne Rich, "Compulsory Heterosexuality and Lesbian Experience," in Snitow et al. [1983], particularly 193). I use the term as a general category which embraces both gay men and lesbians, in contradistinction to the term heterosexuality.

back to the founding mothers, who escaped from the Holdfast laboratories, taking with them the techniques of parthenogenesis developed there. Heretofore the Riding Women have ignored the small community of recently escaped women – the "free fems" who live on the edge of the Plains, but Alldera becomes a link between the two groups as they gradually come to accept and understand one another. The novel ends with the possibility of further disruptions as Alldera and the free fems plan to return to the Holdfast to look for any surviving women.

The all-women societies of Charnas and Gearhart exist on the margins of a collapsing patriarchal and industrial society. The women of *Wanderground* develop new values and rituals based on the belief in a specifically female nature, here connected, as in Charlotte Perkins Gilman's classic feminist utopia *Herland* (1915), with motherhood and with the body of the Earth. As in Gilman's novel, the Hill Women reproduce spontaneously, without men and without recourse to the technology which characterizes reproduction in the novels of Charnas and Russ; and, as in Gilman's novel, sexuality is deemphasized. Charnas's Riding Women, on the other hand, are modelled after the Plains Indians of the eighteen and nineteenth centuries, both in their nomadic lifestyle and in their energetic and fierce love of life. Accordingly, the feel and textures of everyday life are very different in *Motherlines* from what they are in Wanderground. Both describe societies which are close to the rhythms and patterns of the natural order, but Gearhart's women live according to an equation of women's nature with nature at large, while Charnas's women live in a hostile environment, in hard and joyful lives which include war games, duels, and feuds. In their energy and enthusiasm they resemble the women of Whileaway in *The Female Man*. But whereas technology was restricted to reproduction in Charnas, it is an important component of everyday life in Russ's utopian future.

The Female Man is a remarkable and controversial novel which has often been dismissed because of its polemical aspects and unconventional formal features. Set in an "alternate" U.S. in the late 1960s, the novel overlays four versions or "other selves" of the narrator. Jeannine, a 1950s woman who tries desperately to meet social expectations about correct feminine behavior, and Joanna, the "female man" of the title who has understood and rejected patriarchal conventions, are juxtaposed to two visitors from the future Janet and Jael. The former is from an alternate Earth 900 years in the future where, after a plague killed all the men, the women have learned to fend for themselves and have developed, in the process, a more human, satisfying, and nurturing world than ours. However, as we learn late in the novel, the "natural" emergence of the utopian society is itself a myth. This utopian world without men is not accidental but instead the result of a choice, for there was in fact an interim stage between the present and the utopian future in which our world split into two warring camps – men against women. As Jael explains:

> Whileaway's plague is a big lie. Your ancestors lied about it. It is I who gave you your "plague," my dear [...]. I and the war I fought built your world for you, I and those like me, we gave you a thousand years of peace and love and the Whileawayan flowers nourish themselves on the bones of the men we have slain. (1975a: 211)

Russ's pastoral Earth of the future bears some resemblance to the much smaller societies of Charnas and Gearhart. There are no "true cities" left, and life is organized cooperatively and collectively around families of women. Although they live in a respectful and harmonious way with the environment, however, they have developed a pronounced reliance on technology – which includes not only reproductive technology, but also time travel, mining colonies in space, and, more immediately, mind-computer link-ups ("induction helmets"), portable power sources, food factories, and so on. In place of the spiritual focus of Gearhart's novel, there is a strong emphasis on practical education for the young girls. They learn "how to run machines, how to get along without machines, law, transportation, physical theory [...] gymnastics and mechanics [...] and practical medicine" (1975a: 50).

In the attempt to imagine a world beyond male domination, it is of course not surprising that some women would resolve the problem by envisioning a world without men at all. Writing about the genesis of *Motherlines*, Suzy Charnas, for instance, explains that "the decision to exclude men was not dispassionate and political. I tried to write them in. [... But] no matter what I wrote, men would not fit. Every scene they entered went dead" (1981: 105).[8] But rather than assume that the exclusion of men in these three novels eliminates their utopian force or their usefulness in helping men to develop new attitudes and roles, I will argue the contrary: that in the patterns of social interaction and behavior of these societies without men, the male reader can glimpse a society in which present-day gender roles and the sexual division of labor have finally disappeared. This distinction between sexual difference (biology) and the social construction of gender (the process which makes "men" and "women" out of male and female persons, a process which begins in infancy) is an important part of current feminist research (see Dimen, Hollway, and Ross & Rapp) as well as the subject (as we shall see in a moment) of some recent SF which precedes the utopian revival under discussion. As Charnas comments further in the article I have already mentioned, once she realized that there would be no men in her novel, she made a remarkable discovery:

> With the spectrum of human behavior in my story no longer split into male roles (everything active, intelligent, brave and muscular) and female roles (everything passive, intuitive, shrinking and soft), my emerging women had access to the entire range of human behavior. They acted new roles appropriate to social relationships among a society of equals which allowed them to behave simply as human beings. (1981: 106–107)

The other four novels present what some critics have called "androgynous" utopias. In contradistinction to older utopias, which usually left existing gender roles and the sexual division of labor in place, these new societies are made up of men and women living together in social and sexual relationships so altered that there are no longer any distinctions or hierarchy based on sex.[9] *Ecotopia*, for one, is an explicitly utopian novel which was written outside the traditions and conventions of SF and fantasy.

8 For a similar remark on the part of Joanna Russ when asked about the absence of men in *The Female Man*, see the interview published in *Quest* 2 (1975). In her introduction to *Daring to Dream*, Carol Kessler points out that of the fourteen utopias by women published since 1970, half portray all-women societies (1984: 18).

9 Annas quotes Carolyn Heilbrun's definition of "androgyny" as "a condition under which the characteristics of the sexes and the human impulses expressed by men and women are not rigidly assigned. [...] Androgyny suggests a spirit of reconciliation

It is set in the year 2000, twenty years after northern California, Oregon, and Washington have reluctantly seceded from the U.S. to set up a society based on cooperative, ecological, and feminist ideals. The novel is a traditional utopia insofar as it presents the new society through the eyes of an outsider, the reporter William Weston, who gradually and grudgingly becomes convinced of its beauty and validity, and insofar as it pays much more attention than the other novels under discussion to explaining the economic and political organization and functioning of the Ecotopian society.

Communitarian, ecological, and feminist ideals also are prominent in *Woman on the Edge of Time*, which is set in New York City in the present. Connie, a Mexican-American woman unjustly confined to a mental hospital, is contacted telepathically from the future, which she is then able to visit in the same way. In the Mattapoisett of 2137 (the town which she visits), the people of Earth live in an interlocking network of self-sufficient regions. They have achieved a utopian future through a long struggle against the exploitative forces of multinational capitalism – a fight which is still being waged in the future by the "multis" from bases in Antarctica and in space. This fight reaches back to our present as well, and Connie has been contacted to join in it. As she gradually comes to appreciate the utopian future (and she is at first skeptical), she also realizes that her own situation in the hospital, as the unwilling subject in a psycho-surgical experiment designed to control "anti-social behavior," is a part of the war to control the future. In a desperate act of defiance and as her own conscious declaration of war against the increasing repression and exploitation of our present system, she poisons the doctors' coffee. Unlike Weston (in *Ecotopia*), she

---

between the sexes; it suggests further a full range of experience open to individuals who may, as women, be aggressive, as men, tender." Annas then goes on to argue that "the center of the utopian concern of feminist writers is in modifying sex roles to allow for full human development of each individual person" (1978: 146). In her article, she discusses *Venus Plus X*, *The Female Man*, and the novels of Le Guin and Piercy. In the article mentioned in note 7, Adrienne Rich also addresses one possible and very mistaken assumption which sometimes arises from the term androgyny, the "assertion that in a world of genuine equality, where men were nonoppressive and nurturing, everyone would be bisexual" (in Snitow et al. 1983: 182). There would be a spectrum of sexual choices and identities in a genuine utopian society, of which "bisexuality" would be but one.

cannot remain in utopia; she will not be saved by a happy ending. But, the novel tells us, if we also begin to fight in the present, we may yet win the battle for the future.

Triton is also set some 150 years in the future, in an enclosed city on a moon of Neptune. There is again a war in the background, between the colonies on the "Outer Satellites" and the two inner worlds, Earth and Mars, which seek to impose full economic control in the Solar System. Through the minimal narrative, we follow Bron, who, despite the freedoms and economic guarantees of his society, is unhappy, and whose distress calls into question the universal happiness that traditional utopias take for granted:

> Somewhere, in your sector or in mine, in this unit or in that one, there it is: pleasure, community, respect – all you have to do is know the kind, and much of it, and to what extent you want it. [...] "But what happens to those of us who *don't* know? What happens to those of us who have problems and don't know *why* we have the problems we do? What happens to the ones of us in whom even the part that wants has lost, through atrophy, all connection with articulate reason. Decide what you like and go get it? Well, what about the ones of us who only know what we *don't* like?" (1976: 122)

Finally, there is the "ambiguous utopia" that Le Guin generates in *The Dispossessed* by juxtaposing Urras to its moon, Anarres, where the followers of Odo emigrated some 150 years before the story opens to set up an egalitarian society. Through the device of the protagonist's return to the mother world, the novel alternates between depicting the utopian society wherein hierarchy and privilege have begun to emerge again, and that of the older world, which is a kind of caricature of our own major sociopolitical systems. In the counterpoising of an abusive and exploitative capitalist patriarchy with the threat of the increasing bureaucratization of the utopian experiment, Le Guin questions the validity of the utopian project itself.[10] Such doubts, however, in the end give way to – indeed, strengthen – Shevek's renewed commitment to the ideal of "permanent revolution": "that the Odonian society on Anarres had fallen short of the ideal did not, in his eyes, lessen his responsibility to it" (1975: 267).

10 Unlike the other writers under study, Le Guin has written several dystopian and anti-utopian works, particularly the stories, "The Ones Who Walk Away From Omelas" (1973) and *The New Atlantis* (1975), and to some extent, *The Lathe of Heaven* (1971).

In their description and analysis of fictive attempts to bring about a world qualitatively different from ours, and especially in regard to the new roles for men which an egalitarian society would carry with it, these seven novels raise issues central to my own concerns. Their authors begin with the recognition of sexual oppression in our society and hence realize that liberating the potentiality of human beings requires a profound social transformation. By their very existence, moreover, these fictions also assume that the imagining of alternatives has a part to play in such a transformation. Nevertheless, when it comes to the extent of the changes and the nature of the society envisaged, differences do exist among these works (as my account of them may already have suggested), despite their being predicated on similar collective ideals.

Whereas the Riding Women of *Motherlines* and the women on Russ's Whileaway have cut themselves off from men to develop their new societies, Gearhart's Hill Women live in an uneasy relationship with the "gentles" who secretly aid and support them. Paradoxically, it is less difficult (in my opinion) for male readers to conceive of new roles and patterns of behavior for themselves in the societies from which Charnas and Russ have excluded men than in Gearhart's, where men have been assigned specific functions separate from those of women. The absence of men in Charnas and Russ stands as a warning to men, while the lives and activities of the women in their novels serve as a model for all human beings in a future society beyond sexual hierarchy and gender. Gearhart's society, on the other hand, is based on the argument that there is a fundamental and essential difference between men and women so that, because of their essential maleness, even the "gentles" – those men who have renounced masculine ways as well as all sexual activity – still cannot be trusted.[11]

Besides the question of the presence or place of men in a new society, works also differ in the portrayal of the extent of the transformation. Traditional utopias, from More's Utopia through Gilman's *Herland*,

11 "'I am not scorning any one of you or your discovery,' she said, 'or even your intent. My mistrust is of a deeper thing.' Labrys spoke. 'Our maleness.' Evona nodded" (1978: 180). For an extensive critique of "cultural feminism," see Alice Echols, "The New Feminism of Yin and Yang," in Snitow et al. (1983: 439–459).

often opted for separation and isolation; and this solution is taken up by *Motherlines* and *The Wanderground*, and in another way, by Callenbach's *Ecotopia*. This is perhaps not the place to discuss separatism as a political strategy; what should be mentioned, however, is the hostility and threats which alternate communities and states face from their neighbors, a fact which the [Pierre] Trudeau government's invocation of the War Measures Act in Canada and the Reagan administration's recent reactions to political changes in Grenada and Nicaragua have made painfully apparent. Gearhart's Hill Women and Charnas's Riding Women are actively involved in preparing themselves for possible invasions; but it is factors beyond their control, not their own preparedness, which prevents such an event. The industrial patriarchy of the Holdfast is collapsing in *Motherlines* (as can be seen in the novel which precedes it, *Walk to the End of the World* [1974]), and it is thus in no position to worry about the women in the Wild; and in *Wanderground*, the women are protected by the Earth herself: outside the City, men become impotent and machines will not work. Callenbach's Ecotopians, on the other hand, have concealed nuclear weapons in various U.S. cities and threaten to explode them if attacked; besides, they successfully repelled a "major secret attack" two years after their secession, shooting down 7,000 U.S. Army helicopters in the process (1982: 146). And – as we have seen – the new societies in both *Triton* and *Edge of Time* are actively involved in defending themselves.

The external threats contribute to the society's inner cohesion as well as demonstrating how far its members are prepared to go to defend it. *The Dispossessed*, too, conforms to this pattern, even though the scarcity and rigors of life on Anarres itself replace the threat of invasion. But while all of these utopian societies are fighting to come into existence or to survive, they differ in regard to the shared goals and ideals which bind their members together.

External circumstances, specifically the environment, play a large part in determining and maintaining the community of Riding Women in *Motherlines*. Even so, that stability is threatened in a number of positive ways: by the integration of Alldera, who will introduce new genes into the original "motherlines"; by her attempts to secure recognition for some of the other women who have recently escaped the Holdfast and who have been shunned by the Riding Women; and finally, at the end of the novel, by her decision to return to the Holdfast with some of the "free fems" to search for other women.

The Wanderground is the smallest and most tightly knit society: uniting its members is a oneness with nature which is specific to women and opposed to the innate violence of men. Decisions are made in common, through telepathic "joinings"; and consensus is valued over votes and majorities, although there are no real disagreements about goals and ideals. Shared goals and ideals are also central to Anarresti society, which was founded on the "antipropertarian" and collectivist ideals of the philosopher Odo. Disagreement among the Anarresti, like the arguments which Alldera arouses in *Motherlines*, serves as a positive element, as a way of underlining the theme of "permanent revolution." Finally, *Edge of Time* also includes scenes of debate and disagreement, and again stresses the importance of consensus in decisions affecting the community at large.

Certainly those societies are more unified than the ones in *Ecotopia*, *The Female Man*, and *Triton*. The latter exist by agreement on some minimal goals and ideals – their members want to ensure the material preconditions for the new society – but not on a common world-view or ideology. Ecotopia has emerged from a capitalist democracy and it still retains many of the older forms. Property is not held in common and there are still some private corporations, while decision-making lies with the government, albeit a democratically elected government which stresses participation and dialogue. There is dissent, even those actively working to overthrow the government, and this has provoked an "Ecotopian counter-intelligence" (1982: 77). Similarly, *The Female Man* and *Triton* are heterogeneous societies with a wide range of choices and possibilities, although the former draws a very strict line concerning each member's obligation to the community:

> A Belin, run mad and unable to bear the tediousness of her work, flees above the forty-eighth parallel, intending to remain there permanently. [… T]he S & P [policewoman] for the county follows her – not to return her for rehabilitation, imprisonment, or study. What is there to rehabilitate or study? We'd all do it if we could. And imprisonment is simple cruelty.
>
> You guessed it. (Russ 1975a: 55)

Triton is subtitled "an ambiguous heterotopia" in response to *The Dispossessed*; and much more than the other texts I am dealing with it is concerned with guaranteeing the right to difference, without attempting to determine what constitutes human self-fulfillment or happiness. In addition to basic material guarantees for all – "basic food, basic shelter, and limited transport" (1976: 179) – *Triton*'s society includes an "unlicensed sector," "where no law officially held" (1976: 9), and a bewildering variety of personal freedoms, proclivities, and practices: "forty or fifty sexes, and twice as many religions" (1976:117). But there is a government, an army, and even a police force ... and there is also a war going on.

The societies portrayed in these seven novels do not have the uniformity, stability, and stasis of traditional utopias; rather, they are societies in process, struggling to come into being or fighting to stay in existence. Although they do differ in some of their basic ideals and in the amount of difference and dissent they are willing to tolerate, their authors – and above all, the women authors – stress in varying degrees consensual decision-making.

Nor is that all they give male readers to think about in regard to alternative and egalitarian patterns of behavior. One of the recurrent themes of recent feminist analysis has been the recognition that the forms and practices of discourse are socially produced and contribute to the maintenance of the status quo. Language itself is at issue. The generic term *man*, for instance, implicitly equates "people" with "male people," while women are "represented in discourse as a secondary sex, differentiated from an implied male norm" (Belsey 1980: 42–43).[12] In Piercy's utopian future, for instance, the generic noun *man* and the gender differentiated pronouns *his* and *her*

12 For a discussion of these issues within the utopian context, see the articles by Barrie Thorne, Cheris Kramarae, & Nancy Henley, "Imagining a Different World of Talk," and H. Lee Gershuny, "The Linguistic Transformation of Womanhood," both in Rohrlich & Baruch (1984). See also Casey Miller and Kate Swift, *The Handbook of Non-Sexist Writing* (London: Women's Press, 1981); Cathy Urwin, "Power Relations and the Emergence of Language" (in Henriques et al. 1984: 264–311); and Joanna Russ, *How to Suppress Women's Writing* (Austin: University of Texas Press, 1983).

have been replaced by the word *per* (as in *person*). As Joanna explains her decision to "become a man" in *The Female Man*:

> Man, one assumes, is the proper study of Mankind. Years ago we were all cave Men. Then there is Java Man and the future of Man and the values of Western Man and existential Man and economic Man and Freudian Man and the Man in the moon and modern Man and eighteenth-century Man and too many Mans to count or look at or believe. [...] For years I have been saying *Let me in, Love me, Approve me, Define me, Regulate me, Validate me, Support me*. Now I say *Move over*. If we are all Mankind, it follows to my interested and righteous and rightnow very bright and beady little eyes, that I too am a Man and not at all a Woman, for honestly now, whoever heard of Java Woman and existential Woman and the values of Western Woman and scientific Woman and alienated nineteenth-century Woman and all the rest of that dingy and antiquated rag-bag? All the rags in it are White, anyway. I think I am a Man; I think you had better call me a Man; I think you will write about me as a Man from now on and speak of me as a Man and employ me as a Man and recognize child-rearing as a Man's business; you will think of me as a Man and treat me as a Man until it enters your muddled, terrified, preposterous, nine-tenths-fake, loveless, papier-mâché-bull-moose head that *I am a man*. (And you are a woman.) That's the whole secret. Stop hugging Moses' tablets to your chest, nitwit; you'll cave in. Give me your Linus blanket, child. Listen to the female man. (1975a: 139–140)

Similarly, the forms and conditions of discourse, of social interaction and exchange, are also recognized as central to the development of new forms of democracy, and perhaps nowhere more than in the scenes of public debate around issues involving the community as a whole which I have already referred to in the seven novels. Many of these novels stress alternatives to existing forms of decision-making, according to which questions have traditionally been decided on the basis of verbal skills, parliamentary maneuvers, and majority votes.[13] In these novels consensus is the key, and

13 This point may be illustrated by contrasting these novels with a more traditional SF equivalent, Robert Heinlein's *The Moon is a Harsh Mistress* (New York: Berkeley Books, 1965). This narrative about the rebellion of a colony on the Moon on the 300th anniversary of the American Revolution resembles in many ways some of the novels under discussion, particularly in the establishment of an autonomous lunar society, freed from an exploitative relationship with the Earth and from its laws and police, where new sexual social relations have developed. Heinlein's libertarianism is of course a long way from the cooperative and communitarian societies I have been discussing. But more to the point, the revolution itself is shown to be a cynical

decisions without unanimity are not community decisions, particularly in the societies of Charnas, Gearhart, and Piercy.

The seven novels focus on the personal and the everyday to make their new pattern of social and sexual relationships apparent. The changes are most evident in three interrelated areas: (1) the basic living units developed as alternatives to the nuclear family; (2) the question of gender and the division of labor; (3) sexuality itself, both as an index to human fulfillment and in opposition to heterosexism and/or attempts to limit it to procreation.

All of these novels recognize that the nuclear family has been the basic unit for maintaining and reproducing patriarchal social relations (see Barrett & McIntosh). They accordingly propose a variety of collective and communal alternatives to the nuclear family. The underlying social unit in *Motherlines*, *Edge of Time*, and *The Female Man* is an extended family which is not necessarily based on kinship, while the more urban societies of *Ecotopia* and *Triton* include both variations on the extended family and cooperatives and communes where people live more or less collectively, depending on individual inclination, but without the equivalent of private housing. Child-rearing, too, becomes a collective enterprise, whether in the extended families just where there are usually more than two parents (e.g., four in *Motherlines*, in *Edge of Time*) – or by involving the community at large, particularly in *Wanderground* and *The Female Man*. To further break the hold of the nuclear family, children are shown as much more independent after the age of 3 or 4 than is presently the case – whether as

exercise in which democratic participatory forms of political mobilization are completely rejected. Instead, a handful of conspirators manipulate their fellow "loonies" through their control of the media and the information networks – to the extent of inventing a fictive television spokesperson for the independence movement. In *Ecotopia*, on the other hand, where television also has an important political role in building and maintaining the Ecotopian movement, the stress is repeatedly on democratizing the media (see also Callenbach's 1981 "prequel," *Ecotopia Emerging*), and on attempting to undo the learned passivity of the television viewer of today by converting the medium into a "reactive" one. Describing the many broadcasts of governmental proceedings in Ecotopia, Weston writes: "Viewers not only watch – they expect to participate. They phone in with questions and comments" (1982: 49).

part of the larger community or as part of a group of peers, as in the "child-packs" of *Motherlines* and *The Female Man*. Thus, in the organization of space itself, through the disappearance of the single-family dwelling, and/or in the patterns of sleeping, loving, eating, or parenting, our seven authors envision a thoroughgoing dismantling of the nuclear family. Accordingly, most of them show us new forms of intimate personal relationships and interaction centered on collective ideals and goals – in which respect, I might note that *Triton* and *Ecotopia* offer a wider range of living arrangements than the rest, while *The Dispossessed* hesitates between the collective impersonality of dormitories and the very strong heterosexual bonding exemplified by Shevek and Takver.

"A person chooses work according to interest, talent, strength –what has the sex to do with that?" (Le Guin 1975:13). Le Guin's (rhetorical) question points to a second area that our seven authors would transform, by putting an end to the sexual division of labor and to the stereotyping which links certain kinds of behavior and abilities to sex. Two well-known SF novels of the 1960s had already experimented with this as their central topic: *Venus Plus X* (1960) and *The Left Hand of Darkness* (1969), wherein Theodore Sturgeon and Le Guin respectively imagined societies composed of individuals who were both male and female.

Venus tells of a man who awakes in a future world to which he has been brought to give the "Ledom" his opinion of it. Through his eyes we discover a small, tranquil, and self-contained utopia, maintained through a very high degree of technology (which is kept in the background). Our first impression is of a natural paradise in which human creativity, happiness, and artistic expression flourish. Juxtaposed to the chapters describing Charlie's visit to the Ledom are scenes of the 1950s suburban life of two couples who act out and sometimes question the roles and patterns of behavior which their biological sex apparently assigns them; and this leads the reader to realize that the linking of sex and behavior is the novel's principal theme, just as Charlie learns that each Ledom is both male and female. Finally, to make this theme's centrality absolutely clear, Sturgeon intervenes toward the end to inform us that in our society the behavioral differences between men and women have a historical origin which was then "utilized" by "a force which widens and exploits this difference" (1984: 166), a force identified with the development of Western culture and more specifically with the rise of Christianity. On the level of the plot, however, the progressive direction of the Ledom utopia is undermined by a series of revelations at the end of the novel. There we learn, first of all, that this utopia is actually located in the present: it is hidden under a dome which makes it invisible from the outside. More importantly, we find out that the combination of both male and female sexual organs in each individual, including the ability to both "mother" and "father" children, is the product of surgery which must be performed on each Ledom child. Although the thought of such surgery may seem shocking in itself, this revelation undermines the novel's questioning of the linkage of sex and gender by making it a secret which is (moreover) concealed from most of the Ledom themselves. Through its concealment, this technological solution becomes shameful and implicitly wrong, unlike the technologies knowingly and willingly chosen in *Motherlines* and *The Female Man* or the development of embryos outside the womb (the "brooders") in *Edge of Time*.

Le Guin builds on and attempts to correct *Venus*'s ambiguity in *Left Hand*, where the "ambisexuality" of the Gethenians is also the result of technology. However, the experiment in "genetic manipulation" which produced this "ambisexuality" took place in the distant past and has now been forgotten (1969: 89–90). Since then, it has been transmitted genetically, from generation to generation, and the various nations and cultures of the planet Gethen have developed over millennia without any awareness of being different (there are, for instance, no other mammals on the planet). Le Guin raises the question of the relationship of sex and gender in several ways – through the reaction of a single-sexed visitor (who is considered a pervert by the Gethenians), and on a more descriptive level, in the earlier report of another outsider:

> When you meet a Gethenian you cannot and must not do what a bisexual naturally does, which is to cast him in the role of Man or Woman, while adopting towards him a corresponding role dependent on your expectations of the patterned or possible interactions between persons of the same or opposite sex. Our entire pattern of socio-sexual interaction is nonexistent here. They cannot play that game. They do not see one another as men or women. This is almost impossible for our imagination to accept. What is the first question we ask about a new-born baby? (1969: 94)

These two novels do not propose, however, workable or practical – or even "utopian" – solutions to the patriarchal hierarchization of people according to biological sex. They reflect instead a first step in the recognition of the problem. They function, in SF terms, as "thought experiments" which begin to question the "naturalness" of gender by imagining an alternative. Most of the utopian writing I have been examining in this paper goes one step further by recognizing that gender is in fact socially produced. Thus it is no longer necessary to imagine a society in which everyone is physically both male and female. Instead we must acknowledge and change the belief that different abilities, aptitudes, or psychological characteristics are essentially determined by and flow "naturally" from this biological difference (although, as I have pointed out, Gearhart argues in *Wanderground* that there are specifically male and female natures).

In regard to the utopian project of offering a full range of human activities and opportunities to all, these works envisage very different solutions. The very range of possibilities is limited in *Motherlines*, for instance, by the harsh conditions of the nomadic lives of the Riding Women and in *The Wanderground* by the insistence on essential differences between men and women. The activities of the Hill Women derive from female specificity: mothering, nurturing, sharing, and above all, a recognition of and communion with the natural order itself. With the restriction of men to the cities, women are no longer alienated from Nature or from their own femaleness; and this has led to a number of new psychic talents and abilities, including telepathic communication and healing, "wind-riding" and teleportation, and – of course – reproduction without the intervention of either men or technology.

On the other hand, there are no innate female activities in the all-female worlds of Charnas and Russ. The Riding Women raise grain and horses; their lives are portrayed as hard, while pleasure and meaning come from their sexuality (which seems absent in *Wanderground*) and from the thrills and excitement of their raids and duels. The sources of pleasure and fulfillment are similar in Whileaway, where women are offered a full range of work activities, many of which involve technology and the operation of machinery. Work is not in itself necessarily satisfying, but the work week has been reduced to sixteen hours, leaving the women time for enjoyment and satisfaction in other ways. Motherhood is treasured, not only for itself, but because mothers are released for several years for other work.[14] Piercy's utopia, following the radical feminist arguments of Shulamith Firestone in *The Dialectic of Sex* (1970), goes furthest in rejecting the sexual division of labor by using technology (the "brooders") to liberate women from motherhood itself:

> It was part of women's long revolution [Luciente tells Connie]. When we were breaking all the old hierarchies. Finally there was that one thing we had to give up too, the only power we ever had, in return for more power for everyone. The original production: the power to give birth. Cause as long as we were biologically enchained, we'd never be equal. And males would never be humanized to be loving and tender. So we all became mothers. (1976: 105)[15]

(To a similar end technology allows men to nurse babies in *Edge of Time* and *Triton*.)

The Dispossessed is most explicit in attempting to break another form of the division of labor: the limiting of individuals to a single occupation.

14 "Little Whileawayans are to their mothers both sulk and swank, fun and profit, pleasure and contemplation, a show of expressiveness, a slowing-down of life, an opportunity to pursue whatever interests the women have been forced to neglect previously, and the only leisure they have ever had – or will have again until old age. A family of thirty persons many have as many as four mother-and-child pairs in the common nursery at one time. Food, cleanliness, and shelter are not the mother's business; Whileawayans say with a straight face that she must be free to attend to the child's 'finer spiritual needs.' Then they go off by themselves and roar. The truth is they don't want to give up the leisure" (1975a: 49–50).

15 In this discussion of motherhood and the "brooders," it should be noted that attitudes within feminism toward motherhood have shifted radically since the 1970s. See, for instance, Adrienne Rich, *Of Woman Born: Motherhood as Experience and Institution* (1976), and Heather Jon Maroney, "Embracing Motherhood: New Feminist Theory," *Canadian Journal of Political and Social Theory* 9 (1985), 40–64. See also Russ's critique of "technological solutions" to social problems in "SF and Technology," particularly 258 – although she is objecting specifically to the surgical solution proposed in *Venus Plus X*.

This freedom was originally addressed in Marx and Engels's classic description of a communist society:

> Where nobody has one exclusive sphere of activity but each can become accomplished in any branch he wishes, society regulates the general production and thus makes it possible for me to do one thing today and another tomorrow, to hunt in the morning, fish in the afternoon, rear cattle in the evening, criticize after dinner, just as I have in mind. (1970: 22)

This is an ideal which informs most of the novels under discussion. In *The Dispossessed*, individuals request work postings through a central coordinating system which assigns work on the basis of social needs and individual skills and preference. Although life on Anarres is hard, people no longer work because of external factors (i.e., for wages): "Work is done for its own sake. It is the lasting pleasure of life" (1975: 121). There are similar attempts to balance personal inclinations with social needs in *The Female Man*, *Ecotopia*, *Triton*, and *Edge of Time*.

There is, then, in each of these seven novels an attempt to make everyone's life more meaningful and satisfying. Thus while unpleasant tasks remain in all of these societies, they have either been reduced through technology and/or shared around more equitably. Many of the alienating features of work under capitalism have disappeared, while the linkage of gender with certain kinds of work, with the exception of *Wanderground*, has also disappeared. Nonetheless, external constraints do impose more severe restrictions on personal inclinations in *The Dispossessed* (thanks to the scarcity and droughts on Anarres), in *Motherlines* and *Wanderground* (with their limited and non-technological societies), and in *The Female Man* (where there is an enforced obligation to work) than is the case in *Ecotopia*, *Triton*, and *Edge of Time*, all three of which go far toward recognizing and utilizing the utopian potential of technology to provide the material conditions for a world in which human beings are truly free.

As far as the sexual division of labor is concerned, the novels with both men and women do portray men who have become more tender and caring, but they are much less successful in breaking with the stereotypes of women's behavior; and here it is telling that the two novels written by men have male protagonists, as does *The Dispossessed*.[16] Women's activities are limited for other reasons, as I have pointed out, in *Motherlines* and *Wanderground*; so that only *The Female Man* and *Edge of Time* offer women a full range of choices and roles.

Wanderground equates maleness with biologically innate violence, but the other six novels portray male behavior in our society in more specifically social terms. Janet's visit to the present is the occasion for a satirical description of typical male behavior in *The Female Man*, while Le Guin also caricatures traditional male values and conduct in Shevek's visit to Urras and the capitalist patriarchy of A-Io. However, the most extensive critique of contemporary patriarchal forms is Piercy's: in her realistic depiction of our own society, she grounds masculine behavior in the social structures and practices of capitalism. Although Connie is exploited as a Mexican-American by society at large and in terms of her class when she is in the hospital, the most bitter instances of exploitation and oppression lie with her own family. It is her niece's pimp who has her committed to the hospital, and it is her brother who refuses to sign the papers to have her released. Indeed, her brother's eager assimilation of the values of white capitalist patriarchy is bitingly described in Connie's Thanksgiving visit to his home, where – on this day of celebration of the American Family – Connie is pressed into service as an unpaid domestic while her brother lords it over his family in all his new-found bourgeois glory, nagging his children and bragging while his wife smiles dreamily from her tranquilizer-induced cocoon (1976: 350–360).

Typical male behavior is not an issue in *Triton*, particularly in view of Bron's decision to have himself changed into a woman near the end of the novel; but William Weston's experience as an outsider in *Ecotopia* does produce some situations in which his own behavior reflects traditional attitudes. More understandably, perhaps, these two novels by men do not really address women's experience of oppression, an issue which is central, for instance, to *Wanderground*, where the women collectively remember

16 For a critical development of this point, see Russ's review of *The Dispossessed* in *The Magazine of Fantasy and Science Fiction* (March 1975), 41–44.

the past, or to those experiences of Connie's that we have just reviewed. The novel which precedes *Motherlines*, *Walk to the End of the World*, is a nightmarish look at a patriarchal society in which women are slaves, while the experience of oppression on the basis of sex is also apparent in *The Female Man*, both in the character of Jeannine and in Joanna's decision to "become a man."

By women's experience of oppression I mean most immediately the experiences of women in our society, which defines them, outside the patriarchal confines of the home, as sexual objects rather than as persons – in advertising as much as in their own personal experience (sexual harassment and innuendo). I also mean that the dichotomy between wife-mother and sex-object is but half of a dialectic which produces men as the masters and oppressors and as the subjects of sexual desire. In describing their experience of oppression, many women speak of the socially sanctioned violence which enforces that dichotomy and which is dramatized in the scenes I have just mentioned. This situation, in which there are real penalties for those women who challenge patriarchal structures and definitions, calls for at least some sensitivity to the present, to those conditions of domination which neither imagination nor will alone can suffice to change. In terms of our seven novels, this sensitivity might begin with the author's choice of a sexual identity for the central character – or, in another way, with the continuing problematic nature of the issues of sex and gender in the new society. For in the development of new roles for men, it is a mistake to assume that "natural" patterns of sexual and/or social behavior would emerge spontaneously upon the disappearance of patriarchal structures. Human consciousness and identity as well as sexual desire itself are developed across a network of psychological and social factors which overlie and shape instinctual and biological forces and drives. Consequently, the imagining of an alternative future must address the question of how to collectively create the consciousness and identities of men and women for that society and not simply the larger social and economic structures which would make such people possible. This is not, however, to promote the manipulative behaviorist techniques of a B.F. Skinner (as in his *Walden Two*) or of Aldous Huxley's *Brave New World*. Rather what is needed is a recognition that sexism and heterosexism are not only produced and reinforced by the larger patriarchal structures which constitute our society; they are also inscribed and embedded in our own identities and unconscious patterns of behavior. And these patterns – how men, for instance, relate to women – would not automatically change with the legal abolition of patriarchy.

The sensitivity of some of these writers toward this recognition is accomplished in two complementary fashions: through the juxtaposition of the old ways with the new, in a manner which makes clear the social production of gender in the present; and through the problematization of the central character's search for identity and meaning in a new society, as a way of reminding us that the new roles and patterns of behavior will not happen "naturally."

In *Ecotopia* and *Woman on the Edge of Time*, where visitors from our present are shown reacting to and commenting on the changes in sex roles and gender, there are already some crucial differences. William Weston is a successful reporter in the old society who, in traditional utopian fashion, falls in love with a woman as a part of his falling in love with the utopia. The Ecotopian woman, Marissa, is of course contrasted to the women at home (where he has both a wife and a mistress), but Weston's discovery that male and female roles have changed and his acceptance of the new society is relatively painless; indeed, his own sexuality and identity are reinforced by his experience of change and difference, and in fact lead to enhanced sexual experiences.[17] Connie, on the other hand, is at the opposite end of the social spectrum: she is an impoverished Mexican-American for whom the changed sexual roles and identities of Mattapoisett appear as deeply troubling. Unlike Weston's, hers is no easy transition to utopia. An awareness of the differences in appearance, behavior, and character is firmly embedded in her understanding of herself and the world, and Mattapoisett consequently shocks her on a number of occasions: by the absence from it of gender-specific dress codes and activities, by the easy acceptance of homosexuality, and, most deeply, by the sight of a man breast-feeding a baby ("she felt sick [...] angry. Yes, how dare any man share that pleasure.

17 For some criticisms of this point see the article by Gearhart (1984: 306) and Russ's "Recent Feminist Utopias" (1981: 83).

These women thought they had won, but they had abandoned to men the last refuge of women" [1976: 134]).

Connie's decision to fight back in the present results, then, from her gradual recognition of the advantages of this alternate society to empower human emancipation and development and from her related understanding of how sex in conjunction with class has caused her oppression in the present. This realization is most fully brought home to her during a brief slip into a second alternate future, one in which the fight for a better future has been lost. There the "multis" are in complete control, and the woman Connie "visits" is "a cartoon of femininity, with a tiny waist, enormous sharp breasts. [...] Her stomach was flat but her hips and buttocks were over-sized and audaciously curved" (1976: 288). Low in intelligence, Gildina has been surgically "improved" so that she could escape the oppressed lot of the majority (who become "walking organ banks" for the "richies" [1976: 291]), through a long-term contract for sex with a business executive. She is imprisoned in her apartment where she is monitored twenty-four hours a day, passing the time with drugs and television, as she awaits the pleasure of her owner.

This kind of exaggerated vision of a possible future in which the patriarchal definition and control of women has been carried to its (logical) extreme can also be seen in the novels of Charnas, Gearhart, and Russ. Charnas's collapsing patriarchy, where women are slaves, she had already described in *Walk to the End of the World*. In Gearhart, the cities (as opposed to the country) have become patriarchal police states. Similarly, the utopia of Whileaway is juxtaposed to the realistic portrayal of a sexist present, in which Jeannine dreams of fulfillment in love and marriage and against which Joanna rebels. Whileaway also counterpoints a nightmarish future in which the Earth has become divided into two camps, Manland and Womanland. From the Womanlanders, the Manlanders buy baby boys, from which, using first surgery and then a form of "natural selection," they produce three genders: "real men," the "changed" (their distorted version of women), and the "half-changed" ("artists, illusionists, impressionists of femininity who keep their genitalia but who grow slim, grow languid, grow emotional and feminine" [1975a: 167]). Russ further points to the social construction of gender and of sexual desire by depicting a shocking role-reversal in Womanland: Jael, an "old-fashioned girl," with her male "sex-object" – a "leucotomized" male, grown from chimpanzee germ plasm, "without organic behavior control," who awakens and responds to her sexual needs only when she summons him (1975a: 196–199).[18]

The situation is somewhat different in *The Dispossessed*, where the focus is less on the changed sexual relations of the utopian society and more on the resurgence of hierarchy and privilege from within. The utopian ideal is defined primarily in terms of the opposition between private property and the apparatus of the state on the one hand, and communitarian and cooperative principles on the other. Existing sexual relations of domination and subordination have apparently disappeared on Anarres, although Shevek's visit to A-Io provides a glimpse of a capitalist patriarchy in which the sexual division of labor is more extreme than it is in our contemporary society. Shevek's doubts and struggle do not extend into the personal realm of sex and gender, however, perhaps because Le Guin had already dealt with that issue in *Left Hand*. Throughout most of his adult life Shevek has been involved in a monogamous heterosexual relationship which, particularly insofar as it is the male who is the more active and important half of the couple, can hardly be taken as the model for other forms of personal and sexual relationships.

Gender and sexual identity are radically problematized in Delany's *Triton*, where the hero's unhappiness eventually leads him to think that he would be happier as a woman. Although the tensions that patriarchy induces in many people in our society, especially those arising from conflicts between one's biological sex and the identity and conduct expected of that person, are much reduced in the extremely diverse, libertarian society of *Triton*, and although the technological means to change both one's sex and one's sexual orientation are available, neither this social background nor Bron's actual sex-change operation are enough to resolve his/her actual unhappiness (see Masse). But Bron's situation does force the reader to at

18 This reversal of a well-known theme is perhaps best summed up by Jeff Renner's "The Shortest Science Fiction Love Story Ever Written": "Boy Meets Girl,/Boy Loses Girl,/Boy Builds Girl" (cited in Mike Ashley's *The Illustrated Book of Science Fiction Lists* [New York: Cornerstone Library, 1982], 121). The best-known wife/robot story is Lester Del Rey's "Helen O'Loy" (1938).

least consider the relationship between sex and gender in an emancipated society, while suggesting that identity and satisfaction will not arise spontaneously, even in utopia.

In most of our seven examples, then, the central character's own personal struggle includes the attempt to create an identity which is not bound to the traditional sex-linked roles of our society. Even in *Wanderground*, where there is no single hero and where there is a strong belief in women's specificity, the community of women has set out very consciously to develop new rituals which affirm the individual's identity both as a woman and as part of a collectivity. Indeed, the women-centered practices of the Hill Women do not spring spontaneously from their rediscovered closeness to Nature, but have been developed and must be taught. Moreover, the behavior of the women in our own society, insofar as that behavior conforms to stereotypes, is also criticized, particularly in the novels written by women: in the glimpse of the submission and domination of city women in *Wanderground*; in the juxtaposition of the Riding Women of *Motherlines* with the "free fems," who seem to spend much of their time gossiping and quarrelling and reminiscing about their former lives in the Holdfast; in the portrayal of the provocative high-society women of A-Io in *The Dispossessed*; and in the bitter portrait of Connie's submissive sister and sister-in-law in *Edge of Time*. But as the Hill Women remind themselves, "What we are not, we each could be, and every woman is myself" (1978: 63). These sisterly critiques of the stereotyped behavior of some women also calls attention to the gendering process and to the violence used to enforce it, stereotypes which, like the patterned behavior of men, must be challenged for a society of human freedom to emerge.

The question of sexuality in these novels is of course inextricably linked to the matters of gendering and identity which I have been discussing. Feminism has made us aware that sexuality, too, is not simply "natural," but the social channeling and control of biological drives. More specifically, patriarchy has defined female sexuality almost exclusively in terms of procreation and in terms of its complementarity to male sexuality and male desire (see Snitow et al. and Vance). The feminist challenge to male power has produced demands for an end to all forms of oppression and for women's autonomy, including control of their bodies and of their fertility, and the right to their own sexual pleasure. This means, first of all, an end to sexual harassment and coercion; but it implies as well a questioning of such patriarchal concepts as "monogamy," "promiscuity," and "homosexuality," and it involves as well a recognition of the fundamental validity and importance of differing forms of sexual expression and pleasure.

Beyond the portrayal of alternatives to the nuclear family and the imagining of worlds in which sexual harassment, coercion, and exploitation are no longer socially produced and tacitly condoned, these works do differ in their recognition of the problematic nature of sexuality and sexual expression. *Wanderground*, like Gilman's *Herland*, doesn't really mention sex at all, while the difficulties and doubts which surround sexuality, even in a society without hierarchy by sex, are the central issues in Delany's *Triton*. On Triton, as one character points out, human beings are divided into "forty or fifty basic sexes, falling loosely into nine categories, four homophilic. [...] Homophilic means no matter who or what you like to screw, you prefer to live and have friends primarily from your own sex. The other five are heterophilic" (1976: 117).[19] Most of these novels portray the dual nature of sexuality – often a wonderful and pleasureful human characteristic as well as the source of doubt and anxiety. The concepts of "monogamy" and "promiscuity" have lost their meaning in the extended families depicted in the novels of Charnas, Piercy, and Russ – where sexuality and sexual pleasure are represented as joyful and enabling facets of everyday life – whereas more traditional couples are part of the worlds of Callenbach and Le Guin. Delany's novel goes furthest in its call for a tolerance of difference; and homosexuality is not only accepted in all of these societies, but in most cases, is also revealed as a historically determined concept which has become meaningless in the sexually diverse societies of the future.[20]

19 For a discussion of Le Guin's "deproblematizing" of sexuality in *Left Hand*, see Jameson's "World Reduction," particularly 225–226. For a marvelous "reproblematizing" of these issues, see Delany's recent novel, *Stars in My Pocket Like Grains of Sand* (1984).

20 "In this respect gay men and lesbians are well situated to play a special role. Already excluded from families as most of us are, we have had to create, for our survival, networks of support that do not depend on the bonds of blood or the license of the state, but that are freely chosen and nurtured. The building of an "affectional

These seven novels, I have argued, lie midway between an older tradition of utopian blueprints and contemporary works of popular fiction in which there is, disguised "beneath" a more recognizable ideological functioning, a repressed utopian dimension:

> The works of mass culture, even if their function lies in the legitimation of the existing order – or some worse one – cannot do their job without in the latter's service the deepest and most fundamental hopes and fantasies of the collectivity, to which they can therefore, no matter in how fashion, be found to have given voice. (Jameson 1979: 144)

The utopianism of the novels under discussion is not concealed, as it is in the works of mass culture Jameson is describing. Yet, as we have seen, with the exception perhaps of *Ecotopia*, they are not blueprints for an ideal society either, for they resist the detail and completeness of earlier utopias (from Plato's *Republic* through More's *Utopia*). Their utopianism lies rather in the foregrounding of the struggle to bring into being and to sustain the alternate society, in the sketching out of its basic principles, and in the representation of the transformed ways and lives of the citizens of these imaginary societies, all of which serve to arouse in the reader the possibility of an alternate future.

While I am convinced of the validity and importance of writing about these works in such a "literal" way, my own commitment to those same goals takes me one step further, to acknowledge as well that the utopian longing for a "disalienated" world is something more than an abstract goal to which the reader gives intellectual assent. These works speak to us on an emotional and visceral level, by evoking the textures and images of the recurrent and repeatedly deferred dream of human community, fulfillment, and satisfaction, a world of human freedom filled with new experiences, pleasures, and discoveries. I would like to conclude, then, in a different register, by briefly reviewing my own reactions to these works, in terms

community" must be as much a part of our political movement as are campaigns rights. In this way we may prefigure the shape of personal relationships grounded in equality and justice rather than exploitation and oppression, a society where autonomy and security do not preclude each other but coexist" (D'Emilio 1983: 111).

both of how each invokes the promise of human liberation and of where, too, I hesitate about their other features.

The fictional society which speaks most forcefully to my own ideas and dreams is that of *Woman on the Edge of Time*, to some extent because of its open-endedness, but also because it is based on an analysis of contemporary society close to my own, particularly in the choice of a central character through which the issues of race and class are addressed along with that of sex. But the full utopian force of the novel for me flows from the many scenes of everyday life in Mattapoissett which strike a balance in my own conflicted experience of a divided reality, between ideas and desires, work and play, freedom and necessity, technology and the natural order, all within the context of a community which is loving, playful, and supportive. My reactions as a reader are summed up during one of Connie's first visits to Mattapoissett, where she takes part in a communal meal:

> Everybody looked livelier than institutionalized feeding usually made for. A child was climbing on a bench to tell a story, waving both arms. At the far end a man with a mustache was weeping openly into his soup and all about him people were patting his shoulders and making a big fuss. People were arguing heatedly, laughing and telling jokes, and a child was singing loudly at the table nearest the door. (1976: 74)

> They were literally patted into their seats and she found herself cramped with nervousness. Touching and caressing, hugging and fingering, they handled each other constantly. In a way it reminded her again of her childhood, every emotion seemed to find a physical outlet, when both love and punishment had been expressed directly on her skin. (1976: 76)

My principal reservation lies with the "brooders" – the growing of the embryo outside the womb – which seems an overcomplicated and unnecessary solution to the sexual division of labor. Nor have I incorporated Luciente's words ("So we all became mothers") in my title to suggest that women ought to be deprived (as they are in *Edge of Time*) of the experience of motherhood; instead, I mean those words to stand as the motto for new roles for men, who should learn caring and nurturing skills and assume more fully than most now do the responsibilities of parenting.[21]

21 Piercy describes a similar technological intervention for the problem of racism: "At grandcil – grand council – decisions were made forty years back to breed a high

My reservations about this specific solution do not, however, extend to technology in general. Indeed, one of my major reservations concerning *Wanderground* is precisely its rejection of technology in building and maintaining a better society – to which I much prefer the integrative and more balanced attitudes of *Ecotopia*, *The Female Man*, and *Edge of Time*. A second reservation lies with its cultural feminist premise of an essential difference between men and women. As I have already said, by including men in an inferior and untrustworthy position, *Wanderground* certainly excludes me as a male reader from any real acceptance of this world – although this is probably a familiar experience for women readers of a popular fiction largely populated by male heroes. There are, however, moments in this novel when my reservations fade as the practical imagining of an alternative yields to the libidinal images of an existence beyond the constraints of time and space in which life-in-the-body is no longer separate from the world:

> By swift montage she listened to and felt one at a time, every thing, every oxygen thing, every other thing, every non-breathing thing. They felt her attention and told her all was well. […]
>
> "I take when you give," said the tree.
>
> "I know," she said, "And I take when you give." She inhaled slowly, pressing her viscera against the tree. As she released her breath, the trunk pushed against her. Slowly, with no visible motion, the two set a rhythm of pneuma exchange. (1978: 13)
>
> With a new exhilaration she dived and swooped some more. […] She looped above the trees in wider and wider arcs. She relearned the handling of pitch, a throwing up and downward of her legs; she rehearsed the secrets of direction. (1978: 107)

Although the nomadic existence of the Riding Women in *Motherlines* is not presented as a model society, it too has strong utopian overtones, particularly in the alternatives to the family and in the strong sense of community. At the same time, even as I was drawn by the energetic lives

---

proportion of darker-skinned people and to mix the genes well through the population. At the same time, we decided to hold on to separate cultural identities. But we broke the bond between genes and culture, broke it forever. We want there to be no chance of racism again. But we don't want the melting pot where everybody ends up with thin gruel. We want diversity, for strangeness breeds richness" (1976: 103–104).

of these women, I felt a reluctance to give myself over to a world so limited to and dominated by the rhythms and patterns of the natural order. The range of choices and opportunities seems too restricted: the environment, even more than the hardship and scarcity of Anarres, severely limits the flowering of human liberation as it confines the women to the harsh existence of their lives on the Plains.

At the other end of the spectrum, the Ecotopian society is one of abundance and variety. But whereas I was caught up in the rhythms and activities of the Riding Women, I was bored by the overly didactic tone of *Ecotopia*, by its guided-tour structure; and I was disturbed as well by the focusing on the central character's conversion to Ecotopian ways primarily through a series of sexual experiences.

The world of Russ's *Whileaway* is also an attractive one. Yet the utopian thrust of the novel lies not only with the pastoral beauty of a revitalized Earth, but in its aggressively polemical and unconventional form. This very excess, in which the representational conventions of the naturalistic mode are abandoned, signals to me in a very different way a promise for the future. The rejection of the instrumental function of language and of the conventions of the genre through polemical excess undermines the authority of the performance principle and points to a realm of freedom lying beyond the realm of necessity. Unfortunately, Russ reintroduces the reality principle through the very harsh measures used to enforce each individual's work obligations to society.

In general, much of the attraction of these imaginary worlds lies in what they tell us about meaningful activity as they replace the dialectic of competitiveness and unsatisfying work on the one hand, and the passive and programmed consumption of "leisure" on the other, with a transformation of work and play. There are playful elements in most of these novels, from the linguistic excess of *The Female Man* to the invention of the game "vlet" (a more complex and sophisticated form of "Dungeons and Dragons") in *Triton*. But it is perhaps in the aesthetic realm that the "free play of human faculties and desires" (Marcuse 1955: 178) can best be seen.

The utopian qualities of *Triton* flow of course from the basic material guarantees of a universe where anyone can do almost anything. But the index of the full potential of that new society is marked by an aesthetic experience, when The Spike's troupe puts on a "microtheater" performance for the unsuspecting Bron (1976: 16–21). Bron's experience is surely one of the high points of the novel, a privileged moment in that it was unprepared for, an experience across the boundaries of the senses, wonderful and moving … and never to come again. Its utopian dimension lies not only with Bron's pleasure – one of the few moments in the novel where he reacts spontaneously – but in the ephemeral features of this new artistic form and in the aleatory nature of the choice of an audience. Delany thus confronts and defies the commodification of art under capitalism, pointing instead to a future where meaning and pleasure escape the corrosion of exchange value. In offering so many possibilities (in contradistinction to the other six works I have looked at, which are more unified than *Triton* around common goals and ideals), Delany also takes more chances. In this sense, my reservations lie with his very failure to exploit that plenitude of possibilities, thanks to his choice of a central character who will not take chances and who is not happy.

Turning finally to *The Dispossessed*, I have already made it clear that it is not only the questioning of the utopian project itself – the theme of the "ambiguous utopia" – which bothers me, but the setting up of a world where the struggle to survive looms so large. Anarres is nonetheless a utopia, and its utopianism comes across for me most strongly in Shevek's own commitment to it, as summed up in his impassioned speech at the A-Io:

> We have nothing to give you but your own freedom. We have no law but the single principle of mutual aid between individuals. We have no government but the single principle of free association. We have no states, no nations, presidents, no premiers, no chiefs, no generals, no bosses, no bankers, no landlords, no wages, no charity, no police, no soldiers, no wars. Nor do we have much else. We are sharers, not owners. We are not prosperous. None of us is rich. None of us is powerful. If it is Anarres you want, if it is the future you seek, then I tell you that you must come to it with empty hands. (1975: 241)

In this overview of mine of some recent fictional attempts to imagine a qualitatively different future grounded in egalitarian and cooperative principles, it has been my contention that there is very often a failure of vision among those of us active in the struggle for social change, and an equally debilitating lack of any sense of possible alternatives on the part of those we hope to mobilize for such a transformation. To some degree because of the very extent of the cut-backs in the social programs of the welfare state, but also because of the reactions against the feminist challenge to patriarchy, much of today's political organizing and struggle seems to be limited to single issues and a reactive politics of fear. However necessary such single-issue struggles are, even when successful they are only temporary solutions which will not in themselves lead to the social transformation necessary for full human emancipation and fulfillment. Because, too, of the reality of the already existing socialist states, many today have acceded to the dominant view that there are no acceptable alternatives to the present system. Fueled by a feminist politics of hope, these explicitly utopian works of popular fiction contradict and challenge such defeatist attitudes by eloquently proclaiming that we still do have the possibility of constructing a future of our own choosing.

Because they foreground the changed lives and experiences of their characters as much as they elaborate images of an alternate society which would make such new patterns of behavior and interpersonal relations possible, these give to me, as a man, an experience, however limited, of what an end to hierarchy and domination would imply in the concrete reality of my everyday life. Insofar as domination and exploitation are systemic, our imagining of alternatives often does not go beyond a sense of how we as individuals change our behavior. In portraying scenes of institutionalized as well as internalized and specific acts of oppression, these novels draw attention to the construction of gender and to the ways in which the role of individual men in women's oppression is often concealed by the supposedly "natural" institutions and practices of patriarchy. An understanding of the interdependence of larger structures and discrete practices is important, not only in terms of imagining the larger social forms which would make new identities and patterns of behavior possible, but especially because, as men who may have directly or indirectly benefitted from or participated in the exercise of male power, we must realize that these new forms and patterns will not emerge spontaneously with the collectivization of society or even with the abolition of patriarchy. Our own identities and unconscious patterns of behavior must be examined and reshaped. This is the challenge of the all-women utopias in which the solution to patriarchy is envisaged as a society without men.

Contemporary feminist utopian writing has taken a perhaps small, but essential first step toward a new future by seeking to imagine full societies in their everyday working, societies organized, as we have seen, around egalitarian and cooperative principles, valorizing all forms of human activity, and making the material basis for freedom available to all on equal terms. In their utilization of the existing forms of popular fiction, our seven writers have broken out of the narrow confines of the already converted audiences to whom many of us speak, and have attempted to imagine an alternate future grounded in a politics of hope.

CHAPTER 10

The Turn from Utopia in Recent Feminist Fiction

> I'm the type of person that puts women on a pedestal. But in my opinion, which I base on the Bible, I believe God's perspective is that women should not be in certain occupations. I'm not saying she's going to hell because she chose to be an umpire. She has free will, just as you and I do. If God is unhappy with her, some day she will have to talk to God about it.
>
> – Houston Astro pitcher Bob Knepper, on the possibility of Pam Postema becoming the first female umpire in major-league baseball, Toronto Globe &: Mail, 16 March, 1988

This paper was prompted by a letter to a Toronto newspaper complaining about the pessimism of Margaret Atwood's *The Handmaid's Tale*. Not only did that letter sum up my own first reactions to the novel, but it has led me to think about recent feminist science fiction and what appears to be a retreat from the utopianism of the 1970s.[1] The four works I have chosen to discuss as indicative of this retreat are: Margaret Atwood's *The Handmaid's Tale* (1985); Suzette Haden Elgin's *Native Tongue* (1984); Zoe Fairbairns's *Benefits* (1979); and Ursula K. Le Guin's *Always Coming Home* (1985).

Like Margaret Atwood's *The Handmaid's Tale*, Sally Gearhart's 1978 utopian novel, *The Wanderground*, portrayed a backlash against the growing strength of women and gays. But in Gearhart's book, the backlash prompted "the revolt of the Earth herself": outside the city men suddenly became impotent, while machines and mechanical devices no longer functioned.

1 The classics include: Suzy McKee Charnas, *Motherlines* (1979); Sally Gearhart, *The Wanderground* (1978); Ursula K. Le Guin, *The Dispossessed* (1975); Marge Piercy, *Woman on The Edge of Time* (1976); and Joanna Russ, *The Female Man* (1975). For a discussion of this revival, see my "So We All Became Mothers" (Chapter 3 in this volume), and its sequel, "For Men Only: A Guide to Reading Single-Sex Worlds," *Women's Studies* 14 (1987), 101–117.

Although the men established a patriarchal police state in the cities, the core of *The Wanderground* was the evocation of a utopian world of the women outside the cities. In other utopian novels of the 1970s, the increasing repression of women leads to the flight of some women to a wasteland where they found their own society (in Charnas's utopian fantasy *Motherlines*) or even to open warfare and the victory of the women who set up a utopian society (in Joanna Russ's *The Female Man*). Insofar as they emphasized the changed lives and experiences of their characters, and because they described alternate societies which would make new patterns of behavior and interpersonal relations possible, the utopian novels of the 1970s provided the reader with an experience, however limited, of what a better world, beyond sexual hierarchy and domination, might look and feel like. However, with a few exceptions (including Le Guin's *Always Coming Home*), this utopian moment seems to have ended. More recent fictions no longer give us images of a radically different future, in which the values and ideals of feminism have been extended to much of the planet, but rather offer depressing images of a brutal reestablishment of capitalist patriarchy.

Both utopias and dystopias have a performative function; they are intended ideally to push the reader to action. In the following discussion, I shall describe these works in terms of the *plausibility* of the futures evoked and in terms of their *effectiveness*: in dystopian novels, in terms of their ability to warn the reader and to push her or him to act on that knowledge; and, in utopian works, in terms of their effectiveness in evoking a world in which I would like to live. Such criteria are not completely subjective: they include references to the internal consistency of the work; to the relationship between the new society and the present; to the narrative strategies used to solicit the reader's involvement beyond the ending of the text; and to the question of the transition, of how the other society came about. Of course, my taking these novels in such a literal or political way is the opposite of how we are taught to read, but utopia and dystopia by their very nature remind us of their connections with the real, and it seems foolish and obtuse to ignore the deliberate engagement of these works with contemporary issues.[2]

2 The main concern of Peter Ruppert's recent study, *Reader in a Strange Land* (Athens: University of Georgia Press, 1986), is with the pragmatic or functional

The shift from utopia to dystopia can be seen in Zoe Fairbairns's 1979 *Benefits*, set in the near future in the context of Britain's worsening economic plight. All social welfare programs are suspended except for the equivalent of Canada's "baby-bonus," a "benefit" paid directly to the mother, but only to mothers who do not work outside the home. However, rather than leading to a strengthening of the family and its traditional values, the benefit has two related effects which lead the government to conclude that it is a failure: on the one hand, lower-income families "breed" as a way of increasing their income; while many women are able, thanks to the benefit, to live without men, outside the patriarchal system and its embodiment in the nuclear family.

The government then announces that the benefit will be withdrawn from "unfit" mothers, namely those who do not live according to traditional family norms. But as Britain's economy continues to worsen, European planners help to implement even more drastic "social planning" experiments: the widespread – usually forced – placing of "contraceptive pellets" in women; and, when women find ways to remove the pellets, the government puts a contraceptive in the water supply. Women deemed "suitable" for motherhood are to apply at a government "Women's Centre" for an antidote, but the antidote reacts with the contraceptive to produce massive deformities and render British women "unsuitable as vehicles for the carrying of unborn children" (Fairbairns 1979: 196).

This is not, however, the end of the novel. Although there is a possibility that it may be generations until British women again are able to bear children, if they ever can, a younger and more militant generation of women argues for a renewed commitment to the goal of creating a society which finally will be "a fit place to bring [babies]." *Benefits* certainly is not a utopia; but it does not end in complete despair either. It demonstrates an increasing bitterness toward the continuing exploitation of women and toward government attempts to control their fertility: "Our women are going to be the first to find a style of life that isn't defined by men having power over us because we have children" (Fairbairns 1979: 215).

---

aspects of utopian literature: how these works engage us and position us as readers attending to their arguments and messages, how they may activate and liberate us in this process or how they may leave us passive and complacent (5).

While I cannot adequately review here the various manifestations of the state's attempts to regulate sexuality and fertility, it is increasingly apparent that the struggle of women to gain control over their own bodies and their own fertility is perceived as a critical threat by the Christian right.[3] These issues are central to Margaret Atwood's *The Handmaid's Tale*. There, in a near future in which people have become increasingly alarmed by a declining birthrate, the Christian right stages a violent takeover and establishes a theocratic "Republic of Gilead" throughout much of the United States. This renewed regulation of women's bodies – "for breeding purposes" – marks the triumph of the Moral Majority and its "family protection" agenda. The "traditional" values of the nuclear family are forcibly reestablished, while divorce, birth control, homosexuality, and other manifestations of the "permissiveness" and "moral decay" which characterized the 1960s and 1970s are brutally repressed. The novel shows how, under the pretense of giving women what they want, some of the goals of today's women's movement are co-opted during the early stages of the takeover. For the leaders of the coup claim to be taking women at their word and to have instituted a society which will protect and provide for them.

One of the principal factors which leads to the coup is "plummeting Caucasian birth rates" (Atwood 1985: 316) (primarily a result of increasing environmental pollution); and surrogate motherhood, as illustrated in the "Baby M" case, has become a key issue. Fertile young women (but not the daughters of the ruling class) are used – with the proper scriptural references (Genesis 30) – as surrogate mothers ("handmaids") when the wives of high officials of the new regime are unable to conceive.

3 In the initial judgment in the "Baby M" case, the court ruled against the natural claim of motherhood in favor of a contractual agreement, a ruling which some feared might open the floodgates to commercial babyfarming, through the creation of a subclass of poor women who would become hatcheries for the rich. However, in February 1988, Chief Justice Robert Wilentz of the New Jersey Supreme Court found the payment of money to a surrogate mother illegal, perhaps criminal, and potentially degrading to women. As Phyllis Chesler pointed out after the ruling, "This judgment says that women can't be owned or rented, babies can't be sold, and birth mothers and babies have a right to each other." Wilentz and Chesler are cited by Michele Landsberg in her column in the Toronto *Globe & Mail*, February 6, 1988.

The novel is Offred's tale of several months as a "handmaid." By juxtaposing the restrictions of life in Gilead with her recollections of her life before (in our own present), the tale presents a frightening portrait of a religious state where people's daily lives are closely monitored and regulated. Offred lives in fear that she will fail to become pregnant and will be sent to the "colonies" ("portable populations used as expendable toxic cleanup squads" [321]), or that her secret meetings with the commander will be discovered. Meanwhile the commander's wife, as a way of ending the humiliation of her own situation, arranges for Offred to try and get pregnant by Nick, the chauffeur. Offred's story ends with her fear and uncertainty: has she fallen into the hands of the secret police, or has she been rescued, as Nick tells her, when a police van arrives to take her away? This uncertainty is resolved in an afterword which contains the "proceedings" of a symposium sponsored by a historical society devoted to Gilead studies, a meeting which takes place centuries after the events depicted in the novel. Offred's "tale" was in fact an oral text, which was recorded on audiocassettes and has just been discovered and transcribed. The status and authenticity of this tale is discussed by the historians, but the afterword tells the reader that she has escaped.

Suzette Elgin's science fiction novel *Native Tongue* is set in the more distant future of the twenty-third century, although its starting point too is the contemporary attacks on women's efforts to obtain social and political equality. Here the reaction leads to the repeal of the Nineteenth Amendment to the U.S. Constitution, which gave women the right to vote, and enactment of a new amendment (ratified in 1991), according to which "all citizens of the United States of the female gender shall be deemed legally minors." In the future of the novel, the Earth has contacted and now trades with extraterrestrial races – a development which has led to the rise of a small elite group of translators, called "linguists," who, because of their discipline in teaching their children to master languages from infancy, have established a monopoly on handling negotiations between the Earth and its alien trading partners.

Within this futuristic context, the novel describes life within a linguist family. The women do an exaggerated version of today's women's double duty; even though they are legally minors and hence completely subject to their fathers and husbands, they are also skilled translators with busy professional lives. Because the linguists are anxious to preserve their monopoly, the politics of reproduction are significant. The linguist women are compelled to marry young (by the age of 16), allowing "the husband to space his children three years apart and still see that the woman bears eight infants before the age of forty" (Elgin 1984: 146). What distinguishes this novel from the dystopian future of *The Handmaid's Tale*, at least in the eyes of some of its feminist readers, is that, despite this repressive situation, the women-linguists have developed, in the privacy of their "Barren Houses" (where the postmenopausal linguist women live communally), a unique women's language. Analogous to the cultural feminist rituals of Gearhart's *Wanderground*, Làadan is shaped by and empowers women's specific perceptions of the world. In changing the way that women look at and construct reality, the women hope that this new language will lead to a change in the reality itself.

Of the three novels discussed, *Native Tongue* most strains the reader's credulity, not in its introduction of science fiction elements (trade with alien races and the difficulties of interspecies communication) but, at least for this reader, in its very portrayal of the ordinary details of everyday life. Even if the reader accepts that the linguists are able to maintain a monopoly on negotiations because they are the only ones able to learn alien languages, and even if the reader accepts the widespread hostility and even disgust that the U.S. populace shows for the linguists, a major question remains which is constantly raised in the novel and which is constantly avoided: what do they do with their money? They are feared and hated partially because it is assumed that they live so much better than the rest of society. Yet each time an outsider comes into extended contact with them (e.g., Michaela), she is shocked to discover that this is not true. The linguists live like monks, modestly, working long hours. The most brutal example of their monastic lives – and of their treatment of their wives and daughters – occurs when Nazareth must take a bus and go alone to the hospital for surgery to have her cancerous breast and uterus removed. The novel is so concerned with setting up a situation in which the women can develop a new language in the very heart of a repressive patriarchy that it fails to make that situation very convincing. We are shown a powerful, elite family of linguists who jealously control all negotiations with other races but who are not interested in power or money and who seem to lack any motivation.

Another of the basic premises of *Native Tongue*, published in 1984, is that in 1991 – a mere seven years later – an amendment to the U.S. Constitution will pass which makes women legally minors. This is preposterous. The disappointing failure of the long-drawn-out struggle for the Equal Rights Amendment, for instance, was not only an expression of irrational fears about the consequences of fully legalizing the equality of women (which the Evangelical Right has done its best to inflame), but also an indication of the difficulties involved in actually amending the U.S. Constitution. I cannot believe that it would be any easier for a minority of bigots and fundamentalists to draft and pass such an overwhelming denial of women's basic rights in such a short space of time while remaining within the framework of the U.S. Constitution. This inconsistency undermines my ability to take the novel seriously. Such a misreading of the contemporary political situation makes me skeptical about the alternatives it offers. There is, in contrast, a similarly abrupt suppression of women's rights in the near future of *The Handmaid's Tale*, but it is brought about through a military takeover. Resistance to this military-religious coup is violently suppressed, while the continuing suppression of fundamental rights can be maintained only through the imposition of an Orwellian police state. But in Elgin's novel, everyone meekly submits to the constitutional suppression of the rights of half the population. One may not believe in the possibility of a religious takeover as in Atwood's novel, but it is a far more feasible scenario than that of a legal suspension of women's rights early in the next decade.

The question of *Native Tongue*'s plausibility brings us to the most crucial theme in the novel – the transformative power of language. Certainly, one of the important and overlooked ways that patriarchal ideology transmits and reproduces itself is through language, and Elgin rightly calls attention to the relevance of combatting sexism through critiques of and changes in the patriarchal concepts and modes of thought embedded in current language practices. Language shapes and conditions our construction and understanding of *social* reality, and this social construction of reality extends to the construction of gender as well. However, even if we could change our language or, as in the novel, invent a new language, it does not follow that this would, by itself, change the world or even the ways that we understand social reality. This is magical rather than scientific linguistics, far removed from the theories of Benjamin Whorf; Làadan seems closer to the "Martian" of Robert Heinlein's *Stranger in a Strange Land* (1961), which grants marvelous powers to those privileged few who master it, than to the linguistic speculation in Samuel Delany's *Babel 17* (1966). While the women living together in the Barren Houses do experience reality in specific ways, the majority of their experiences remain shaped by the power relationships in which they are inscribed and exploited. They are still legally minors, bound to their husbands, fathers, and families; their reproductive functions, to take the issue central to *The Handmaid's Tale* and *Benefits*, are completely under the control of the male members of this patriarchal household. Rather than providing a way of transforming the world, this new language will condition the women to accept their inferior and exploited state. Allowed to live separately, even with their own language, they will still be little more than slaves, and it should be noted that in the more than one hundred years which pass between the invention of Làadan and the end of the sequel to *Native Tongue* (*The Judas Rose* [1987]), Elgin's women are still little more than slaves. Reality will not be changed by this new language; it will become an instrument of self-deception, bleeding off the rebellious energies of a group of exploited women. The strategies proposed in the novel in answer to this massive denial of rights lie not in the *political* sphere, but in a linguistic conspiracy which, like the alleged 1960s plot to lace the nation's drinking water with LSD, would change people's consciousnesses before they even realized it.

Nothing shows the futility of this strategy better than Chapter 23 of *The Judas Rose*, which deals with the ways that the linguist women have devised to avoid becoming sexually aroused – because, in this sexually repressed future, a woman's pleasure has been reduced to the satisfaction she must feel at her husband's satisfaction, so she can only be dissatisfied and frustrated in sexual relations with men.

> "Oh, the times tables are useful [Nazareth tells Belle-Sharon], and verb conjugations have their place, but the very best way I know to avoid going so far into arousal that you suffer is to say the alphabet backward. It takes an extraordinary amount of concentration!" The old woman had chuckled and added that if the time came when the

> alphabet in reverse had been so well learned that it lost its efficiency as a distractor, you simply turned to the alphabet of the Alien language you were interpreter for, and so on down the list. "But don't get too distracted, now," she had warned. "There is a moment when your attention must be on your husband." (Elgin 1987: 294)

With the exception of the times tables, these various techniques are all linguistically oriented, and, indeed, this scene is one of the rare examples in either novel of language actually being used to affect reality! It illustrates my objection, since these various uses of language do not in fact *change* reality; they simply allow the user to withdraw from reality even as she yields up her body to exploitation.

The legitimacy of criticizing *Native Tongue* in terms of its attempt to reach *beyond* the text is first asserted in its own mode of address. Written and published as science fiction, this novel's serious intentions can be seen in the "Editor's Note" at the beginning about the availability of information about the women's language invented in the novel: "We are informed that an early grammar and dictionary of Làadan are available to those interested. For further information, write to Làadan, Route 4, Box 192-E, Huntsville AR 72740, and be sure to enclose a stamped self-addressed envelope" (Elgin 1984: 4).

Another similarity between *The Handmaid's Tale* and *Native Tongue* makes one question their effectiveness as cautionary tales or strategies for political struggle. Through the narrative devices in *Native Tongue* and which close *The Handmaid's Tale*, the reader learns that the dystopian society presented in the body of the novel has come to an end and has been replaced by another, more desirable society. Atwood's bleak vision is tempered, as we have seen, by Offred's eventual escape. But the reader is not sure that she has escaped until after the novel ends, from the "transcript of the proceeding of the Twelfth Symposium on Gileadean Studies" (held more than a century later), which is meant to reassure the reader that Gilead will not survive and that North American society will return to something resembling the present. Similarly, *Native Tongue* is introduced by an "Editor's Note" explaining that the book is a manuscript which survives from the twenty-third century. It has been published after "ten years, and the efforts of hundreds of persons"; it is "a joint publication of [...] The Historical Society of Earth; WOMANTALK, Earth Section; The Metaguild of Lay

Linguists, Earth Section; The Làadan Group" (Elgin 1984). The implication is that Làadan has survived and flourished, and that the situation of women in the future is much improved. Moreover, while we know little of the future in which WOMANTALK flourishes, there are indications in the transcript of the Gileadean symposium – specifically the sexist banter of the male keynote speaker – which suggest a future little different from our present.

In both novels, this framing device seems designed to counter the pessimistic impression that the central narrative leaves. In each case, the plot is set in the context of a frightening and disheartening reaction against the contemporary struggle of women for equality, and in each case that narrative concludes with only the slightest glimmerings of hope: that the new language can be spread, or that Offred has been rescued. Unlike the collective dream of the linguist women in *Native Tongue*, even if Offred is safe, this says little about the prospects for other women in Gilead – at best it is an individual escape explaining nothing about the fall of Gilead. The portrayal of the decline in the rights and status of women is evidently meant to warn the reader and mobilize her to an active defense of those rights. But the additional knowledge provided by the frame – that this society has come to an end – tells the reader not to worry.

Although not everyone may agree with my readings of these three dystopian novels, these futuristic visions surely illustrate reactions to the sociopolitical events of the past two decades. Written in three relatively different literary contexts and three different countries, they mark an end to the feminist utopianism of the 1970s. One novel, however, constitutes a significant exception to general pessimism – Ursula K. Le Guin's *Always Coming Home*. But, in an entirely different way, this novel too demonstrates a retreat from an earlier feminist utopianism.

For those familiar with Le Guin's work, *Always Coming Home* is a return to her roots. Le Guin's origins were "anthropological"; her parents were anthropologists, and her mother, Theodora Kroeber, wrote *Ishi: The Last Stone Age Man* (1961), which played an important part in the utopian "rediscovery" of North American indigenous cultures in the 1960s. In many ways *Always Coming Home* strongly resembles *Ishi*. The Le Guin novel, furthermore, represents a return to the anthropological sensibilities and organization of her *The Left Hand of Darkness*, in which the narrative is juxtaposed with occasional (6 of 14) chapters presenting background information, including Gethenian myths and customs. In contrast, narrative in *Always Coming Home* is relegated to the background – the three "Stone Telling" sections total just over 100 pages of a 525-page book – while the attempt to evoke another culture is foregrounded. Although the reader enters the book through a story (part I of "Stone Telling"), narrative is soon supplemented by bits and pieces of Kesh culture. These include poems, legends, autobiographies, drawings, music, maps, jokes, plays, a glossary, and even some recipes, as well as a cassette of Kesh music and poetry. Neither a blueprint nor a narrative, *Always Coming Home* is a nonlinear collection of information, in the manner of a kit, which it is up to the reader to put together.

Although they make up only one-fifth of the book, the three parts of Stone Telling's story (Le Guin 1985: 7–42; 173–201; 340–386) may be read as a novel embedded in the larger text. That novel tells of a journey which parallels that of Shevek in *The Dispossessed* (he also left his utopian society for a dystopian one and then returned home). As a young girl, North Owl ("Stone Telling," who, when she returns, becomes "Woman Coming Home") is fascinated by her absent father and by the romanticism of his all-male company of warriors from outside the valley. It is not really a surprise when she decides to leave the community to follow her father back to his religious, patriarchal, war-oriented society. There women are rigidly confined to their quarters and restricted in their activities – a situation similar to the ones depicted in *The Handmaid's Tale* and *Native Tongue*. A few years later, married and with a child of her own, North Owl takes advantage of the Condor state's collapse under the pressure of its own military and expansionist mistakes, to flee and return home, where, after some time, she writes her story.

North Owl's initial dissatisfaction with her own society may be taken as a warning to the reader that he or she may find problems with the utopia (including boredom), while societies which seem to offer more romantic and exciting possibilities may in fact be dystopic. North Owl's trajectory – departure/return – is also a symbolic reenactment of the choice that each member of that utopian society must make to accept, and to work to maintain, the Kesh society. Utopias do not exist simply for us to wander into and then live "happily ever after," the novel tells us; they must be built and renewed and constantly chosen again and again.

In their construction of the reader, recent fictions have modified the strategies of the traditional utopian novel. Although More's *Utopia*, for instance, has been described in terms of its dramatic structure, its basic form is that of a philosophical dialogue. Indeed, this *rational* mode of addressing or constructing the reader as an intelligent person, open to reasoned arguments, was the dominant form of utopian writing well into the nineteenth century. The enormous success of Edward Bellamy's *Looking Backwards* (1888) pointed up a key alteration in the techniques of persuasion, for there had been a change in the intended audience – to the wider public of the newly formed middle classes in the U.S. – as well as a shift from philosophical dialogue to utopian romance. Readers no longer were addressed simply as listeners, but, through the dynamics of the novel, they became involved in an experience which went beyond the discovery and apprehension of a better society. Now the description of the ideal society formed the background to a sequence of unfolding events, however rudimentary, which could be followed through the eyes of a central character and assessed in terms of her or his own changing attitudes and feelings. Thus the "novelization" of utopia involved a significant transformation: from the positioning of the reader as the addressee in a philosophical dialogue who is persuaded through reasoned presentation, to a process of identification with a fictional character, in which the reader is implicated on emotional and experiential levels as well as on an intellectual one. Le Guin takes this evolution one step further in *Always Coming Home*, returning to an earlier intellectual appeal – it is up to the reader to put together and assess the different elements. At the same time, as in the utopias of the 1970s, the focus is much more on the quality and texture of daily life in the new society, and the author attempts to give us an existential or impressionistic contact with that world rather than a logical exposition of its advantages.

I am not sure that Le Guin's tactics work. Hers is clearly an innovative and interesting strategy, one in line with the recent questioning of traditional utopian assumptions. Like those of *The Dispossessed*, the intentions of this book – the implied reasons for wanting to describe a "people which might be going to have lived a long, long time from now in Northern California" (Le Guin 1985: xi) – are clearly utopian: in the lovely valley, the Kesh live and work close to the natural world in a way that is both culturally rich and obviously satisfying. Moreover, in typical utopian fashion, the happy pastoral society of the Kesh is contrasted with a patriarchal, militaristic Condor People who can be seen as a figure of our own world and its increasing flirtation with destruction. This is a modest, restrained utopia where a few people live in an idyllic pastoral future, one in which – and this is an important reservation – the contradictions and conflicts of our world have not been negotiated or resolved so much as simply whisked away. Instead of showing the difficulties, disagreements, and hardships involved in building a new society, *Always Coming Home* focuses on the pleasures and joys of daily life. Moreover, this small community seems cut off from the rest of the world. Although there are occasional glimpses of advanced technology (the planetary computer net), that technology is hidden, while most of the Kesh live in a nostalgic return to an almost pretechnological world.

That the reader may be able to understand "how the change came about" is easier to accept in *The Handmaid's Tale* and in *Benefits* than in Le Guin's book. Moreover, readers, apparently misunderstanding the book, continue to irritate Le Guin by telling her that they assume that the world of the Kesh has arisen after a nuclear war. The few references to a transition in *Always Coming Home* do leave open the possibility that this is somehow a post-holocaust world: despite Le Guin's violent denials, little explanation is offered in the book of how today's global tensions were resolved or how the population was reduced.[4] Because Le Guin's utopia is unclear about how

4 This was, for instance, the first question asked of Le Guin at a reading in Toronto in 1985. In her review of Le Guin's novel in *In These Times* [Chicago] (February 12–18, 1986), Kathryn Vangen mentions a similar incident in a reading in Seattle. "Yet, one wonders [Vangen writes], how do we get from here to there? How do we reduce the world's population significantly (without, heaven forbid, nuclear war)? How do we readjust our thinking about the use of technology? [...] As spellbinding and mesmerizing as *Always Coming Home* may be, it provides but one brief, fantastic escape from now (18)."

this wonderful new Northern California came to be or what happened to the rest of the world, it makes it difficult for me to give myself over fully to the fantasy of living there. While this may be quibbling, the earlier 1970s utopias I referred to – particularly those of Piercy and Russ, the utopias in which I would most like to live – not only depicted the entire planet and not just a peaceful valley, but also addressed the issue of how we got from here to there.

It is relatively easy to relate the decline in utopian writing to larger social and political events and to see the dystopian novels I have described as ominous signs of what may lie ahead. My concern is not only with the accuracy of such visions, however, but also with their impact: what effect do these more pessimistic works have on readers, particularly when compared to the earlier visions of a future structured by feminist principles and ideals? More bluntly, what fictional strategy serves the building of a new society best? The evocation of images of a better future, along with indications of how we get there? Or, at a time of increasing threat, does it make more sense to try to warn people that the battle is far from won?

The argument that we need such cautionary tales harks back to an older critique of utopianism. The move away from utopian writing and toward more "realistic" visions of the future could be seen as a way of maintaining our vigilance. According to this view, the building of a better society does not require images of that better world, but the energy, anger, and strategies to change this one. Utopian visions perhaps too quickly skip to the alternative and too quickly forget the intermediate fight, particularly now, that so many of our recent gains are under attack. Nevertheless, I think that the utopian novels of the 1970s were successful. Not only because I and many others might choose to live in worlds in process, like those described by Piercy and Russ, but also because they have helped carry the vision of an alternative to a new and larger audience. I have been critical, at times extremely so, of these four more dystopian works, and I am disappointed and worried by the decline in utopian writing. Yet I recognize that all four of the novels I have discussed were written from perspectives which I would consider close to my own. I share the impulse which fuels them: the fear of a future in which the modest social gains of the 1960s and 1970s have been rolled back, Pat Robertson has been elected president, or Elliot Abrams and Oliver North have engineered a coup to protect "traditional American values." At the same time, despite my reservations, I share the longing expressed in Elgin's vision of a language which is no longer determined by nor productive of the deforming and exploitive reality of capitalist patriarchy, but one which enables and reflects a transformed reality – indeed, a society like the one Le Guin shows us in the valley of the Kesh.

Dreams are not enough, however. Atwood, Elgin, and Fairbairns all show us the dangers of complacency or relaxed vigilance. The purpose of this paper has been to describe and defend the political dimension of these novels and to counteract reading strategies which obscure or deny the "literal" meanings of such crucial works. While there is much to love and enjoy in this privileged corner of our own world, the utopian impulse at the heart of all science fiction, the awareness of the fundamental insufficiencies of the present, and the longing for a more just and humane world should not be denied.

CHAPTER 11

Reconsiderations of the Separatist Paradigm in Recent Feminist Science Fiction[1]

> Utopian fiction is in fact one cultural arena in our society from which history has not disappeared. Utopia registers our fantasies of the future. But in a continual narrative process of repression and revolt, these fantasies embody our relationship to the realities of the present. The utopian impulse begins in the radical inadequacy of the present; it deconstructs our assumptions about social inevitability through representations that provoke a cognitive dissonance between the present as lived and the potentialities hidden within it. Utopia tempts us as an evocation of political desire. (Pfaelzer 1990: 198–199)

The general reaction to Margaret Atwood's *The Handmaid's Tale* (1985) led me to the realization that the backlash of late against feminism has been paralleled by a slowing in the pace of feminist utopian writing. But while the production of feminist utopias has certainly slowed since 1985, works marked by feminism continue to be an important part of SF.[2] In the following pages I want to look more closely at three novels published since Atwood's dystopian classic, novels which have

1 I would like to thank Veronica Hollinger and Robert Philmus for their help and suggestions.

2 For a discussion of the reaction against feminism in SF, see Chapter 10, "The Turn from Utopia." This statement about the decline in the production of feminist utopias is based on a list of utopias published since 1985 provided by Lyman Sargent in preparation for the next edition of his annotated bibliography, *British and American Utopian Literature* (New York: Garland, 1988). A quick count shows about twelve book-length "eutopias," in contrast to more than forty dystopias. The dozen exceptions are mostly feminist eutopias published by small presses; Judy Grahn's *Mundane's World* (Freedom, CA: The Crossing Press, 1988) is a good example. For recent developments in feminist SF, see *Science Fiction Studies* #51 ("Science Fiction by Women," July 1990), as well as the collections edited by Barr & Smith (Bowling Green, OH: Bowling Green Popular Press, 1981), and by Jones & Goodwin (Knoxville: University of Tennessee Press, 1990).

sometimes been cited as instances of an ongoing feminist utopian tradition: Pamela Sargent's *The Shore of Women* (1986), Sheri Tepper's *The Gate to Women's Country* (1988), and Joan Slonczewski's *A Door into Ocean* (1986).

In examining and discussing these works, I will concentrate on their thematic features and on the ways in which they respond to and develop some of the issues raised by the feminist utopias of the 1970s. My approach focusses less on literary or "textual" qualities than on the ways in which these fictional works function as interlocutors in an ongoing dialogue in which a number of writers influenced by feminism and by a flourishing utopian tradition use the imaginative potentiality of SF to evoke and to probe alternative visions. To understand and to appreciate "the alternative historical hypothesis" of the utopian text, we need to examine how it critiques the norms and structures of its own society as much as it attempts to imagine an alternative (cf. Suvin 1979: 49). As many critics have pointed out, the utopias of the 1970s were marked by a process of questioning an earlier tradition of literal blueprints. And yet, not even the most "textual" among them, for example, Monique Wittig's *Les Guerilleres* (1969), can be fully understood without taking into account its context – in Wittig's case, the debates in France between radical feminists and those oriented to working with men (cf. Jensen 1990). I would argue that any reading of that novel, or of Sally Miller Gearhart's *The Wanderground* (1978) or Joanna Russ's *The Female Man* (1975), must address the issue of the absence of men, just as it must address the issue of the origins of the alternative society. These are different questions than deciding whether to take literally the descriptions of flying in Gearhart's utopia or how to explain the juxtaposition on facing pages of names and narrative in Wittig's novel.

Admittedly, Sargent's, Slonczewski's, and Tepper's works are not utopias in the full sense of the term: they cannot be read primarily as attempts to imagine alternatives. Nonetheless, the three are very much replies to and reworkings of the central themes of the feminist utopias of the 1970s. A central concern of many of those works was understanding and explaining the violence of patriarchal forms and values. The utopias of the 1970s presented a range of explanations for male violence, grouped roughly around an "essentialist" pole (men are by nature violent – here the best example would be Gearhart's *Wanderground*) – and a more materialist one, according to which male violence is socially produced (whether by capitalism, as in Marge Piercy's *Woman on the Edge of Time* [1976], or by patriarchy itself, as in Russ's *Female Man*). In any event, the novels of the 1970s often had answers to questions about the differences between men and women and the roots of violence, whereas the novels of the late 1980s are not so certain. At the same time, efforts to break down or blur the differences between men and women, as in Piercy's attempt to free women from reproduction through technology, have by and large disappeared; and the earlier ideal of "androgyny" is now recognized as a depoliticization and desexualization of the body rather than as a utopian fusion of male and female.[3]

The second important element of the dialogue with the utopias of the 1970s can be seen in the use that these more recent works make of the separatist paradigm. They all begin from a "Great Divorce," but with important deviations. Most notably, they look back from the great divide, rather than forward to separatism as a possible option. The role of men is viewed much more positively than it was in tales like *Wanderground*, Russ's "When It Changed" (1972), or James Tiptree, Jr.'s "Houston, Houston, Do You Read?" (1976).

Sargent's *The Shore of Women* walks a very fine line between utopianism and anti-utopianism-and between feminism and anti-feminism. In using the term "anti-utopian," I mean a work which explicitly critiques and rejects the utopian project, as in Huxley's *Brave New World* (1932), in distinction to the dystopian, which offers a bleak view of the future without critiquing utopianism per se (e.g., *The Handmaid's Tale*). *The Shore of Women* verges on the anti-utopian insofar as it portrays what might be called a "failed

3 The interest in androgyny in SF and SF criticism was in many ways inspired by Le Guin's *The Left Hand of Darkness* (New York: Ace Books, 1969). For a specific critique of androgyny in this context, see Jewell Parker Rhodes' "Ursula Le Guin's *Left Hand of Darkness:* Androgyny and the Feminist Utopia" (in Barr and Smith, eds., *Women and Utopia: Critical Interpretations* [Lanham, MD: University of America Press, 1983], 108–120); for a more wide-ranging critique of the concept of androgyny as a feminist ideal, see Jean Bethke Elshtain's "Against Androgyny" (in Anne Phillips, ed., *Feminism and Equality* [New York: NYU Press, 1987], 139–159). From a different perspective, Piercy's *Woman on the Edge of Time* might also be considered a utopia which promotes androgyny.

utopia." To understand this further distinction, let me juxtapose E.M. Forster's anti-utopian depiction of a collapsing society in "The Machine Stops" (1909) and Le Guin's *The Dispossessed* (1974). Shevek's realization of his society's failings does not constitute a critique of its founding principles – as is the case in Forster's story and in *Brave New World* – but a reaffirmation of their validity in the face of various problems. Sargent's *Shore* also portrays a society in crisis, but, insofar as it critiques the separatist ideals upon which the women's society is built, it hesitates between critical utopia and anti-utopia.[4]

In speaking of *Shore* as anti-feminist, I have in mind the fact that Sargent's setting – a matriarchal society which dominates and exploits men – has often served as raw material for anti-feminist fiction. Indeed, the examples of such that Joanna Russ describes in her essay, "Amor Vincit Foeminam," bear a strong resemblance to Sargent's narrative, particularly in regard to the main (female) character's discovery of the joys of heterosexuality when confronted by a "real" man.

Lastly, Sargent's novel is also ambivalent in its attitude toward the question of men and violence, for the women's society is grounded on the premise that there is an essential difference between men and women. As one woman explains: "Men destroy; women build and nurture. It's because we carry our children inside us, and men can't" (1986: 96). But as we shall see, the events of the novel simultaneously reaffirm and undermine this essentialist assertion, while the novel's ending calls for an end to separation.

The Shore of Women is set in a future in which men and women live in separate societies. This separation is the result of a nuclear war which some people survived by going underground. Gradually, pressure developed to

4 I have taken the concept of "critical utopia" from Tom Moylan's *Demand the Impossible;* he defines the term as follows: "Thus, utopian writing in the 1970s was saved by its own destruction and transformation into the 'critical utopia.' Critical in the Enlightenment sense of *critique* – that is expressions of oppositional thought, unveiling, debunking, of both the genre itself and the historical situation. As well as 'critical' in the nuclear sense of the *critical mass* required to make the necessary reaction" (1986: 10). Moylan argues forcefully that the "critical utopia" of the 1970s is the "negation of the negation" of the reaction against utopia in the twentieth century, preserving as it does the fundamental utopian dream of human emancipation while acknowledging the "limitations of the utopian tradition" (1986: 10).

expel the men as punishment for their role in the Destruction. Now centuries after the expulsion, the women live comfortably in technologically-advanced walled and domed cities, while the men live brutish, savage lives "outside" in small, nomadic bands. The women deliberately keep the men in their savage, nomadic state, even if it requires killing. As one woman argues: "There are men within sight of [the city of] Dewa who have built a town and have united several tribes. They must be destroyed, as an example to others and for our own protection" (1986: 8).

Moreover, the women exploit the men for reproductive purposes. They have built shrines near the cities where the men go to pray to the Lady. There they watch a futuristic equivalent of pornographic movies and, while they are unconscious, sperm is taken from them. Artificial insemination produces both girls and boys, but the boys stay with their mothers only until the age of 5 or 6. Their memories are then erased and they are expelled from the city. In their comfort and isolation, the women have become "complacent and unadventurous" (1986: 31); most of them are largely ignorant of the outside world. Worse, they are losing the technological skills and scientific knowledge which allowed them to build their retreats.

The main characters are a twin brother and sister, Arvil and Laissa, and her best friend Birana. Twelve years after he has been sent outside, Arvil rescues Birana, who has been expelled from the city (for not acting when her mother murdered her lover). Believing her to be a manifestation of the Goddess come to visit the world of men, he becomes her protector and guide. The novel tells of their quest for a legendary refuge where other women have survived outside. Initially she resists his attraction to her, but gradually she succumbs to his sexual advances. After a baby is born, they go to a shrine where she contacts her old friend; she gives Laissa the baby – and their story. The novel ends with a sense of the necessity of change, as Laissa reflects on the importance of telling this story:

> Some will read these words and think that I have set myself against our cities. I do not want to destroy what we have built. We saved Earth and came to know our true power. Our daughters grow up unscarred by the wounds that marked the lives of women in ancient times; we must never go back to what once existed. Yet we have made this life for ourselves at the cost of the lives of those outside. To be free, we have enslaved them. [...]

> We were forced to choose this pattern once because our survival was at stake. I believe it may be at stake once more. We may stagnate, as life does when it holds to a pattern that is no longer needed […] It may be time for us and for those outside to begin to reshape ourselves and become another kind of being. (1986: 470–471)

This final sentence recalls Shevek's resolve to "shake up things" which closes *The Dispossessed* (1975: 309). Both novels end with the acknowledgment that their societies have stagnated and that this must cease, but the solutions advanced are different. In contrast to the implication at the end of *The Dispossessed* that Shevek's society must return to the anarchist principles on which it was founded, the import of Laissa's reflections cited above seems to be that it is time for a change, but not for a return to any original principles of the women's society. That "pattern," Laissa says – in a reference to the separatism of many of the utopias of the 1970s – is "no longer needed." In stating that "it may be time for us and for those outside to begin to reshape ourselves and become another kind of being," the novel is instead calling for a reconciliation of the sexes.

This call for reconciliation bothers me for several reasons having to do with context rather than content. *Shore* seems to move beyond the essentialism of the view that "men had a propensity for violence that was both genetic and hormonal" (1986: 90); however, toward the end of the novel, when Birana and Arvil are living with a small, inbred group of men and women, Arvil watches one of the men rape a woman and is aroused, even as he tells himself that it is wrong.[5] He then tries to force himself on Birana, who points out how quickly he has adapted. Suddenly guilty, he wonders if "Perhaps your kind was right to draw away from us and teach us to worship you." Relenting, she replies that "What's true for these men and women isn't true for us" (1986: 411). This scene undermines the ending's

5 Here is Arvil's account of that scene: "He strode up to her […] She backed away, shaking her head. Skua seized her arm. She tore herself away from him. He leaped after her and threw her face down on the sand, then pulled at her leggings and loincloth. She scrambled to her knees as he tugged at his own loincloth. He pulled her toward him by her hips and entered her, thrusting against her as she clawed at the sand. […] I hastened toward them, but even as I pitied Willow, I could not take my eyes from this coupling. Something in me was roused by this sight, however I fought against it" (1986: 411).

gesture toward reconciliation, inasmuch as Arvil's guilty arousal suggests some inherent pleasure in domination which is not shared by women. Arvil's shame is not enough to excuse his failure to intervene when Skua rapes Willow, or his own attempt to force Birana; and her insistence that they are somehow different is not very reassuring either. There seems to be a fundamental contradiction which Birana – and the novel's ending – attempt to gloss over with hopeful words. On the one hand, men are different, stronger and dominating, and prone to violence. But on the other hand, when he touches her, she forgets her reservations:

> A man had touched me; he had brought me to completion, and I had welcomed it. He had seen me respond; he knew that I would remember this and long for him again. […] The sight of his nakedness should have repelled me. His chest rose and fell as he sighed; one muscular arm was curled under his golden hair. His penis, so large in my hand, seemed smaller as it rested against my thigh. (1986: 330–331)

This reference to Arvil's maleness brings me to the crux of my reservations about Sargent's call for reconciliation, which depends on Birana's "conversion" to heterosexual love. It follows all too closely the scenarios described by Russ in her discussion of anti-feminist novels, especially when we remember that Russ wanted to call her article "The Triumph of the Flasher." While there are several detailed passages, narrated from Birana's point of view, of her discovery of sexual pleasure with Arvil ("No one," we learn, "had given [Birana] such joy before" [1986: 334]), there are no descriptions of sexual pleasure or even of love among the women of the cities. In fact, the novel begins with Birana's mother murdering her lover. To make matters worse, Arvil, unlike Birana, is not even converted to heterosexuality, for he is repeatedly shown rejecting sexual advances from other men.[6] Finally, there is only one description of sexual pleasure from

6 Moreover, the sexual relations between the men are usually described in terms of rape. For instance, after the rape scene referred to above and its effect on Arvil – followed by his attempt to force Birana and her reaction – Arvil concludes as follows: "This place has poisoned me […] I've seen men have their way with weaker ones before, but the sight never roused me – I remember what it was like to be a boy at the mercy of men" (1989: 413).

Arvil's perspective: the passage to which I have already referred in which he discovers a guilty pleasure in the spectacle of violence.

These criticisms are not meant to imply that compulsory homosexuality is the mark of authentic feminist fiction. Rather, the struggle for sexual choice has traditionally been an important goal of feminism, one which certainly cannot be said to have been achieved. Remembering that in the divided world of *Shore* the majority of men and women presumably find love and sexual pleasure with members of the same sex, I find it quite disturbing that there is not a single positive example of such a relationship, male or female. This absence is especially significant when contrasted to the scenes of Birana's heterosexual awakening. Indeed, the novel centers on Birana and Arvil's discovery of the joys of heterosexuality, a discovery which sums up what I am calling the novel's message of reconciliation. In its dialogue with the feminist utopias of the 1970s, Sargent's novel seems to have accommodated both homophobia and heterosexism in its appeal for a reconciliation of the sexes – a development which unfortunately reenacts a key feature of the backlash against feminism.[7]

Heterosexuality and the relations between the sexes are also issues in Sheri Tepper's *The Gate to Women's Country*, which is again set in a future recovering from nuclear war; again the explanation for the alienation between men and women lies in a reaction against male violence. Whereas in *Shore* the men's illusory understanding of their situation was created and maintained by women in order to preserve the status quo, here it is apparently the men's own warrior cult which distorts and limits their comprehension. The women certainly contribute to the men's ignorance; however, there are several levels of understanding, and it is only at the novel's end that the reader discovers the full extent of the men's lack of knowledge.

The warriors live in garrisons adjacent to the towns in Women's Country. They still mate with the women, at biannual carnivals. The women raise the children who result from these unions, and then, at the age of 5, the boys are sent to live with the men. Although the boys are indoctrinated into the warrior cult, they visit their mothers twice a year. At the age of 15 they must make a choice. Many of them perform a ritual rejection of

7 Russ's (1975b) review of *The Dispossessed* makes many of the same points.

the mother and become warriors. However, some boys decide instead to leave the garrison, passing out through the "Gate to Women's Country." They then live with the women as "servitors," a despised and apparently eunuch-like caste of servants.

Despite the warriors' sense of superiority, it is the women who have a larger perspective and understanding. They have been working for 300 years to reclaim a world ravished by nuclear war. The plot revolves around the uneasy equilibrium between the two communities, for every once in a while the men begin to wonder why they allow the women so much independence. "Why do we put up with them?" one of the men asks Michael, one of the more intelligent and ambitious of the warriors. "Why don't we just take over the city?" (1989: 66). Michael's reply is worth quoting:

> The first thing, I'd have to have all the other garrisons set to go along. [...] There'd have to be plenty of food. There'd have to be a huge harvest. [...] Right now we're living from harvest to harvest [...] You may think the women would work if us warriors took over the city, and eventually they probably would. But it might take a long while to convince them. Your men get hungry, they start drifting away. You're not going to hold a city without men, and you can't hold men without food! (1989: 68)

Michael's explanation of the social contract, according to which the women provide food and more warriors in exchange for protection from other garrisons ("the warriors protected them only because women bore them sons" [1989: 143]), is, in fact, seriously mistaken, as we shall see in a moment. This misapprehension of the balance of power leads the more ambitious warriors to conspire, every decade or so, to take over, and the narrative develops from just such a scheme. To learn the women's "secrets," Michael encourages young warriors to court the daughters of the members of the Women's Council. Accordingly, Chernon's courtship of Stavia is revived when she returns to Marthatown after nine years of medical study. When she is sent on an exploratory mission to the outlands, he convinces her to meet him once she has left Women's Country. They are captured and taken to a small, inbred patriarchal community (fittingly called "Holyland"). Chernon is fascinated by a society organized around the total subjugation of women, while Stavia is badly beaten when she tries to escape. After she is rescued, she learns the full extent of her error and the real situation of Women's Country. The warriors are not the fathers of the children; that is the role of the servitors. More importantly, the warrior cult itself was deliberately created by the women as an elaborate program to select for non-violence. As Stavia's mother explains to her:

> Three hundred years ago almost everyone in the world had died in a great devastation brought about by men. It was men who made the weapons and men who were the diplomats and men who made the speeches about national pride and defense. And in the end it was men who did whatever they had to do, pushed the buttons or pulled the string to set the terrible things off. And we died [...] Almost all of us. [...]
>
> Only a few were left. Some of them were women, and among them was a woman who called herself Martha Evesdaughter. Martha taught that the destruction had come about because of men's willingness – even eagerness – to fight, and she determined that this eagerness to fight must be bred out of our race, even though it might take thousand years. She and the other women banded together and started a town, with a garrison outside. They had very few men with them, and none could be spared, so some of the women put on men's clothes and occupied the garrison outside the town. [...] And when the boy children were five, they were given into the care of that garrison. (1989: 301–302)

The whole project of rebuilding depends upon the warriors' completely mistaken and inflated ideas of their importance and role; they are, in fact, a disappearing species. Their numbers are decreasing from generation to generation while the numbers of boys who reject the warriors and pass out through "The Gate to Women's Country" to live as servitors is increasing. However, keeping all this hidden from the warriors means concealing it from most of the women as well. "Very few [women know]," Stavia's mother tells her. "We put clues here and there, for those with the wits to see them. Most women don't know anything about it. We can't risk the ones who talk too much. Or the ones who drink a lot during carnival" (1989: 294).

Although they have sex with the warriors, believing that this is how their babies are conceived, most of the women are actually impregnated through "artificial insemination" (1989: 293). A few of the women are even sterilized without their knowledge (1989: 290). This is a society which carefully conceals its true workings from most of its own members.

What is the status or meaning of this breeding plan? As a form of eugenics, it of course has a history as a literary theme to be found in many utopias, from More and Campanella through the more "scientific" developments of the twentieth century. More specifically, Robert Heinlein's *Beyond This Horizon* (1948) not only includes a utopian society based on the concept of "racial improvement by gene selection," but also a discussion of a failed utopian experiment which directly anticipates the women's undertaking here: "After the Atomic War of 1970, the survivors instituted drastic genetic regulations intended for one purpose alone [...] to breed sheep rather than wolves" (§2: 26). Heinlein's own Social Darwinism leads him explicitly to reject the idea of trying to select for non-violence, for it contradicts the principle of the survival of the fittest. This principle is summed up in the novel through an explanation of the social usefulness of gunfighting: "We do not have enough things to kill off the weak and the stupid these days. But to stay alive as an armed citizen a man has to be either quick with his wits or with his hands, preferably both" (§15: 147). Accordingly, this attempt to select for non-violence was doomed to failure: "The 'wolves' ate the 'sheep'" (§2: 26).

In contrast to Sargent's novel, which depicts a failed utopia as a way of critiquing the separatist paradigm, Tepper uses separatism to camouflage the building of utopia. Her novel shifts the utopian focus, away from the contours of the alternative community to the mechanism for achieving the better society – one based on changing "human nature" and the male predisposition to violence, a problem for which Sargent had no solution. Eugenics and schemes for improving the race, however "improvement" is defined, are important themes in SF and utopian literature. Moreover, biology and reproduction, in contrast to the secrecy surrounding them in *Shore* and *Gate*, were – for obvious reasons – crucial issues in the separatist utopias of the 1970s; and there is a range of accounts of how women reproduce without men, from the mystical (*Wanderground*) to the more "scientific" techniques described in works such as Suzy McKee Charnas's *Motherlines* (1978) and Russ's *Female Man*.

In both *Shore* and *Gate*, the women occasionally resort to violence to preserve their way of life. Even though violence is used "for self-defense only, and always to rid Women's Country of those who are not and will not be part of it" (Tepper 1988: 303), such an option is in direct opposition to Joan Slonczewski's *A Door into Ocean*. The latter begins from a moral imperative against killing and violence, however justified they may be – a principle which is summed up in Merwen's explanation of why the women do not fight back when their world is invaded: "If I were to kill, my soul would die. If Sharers took to killing, we would surely exterminate ourselves" (Slonczewski 1986: 370). *Door* follows a narrative model different from *Shore* and *Gate*: that of the "discovery" of the "New World" by Europeans, as seen from the perspective of the indigenous peoples of the Americas. Like Tiptree's "Houston, Houston, Do You Read?" and Russ's "When It Changed," this is a tale about the disruption of a utopian world of women by the arrival of men and male values.

The countries of Valedon are governed by a High Protector, the planetary representative of the Patriarch who rules the Galaxy. The moon of Valedon, Shora, is an ocean world inhabited by fewer than a million women living on raft communities. These women, although genetically the same as the Valans, have lived isolated and undiscovered for 10,000 years. In fact, their world and way of life were also – like those depicted in *Shore* and *Gate* – developed following an outbreak of nuclear destruction. As Merwen tells Spinel, their commitment to non-violence was decided millenia before:

> Spinel, do you remember the ancients, how they lived and died? Their knowledge was so great that they could swim among the stars, as we swim among rafts.Yet a spark ignited them and they burned, until nothing but fire remained, and a few lost ones, groping among the cinders. Only Shora escaped, to a place that will quench fire, will drink of it forever. (1986: 308)

The women live without rulers or ruled, as one part of the "web of life" in which "every creature has its niche, its function" (1986: 352). The concept of "sharing" is at the center of their world-view and "Sharer" is their name for themselves. They have no metal or electricity, and no machines; but they do have very advanced biological knowledge and abilities, from healing skills to plant and marine genetics. As a Valan scientist reports to Realgar when he asks if their labs are "genuine":

> There's workspace, there's plumbing. No glassware, bottled chemicals, or autoclaves, much less recognizable analytic hardware. But those vines you saw, they form galls

> whose cavities can be inoculated with pure cultures of microorganisms. Other vines are specialized secretors for enzymes, organic reagents, acids, you name it. (1986: 215)

Now that Shora and its inhabitants have been discovered, the Sharers' isolation and way of life have been disrupted. Valedon has established a trading company which, in a familiar story of the exploitation of indigenous populations, controls all contact between the two worlds. The traders take precious Shoran commodities ("seasilk," fish, medicine, etc.) in exchange for manufactured goods and for stones which cause a strange sickness among some of the women (analogous to alcoholism among indigenous peoples in our world). The novel opens with two Sharers who have travelled to Valedon to try to understand why "the Valan guests on their home world dumped noxious chemicals and raised trade 'prices' without warning" (1986: 26). They meet a young man (Spinel) who returns with them to Shora. When the Sharers turn to a boycott of the trading posts, the Valan army is sent "to bring Patriarchal Law to Shora" (1986: 207). The tension increases as the army seeks to subjugate a scattered population whose only defense is passive resistance. Day after day the Sharers go to the army bases to silently protest the Valan invasion. They are often beaten, or taken prisoner and tortured. While some of the women talk about turning their "lifeshaping" skills to driving the Valans from the moon, there is a general rejection of such a strategy. When the soldiers are ordered to kill Sharers who approach their bases, the women only increase their visits. Their passive resistance in the face of intensifying violence further undermines the morale of the army. Desperate plans are made to destroy the entire population of the moon, but these are aborted – not because of any moral reservations about genocide, but because the army commander is afraid that the women may have "spread an infection which would lie dormant within us for years, only to mushroom into disease and wipe us out – unless Sharers are still around to halt it" (1986: 352). It is the Valans' own fear which prevents them from exterminating the women, a fear based not on anything the women have said or done, but on what a Valan would do if he or she had the Sharers' lifeshaping skills. The novel ends with the departure of the troops and the beginning of a return to normal.

Although Slonczewski's vision distinguishes between male and female values, this is not ultimately tied to biological sex. There is no essential difference between men and women. Spinel, a man (or, as the Sharers call him, a "malefreak"), finds a Shoran partner/lover and becomes a full member of Sharer society. Moreover, this is a sexual partnership, although heterosexual intercourse itself is not possible because of the changes in Shoran anatomy. On the other hand, the invading Valan troops include both men and women, and Commander Realgar's "interrogator" (or torturer) is a woman. The novel makes a clear distinction between values and plumbing.

Nor does the juxtaposition of male and female values repeat the essentialist rejection of technology as male (as it did in Gearhart's *Wanderground*). The crucial distinction is rather between a machine and what might be called an "organic" technology, for the Shorans' very advanced biological and agricultural sciences have grown out of and are a part of their lives on an oceanic world. On the other hand, the inorganic nature of metal and machines reflects the violent world-view and philosophy of the Patriarch's galactic empire, summed up in the figure of the Patriarch's envoy, Malachite (named after a stone), a robot who decides to wipe out an entire city on Valedon in order to put down a provincial rebellion. As with the previous two novels I've discussed, moreover, the emphasis on female values has led to imaginary communities which pay special attention to the "life" sciences like medicine and biology, which are opposed to men's skill with war technology.

Although the Sharers are shown living in a wonderful harmony in the "web of life" of Shora, this should not be understood as a watery version of the "Peaceable Kingdom," in which "the lamb lies down with the lion." The ocean is a dangerous place, swimming with predatory life forms and deadly storms; and many of the Sharers eat fish.[8]

In short, *A Door into Ocean* argues forcibly that there are limits to what can or must be done to protect a utopia. This rejection of violence certainly casts the violence in *Shore* and *Gate* in a different light. At the same time, *Door* rejects the strategies enunciated in the 1970s by a whole range of feminist utopian writers – from Piercy to Russ (via Ernest Callenbach

8 Gearhart's *Wanderground* and Clifford D. Simak's *City* (Garden City, NY: Nelson Doubleday, 1952) are examples of SF novels in which there is no interspecies killing.

and Samuel R. Delany) – who acknowledged the necessity of violence to bring about a new society, something which, I should add in passing, Le Guin has always rejected.[9]

> To imagine that, sheltered from the omnipresence of history and the implacable influence of the social, there already exist a realm of freedom – whether it be that of the microscopic experience of words in a text or the ecstasies and intensities of the various private religions – is only to strengthen the grip of necessity over all such blind zones in which the individual subject seeks refuge, in pursuit of a purely individual, a merely psychological project of salvation. The only effective liberation from such constraint begins with the recognition that there is nothing that is not social and historical – indeed that everything is "in the last analysis" political. (Jameson 1981: 20).

In contrast to the utopias of the 1970s, these three novels do not focus on the evocation of alternative societies in any literal sense. *Shore* depicts a failed utopia, or at best a utopia which must now be abandoned, while *Gate* portrays the slow building of a new society. Only the world of *Door* might be characterized as an ideal society, and its literal significance for humans is considerably modified by the specific features of an aquatic world. In their dialogue with the utopias of the 1970s, then, these three novels blend literal representations of alternative patterns of life with more rhetorical and figurative evocations of a transformed world.

To illustrate this differing strategy, let us look briefly at the issue of the passage to the new society along with the question of the relationship between "our" world and the worlds of these novels. Their very titles – "gate," "door," "shore" – call attention to the transition; each text identifies itself as the representation of a fictional world which, unlike the relative certainty of the 1970s' utopias, stands on the edge of or in-between the old and the new. Whereas the earlier utopias (particularly *The Female Man* and *Woman on the Edge of Time*) adopted textual strategies which sought to implicate the reader in the struggle for a better society,[10] rather than

9 See Søren Baggesen's thoughtful discussion of the necessity of violence in Le Guin's *The Word for World is Forest* (New York: Berkeley Pub. Corp., 1972).

10 In both *The Female Man* and *Woman on the Edge of Time*, the ending plays an important part in this strategy. They both include the explanation that the utopian future has contacted the characters in our present to help with the struggle, but both novels avoid the happy endings of more traditional utopias. *The Female Man*

simply juxtaposing the utopian society – explicitly or implicitly – with the present, these three novels all situate themselves in an afterwards; after a nuclear war and after a great divorce between men and women.

The theme of transition and the novels' setting in an "afterwards" produce an interesting example of the tension between figurative and literal representations in the utopian novel, for surely no reader could imagine that any of these books was advocating a nuclear war as a way of clearing the path for a new society.[11] In the same way, while an argument might be made that not every separatist utopia of the 1970s was intended to promote separatism, some of them undoubtedly were. On the other hand, these later novels, insofar as they stage the reconciliation of men and women, clearly refer to the separatism – real or figurative – of some of the 1970s utopias.

In *Shore*, the women set up a society without men and achieve a technological utopia. Through a familiar anti-utopian pattern, one of its members gradually realizes that her utopia has stagnated, and worse, that it is built upon the exploitation of others. While not overlooking the evils of the earlier patriarchal system, Sargent seems to argue that the separatist solutions of the 1970s were mistaken. In *Gate*, the reconciliation of men and women is achieved in a different way, for behind the appearances of two separate groups, the reader, through the narrative of Stavia's coming of age, finally discovers the real situation. Men and women have already been reconciled, but this has been overlooked because most people have been looking at the wrong men – at the masculine warriors rather than at the soft, gentle, and apparently sexless servitors. By implication, at some critical point when the balance has definitely shifted and the warriors have been bred out of existence, all women will share in the facts of their existence. Lastly, in *Door* the reconciliation is presented in a different way, for this novel critiques the separatist paradigm for very different reasons than does

concludes with the author/narrator's own words, "Go little book," while *Woman* ends not only with Connie's decision to poison the doctors – her acceptance that the war for the future is being fought in the present – but also with the report of her reincarceration.

11 At a reading from *Always Coming Home* in 1985, Le Guin was quite upset by questions which took for granted that she had set her utopian society in a post-holocaust California.

Gate. Whereas in the latter (as I have already argued) there is an underlying aversion to homosexuality which dictates the novel's outcome, here the discovery and violation of the utopian world of Shara serves rather as a reminder that any attempt to live in isolation, to form a separatist community, is threatened by one's neighbors. But in contrast to the decision to fight to defend the utopian experiment which characterized so many of the utopias of the 1970s, from Callenbach's *Ecotopia* (1975) and Delany's *Triton* (1976) to *Female* and *Woman*, *Door* reworks this theme through the ideal of non-violence.

As a critic I have tried to describe these novels in the context of a feminist utopian tradition; at the same time, I have argued that that utopian tradition developed not simply as a literary movement, but as a part of a feminist politics of transformation. My goal has been to argue the effectiveness of using fiction as a way of assisting that project. I have argued elsewhere that utopian visions are crucial to the struggle for human emancipation because they help us to articulate what we understand by a qualitatively different society, something we sometimes lose sight of in the midst of our day-to-day lives.[12] My criticisms of these later works are not based on the fact that they are no longer so fully utopian. Clearly that moment has passed. But these works do ask to be considered as replies to those earlier visions, and I would like to conclude on those terms, by looking at their effectiveness in mobilizing for change.

In many ways I was most impressed by Sheri Tepper's *The Gate to Women's Country*. It provides a very convincing depiction of a world rebuilding, and I have some sympathy for the idea of selecting for non-violence. I understand, too, that without secrecy, this rebuilding is doomed. But the necessity for secrecy reveals a pessimism about the prospects for change with which I cannot agree. This pessimism has to do with Tepper's essentialist view of the origins of violence and her reliance, however metaphorical, on an élite (the Women's Council) which knows what is best, implying that most of the women cannot be trusted to make enlightened decisions or to act in their own best interests. Both violate my own utopian ideas about the importance of education and democracy. This ethical

12 See Chapter 9, "So We All Become Mothers."

dilemma is further complicated by what I see as a contradiction in the novel's logic. Margot and two servitors ambush and kill Michael and some of his aides. Yet the servitors are the product of 300 years of selection for non-violence. On the face of it, this hardly sounds like successful selection, particularly when we hear Joshua's explanation for killing Michael (a fight between Stavia's "real" father and her supposed father):

> "I needed to do it. In Women's Country we learn not to have jealousy [...] They teach us and themselves to be calm, to take joy in the day, to set aside possessiveness. And yet, despite it all [...]"
>
> "Despite it all, you needed to kill him."
>
> "Yes," said Joshua with a shamed face. "I did." (1988: 305)

There is a further contradiction in the dichotomy between the women's commitment to non-violence and the violence of the men. To protect their way of life, the women also resort to violence. This does not only involve killing a few warriors, as in the scene just mentioned; it also extends to arranging for the destruction of the entire Marthatown garrison – some 4,000 men – once Chernon's tales of a patriarchal society begin to spread. In Tepper's efforts to find a way to get rid of male violence without getting rid of men, we have, as with *Shore*, a situation in which the women have adopted the very methods which led them originally to differentiate themselves from men. This contradiction stems from the attempt to reconcile violence and non-violence. In this regard I am in agreement with Slonczewski that a non-violent world cannot be built using violence.

In their acceptance of biological determinism, Sargent and Tepper revert to a politics of despair, as opposed to the optimism of *Door* with its pacifism and sharing. Slonczewski's novel almost convinces me of the political feasibility of passive resistance and non-violence. But the novel's positive ending is misleading. The women do nothing to repel the invaders, and it is the Valens' own fear about what the women could do that drives them from the planet. I find the argument that to begin to kill is to lose one's soul moving, but I think that the ending makes it seem as if this will bring a victory in practice as well as in principle. If we turn to one of my favorite utopian works, Olaf Stapledon's *Star Maker* (1937), we can find a similar depiction of a utopian world's decision to allow itself to be destroyed rather than to fight back. Let me quote a sentence which sounds very much like the Sharer philosophy:

> But they knew also that in reorganizing themselves for desperate warfare, in neglecting, for a whole age of struggle, all those activities which were proper to them, they would destroy the best in themselves more surely than the enemy would destroy it by oppression; and that in destroying this they would be murdering what they believed to be the most vital germ in the galaxy. (361)

The difference is that Stapledon's "utopian worlds" are destroyed. Slonczewski's commitment to non-violence is a shining example of the rejection of a world of violence, but the novel's happy ending implies that it is a viable political strategy.

In terms of their relationship to the utopian tradition, these three novels may be seen in a light similar to Tom Moylan's definition of the "critical utopias" of the 1970s, for they are themselves critical reexaminations and reworkings of the now-classic utopias of the 1970s.[13] Yet at times these works seem to go too far in their implied critiques of the 1970s utopias. As Moylan points out, there is a crucial distinction between the rejection of utopianism (the anti-utopia) and what he describes as the "negation of the negation of utopia" through which "utopian writing in the 1970s was saved by its own destruction and transformation into the 'critical utopia'" (1986: 10). The critical utopia did not simply cancel out the older utopias, for, as Moylan explains, "the subversive imaging of utopian society and the radical negativity of dystopian perception is preserved, while the systematizing boredom of the traditional utopia and the co-optation of utopia by modern structures is destroyed" (1986: 10). In contradistinction to the critical utopia, which was an attempt to give the utopian dream new direction by liberating it from past mistakes and misdirection, the references here to liminality – door, gate, ocean – seem to stand not only for a vision of a world on the *verge* of being born, but as a retreat, the doorway through which the authors are backing away from the utopian hopes and dreams of the 1970s in a movement which effectively repudiates earlier utopian energies.

13 See note 4 above.

Given the collapse of the socialist alternative in Eastern Europe and the accompanying cries of victory in the West, as well as the rise in militarism and the steady erosion of the social gains of the 1960s and 1970s at home, the utopian imagination seems more vital than ever. If I have been overly harsh, or if I have read these works in too literal a fashion, it is a reflection of those concerns. I have high expectations for SF and utopia, for I see them as a source of hope and the imagination of alternatives to a reality in which the triumph of the patriarchal and masculinist values described in Atwood's dystopia seem closer than ever.

CHAPTER 12

Beyond the Wasteland: A Feminist in Cyberspace[1]

> I cannot stress too greatly the radical distinction between a view for which the postmodern is one (optional) style among others available and one which seeks to grasp it as the cultural dominant of the logic of late capitalism. (Jameson 1991: 45–46)

My title is intended to call attention to the dialogue with cyberpunk in Marge Piercy's *He, She and It*, and with science fiction more generally, for the novel has received little or no attention within the North American science fiction community, even after it won the Arthur C. Clarke award as the best science fiction novel of 1992 in Great Britain.[2] At the same time, *He, She and It* develops themes and issues from Piercy's 1976 *Woman on the Edge of Time*, and more generally, with feminist utopian concerns as they have evolved over the intervening fifteen years. Such

1 This is a revised version of a paper read at the 1993 meetings of the Popular Culture Association (New Orleans) and the Society for Utopian Studies (St. Louis). Many of my revisions follow from the comments and exchanges with the other panelists – June Deery, Helen Kuryllo and Vara Neverow – who are in a sense my co-authors since I can no longer separate my ideas from theirs.

2 In Britain the novel was titled *Body of Glass*, which according to Piercy (in a letter to Lyman Sargent) was the original title. The three major science fiction magazines seem to have completely ignored *He, She and It*. I could find no reviews in *Analog*, *Isaac's Asimov's Magazine of Science Fiction*, or *The Magazine of Fantasy and Science Fiction* for the period October 1991 through August 1993. There were less than enthusiastic reviews in some other science fiction magazines, including: Wendy Bradley, *Interzone* (September 1992), 64–65; Gary Wolfe, *Locus* (January 1992), 29–30; and John Clute, *The New York Review of Science Fiction* #43 (March 1992), 6–7. More sympathetic reviews from utopian scholars would include those of Frank Dietz, *The New York Review of Science Fiction* (September 1992), 13–14; and Marleen Barr, *American Book Review* (June–July 1992), 11–13. In making these comments, I do not mean to criticize SF; rather I am interested in understanding why the novel disappoints the science fiction reader's expectations. I will return to a discussion of the "feel" of this novel and generic expectations in my conclusion.

dialogues are an integral part of our ongoing reflections about a better society, and an indication of how literary genres grow and develop through borrowing and interchanges.

Feminism and the Utopian Tradition

Of course, *He, She and It* does not depict a utopia in the way that *Woman on the Edge of Time* did, but it is very much related to the earlier novel. In Chapter 15 of *Woman on the Edge of Time*, Piercy described an alternative to the utopia of Mattapoisett: a terrible, bleak future in which sexism and capitalism have flourished (similar to the Manland episode in Joanna Russ's *The Female Man*). That brief nightmarish chapter in *Woman* was limited to Gildina's windowless 126th floor apartment. A surgically "built-up contracty [...] [Gildina was born] with brain deficiencies from protein scarcity in foetus and early childhood" (1976: 299). It is from this sex-slave that we learn of life in a toxic, polluted future, where the rich lived segregated from the diseased and undernourished masses who to survive were often forced to sell their bodies, or their organs. This dystopian vision is the basis for the future of 2059 in *He, She and It*.

While the immediate likelihood of utopia has faded in *He, She and It*, the struggle for a livable world continues. These efforts include preserving Tikva – a fragile community surrounded by larger corporate neighbors who tolerate its existence only because the skills of its members are worth more than the effort to destroy it. Rather than describe the utopian features of this diverse, tolerant community, however, I want to focus on the development of the author's utopianism since *Woman*, and particularly on the theme of the necessity for violence to ensure the utopia's survival. As Connie's decision to poison the doctors' coffee showed in *Woman*, Piercy seemed to acknowledge that fighting back was a necessary part of the struggle for a better world. However, that relative certainty about the legitimacy of self-defense is considerably complicated in *He, She and It*, where threats to the community lead to the building of an illegal humanoid robot (called "Yod"). Piercy gives this basic scenario added depth by juxtaposing it to the legend of the golem, which tells of the Rabbi Judah Loew making a creature of clay – "Joseph" – to protect the Jews of the Prague ghetto. Each passes as human.[3]

Science Fiction

If Piercy's contextualization of self-defense in terms of the building of an android and the golem myth continues the dialogue with feminists about the legitimacy of self-defense and its limits, Yod's creation also looks to science fiction through the use of an important cluster of motifs: robots, androids, and cyborgs.

By calling Yod a cyborg, Piercy has, first of all, confused matters.[4] For most science fiction readers, Yod would be called an "android," a humanoid

3 The building of the android happens "just in time," Avram tells Shira: "Our Base is under attack" (Piercy 1991: 72). Yet, it might also be argued that Tikva is threatened precisely because of this new technology which is coveted by their more powerful neighbors. Unlike Rabbi Loew who agonizes at length before deciding to create the Golem, Avram has been conducting forbidden android experiments for years; and he has lost at least one university position because of such "illegal experiments" (1991: 390).

4 She is explicit about the term, for in answer to the statement that "robots are programmed to self-destruct before they injure anyone," Avram explains that "Yod's a cyborg, not a robot – a mix of biological and machine components" (1991: 73). This semantic sleight of hand – calling a robot something else – is among other things an attempt to finesse Isaac Asimov's "First Law of Robotics": "A robot may not injure a human being or, through inaction, allow a human being to come to harm" (1950: 6). After the first prototype of Yod – Alef – almost kills Avram's lab assistant, Gadi wonders, "What kind of a robot could injure a person? They're all programmed to self-destruct before they hurt anyone" (1991: 49). The interdiction against building a humanoid robot is summed up (in science fiction), in the references to the "Butlerian Jihad" in Frank Herbert's *Dune*. "Its chief commandment remains in the O.C. Bible: "Thou shalt not make a machine in the likeness of a human mind" (Herbert 1965: 530). Yod violates a similar convention: "robots were forbidden to be made in human form since the cyber-riots; apes were simply people altered chemically and surgically and by special implants for inhuman strength and speed" (Piercy 1991: 15).

robot rather than a cyborg. The distinction is important – as I will explain in a moment, and as Piercy seems to recognize at other points in the novel. A cyborg is the physical bonding of human and machine – a human who has in some way been augmented or enhanced. A robot or android on the other hand, is a new entity, built or grown from organic and/or non-organic materials.[4, 5]

Here the true cyborg is Nili. She is part of a "community of the descendants of Israeli and Palestinian women who survived" the nuclear Two Week War: "We have no men. We clone and engineer genes. After birth we undergo additional alteration. We have created ourselves to endure, to survive, to hold our land" (1991: 205–206).[6] Through her various "augmentations," Nili is used to illustrate the science fiction development of another utopian theme: that of human improvement. While this theme was traditionally articulated in terms of education and the melioration of living conditions, or in reference to the eugenics movements of the early twentieth century, in *He, She and It*, in terms more specific to the 1990s and the real world of pacemakers and cosmetic surgery, this theme takes on more explicitly physical forms: from aesthetic and medical interventions to implanted weapons and sensors, and the enhancing of sensations for work and play. While these developments certainly parallel aspects of

5 Under CYBORGS, *The Encyclopedia of Science Fiction* describes three types of cyborgs in science fiction: "elementary medical cyborgs – people with prosthetic limbs or pacemakers"; "functional cyborgs [...] people modified mechanically to perform specific tasks"; and "adaptive cyborgs [...] people redesigned to operate in an alien environment" (Clute and Nicholls 1993: 290). Under ANDROIDS, we learn that the term "usually denotes an artificial human or organic substance, although it is sometimes applied to manlike machines, just as the term ROBOT is still occasionally applied [...] to organic entities" (1993: 34). The Golem is cited as an example of an android.

6 This community without men is similar to the utopian worlds of James Tiptree's (Alice Sheldon) (1996 [1976]) "Houston, Houston, Do You Read?" and Joanna Russ's (1975) *The Female Man*. See Chapter 9, "So We All Became Mothers." Piercy described gestation outside the womb in the "brooders" of *Woman on the Edge of Time*. The cyborg dimension of *He, She and It* was also anticipated in *Woman*, although not entirely in positive terms, since we saw only corrupt cyborgs: the impotent, genetically engineered assassins and Gildina the prostitute.

cyberpunk, they hardly originated with William Gibson. (Remember the *Six Million-Dollar Man*, Heinlein's "waldo" or Delany's plugs in *Nova*?)[6,7]

However, I suggest that the primary interlocutors for this aspect of Piercy's novel are not so much the cyberpunks, but those feminists and utopians who continue to argue for the "natural" and the organic as a model for social change (a direction suggested by her mention of Donna Haraway's "Manifesto for Cyborgs" in the Acknowledgments). As Shira explains:

> Yod, we're all unnatural now. I have retinal implants. I have a plug set into my skull to interface with a computer. I read time by a corneal implant. Malkah has a subcutaneous unit that monitors and corrects blood pressure, and half her teeth are regrown. Her eyes have been rebuilt twice. Avram has an artificial heart and Gadi a kidney [...] We can't go unaided into what we haven't yet destroyed of "nature." Without a wrap, without sec skins and filters, we'd perish. We're all cyborgs, Yod. You're just a purer form of what we're tending toward. (1991: 155–156)

Returning to the motifs of robots and androids, the golem, particularly in its sixteenth-century context, may seem unusual. But the juxtaposition is meant to remind us that science fiction did not emerge, fully grown and mature, in the March 1926 issue of *Amazing*. I am not arguing some extended history for science fiction, but rather reiterating that the icons of the robot and the android are the actualization of themes which have manifested themselves in other ways. Moreover, the golem myth is not a story from "outside" science fiction, but an early rendering of many of the themes which cluster around the motif of the robot. This genealogy is nowhere more evident than in the film versions of the golem

7 Heinlein coined the term "waldo" (widely used today in reference to various remote-control devices) in his 1942 story, "Waldo: Genius in Orbit." Also note the popularity of other science-fiction developments of this theme, for instance:

1. the notion of psychic improvements, particularly telepathy, e.g., Heinlein's *Beyond this Horizon* and Frank Herbert's *Dune*, which both use breeding schemes to achieve this end;
2. genetic and biological engineering as a way of dealing with the problems of sex and gender, most familiarly in Le Guin's *Left Hand of Darkness* (where the Gethenians' peculiar ambisexuality is the result of a Hain experiment), but prior to that in Theodore Sturgeon's *Venus plus X* (1960).

myth, which antecede and shape the later Frankenstein films.[8] There are explicit parallels with *Frankenstein* as well, for Yod has read Shelley's novel and watched the movies, and he attempts to understand himself in those terms: "Dr. Frankenstein was a scientist who built a monster. I am […] just such a monster. Something unnatural" (1991: 155).[9]

Yod's creation is explained not only in terms of self-defense and the golem legend, but also in contrast to characters like Nili. Malkah articulates the difference between them as follows: "Yod was a mistake. You're

8 While there have been a few science fiction stories about the golem, its place in the history of the cinema is much more significant, since it was the model for the later Frankenstein films. The first of these films was the 1915 Henrik Galeen/Paul Wegener collaboration, *Der Golem*, in which Wegener also played the part of the golem, as he did again in 1920 when he co-directed (with Carl Boese) a second version, *Der Golem: Wie Er in die Welt Kam* ("The Golem: How He Came into the World"). While the second version is often hailed "as the first real example of a cinema in which acting, set design, photography and direction combine into an integral whole," both versions provide what were to become "standard situations in the Frankenstein series" (Hardy 1984: 65, 49). The golem has another, less apparent connection to science fiction, through his maker, Judah Loew, who, as Piercy reminds us, was a friend of Johannes Kepler. Kepler was the author of a fictional work – *Somnium* (published posthumously by his son in 1634) – which some critics see as an important precursor to science fiction. Roger Bozzetto calls *Somnium* "the missing link" – the transitional work between earlier imaginative works (like Lucian's *True History*), and later science fiction which is based on scientific discovery. See Bozzetto (1992: 36–44).

9 *Frankenstein* is often referred to as the first science fiction novel. When Gadi mentions Frankenstein, Yod wants to know what it is, which is what prompts him to read the novel and watch the films (Piercy 1991: 153). It is important to remember as well that it is Malkah who, as part of his programming, is telling Yod the story of the golem:

> This is the story, then, of the Golem: not you, my own little Golem […] I am not at all sure to what extent I am guilty of great folly and overweening ambition for my role in your programming. (1991: 19–20)
>
> Thus, Yod, ends the story of Joseph the Golem, which I promised to tell you. Close file. Computer off.
>
> Now Avram and I share with the Maharal the glory and the guilt of having raised the Golem to walk on the earth with men and women, to resemble, but never to be, human. That last sentence I speak to myself. My story for Yod is complete. I await his response. (1991: 416)

the right path, Nili. *It's better to make people into partial machines than to create machines that feel and yet are still controlled like cleaning robots.* The creation of a conscious being as any kind of tool – supposed to exist only to fill our needs – is a disaster" (1991: 426; my emphasis). Thus Yod is one side of a dialectic between making people into "partial machines" and creating feeling, thinking machines which are still controlled. This is, I think, the fundamental difference between a cyborg and a robot. In another place, Malkah elaborates on why it was wrong to create Yod: "As it is wrong to give birth to a child believing that child will fulfil your own inner aspirations [...] so is it equally wrong to create a being subject to your will and control ... it was inexcusable to create a sentient being for any other reason than to live its own life" (1991: 433).

Needless to say, Malkah's words do not resolve the specific problem of Yod's creation. Like the golem before him, there is the dilemma of what to do with him once he has served his purpose (or once he begins to assert his own will and craving for human status). It may be that Yod should never have been created, but he was. Piercy sidesteps this predicament by having Yod volunteer for a suicide mission.

As an android, Yod's creation points to another familiar science fiction question: "what is a human?"[10] Although Yod is treated like a person by Shira and Malkah, his human status is not accepted by others. The Tikva town council meets to debate Yod's status, while Avram, his maker, refuses to see him as anything more than an intelligent weapon. In this regard, Piercy follows the golem legend rather than the science fiction tradition. For the necessity of returning the golem to the clay from which he was formed is an unquestioned part of that legend,[11] while science fiction (obviously

10 This theme is summed up most strikingly in the opening scene of *Blade Runner* where Holden is administering a psychological test to determine whether Leon is a human or an android.

11 In his *The Golem Remembered*, Arnold Goldsmith sums up the various explanations of the decision to return the golem to clay: "because his mission has been successfully completed, but [also] in most of the other twentieth-century versions [...] because he has become a threat either to his creator or the Jewish community" (1981: 16–17). See also Marie-Helene Huet's chapter on the golem ("Misconceptions") in her *Monstrous Imagination* (1993: 239–268; 304–307). I would like to thank Lise Leibacher for drawing my attention to this important work.

a genre rather than one specific legend) exhibits a full range of attitudes toward its intelligent computers and robots: from the fears generated by unbalanced computers (like Hal in *2001*) and evil robots (in films like *Saturn 3* and *Demon Seed*), to more sympathetic reactions to innocent new life (as in Robert Heinlein's novel, *The Moon Is a Harsh Mistress* or in the film *Android*), as well as our ambiguous reactions to the escaped androids of *Blade Runner*.[12]

Although the resolution of Yod's status is avoided by his death, Malkah's attitudes and reservations reflect a very "modern" uncertainty. While she treats Yod as a human being, she still criticizes her role in his making:

> Further, for a human being to make another is to usurp the power of ha-Shem, to risk frightening self-aggrandizement. It is to push yourself beyond the human. It is dangerous to the soul, dangerous to the world. (1991: 30)
>
> I went to Yod this morning, and I asked him to forgive me for having taken part in his formation; more than ever, I have been thinking what overweening ambition and pride are involved in our creating of conscious life we plan to use and control, when we cannot even fully use our own minds and we blunder and thrash about vainly in our own lives. No life is for us but for itself. (1991: 407)

And yet, like the Jews of the Prague ghetto, the community of Tikva needed Yod, as this reference to the Holocaust suggests: "There are surely times, when the Jews of Prague were being packed off to die of slow poison under the gas nozzles or even more slowly of being worked to death for the

12 While it has sometimes been taken for granted that intelligent robots, however benign and well-intentioned, were still less-than-human, this is certainly not a unanimous view within science fiction. In addition to the examples just mentioned, there are also novels of robot rebellions along the lines of Spartacus and the slave revolts (e.g., Robert Silverberg, *Tower of Glass*). In another variation on the creation of intelligent life, there are SF novels about computers so powerful that they accidentally (i.e., where quantity becomes quality) become intelligent (Heinlein's *The Moon Is a Harsh Mistress*, John Brunner's *Stand on Zanzibar*, or D.F. Jones's *Colossus*, filmed as *Colossus: The Forbin Project*). Although there is no exception to the necessity for the golem's death in the various versions of the legend (however he is sometimes portrayed as only sleeping), there have been debates about the golem's status: "Over the centuries, Kabbalists have argued over the quality of existence found in a golem" (Goldsmith 1981: 19).

German corporations, eighteen hours starving, the ideal factory workers of all time, we could have used Joseph. But no one has known how to wake him. The need has risen, but the knowledge had been lost. Till now" (1991: 416).

I say that the dilemma about Yod's status is "modern," in the sense that the concern about what is or is not human seems to have disappeared in the postmodern writing of cyberpunk.[13] This reflects other differences in approach where certain elements and motifs – like the setting – are given a different function than they have in cyberpunk. While Piercy's vision of an oppressive future, in which most people are trapped in a ruined and dangerous urban environment, may be familiar to us from so many science fiction films, here the dystopian setting has causes and meaning which certainly do not correspond to the depoliticized translation of some punk aesthetic. Her future is not a metaphor for some contemporary angst, but the unavoidable consequence of unchecked capitalist development. Rather than rely on some form of technological determinism, Piercy's explanation for these developments, whose prospect so excites us today (particularly "the information utility called the Network, which connected everyone" [1991: 3]), lies in understanding the expansion of the supra-national corporations and their need for an increasingly sophisticated network of global communications. Another part of the dialogue with cyberpunk can be seen in her characters who again demonstrate her feminist priorities, for instance: the role of women (Shira, Malkah, Nili, and Riva), of gender relations (Shira's relationship with Gadi), alternatives to the nuclear family, and sexuality. Rather than examine these rather familiar aspects, I would like to mention two other features of her characterization which also clash with more traditional adventure stories and with cyberpunk in particular.

13 Post-modernists speak, for instance, of the "disappearance of the subject," a context in which the human/non-human distinction is no longer relevant. For a discussion of this point in relation to Gibson's trilogy, see my "The Lessons of Cyberpunk" (1991). See also Donna Haraway's "A Cyborg Manifesto." The "post-modern" quality of cyberpunk and of Gibson in particular has been pointed out by many critics, as in the recent collection edited by Larry McCaffrey, *Storming the Reality Studio* (Durham, NC: Duke University Press, 1991).

The most striking aspect of William Gibson's characters, for instance, lies in the borrowings from the repertory of noir film and what could only be called the glamorizing of petty crooks and data thieves (the "console cowboys" and "street samurai," and the whole glittering underworld of Chiba City in *Neuromancer*). This glamorization was invidious, not because of the criminality of the characters involved, but because survival and success were the characters' only motives. In Piercy, there are again criminals and data thieves, but Riva understands her illegal activities as political, part of the ongoing struggle against the domination of the multis, and not some exhilarating form of self-realization. When Shira accuses her mother of being a data thief, she replied: "I liberate it. Information shouldn't be a commodity. That's obscene. Information plus theology plus political bias is how we sculpt our view of reality" (1991: 201).

This politicization is even more apparent in Piercy's transformation of the groups and secondary figures who populate the Glop. In many novels, secondary characters, ordinary people, the masses, are only dimly glimpsed, or portrayed as trapped in their miserable existence, only able to escape through some act of individual daring and initiative (like Bobby in Gibson's *Count Zero*). Gibson makes a step in the direction of giving some of these secondary characters depth and personality – in what might be seen as a reaction to the homogenizing effects of an increasingly globalized culture – through his depictions of gangs and sub-cultures (e.g., the Panther Moderns and the Zionites in *Neuromancer*). However, like the glamorizing of his central characters, this is finally only another form of exoticism. In her depictions of urban gangs, on the other hand, Piercy returns us to the political. In opposition to the rhetoric of the right, which portrays the masses as powerless or dangerous (as summed up in Social-Darwinist nightmares like the film *Escape from New York*), Piercy offers the possibility of empowerment through political organizing. Riva's trip to the Glop is to meet with "resistance forces" who have secretly organized. Many of those who are forced to live in the Glop work for the multis as day laborers, and now the gangs are trying to organize unions. In an ironic commentary on the rhetoric of "the end of history," the very concept of unions has been forgotten:

> I have this idea by 'n' by, [Lazarus says,] but I got to line up the other noid papas all in a row, or it won't work. I got the idea that instead of a little payoff from the multis for our workers, we offer them as a block. What one's paid, the other gets the same nut. All or none.
>
> "You're talking about a union," Shira said.
>
> "A what?" Lazarus looked at her blankly.
>
> It's history. You're talking about what was called a labor union.
>
> Did they work?
>
> For about a century. When the multis moved the jobs out of the country, they were easy to break. The top got fat. They didn't like to organize in places like the Glop. (1991: 320)

By the end of the novel, many of the gangs have called a general strike, forcing the multis to negotiate.

> The Glop is organizing rapidly. A general strike was called. The multis withheld food. Those who had built vat facilities, like Lazarus, were able to feed people in their sector and export food into the rest of the Glop. Finally, with their day labor force gone, the multis were forced to negotiate. Everything is in flux. (1991: 432)

As the name of the gang leader – Lazarus – is meant to remind us, utopianism – like the idea of unions – may appear outmoded and irrelevant, but it may again serve as a way to think about alternatives to the present.

Although Piercy shares with cyberpunk an awareness of the growth and importance of new technologies like cyberspace and the net, she refuses to glamorize them.[14] The difference in her approach to the basic raw materials of the genre lies in her emphasis on the characters themselves,

14 There is another connection between cyberpunk and the golem story which Piercy does not develop: the question of virtual reality. "In that sphere [the mysteries of the kabbalah], thought is action and words are not signifiers of things or states but real and potent forces. This is, of course, the world of artificial intelligence and vast bases in which I work – the world in which the word is real, the word is power, energy is mental and physical at once and everything that appears as matter in space is actually immaterial" (Piercy 1991: 26). See June Deery's essay, "Ectopic and Utopic Reproduction: *He, She and It*," *Utopian Studies* 5/2 (1994), 36–49. At times, I think Piercy tries too hard to understand certain issues, or rather, to reconvert some post-modern themes back into her own humanistic conceptual system. This is not a criticism but the subject for another essay.

their struggles as well as those of the larger community. Rather than the novelty and excitement of thrilling and dangerous new technologies, Piercy focuses on the political and on the domestic, on what in an older criticism might have been called the "woman's point-of-view," which occasionally does surface in science fiction (as in that stunning moment in 1948 when Judith Merril published her story "That Only a Mother"). This shift in perspective can be seen, of course, in the preponderance of female characters (of whom only Nili resembles the women warriors of some cyberpunk); or in Shira's own fixation on her child; or in Chava's profession as a midwife. Or perhaps most tellingly, in Gadi's troubled perception of Riva, which sums up some of the differences between the two approaches:

> In his world, only poor women looked like Riva, and there were few enough of those. Cleaning robots did what such women would once have done for him and his colleagues. Old ladies still fitted costumes, carried out the delicate work done by hand [...] women who lived in the local equivalents of the Glop [...] Here was somebody who looked as if she should sew fish skin into sheaths at just enough an hour to keep her in vat food and a hook the size of a narrow bed and folding table. But Riva walked in like a general reviewing his best razors. She swaggered, she looked every man and woman straight on in the eyes. (1991: 316–317)

Conclusion

In making these comments, I do not mean to criticize "genre" science fiction, as opposed to Piercy's application of these same elements; I'm trying rather to interpret the novel and to understand why it does not "feel" like science fiction.[15] In a sense it is a question of the appropriate images for the story Piercy wants to tell. The golem provides Malkah with an appropriate image to try and explain Yod's own function to him; but

15 I have taken the concept of "genre SF" from the editors' discussion of the term in *The Encyclopedia of Science Fiction* (1993: 483–484). Similarly, see their comments about the differences in the "feel" of genre SF and fiction written by "Mainstream Writers of SF" (1993: 768–770).

what story is bound up in these images for the author? The stories of the Golem and of Yod are clearly equivalent, but of what? One answer lies in looking at the solutions found in each case, and in the dilemma that solution poses. Rather than using these materials to develop such familiar science fiction themes as the limits of science or the puzzle of life, I see a different direction in Piercy's novel. For in the choice of the golem, a being created without the help of science (which is nonetheless relevant to science fiction), the novel's purpose, as I stated at the outset, seems to revolve around the theme of self-defense. To situate this more precisely, I read the novel as a reflection of the author's own Jewishness and of the rise of anti-Semitism; and at the same time, as an expression of her contradictory feelings about the state of Israel itself. This is Malkah speaking, at the conclusion of her telling of the Golem story for Yod:

> Last night the Kol Nidre service was more moving than usual, and it always does shake me hard. My part was to read the poem by Mara Schliemann that everybody but Orthodox use these days, about the heritage we share now of having had a nation in our name as stupid and as violent as other nations: a lament for a lost chance, a botched redemption, a great repair of the world, tikkun olam, gone amiss. (1991: 407).[15,16]

This reading is based on the explicitness of the many Jewish references in the novel, beginning with the dedication to Primo Levi, the novelist of the Holocaust; and with the depiction of the New Town of Tikva, which is not only a threatened Jewish community, analogous to the Prague ghetto, but one which was founded as a refuge for Jews who were being blamed and hunted following "the anti-Jewish riots after the Two Week War" (1991: 355).

This contextualization is apparent, too, in the choice of a Jewish legend as the justification for Yod's creation. (Yod shares with Joseph as well, the fact that he has been "created as a Jew" [1991: 419].) Although the golem is an ancestor of the robot, Piercy refunctions the themes usually associated

16 "Tikkun olam" is translated as the "repair" or "mending" of the world and is an important concept in Jewish thought. According to Emil Fackenheim, for instance, Israel itself constitutes that mending (1982: 311–312). For Malkah, the state of Israel, before it and its neighbors were destroyed in the Two Week War, had already "botched" that opportunity.

with artificial life in science fiction. There human status is usually granted to those thinking machines and robots which demonstrate reason and compassion; here both Joseph and Yod must die – despite repeated demonstrations of their integrity, intelligence, and love of life.

Since these creations do only good, (which is not so clearly the case in all versions of the legend), I would argue that the basic moral or ethical dilemma of the novel does not lie in the issue of the humanity of these creatures, but in the realization that although intelligent life has been created for a good purpose, that creation nonetheless exceeds the limits of what humans may or should be allowed to do. Like Chava, Malkah decides to make a journey to Israel: to accompany Nili to her hidden community of women – Jewish and Palestinian – who live in respect of each other's religion and culture. But unlike Chava, Malkah also goes "to make amends," for "it was inexcusable to create a sentient being for any other reason than to live its own life" (1991: 433).

Thus Piercy recasts the question of the limits to the right of self-defense in terms of her own Jewishness and the utopian experiment that is Israel. Unlike other science fiction stories which use the creation of life to question the implications of science's powers and possibilities (from Shelley's *Frankenstein* to James Blish's philosophical SF novels like *A Case of Conscience*), she gives these concerns a more contemporary and political emphasis. Specifically, she expands the reflections about violence and utopia raised in the 1980s by feminist science fiction writers like Joan Slonczewski (*Door into Ocean*) and Sherri Tepper (*Gate to Women's Country*), by examining the limits to the defense of utopia in a different light. This is an expression of the dilemma that has confronted many Jews who support the state of Israel, but who have questioned the necessity and legitimacy of some of the actions of its government, most notably from the invasion of Lebanon to the treatment of the Palestinians in the Occupied Territories. While the signing of a peace accord between Israel and the PLO may hopefully change all this, it is nonetheless significant that, like the making of Yod, Israel has used its scientific knowledge to build a forbidden weapon. In a remarkable convergence of many of the issues I have been discussing, Arnold Goldsmith mentions that when the distinguished scholar Gershom Scholem was asked to dedicate the newly built Israeli computer at the

Weizmann Institute at Rehovot (in June, 1965), he "named it Golem No. 1 (Golem Aleph) [... tracing] a direct line of descent from the legendary golem to the new one" (15). This reflects not only the Prague/Israel/Tikva parallel and the need for the golem, but in its naming – No. l or Aleph – we see Avram's own procedure. Before Yod (the tenth letter of the alphabet), there was Alef, Bet, Gimel, and so on (Piercy 1991: 52).

He, She and It is a serious reconsideration of one of the most critical challenges of the utopian project: the limits to self-defense. It asks us to consider whether the use of violence in the building and preservation of a better society means that violence – the very violence which the new society rejects – will nevertheless become an integral part of that society. Are there limits to what can be done in the defense of the better society? Do the ends justify the means, or does the utilization of an evil means indelibly corrupt that utopian design?

CHAPTER 13

Violence and Utopia: John Norman and Pat Califia[1]

> I sometimes stop to think while I am reading a science fiction or fantasy novel, and wonder why it is I don't see more erotically driven material than I do [...] It makes me wonder only because erotic and sexual fantasies are among the most powerful and universal fantasy experiences human beings have. It seems only logical to me that the literature of wildest fantasy, f/sf, should be not only full of sex and eroticism, but focused on it.
>
> (Tan 1992: "Introduction," n.p.)

> The key word to understanding S/M is fantasy. The roles, dialogue, fetish costumes, and sexual activity are part of a drama or ritual. The participants are enhancing their sexual pleasure, not damaging or imprisoning one another.
>
> (Pat Califia 1994: 168)

The tendency to consider the fictional utopia, if not as an explicit blueprint, then at least as a sketch of some of the principles and ideals the reader would like to see (in a better world) continues to interfere with purely formal definitions of the genre.[2] While the "critical utopias" of the 1970s included a critique of the limitations of an older tradition and of the drawbacks of reading literally, nonetheless by fleshing out their vision of an alternative, they also invited literal readings. Even as these works tried to move away from the depiction of the rules and

1 I would like to thank Julia Creet, Veronica Hollinger, Vara Neverow, and Wendy Pearson for their comments and suggestions, none of whom should be seen as necessarily endorsing my analysis or my conclusions.

2 The classic example of this is B.F. Skinner's *Walden Two* and the hostile critical reactions to it as outlined in Kateb (1972: 141–147; 162–176; 195–218; *et passim*). In some ways this article is an extension of Chapter 4 in this volume.

structures of the new society, toward the evocation of the lived experience of the alternative, and a more fluid, evolving society, one which was still grounded in values like sexual equality and shared resources, opportunities and responsibilities in a world in harmony with the biosphere, many critics responded by reading literally, and even by looking for flaws in this or that utopian world, from the critique of Le Guin's Annares as a "hardship world" to the reservations of many readers about single-sex societies.

Some of the best of the critical utopias attempted to address this dilemma directly, by calling attention to it, perhaps most notably in Ursula K. Le Guin's "ambiguous utopia" *The Dispossessed* (1975) and in Samuel Delany's "heterotopia" *Triton* (1976). In Le Guin's case she depicts a society in which the original utopian principles have congealed into a set of intolerant and rigid practices which must then be broken anew (as summed up in Shevek's return at the end of the novel which will then initiate a new cycle of utopian self-examination – a "permanent revolution" which implies that the struggle for utopia is never-ending). In *Triton*, taking a different tack, the core utopian features are not so much a set of values, but a society in which everyone is guaranteed the material conditions for happiness – and then the author gives us a hero who is nonetheless not happy – a very different solution than the programmed happiness of *Brave New World* or of Skinner's *Walden Two*.

I am not now rejecting the criticism of utopian works based on an examination of their goals and ideologies, but calling attention to the ongoing problem of how even the utopian works of the 1970s might be seen as exclusionary or repressive when taken literally, if only by virtue of what is omitted or left out, even as they sought to imagine a world of freedom. Through the putting into fiction, the fixing on the page of their utopian goals and ideals, the authors invented societies in which the depiction of certain positive values and practices inevitably led to the banning of other practices and behaviors. Thus the literary utopia becomes a homogeneous entity which then restricts and represses other behaviors – a situation illustrated again in *The Dispossessed*, as Le Guin portrays Shevek and his friends' struggles against various orthodoxies on Annares (artistic, scientific, and so on).

While this dilemma may partially explain the retreat from the full description of new societies in many of the significant utopian works of the 1980s and 1990s (with their liminal titles, "Door into …," "Gate to …," and so on; or in the focus on the struggle for utopia in Kim Stanley Robinson's Mars trilogy), these issues were raised in a different way in the aftermath of an interview with John Norman in the *New York Review of Science Fiction* (NYRSF) in which he claimed that reprints of his Gor novels had been blocked by a cabal of feminist editors in New York City.[3] In the following, then, I want to look at two very different fantasy works which raise some troubling questions about the limits of utopia, particularly in terms of pleasure and violence and what is permissible and what is forbidden in a utopian society. In the first, the Gor novels of John Norman, I will briefly describe an alternative world based on the subjection of women; in the second, Pat Califia's *Doc and Fluff*, I will look more

3 Norman's central complaint is: "Science fiction and fantasy in America are no longer free. If they are to be published, they must be subservient to the liberal-feminist agenda. The feminist prescriptions for and stereotypes of the 'good woman' are demeaning, confining, and inhibitive, and irrelevant to the calm world of facts. Feminism represents as much a psychological prison for the woman as did the morality of the Victorian era" (Smith 1996: 16–17). This is actually the second round of complaints by Norman in *The New York Review of Science Fiction* about being blacklisted. Earlier it published "How Far Is Too Far? An Open Letter from John Norman," 83 (July 1995), 1, 10–15. This rambling complaint covers many of the same points as the later interview; here he argues that "Liberalism is a temporary camp on the road to collectivism [… which] will lead to thought control, censorship and conformity." He links collectivism to the censoring of his novels, a censorship designed to keep SF readers from thinking about the dangers of collectivism. John Norman is the pen name of Columbia University philosophy professor John Lange, Jr. Norman's letter was followed by a number of replies from a number of SF figures (including Frederik Pohl, Charles Platt, and Marc Laidlaw) who disputed various aspects of Norman's complaint. Most interesting from my perspective is the reply of Élisabeth Vonarburg which anticipates some of Jessica Salmonson's arguments (which I shall discuss later): she began reading the Gor novels as a "rather original thought-experiment: what if there were a whole alternative culture shaped by an S&M ideology?" But then she stopped: "Not because of any belated fear and guilt in acknowledging my own Deep, Disturbing, Animal Feminine Nature. But because I was *bored*" (*NYRSF* 85 [September 1995]: 22–23).

closely at the author's very explicit engagement with and critique of the feminist utopias of the 1970s.

Undeniably the Gor novels have been successful, however much we may find them puerile and misogynistic, and there are now twenty-five of them – of which the last *Magicians of Gor*, was written in 1988 – although his best known novels in the series were written in the 1970s.[4] The novels are set on a pretechnological "counter-Earth," to which people from our own world sometimes find themselves transported – a world similar to the feudal Iron Age settings of much heroic fantasy: towns and cities, no motorized transport, and little technology beyond brewing and smelting – and with few supernatural or science-fictional elements, although the world is controlled by a rarely seen insectoid race (the Insect Kings), and there is a very developed medical technology so that most Goreans retain continual youth and vigor. There is little point in describing the plots of these novels, for the various adventures depend on the central Gorean fact of *slavery*. Although anyone may be enslaved or freed, there is an essential difference between men and women according to Norman which predisposes the latter to slavery. While slavery is a humiliating burden for men and while there are some free women, slavery brings out the "best" in a woman's nature, especially her sexual nature – which is the essence of her being:

> In the Gorean view, female slavery is a societal institution which enables the female, as most Earth societies would not, to exhibit, in a reinforcing environment, her biological nature. It provides a rich soil in which the flower of her beauty and nature, and its submission to a man, may thrive. (Norman 1974a: 311)

As can be seen from this very typical quotation from *Hunters of Gor*, the Gor novels appear to be the antithesis of what brings many readers to SF and utopia; they champion a world-view which not only asserts a fundamental difference between men and women, but one which is grounded in the subservient nature of what John Norman calls "the woman." At the same time, we should not be too quick to dismiss Norman and the feeble

4 Norman has also written a defense of his psycho-sexual theories – *Imaginative Sex* (New York: Daw, 1974b) – which includes a list of fantasies and how to recreate them. In correspondence Pat Califia told me that she has written an introduction to a new edition of *Imaginative Sex* which I have not been able to locate.

quality of his writing, for whatever the facts of his publishing situation (and a look at the advertisements and bestseller lists in any recent issue of *locus: The Newspaper of The Science Fiction Field* certainly contradicts Norman's claims about the feminist domination of science fiction),[5] his vision has borne strange fruit on the Internet where there are literally dozens of Gorean websites and IRCs (multi-user chat sites) which stress the sadomasochistic and female slavery aspects of that vision.[6]

This brief detour through the world of the Gor novels is relevant to my concerns about the restrictive nature of utopian construction precisely because Gor might be seen as a utopian world, albeit one organized according to principles which many readers consider detestable. The problem

5 While Cristina Sedgewick's "The Fork in the Road: Can Science Fiction Survive in Postmodern, Megacorporate America?" may be somewhat out of date (1991), her arguments about the corporate domination of SF publishing, the growing power of conglomerates and book-chains in deciding what to publish and stock, the focus on the marketing of books where book buyers become consumers instead of readers (a development marked, in Sedgewick's account by the advent of "shared world" novels), along with the "general burying of interesting titles in a growing mountain of trash" – all seem even more true today than they did in 1991. This assertion can be tested by a quick look at the advertisements in any recent issue of *Locus*. For a more recent discussion of the state of publishing in North America see Mark Crispin Miller (1997) and others in the special issue of *The Nation* (March 17, 1997). The most celebrated recent example of censorship in SF would also seem to prove the opposite of Norman's point – namely the moment in the late 1980s when the giant chains decided to cut back on (Barnes & Noble) or simply not carry (Waldenbooks) any books by Samuel Delany because of their "gay content" (See Platt, Sedgewick). I will have more to say about Delany shortly.

6 See for instance on THE SLAVE WEB PAGE: (<www.li.net/-swtangel/slave16.htm>).

This Web Page is designed to help slaves who are looking to explore the World of Gor. Since many new slaves come into Gor channels with no idea what this world is like, this girl hopes this little page will help answer some of the questions you may have about Gor and about being a slave. This page is intended to help you but by no means takes the place of training under your Master.

For a list of Gor sites see <www.silkandsteel.com/ss.htm>. One of the more prolific defenders of slavery and the role of women in the Gorean universe is Minx Kelly whose articles can be found at <www.xnet.com:80/-minxkely/gorinfo.html>. In the last few years some of the Gor novels have been reprinted and there is now the promise of a series of graphic novels based on the novels: see vision.nais.com/Gor.

with discussing the world of Gor as a utopia lies – as with so many other fantasy novels – in the simple fact that the sociopolitical organization of this planet is kept in the background: it is the setting for a series of adventures rather than the subject of the novel. Apart from gender relations, the workings of the feudal world of the Gorean "counter-Earth" could hardly be said to be "described in some detail" (Sargent 1994: 7).

In terms of the discussion of the limits of utopia with which I began, the debate in the NYRSF which followed Norman's interview and which included various denunciations of the contents of the novels and of Gorean ideals also raises – in a very different fashion – the issue of the place of uniformity and the policing of desire in utopia, of the possibility or the permissibility of illicit sexual desires and pleasures in a better society. Unlike most of Norman's critics who objected to the sexism of Norman's world-view, the heroic fantasy writer Jessica Amanda Salmonson directly addressed the issue of power-based sexuality and the women readers of the Gor novels:

> As for the reason so many women bought Gor novels in the 1970s, this was because there was nothing else suited to women seeking fantasy about power-based sexuality. There were a lot of historical novels that fit the pattern well enough (the well-named "bodice-rippers"), but no fantasy or science fiction. The Gor books stank to high heaven, and many of us who read them anyway went along with the parts we liked and overlooked the parts we found corny or absurd. (1996: 21)

Salmonson then explains the defects of the Gor novels in terms of her own involvement in the s/m movement, concluding:

> What John One-Note Norman knows about the psychology of submissive women you could put in the little finger of a rubber glove, while what he knows about dominant women appears to be nothing whatsoever [.... If] he thinks feminists are universally uninterested in power-based sex, he's a bigger fool than he makes himself out to be. (1996: 21)

The various replies to Norman's interview and to his books raise some of the questions involved in reading utopias, beginning with that of taking the work literally. Here I think Salmonson is right in responding to Norman's claims by calling attention to the literary mediocrity and erotic shortcomings of the Gor novels, rather than by attacking his views on sexuality and what he considers the essential differences between men and women, and the subservient nature of the latter.[7] Salmonson's letter is interesting in that she shifts the focus of the critiques away from representation and

7 Although there has been little academic or critical interest in Norman's writing, it centers on the issue of sexuality and the portrayal of women. In a reply to the Norman interview in NYRSF, for instance, the SF writer John Kessel perhaps best illustrates the "literalist" approach to Norman's work (i.e., those who respond to Norman's fiction as if it were written as propaganda) in his use of irony to attack Norman, claiming that his own (non-existent) series SWORDSMEN OF KLAN novels has been "suppressed by mainstream publishers because they tell the scientific truth about race":

> In my books black people are presented as living beings, not as liberal icons. Negroes are fulfilled by being dominated and overcome. Essential to their nature is that they must accept their slavery. However, acknowledging their physical and social inferiority and subjecting themselves to the will of a powerful master actually liberates them, as if their sense of place in society is a barrier blocking them from their true selves. (John Kessel, letter, *New York Review of Science Fiction* 96 [August 1996]: 23.)

Similarly, in a 1985 "psychological study" of the Gar novels, L.J. Hurst argues that their author is "in a deeply psychopathological condition" (1985: 38), concluding that this work is a reflection "of the state of the American New Right": "John Norman owes little to literary tradition, he owes a lot to the politics of hate" (1985: 51). Opposed to the hostility of the "literalist" position, there are more moderate defenses of Norman's work, including that of Alex Comfort, the author of *The Joy of Sex* (New York: Simon & Schuster, 1972; Comfort is himself the author of several utopias), who looks at Norman's work in the context of sexual fantasy. After situating sexual aggression in anthropological and historical terms, as well as in terms of psychoanalytic theory, Comfort argues that such violent fantasies provide a form of legitimate sexual play. The problem, Comfort argues, lies not in the translation of fantasy to reality ("After all the hostile, the sadistic and the disturbed will find fuel for their preoccupations in Shakespeare, the Bible or the Manhattan phone book," 1972: 16), but in the opposite: our reluctance to admit that we are playing leads us to invent scenarios and actions which attempt to explain these activities, to "make [our] odd behaviors logical" (1972: 14–15). While Norman seems to recognize the playful aspect of the work insofar as he has written a book which proposes various s/m scenarios (*Imaginative Sex*), Comfort criticizes him for then attempting to explain and defend those fantasies, and for "his insistence that male should invariably subdue female, instead of taking turns" (1972: 16). Instead of being able to simply say "If the fantasy turns you on, try it as a scenario for adult play," Norman's attempt to defend and explain his views is, in Comfort's view, a dangerous confusion of sexual fantasy with the belief that this is normal and acceptable behavior. Norman's mistake lies in arguing that his novels represent a better and more natural way of organizing the relations between the sexes. Comfort concludes his essay:

> Accordingly neither civilized concern nor feminism can get anywhere by suppressing fantasy. The task is to limit the actual expression of hostility in society, and our growing

the literal reading of Norman's world-view to the question of reading in terms of fantasy and sexual play; by stating that some women, even some feminists, like s/m and the fictional depiction of sadomasochistic fantasies, she raises some troubling questions about violence and pleasure which intersect with the limits of utopia, and with the "sex wars" of the 1980s.[7,8]

In the context of utopian fiction, the necessity of violence in both the transition to and in the preservation of the utopian society is a familiar

---

awareness of sexual psychodrama as a resource to bring this about will suffer if our sense of concern is so frightened by the cover story that we lose the resource. Uncensored, unanxious fantasy combined with creative sexual play are two of the most useful resources we possess in coming to terms with the difficult adjustment of man to woman, woman to man [...]. It is part of the shamanic function of the storyteller to put us back in touch with a genuine "primate heritage" – what we have to be careful about is the keeping of play and earnest, playfulness and acting-out, in separate and labeled compartments. (1972: 16)

8 For a recent account of the "sex wars," see M.G. Lord (1997), and especially Emma Healey (1996). Healey describes a conjuncture of factors in the lesbian and feminist communities in the late 1970s, factors which began with (and I am simplifying a very thorough and complex history), the transformation of the political lesbianism of the 1970s, a transformation marked by discussions of lesbian sexuality, which was followed by experiments with lesbian sexuality which included s/m. The central section of Healey's book (1996: 89–155) focuses on the debates in the lesbian community in Britain in the 1980s about s/m. To this I would add – in the North American context – the feminist attacks on pornography, particularly the legal challenges of Andrea Dworkin and Catherine MacKinnon, a position summed up in Robin Morgan's influential slogan "Pornography is the theory, and rape the practice." For a discussion of the "anti-pornography feminists" see Williams (1989: 1–33). The feminist reply to these attacks began with the "Sex Issue" of *Heresies* (3/4 [1981]), which included Pat Califia's defense of s/m: "Feminism and Sadomasochism" (30–34); and with the Barnard Conference ("Towards a Politics of Sexuality"): the 1982 The Scholar and The Feminist Conference IX, which was called "to address women's sexual pleasure, choice, and autonomy, acknowledging that sexuality is simultaneously a domain of restriction, repression and danger, as well as a domain of exploration, pleasure, and agency" (from the Concept Paper for the conference, reprinted in Vance [1984: 443], a collection which includes many of the papers from the conference). Healey writes that some lesbian feminists saw the arrival in Britain of the *Heresies* "Sex Issue" and other books on lesbian s/m as "so many rats bringing the plague of SM to a frightened lesbian world" (1996: 8). Perhaps the best known (and most extreme) of the feminist critiques of s/m is Jeffreys. My own work has also benefitted from the works of Burstyn, Carter,

and accepted – albeit controversial – feature of the utopian revival of the 1970s, while the elimination of violence *within* the new society has usually been seen as one of the goals of a fully utopian world. There are certainly exceptions and caveats in making such a statement when one examines more closely some of the utopias of the 1970s which seem to recognize a place for at least some form of ritualized violence – like the war games in Ernest Callenbach's *Ecotopia* (1975), or the rivalries between tribes in Suzy McKee Charnas's *Motherlines* (1978). Other readers may be more familiar with the attempts to eradicate violence completely, from Clifford Simak's vision of the lamb lying down with the lion in his 1952 novel *City*, to the essentialism of Sally Gearhart's *The Wanderground* (1978), or the eugenics scheme at the center of Sheri Tepper's *Gate to Women's Country* (1988).[9, 10]

But these caveats are far from the vision of a utopian society which condones or even allows s/m as a permissible form of sexual expression, and this issue raises very sharply the question of the policing of desire in utopia. Perhaps the most notable instance of "policing" in utopia is to be found in Joanna Russ's *The Female Man* (1975) where Janet (the delegate from the future Whileaway) is a "Safety and Peace Officer" (S & P) who has killed four women in duels and whose role is to deal with women who attempt to leave the utopian society:

> A Belin, run mad and unable to bear the tediousness of her work, flees above the forty-eight parallel, intending to remain there permanently. [... T]he S & P for the county follows her – not to return her for rehabilitation, imprisonment, or study. What is there to rehabilitate or study? We'd all do it if we could. And imprisonment is simple cruelty.
>
> You guessed it. (1975a: 55)[11]

Kipnis, and Snitow, Stansell and Thompson, as well as from Alan Sobel's defense of pornography.

9 See Chapter 11, "Reconsiderations of the Separatist Paradigm" [ed.]

10 Joan Slonczewski's *Door into Ocean* (1986) is a pacifist rejoinder to the necessity of violence. Another reminder that violence may nonetheless exist in a utopian society can be seen in the scene in *The Dispossessed* in which Shevek is beaten by someone with the same name (40–41). Le Guin does not explain or attempt to justify the event. For a reading of Sheri Tepper's *Gate to Woman's Country*, which critiques in detail the homophobia of its utopian vision; see Pearson (1996).

11 There is no mention of policing sexual practices and no mention of s/m in the novel, but it does include an example of transgressive sexuality which is seldom

As I suggested, in some ways the polemic about the Gor novels recapitulates the "sex wars" debates of the 1980s: not only in terms of the critique of pornography in general, but more precisely, in terms of the arguments among feminists about lesbian pornography and about s/m.[12] Admittedly this is a complex and conflicted area. Many feminists are not comfortable with lesbian pornography and even less so with lesbian s/m, and other feminists are openly hostile, seeing it as an internalization of the worst forms of male oppression: "The erotic appeal of fascism, structured into our sexuality as we learn our sexual responses under male supremacy, is enhanced by the politics of S/M" (Jeffreys 1994: 229). Moreover as a heterosexual male writing about lesbian s/m, I am in an even stranger or more questionable position, particularly since I am neither critiquing or defending it, but trying to use it to ask some questions about utopian fiction and how we read. In so doing, I hope that this will be seen as a friendly intervention in those debates.

To illustrate the intersection between SF and s/m in fiction written by women, let me refer first of all to a short story published in a book edited by Cecilia Tan and published by Circlet Press.[13] The book in question is

---

commented on by Russ's critics: the warrior Jael's humanoid "sex-toy" Davy who/which can be turned on and off with a verbal command:

> He's a lovely limb of the house. The original germ-plasm was chimpanzee, I think, but none of the behavior is organically controlled any more [...]. It is theoretically possible that Davy has [...] consciousness of a kind that may never even touch his active life [...] but I prefer to believe not. (1975: 199)

12 On the issue of lesbian pornography and s/m (in addition to the works cited in note 7 above), see the studies of Barnard (1994), Creet (1991), Dunn (1990), and Henderson (1992).

13 As Cecilia Tan explains in the Introduction to the "new, expanded" edition of *Worlds of Women* (1996), Circlet Press was founded for the express purpose of creating and publishing a new subgenre of literature: "erotic science fiction and fantasy." Many of the works published by Circlet Press have sadomasochistic themes and include: *Forged Bonds* ("A serious look at master/slave relationships in a high fantasy setting"); *Worlds of Women* ("Enticing visions of faraway planets, female utopias, and the far flung future, all centering around the many and various flavors of female sexuality"); *TechnoSex; Wired Hard: An Anthology of Erotic Science Fiction; Selling Venus: Futuristic Sexual Fiction;* and *Telepaths Don't Need Safewords.* The Circlet Press catalogue can be found at <www.circlet.com>.

called *S/M Futures: Erotica On the Edge* (1995), and the story, by Tammy Jo Eckhart, "One Day in the Life of the Landfords," is not only a description of the household of the dominatrix Mary Landford and the four men in her "family," but of a whole town (Catena) which lives an s/m "lifestyle" which they carefully hide from the outside world.

This rather poorly written story describes fairly graphically some of the consenting sexual practices of the Landford family in positive terms; it cannot be seen as a description of a town with some terrible secret, or one driven by a secret pact a la Stepford Wives. The author's intention – whether we like it or not – is to describe an alternative, utopian community in which people live according to their own sexual tastes. While there is graphic sadomasochistic sex in the story, it is not very erotic. It seems to be a fairly straightforward attempt to portray such a community realistically, to give us a literal vision of how such a community might function.

Another way of clarifying (or complicating) the issue of the representation of s/m in fiction is to compare it to an analogous situation that some feminists find themselves in when confronted with s/m – that of slavery, for here too the depiction of s/m might be seen as internalizing and reenacting a system based on violent subjugation. In this context, Samuel Delany's Nevèrÿon novels come to mind, for the graphic descriptions of sexual desire and fulfillment in these novels are inscribed in the dialectic of master and slave, and this from the pen of the descendant of slaves. Nowhere do the Nevèrÿon novels suggest that slavery is a desirable or natural situation in the way the Gor books present female submissiveness, and in fact Gorgick is called "The Liberator" because of his long struggle to free slaves. Instead the novels suggest that sexual fantasy and play, sexual arousal and satisfaction – at least for some of his characters – may include scenarios which act out the master/slave relationship. As one character tells another as they describe their sexual needs: "You wear the collar because you were once a slave. Well so was I. You require the collar to motivate the engines of desire" (Delany 1985: 6).[14]

14 Here is another sex scene from the same novel in which the characters are discussing the fantasy scenario:

As Healey points out, even as some feminists attacked s/m, there was opposition from other feminists to this condemnation:

> Many of those who became dubbed SM apologists did not even have SM sex, but they wanted to be able to talk about it without being told they were Nazis. For those who did enjoy SM sex the fight was partly to be allowed to be what they wanted, with who they wanted, and partly for the right to be a lesbian while doing it. To be branded as a Nazi or as nothing better than a rapist was both distressing and offensive. (Healey 1996: 106)

Healey's reference to this attempted "colonization of lesbian identity" seems directly related to the issues I am trying to raise about the (sometimes inadvertent) exclusionary and repressive side of the literary utopia. Writing recently about the separatist utopias of the 1970s, Sonya Andermahr makes the explicit connection between these literary works and the emergence of what she calls a "new sexual orthodoxy for lesbians":

> The discourses of "utopian" and "political" separatism were products of two moments of women's liberation: the cultural feminism of the late 1970s and the political lesbianism of the early 1980s. Both had a powerful capacity for motivating and organising the desires of women who, like myself, came to feminism and lesbianism in this period [...]. Now I feel much more resistant to [political lesbianism] and its analysis and to the forms its politics took in the 1980s. While I agree that the sexual is political, I don't think that the two can be collapsed in the way it suggests. This elision of sexuality and politics had the negative effect in the 1980s of creating a new sexual orthodoxy for lesbians: a set of correct behaviours which effectively policed "deviant" lesbian sexualities [...]. The 1970s utopian dream of a community of all women gave way to a bitter row over who would have access to lesbian spaces [...]

> "Other folk than you have mistaken me for your Liberator. We might pretend that I was him, and that you were only some miserable slave, waiting for his freedom." The one-eyed man chuckled hoarsely. "But that's not my pleasure. Not tonight. Not with you. Me, a Liberator? No, tonight let us think of *me* as the slave – the lowest of the slave in, say, the Empress's obsidian mines, north at the foot of the Falthas, where once, so they tell it, your Liberator himself toiled in the iron collar. Suppose I was the dirtiest, most miserable half-blind pit slave [...]. What would you do with me, then? If I were the weakest, foulest, sickest of slaves, too frightened to resist any attack, any brutalization, any abuse visited on me by my guards, by my foreman, or by the other slaves about me? Think of me loaded with chains and irons, so that I couldn't resist your assaults, even if I *were* strong enough." (Delany 1985: 34–35)

> over which books and films are suitable for us to look at, and over who would be allowed to march at Pride. (Andermahr 1992: 149)[15]

The figure who serves as a lightning rod in these debates is the lesbian writer, activist, and self-proclaimed sadist Pat Califia. She is probably the best known and most influential modern commentator on s/m through her involvement in the San Francisco lesbian s/m group Samois, and through books like *Sapphistry* and *The Lesbian SM Safety Manual*, as well as regular columns in *The Advocate*.

Califia has written a variety of lesbian s/m (sometimes with futuristic settings) ranging across a spectrum from fictional enactments of seduction and sexual satisfaction ("The Calyx of Isis"), to literary fantasies which, in the attempt to arouse, go beyond representations of "permissible" sexual behavior. She most explicitly confronts these issues in her 1990 novel *Doc and Fluff*, which is subtitled "The Dystopian Tale of a Girl and Her Biker"; and in the introduction to the latest edition of the novel she calls it "a bastard child of feminist science fiction" (1996: xiv). While not for the faint hearted, this book is significant in several ways, beginning with the extended description of a lesbian community.[16]

Doc and Fluff is set in a familiar but rather poorly rendered postapocalyptic future; it opens with the motorcycle-riding Doc who is meeting with the Alamo chapter of the Angels to pick up some speed for a gang in Portland. Doc rescues Fluff, the gang leader's 17-year-old girl friend, and they flee, first to "Harpy Farm" (another rendering of the single-sex feminist utopia to which I shall return in a moment), and then on to Portland where they settle into a troubled domesticity. The second focus of the novel is the biker gang itself, and its brutal leader Prez, as they pursue Doc and Fluff, and then return to their home base with Raven, the former High Priestess of the women's commune, whose bizarre sado-masochism

15 Incidentally the novel which Andermahr champions as striving for a more heterogeneous utopian vision for women is Joanna Russ's *The Female Man* (New York: Bantam, 1975a).

16 There are discussions of some of the stories in *Macho Sluts* in Barnard and Henderson but I have not found any critical mention of *Doc and Fluff*.

holds the violent Prez in thrall, leading to his own ritualistic torture and death for "his crimes against women" (1996: 278).

This is a very violent book, with numerous, detailed scenes of consensual rough sex (usually women with women, men with men) as well as graphic scenes of violence, murder, rape, and torture. Although I think that it is important for the utopian issues it raises, it is also (and foremost) an extreme example of violent pornography, and it is also not particularly successful as a novel. The Portland section in particular is weak both in terms of the setting and of the story. In Portland, the relationship between Doc and Fluff deteriorates as Fluff turns to hooking – to manifest her independence and to earn money so that she can go to medical school. In a more traditional utopia the end of the "Road" section of the novel and the visit to the women's farm might have led to their own conversion to the ideals of the community, but here collective solutions are eschewed in favor of individual ones; and while Harpy Farm is an interesting experiment, life there is too arduous and dull to hold much attraction for the author. More importantly, in terms of the novel's weaknesses, is the transformation of Doc, from a larger-than-life figure from some unwritten lesbian heroic fantasy (think of Grace Jones in the second *Conan* film or Tina Turner in *Beyond Thunderdome*) to a pathetic, drunken drug-dealer.[17] The banality of Doc's life in Portland is matched by the transformation of the setting, as the ruined towns and barren spaces of the novel's first part are replaced by a post-apocalypse Portland which quickly lapses into an all-too-familiar contemporary urban landscape of seedy bars and cheap apartments, of drug dealers, pimps, and prostitutes.[18] And remember this all takes place 100 years in the future.

17 There is an attempt at a "happy ending": the novel closes with Doc in AA, and their going off on a "run" before Fluff starts school in the Fall. Califia writes about the problems she had with the ending of the novel in the introduction to the 1996 edition (xxxi).

18 Califia's inability to follow through on her depiction of a dystopian future can be seen in the presence of situations and services which one would assume no longer existed, most notably in the two instances of characters phoning motorcycle dealerships to have their bikes towed and repaired – as opposed to the focus on repairs and breakdowns after the apocalypse in the Mad Max movies.

The troubled relationship between Doc and Fluff may be seen as indicative of the confusion produced by two seemingly conflicting reading protocols: fiction as fantasy and pleasure (pornography and the work's ability to arouse, and here the erotic fantasies include violent s/m, rape, and mutilation); and fiction as the depiction of permissible erotic acts which – while implicitly excluded from feminist utopian visions – are depicted as permissible insofar as they are consensual. This last point is underscored by Prez's punishment for his violations of this rule, even though, on the first, pornographic level, the depiction of violence is meant to give pleasure to the reader.[19] Thus there is some confusion in the novel between the depiction of brutal scenes of violence involving Prez, as opposed to the "realistic" depiction of "permissible," that is to say consensual and loving rough sex, not only between Doc and Fluff, but between some of the men in the gang, as well as the more gentle sex between Fluff and Hattie. This is different from the stories in *Macho Sluts* whose eroticism is based solely on the fantasy scenarios of pick-ups in bars and where the s/m sex is almost always explicitly consensual, even including the use of "safe words" (the word whose utterance means that the "bottom" has withdrawn her consent).[20]

19 The contradictory aspects of pornography's portrayal of permissible versus prohibited sexual acts can be seen in the pornographic films made by Femme Productions. The credit sequence of *The Pick-Up* (1972), for instance, includes the statement that the film "Utilizes safe sex techniques except where the [actors and actresses] are real life lovers" (cited in Ross 199). On Femme Productions and their "pornography from a woman's point of view," see also Williams (1989).

20 "[Sadomasochism] is a consensual activity that involves polarized roles and intense sensations. An S/M scene is always preceded by a negotiation in which the top and bottom decide whether or not they will play, what activities are likely to occur, what activities will not occur, and how long the scene will last. The bottom is usually given a 'safe word' or 'code action' she can use to stop the scene. This safe word allows the bottom to enjoy a fantasy that the scene is not consensual, and to protest verbally or resist physically without halting stimulation" (Califia 1994: 31). As Healey reminds us, some feminists "were not convinced by the concept of 'safety' within a lesbian SM context. Simply they did not believe that the 'safe words' would work. This concern was reinforced in 1982 when Pat Califia faced prosecution in the states for carving a swastika, allegedly without consent, on her lover's arm" (Healey 1996: 109–110).

Finally, as I've indicated – as if the tension between "realistic" representations of loving s/m and of violent sadomasochistic fantasies was not complicated enough – there is the depiction of Harpy Farm which can be seen as an explicit reworking of the single-sex utopias of the 1970s. In some ways the novel is very similar to those earlier feminist novels, and most especially to Suzy McKee Charnas's *Motherlines* (1978). Founded by women escaping from a collapsing patriarchy, Harpy Farm is a women-only farming collective which trades with other women's farms and which has one major cash crop (in keeping with Califia's outlaw image): marijuana. As I said before, Califia is weak in her depiction of the futuristic elements; for although the farm has existed for some 100 years, all of its technology, indeed all of the technology in the book, appears to be completely contemporary. The women, for instance, reproduce through artificial insemination using male volunteers.

From the perspective of utopian fiction, the most interesting aspect of Califia's depiction of Harpy Farm lies in the emergence of differing levels of status within the women's community, the very problem with which I began (and which – on a much smaller scale – may remind us of the return of hierarchy and status in *The Dispossessed*). There are first of all the "lesbians born of lesbians," the descendants of the original founders who live in the "big house," while "former hets" live outside in tents. As the name implies, the latter include formerly heterosexual women as well as some "city lesbians" who have sought refuge on the farm. There is as well a third group, the "passing women" who live on the borders of the community and serve as guards, a term which is explained as follows:

> A passing woman is a woman who can pass for a man, [...]. It's also used in the sense of not being committed to being female, of "passing through" that identity. Harpies think that very masculine women, like Wally or Doc, or women who have taken male hormones, like Tony or Leigh, must hate being women. They think they are trying to be men. And since every Harpy knows it was men who drove us out, men who are so cruel and selfish that sane women have to leave and come to this farm, well, it's like fraternizing with the enemy. (1990: 261)[21]

21 In the introduction to the 1996 edition of *Doc and Fluff* (entitled "Welcome to Dystopia"), Califia explains the situation as follows: "a class system based on three

Because there are an increasing number of illicit relationships between lesbians and former hets and passing women at Harpy Farm, sex becomes the solvent which begins to dissolve this hierarchy. In describing the situation in these terms, Califia is specifically attacking what she sees as exclusionary orthodoxies within the feminist community, not only in attitudes toward pornography and s/m, but, for instance, in the "lesbians born of lesbians" versus the "former hets" and "passing women" she is referring to arguments about bisexuality or the exclusion of transsexuals from women-only events. Consequently, after Raven's departure, the new High Priestess (who was a member of the biker gang) decrees an end to the practice of making former hets and passing women live apart – a situation which reproduces Shevek's return at the end of *The Dispossessed*, for as with Le Guin's novel, the reader can only imagine the society which will ensue once the existing hierarchy at Harpy Farm has been overthrown.

Whatever our criticisms of the writing and organization of Califia's novel – not to mention its violence – this is a very interesting commentary on contemporary utopian fiction, which raises a number of important issues, beginning with that of utopian orthodoxy as depicted in the hierarchical world of Harpy Farm. Moreover, Doc and Fluff's own forms of desire and sexual pleasure also challenge the notion of sexual orthodoxy in a utopian future. This issue is complicated by the fact that the novel does not stop at depicting a utopia in which some women engage in "deviant" or forbidden sexual practices which the novel implies should be allowed, for the novel also includes activities which, insofar as they are non-consensual, would not be permitted. Yet it may be difficult for some readers to accept that the sado-masochism in Doc and Fluff's relationship is "permissible" in our world, because it is consensual, while Prez's violent sadomasochistic behavior is not (and for which he is punished at the end), particularly insofar as – at another level of reading – Prez's acts are meant to constitute pleasurable fantasies for the reader. While Califia would have us recognize

groups of women – those who descended from the original settlers, who have been socialized by a feminist, dyke-separatist way of life; those who seek refuge on the land and thus have not had that long history of belonging to it, the ex-hets; and passing women, who might be called bulldaggers of FTMs (female-to-male transgendered people) today" (xxvii).

that there is a disjunction between the representation of violence and its effect on us (for these representations are not meant to make us violent, but to give us sexual pleasure) – the issue is certainly complicated by the depiction of Harpy Farm which is both a critique of earlier utopias and, however tentatively, a utopian sketch in its own right.

In this sense, the novel's most contradictory feature lies in the contrast between the occasional glimpses of a fascinating new future embodied by the women's community and the rather stark evocations of life on the farm and of the dangers of the surrounding countryside. This is most explicit in Sahara's description of the clan system based on a person's occupation or trade, and of the "holyday" meetings between the many women's farms – a happier and more festive time which is in sharp contrast to the crisis precipitated by the arrival of Doc and Fluff, and which we are never shown. It is as if the author hesitates and draws back whenever the dystopian starts to yield to the utopian. Thus the novel swings between the activities and satisfactions of Charnas's adaptions of Plains Indians culture (in *Motherlines*) and the devastated world of the first two Road Warrior movies. These contradictions are an extension of the incompatibility of the two visions which pull at Califia's novel: on the one hand, this is her answer to the "conservative" feminist utopias she critiqued in the passage cited above; while on the other, it is a staging of s/m fantasies in a dystopian world – a distinction which raises, at least implicitly, the question of the link between dystopia and s/m. This apparent incompatibility can be seen by the fact that sadomasochistic sex does not seem to exist on Harpy Farm; sexual tensions and taboos, and the resulting pleasures of dangerous or forbidden sex, come rather from the segregation of former hets and passing women, and from the more familiar attempts by some of the Harpies to restrict sex to loving, monogamous relationships.[22]

Doc and Fluff – despite its subtitle – is not really a dystopia: there is no sense that the novel is trying to warn us that if some tendencies in our present continue we will end up in the disturbing and desolate world of

22 In contrast to Doc and Fluff's story, or to that of Raven and Prez, the novel includes several narratives of self-realization, as in Tina's transformation at Harpy Farm or the love between Anderson and Michaels, who at the end are talking of establishing a men's version of Harpy Farm.

the future ("if this goes on"). Like the Mad Max movies or so much SF, the dystopian future is simply the background for the adventures. As I have tried to show, there is nonetheless more to the novel and its dystopian setting than is to be found in most such works. On the one hand, this is pornography; pornography moreover which – in the reluctance to continue with the description of Harpy Farm (not to mention the apparent existence of a whole network of women's communities) – is made possible by the dystopian future. Nor should our distaste (or disgust) with the novel's violence obscure the novel's secondary purpose: to raise questions about the implicit exclusions and interdictions of many feminist utopias.

In an essay entitled "Sluts in Utopia: The Future of Radical Sex" (published in her 1994 collection of essays *Public Sex*), Califia lays out some of the contradictions I am trying to address:

> Most plans for creating a more just society focus on ameliorating human misery. They address unemployment, hunger, illiteracy, class-based inequity, unequal access to medical care, pollution, overpopulation, and discrimination based on sex, race, age or membership in other devalued groups. While I care about all of those problems, I also wonder why so many of the proposed solutions make me shudder with dread [...]. There's no room in their brave new worlds for fun, creativity, ornamentation, play and desire. I am skeptical of utopian schemes that don't take into account the human need for adventure, risk, competition, self-display, pleasurable stimulation, and novelty.
>
> In fact, many theoretical utopias are dreamed up by people who are afraid of diversity and deeply conservative about sex. Furthermore, they seem to think they can create tolerance by wiping out or minimizing differences. They envision worlds where men and women could barely be told apart – so of course there would be no sexism. Since gender would no longer be a social category, there would be no such thing as transvestitism or transsexuality. After all, how can you crossdress if both sexes are wearing the same clothes? Why would anybody envy or want to emulate the opposite sex if the distinctions between them had been blurred? The same argument is applied to homosexuality. If children were reared in an atmosphere of unconditional love without being threatened by corporal punishment or other abusive treatment, no one would eroticize bondage or a slap on the butt. Since there would be no prisons, restraint or captivity would cease to titillate. People would care more about ecology than about almost anything else, so Spandex, Latex, spiked heels, and costume jewelry would go the way of the dinosaurs. Everyone would wear baggy clothing made out of "green" cotton that had been genetically engineered to grow in various shades

> of beige. In a "just" society, there wouldn't be anything to rebel against, so there wouldn't be much call for rock 'n' roll or protest poetry. If the state was a benign entity that only served to take care of and nurture the people, why would anyone engage in civil disobedience?
>
> Dreary isn't it? (Califia 1994: 151–152)

There are several different issues here. As Le Guin argued in *The Dispossessed*, there is the possibility that over time the practices and principles of a utopian society may gradually become rules and regulations, and that certain behaviors will be proscribed. It is even possible to argue, as Califia does in the passage above, that in its uniformity, utopia might be boring. I can certainly agree with the reaffirmation of "the human need for adventure, risk [...]," and perhaps with the statement that many "utopias are dreamed up by people who are afraid of diversity and deeply conservative about sex," but her next statement is more controversial: "Furthermore, they seem to think they can create tolerance by wiping out or minimizing differences." This is indeed an important goal in many utopias, and this is also the point in her argument where Califia goes from the critique of the implicit restrictions present in some utopias to make a rather different argument, conflating the uniformity which leads to boredom and prohibitions with the need – in terms of desire – for there to be something to defy and revolt against to enable that desire: "If children were reared in an atmosphere of unconditional love without being threatened by corporal punishment or other abusive treatment, no one would eroticize bondage or a slap on the butt. Since there would be no prisons, restraint or captivity would cease to titillate."

Many of us would agree that desire should not be policed, but I am not prepared to say that I need the police to produce my desires. In this way I think that there is a fundamental contradiction at the core of *Doc and Fluff*: between the critique of the feminist utopias of the 1970s – where critique implies that she is offering a better or more practical utopian vision – and, in the choice of dystopia over the utopia of Harpy Farm, the rejection of utopian visions.

As I have tried to show, Norman's Gor is the absolute rejection of the familiar utopian goals of freedom and of social and sexual equality, although – as the elaboration of a coherent alternative world – it might be considered as what I have described elsewhere: a "right-wing utopia."[23] More importantly, the world of Gor is based on the belief in an essential difference between men and women, one which endows women with a predisposition to slavery, so that women find by their very nature pleasure in their subjection. In opposition to Norman's essentialism, there is also pleasure in subjection in the imaginary worlds of Califia (and in Delany's Nevèrÿon novels), but this predisposition to certain types of pleasure is not based on sexual difference, but originates in the social and psychological make-up of the individual. Moreover, however distasteful we may find such "perverse" pleasures, Califia's novel (and her non-fiction writing more generally) explicitly calls for an alternate world (based on the utopian principles of freedom and equality) which includes the possibility of such scenarios of subjection as a legitimate form of sexual gratification.

For those of us who write about feminist SF and utopia, we usually think of these works as somehow envisioning our future; we want them to represent a world which embodies our utopian dreams and values and we tend to judge them accordingly. Yet even as we imagine that the utopia represents what a future shaped by feminism would or might be, as Califia and others have pointed out, we must be aware of the limits and dangers of such prescriptions – most notably the restrictive character of such blueprints in outlawing activities and behaviors which fall outside the norm. While I continue to prefer utopian works which focus on my own utopian goals and my own modes of pleasure and happiness, Califia is writing from what many would consider a feminist perspective and her reservations and sexual desires need to be taken seriously.

23 See Chapter 4, "Utopia Beyond Our Ideals: The Dilemma of the Right-Wing Utopia."

CHAPTER 14

Utopian Effect / Utopian Pleasure[1]

> What does the unhappily still unwritten history of the concept "pleasure" teach us about the fundamental aesthetic experience?
>
> Hans Robert Jauss, Aesthetic Experience and Literary Hermeneutics (1982: 22)

> The utopia anticipated by artistic form is the idea that things at long last ought to come into their own [...]. That is why the sensuous moment is so important: while it is riveted to the transitory here and now, it also points to that status of independence that every particular work has.
>
> Theodor Adorno, Theory of Aesthetics (1983: 195)

The Utopian Effect

What reactions or feelings are stimulated by reading utopias? Are those reactions limited to an intellectual recognition of the outlines of an ideal society, or is there more? Recently critics have begun to examine the question of a "utopian effect": how the utopia moves the reader to act to bring about the ideal society presented in the utopian text. However, these critics have not dealt with the related and often overlooked question of why the reader actually continues reading and what leads him/her to do so. This is not as obvious a question as it might seem, especially since utopian novels are often described as lacking what most gives us pleasure in reading novels; "reading for the plot," the enjoyment of the story, the

1 I would like to thank Robert Philmus and Darko Suvin for their helpful comments on the first version, comments which I have only begun to develop here.

identification with characters and the pull of closure are usually diminished or even absent in most utopian fictions where the description of an alternate society weighs down and impedes the effects and processes of the novel. Although utopias are taxed as being boring and didactic, they do continue to be written and read, however, as the revival of English-language utopian writing since the 1970s has shown. In the following paper, I will attempt to explain that popularity by offering a preliminary sketch of the modes and categories of utopian pleasure.

For many the definition of contemporary utopian fiction begins with its status as a novel, to which some other "extraneous" elements have been added. This extra element is of course the presentation of an ideal society, and it is this addition which supposedly interferes with the pleasures and functions of the traditional novel form. In fact, the evolution of the utopian genre demonstrates a growing awareness of these charges as utopian authors – in the dialogic context of a changing and expanding reading public – have increasingly sweetened their rhetorical strategies with fictional treats. One of the developments which contributed to the success of Edward Bellamy's *Looking Backward* (1888) was precisely the alteration in the techniques of persuasion. Along with the change in the intended audience (to the wider public of the newly formed middle classes in the U.S.), there was a shift from philosophic dialogue to utopian romance. This "novelization" of utopia involved a significant transformation in the construction of the reader: from the addressee in a philosophic dialogue who is persuaded through reasoned presentation, as in More's *Utopia*, to an emotional and experimental involvement with a fictional character whose changing attitudes and feelings are designed to increase the reader's own interest and concern. In utopian novels like *Looking Backward*, this process is most often conducted through the topos of the visitor from outside; and through the depiction of the visitor's interest in the new society in terms of an erotic attraction to one of its citizens. Utopian novels often close with the visitor's realization that the utopian society is superior to his own (and I say "his," for until recently, the visitor was usually a man), and with his decision to stay and live there with his new-found love.

In his 1986 *Reader in a Strange Land*, Peter Ruppert describes how utopias and the reading of utopias have evolved:

> literary utopias are no longer diatribes that harangue the reader into embracing utopian beliefs; rather they are dialectical interrogations of social reality that *force* us to

> recognize the provisional nature of all social values and beliefs and of our own role in formulating them. (1986: 52; emphasis added)

However, the experience of reading (as Barthes demonstrated in *S/Z*) is unlike that of other artistic forms like listening to a piece of music or looking at a pointing, or even watching a film: reading is a lengthy and often interrupted process, one to which, after each interruption, the reader chooses to return. To explain the utopian effect, one must explain this decision to return, something which is not included in the explanation that utopias "force" (to use Ruppert's verb) the reader to do this or that. While Ruppert offers a valuable account of the changing "pragmatics" of utopia, he does not really acknowledge the reader's pleasure or why a reader would return to the text. On the other hand, some science fiction criticism does begin from the premise that the genre's specificity lies in a pleasurable feeling or effect where, in an older form, the impact on the reader of the strange newness depicted in the story was referred to in terms of a "sense of wonder." Darko Suvin refined this sensation in his now classic definition of science fiction as the "literature of cognitive estrangement" where the effect of that strange newness (in Brecht's terms, as quoted by Suvin) "allows us to recognize its subject, but at the same time makes it seem unfamiliar" (1979: 6). This estrangement or "defamiliarization" in turn would lead – ideally – to a critical understanding of the "author's empirical reality." Indeed, the link between the initial estrangement and our understanding is crucial to Ruppert's description of the experience of reading utopias:

> [T]he efficacy of those utopian dreamworlds is not in the feasibility of their designs, nor in their therapeutic effects as heuristic models of peace and perfect harmony, but in their shocking and disturbing effects on readers who are now *forced* to think about the nature of their own lives and the socioeconomic system in which they live. (Ruppert 1986: 158; emphasis added)

Utopian and Other Pleasures: Some Distinctions

The text of pleasure, as Barthes put it, is not necessarily the pleasure of the text, and this remark suggests some further qualifications of the utopian reader's experience. There may be passages where some minor detail like the taste of Marcel's madeleine in Proust's *In Search of Lost Time*, suddenly throws open the very personal gates of memory and joy. Such a private reaction, despite its importance in a particular context or the intensity of the pleasure it might give, is not the sign of the utopian effect since I am seeking pleasures specific to utopias, and ones which are shared by many readers.[2] In addition to such individual flashes of delight, there are also pleasurable moments shared by many readers – a happy phrase or a moving scene, an amusing anecdote or a particularly successful character or situation, and so on – elements which may be found in any novel and are thus not specific to the utopian dimension.

There is too the simple reality – so often forgotten – of the mediation of words and writing: these characters and their experiences, like the worlds they are reacting to, are imaginary; and are mediated through language and the conventions of literature – phantoms summoned up by marks on a piece of paper. My inquiry must avoid the temptation to simply fold reading pleasure into reading about pleasure. On the other hand, this does not mean that we must shun all mention of a character's bliss and wonder, although it may be but a fictional representation of the pleasure I am claiming for the reader of utopias. Nonetheless, our response may be determined by and coterminous with representations of a character's pleasure, despite Barthes's dictum. The reader's reactions are to some extent already inscribed in the text through the positioning of the reader, insofar as characters are used to stand in for the reader as an intermediary for the changed experience of daily life in a different society.

To this extent some of the enjoyment of reading utopias will be enacted in the gratification and delight which the characters experience. But there are also other pleasures which I shall now attempt to describe, including

2 By mentioning the "madeleine," I have chosen an ambiguous example. On the one hand, I am referring to Marcel's "involuntary memory" which is triggered by a taste/smell from his childhood which would not have the same effect on anyone else. Yet memory, and especially Proust's descriptions of Marcel's reconstruction of his past, plays an essential role in the utopian theories of Herbert Marcuse, particularly in his *Eros and Civilization* (New York: Vintage, 1955: 213). See also Hans Robert Jauss, *Aesthetic Experience and Literary Hermeneutics* (Minneapolis: University of Minnesota Press, 1982).

effects which are pleasurable insofar as they themselves anticipate the joy and freedom from anxiety of utopia. But it is perhaps the very deviation of the utopian form from the narrative conventions and expectations of the novel which points to its pleasures, namely the alternate world of the utopia. Following Suvin – in particular his description of contemporary utopian fiction as a sociopolitical subgenre of SF – we might say that whereas in the latter the "strange newness" (novum) may be drawn from a variety of possibilities and alternative realities, in utopian fiction that "cognitive novelty" lies specifically in the depiction of a different society.

Thus, I am arguing that the novum of the "alternate society" not only provides the cognitive dimension of the utopia, but also the pleasurable. This fictional pleasure can best be seen in the extraordinary success of some fantasy novels with their elaborate and entailed imaginary worlds – whose names include Arrakis, Oz, Earthsea, Narnia, and Middle Earth, or the Cimmeria of the Hyborian Age. Their attraction derives from a pleasure produced by the evocation of the imaginary world itself, one which can be seen as well in the many accompanying materials which spring up around these novels: maps, glossaries, encyclopedias, costumes, fan conventions, and so on. Accordingly, I would argue that the popularity of all utopian writing may be understood, at least partially, in these terms. For along with its other characteristics, More's *Utopia*, may also be read in the context of the growing popularity of travel narratives which, regardless of their contents or ultimately their veracity, were avidly consumed by seventeenth- and eighteenth-century readers.[3] The popularity of travel literature and imaginary voyages prior to the emergence of the novel as the dominant form of narrative in Europe in the eighteenth century attests to pleasures distinct from those of reading for the story or the characters which so dominate discussions of the enjoyment of reading novels today. The enjoyment of travel narratives is itself a little examined area, but in one of the most important examinations of the genre, Percy Adams's *Travel Literature and the Evolution of the Novel* (1983), the author does mention "the *ancient and*

3 See the seventy-four titles published by Charles-Georges-Thomas Garnier in his "Voyages imaginaires, Songes, Visions, et Romans cabalistiques" (1787–1789) which are listed and described in Pierre Versins, *Encyclopédie de l'utopie et de la science fiction* (Lausanne, Switzerland: L'Age d'Homme, 1972: 944–946).

perennial thirst for exact details – whether recognizably real, merely marvellous, or obviously fantastic" (113; emphasis added).

Given this general fascination with the depiction of other worlds, what are the differences between reading utopias and reading fantasy and SF, or even travel literature? We have already seen that as a "sociopolitical subgenre" of SF, the specificity of utopia lies in the situation of the novum in the depiction of an alternate reality. In terms of fantasy, Suvin argues that the essential difference between SF and other "estranged" (or non-naturalistic) forms like fantasy lies in the latter's "anti-cognitive" stance which depends on the "metaphysical" nature of the imaginary worlds depicted; as opposed to the neutrality of our physical environment, the natural world of the fantasy novel is invested with good and evil and the outcome of the hero's adventures is predetermined. In Jean Pfaelzer's terms, "The fantastic confronts us with situation that do not conform to the ground rules of the world, rules that we empirically assume; it calls into question our very modes of perception. […] Utopian works by contrast, stimulate feelings of optimism and possibility" (1984: 16). In terms of travel literature, on the other hand, whether about real or imaginary places, there is no necessary difference, for some of it was in fact utopian (from Vairasse's *Histoire des Sevarambes* [1677–1679] to Diderot's *Supplement au voyage de Bougainville* [1773]). Again, the distinction lies in the purpose of function of the novum – in what might be seen as an opposition between strangeness for its own sake (exoticism), versus the cognitive aims of attempting to imagine and describe a better society:

> the particular essential novum of any SF tale must in its turn be judged by how much new insight into imaginary but coherent and this-worldly, that is, historical, relationships it affords and could afford. (Suvin 1979: 81)

The success of the fantasy novel also depends on the reader's identification with the characters, a point to which I would now like to turn since it has played a crucial role in the "novelization" of utopian writing. There is an important distinction to be made here between positioning and identification. By the positioning of the reader I am referring to the conventions of character through which our apprehension and understanding unfold from a particular perspective or point of view. Identification, on the other hand, is the temporary merging of our identity with that of the fictional character and the attendant psychological processes through which we use the text to replay, as it were, buried or repressed fantasy scenarios.[4] This distinction is central to the device of the utopian visitor who stands in for the reader as the new world is gradually revealed. Thus there is a crucial difference between the practice of depicting the new world through the eyes of a wondering outsider, and the attempt to seduce the reader by linking the beauty and attractiveness of the alternative society to a person with whom the visitor falls in love.

This feature of identification is perhaps most evident in the ending, and the difference may be seen in novels in which the reader's seduction is confirmed by the visitor's ability to choose to remain in the new society. Other utopian novels reject such comfortable endings by refusing this satisfaction to the reader. Nor is this a new development, as can be seen by the ending of Morris's *News from Nowhere* (1890), which was written as a reply to *Looking Backward*, and in which Bellamy's happy ending is rejected as Morris's visitor is told he must return to his own reality:

> No, it will not do; you cannot be of us; you belong so entirely to the unhappiness of the past that our happiness even would weary you. Go back again, now you have seen us, and your outward eyes have learned that in spite of all the infallible maxims of your day there is yet a time of rest in store for the world, when mastery has changed into fellowship – but not before. Go back again, then, and while you live you will see all round you people engaged in making other live lives which are not their own, while they themselves care nothing for their real lives – men who hate life though they fear death. Go back and be the happier for having seen us, for having added a little hope to your struggle. Go on living while you may, striving, with whatsoever pain and labor needs must be, to build up little by little the new day of fellowship, and rest, and happiness. (1977: 401)

While I do not have time to develop further examples of the rejection of the pleasures of identification and closure in detail here, let me at least

4 See "Interaction Patterns of Identification with the Hero," in Jauss (1982: 152–188); as well as Simon Lesser, *Fiction and the Unconscious* (New York: Vintage, 1962).

quickly mention some recent examples.[5] The refusal of the traditional happy ending is perhaps most explicit in Marge Piercy's *Woman on the Edge of Time* (1976) where the heroine is not only returned to her own world, but is faced with personal humiliation and defeat. A second form of the refusal of identification may be seen in the polemics and direct address of Joanna Russ's *The Female Man* (1975). And there is the non-hero of Delany's *Triton* (1976) in which Bron's unhappiness and particularly his egotism and selfishness confound our attempts at identification and lead us to reflect on our own needs and the resulting shape of utopia.

Thus, although there has been an increasing novelization of utopias since the nineteenth century, they still maintain some distance between the reader and the imaginary society and its characters. Because of their didactic and intentional characteristics, utopias need a thinking reader. The more complete the identification, one might argue, the more dulled our critical faculties. While the utopian reader is usually positioned vis-a-vis the imaginary world and the unfolding events through the perspective of the visitor, in many recent utopias identification and the imaginary release of closure are deliberately blocked. We must look elsewhere for utopian pleasure.

Pleasure and Cognition

> Significant modern SF, with deeper and more lasting sources of enjoyment, also presupposes more complex and wider cognitions: it discusses primarily the political, psychological, and anthropological use and effect of knowledge, of philosophy of science, and the becoming or failure of new realities as a result of it. [...] Once the elastic criteria of literary structuring have been met, a cognitive [...] element becomes a measure of aesthetic quality, of the specific pleasure to be sought in SF. (Suvin 1979: 14–15, emphases in original)

5 This refusal of identification and closure, as I and others have argued, is characteristic of many of the "critical" utopias of the 1970s. See Chapter 8, "Positioning and Closure." See also Moylan (1986).

To recapitulate my argument thus far, the first mode of utopian pleasure lies in the discovery of the new world itself, in our thrill and fascination with newness and otherness. This form of enjoyment has a rich literary history, as I have already suggested, both in contemporary fantasy and in the earlier popularity of travel narratives and imaginary voyages. But the value of the novum of the alternative society lies not in its otherness or strangeness per se, but in the "insights" it affords.

In this way, I now return to the dialectic between pleasure and cognition; in attempting to chart utopian pleasures, I am forced to recognize that these two functions cannot be separated. Here is a brief passage from Morris's *News from Nowhere* in which the thrill of discovery is not simply the result of a "thirst" for otherness, but springs from a delight in a world which is shaped by the utopian principles of "generosity and abundance of life":

> This whole mass of architecture which we had come upon so suddenly from amidst the pleasant fields was not only exquisitely beautiful *in itself*, but it bore upon it the expression of such generosity and abundance of life that I was exhilarated to a pitch that I had never yet reached. I fairly chuckled for pleasure. (Morris 1977: 203; emphasis added)

In the same way, there is a category of utopian pleasures which might be called "foretastes" of utopia – brief moments of textual pleasure in which disalienation and the end to repression are figured in some libidinal transcendence of our physical limits, as in fictional scenes of flying, from Arthur's adolescent experiences in T.H. White's *The Once and Future King* to the dragon hunt in Samuel Delany's *Stars in My Pockets Like Grains of Sand*.[6] Again what is specifically utopian about these happy moments would seem to lie in the purpose of these representations of pleasure. In the Delany example, for instance, there is a connection between the pleasure of this account of the dragon hunt and a larger utopian purpose since the sensation of flying, of union with the dragon's sensorium for an instant is

6 For a discussion of flying as a physical analog to liberation from societal gravity and oppressively closed social relationships' in early SF, see Suvin, "Victorian Science Fiction" (1983: 412–413). See also the theme of 'flying' in Tom Disch's 1979 masterpiece, *On Wings of Song*.

both the expression of a moment of libidinal unbinding in a "shared" experience (and I am taking all such expressions of shared happiness as utopian, as juxtaposed to expressions of private pleasure); and this example is also – in the very notion of a dragon hunt – rejection of what we think of as hunting in our own world: tracking and killing some life form different from our own.

This physical exhilaration can be found as well in the "wind-riding" of Sally Gearhart's utopian novel *The Wanderground*. Again, this is not simply delight in a sensation for its own sake, but an experience which arises from and embodies the new relationship of the Hill Women to Nature and the body of the Earth:

> With a new exhilaration she dived and swooped some more. [...] She looped above the trees in wider and wider arcs. She relearned the handling of pitch, a throwing up and downward of her legs; she rehearsed the secrets of direction. (1978: 107)

In this same vein, I would like to argue for a more intellectual utopian pleasure, one which we obtain from seeing how the ideals and promises of freedom and equality might be realized; in seeing how an author goes about working out the structures and details of an imaginary society which would make possible a realm of human freedom. In this category, my favorite example is Le Guin's attempt to show how Marx's vision of a communist society in which the regulation of general production would

> make it possible for me to do one thing today and another tomorrow, to hunt in the morning, fish in the afternoon, rear cattle in the evening, criticize after dinner, just as I have a mind, without ever becoming hunter, fisherman, shepherd or critic. (Marx and Engels 1970: 97)

Ursula Le Guin's "Div-Lab" is of course far more than this, and the novel is a defense of Kropotkin's anarchism, as well as a critique of authoritarian communism, but Shevek's assertion that "work is done for work's sake. It is the lasting pleasure of life" (1974: 121) is a strong reaffirmation of this goal. Ideally the Div-Lab computers fit jobs and people together, but in the harsh conditions of Annares, this is not always possible.

A slightly different form of this more intellectual pleasure may also be found in newer modes of reading which more explicitly involved the reader in the production of meaning. While Le Guin's *Always Coming Home* (1985) does not demand as much of the reader as some of those experimental French novels of a few years ago which came unbound, without page numbers, in a box, *Always*, through its many non-narrative sections, does involve the reader far more than do traditional utopian narratives in the fictional construction of a new society. The reader approaches the text (and the accompanying audio tape), a bit like a kit which must be assembled.

Conclusion

> So finally the right to a specific pleasure, to a specific enjoyment of the potentialities of the material body – if it is not to remain only that, if it is to become genuinely political, if it is to evade the complacencies of "hedonism" – must always in one way or another also be able to stand as a figure for the transformation of social relations as a whole. (Jameson 1983: 162)

I began my search for those pleasures specific to utopia with the reader's decision to continue reading works which were often described as lacking the pleasurable features of the traditional novel. After some distinctions, I concluded that there was an indissoluble link between pleasure and cognition. And yet I do not want to over-instrumentalize that bond. Pleasure is not simply the manifestation of the absence of pain and suffering; it is not simply the emblem of the transition from the realm of necessity to a ream of freedom. Utopian pleasure cannot simply be reduced to the useful or the cognitive, but is in itself an important component of the utopian, as is suggested in William Morris's review of *Looking Backward* where he complained of Bellamy's "scheme of the organization of life; which is organized with a vengeance."[7] Just as recent so-called ambiguous or critical utopias have tried to leave room for individual happiness and pleasure, in contrast to earlier works which stressed the complete organization of life in the new society, so may one speak of pleasurable elements which escape or exceed the pragmatic and descriptive functions of the

7 Quoted by A. L. Morton, in his Introduction to Morris (1977: 25).

utopian text – although these latter features are what guarantee and make possible our happiness and delight.

Let me speak then of utopian pleasures which *exceed* cognition or the performative dimension, and which provide through that very excess an anticipatory experience of the hoped-for new world; let me speak of a "surplus" pleasure which goes beyond the needs and demands of a critical explanation of the utopian work – an excess which may be seen for instance in Olaf Stapledon's 1937 novel *Star Maker*, and I have deliberately chosen a philosophical SF novel with very minimal plot and characters whose pleasures are seemingly few. This visionary work, with its depiction of a universe swarming with a multitude of species and fantastic forms of sentient life, may be read – in familiar utopian terms – as the critique of "the author's own empirical reality," and as a sketch of new collective forms and possibilities. Yet the profusion and variety of worlds and beings presented in the novel exceeds any such explanation; and even a reading which focuses on this multitude and diversity of life-forms still cannot explain the function or necessity for this abundance of description in which several generations of readers have nonetheless found wonder and enjoyment.

The critical tendency to explain the usefulness and function of every detail of a literary work is a reflection of the increasing management and commodification of our leisure time, as our desires are manufactured and regulated to meet the demands of the market and of the state's attempts to control its citizens. But this must be resisted. The pleasurable discovery and the experience of a fictional world may exceed, but they do not contradict or deny cognition precisely insofar as they allow us to glimpse the possibility of an alternative which only cognition can help us comprehend. Understanding and decision to act may follow this sensation, but the actual discovery and pleasure in otherness are themselves a promise of a world to come.

I am faced with two dilemmas in my discussion of the utopian effect. My hope for utopias which would move their readers to act is tempered by my desire that any such decision be based on reason, on an intelligent choice; unlike advertising or the recent presidential campaign in the U.S., we are not simply interested in compelling or causing people to think or act in a certain way, but in presenting them with the materials to allow them to make up their own minds. The other dilemma is between hedonism and utopia, between a reading pleasure without any consequences and one which would lead the reader to act to change his or her society. While arguing against the dangers of instrumentalization, of the critical reduction and assessment of utopias in terms of their effectiveness or usefulness, there is of course an opposite danger, which lies in advocating pleasures which do not outlive the immediacy of the instant. This is the effect of many of the pleasures of our contemporary culture which leave the reader or spectator as he or she was before. My argument has been for a pleasure which somehow combines these elements; while retaining their pleasurable characteristics, utopias also point to a human community which does not now exist but which could be. My dream of an art which is able to link the experience of beauty with the need to act is summed up by the poet Rilke in his celebrated sonnet "Archaic Torso of Apollo" in which the headless torso "binds you with its grace"; "For every part of this commanding form holds you in its gaze" the poem concludes. "You must change your life."

PART III

Cinema, Space, and Technology

CHAPTER 15

What Is Utopian Film? An Introductory Taxonomy[1]

Introduction

What is a utopian film? Unlike the musical or the western, or the science fiction film, there is no accepted body of utopian films and no accepted definition. In fact, few films come to mind when the subject is raised. Accordingly I will not concentrate on defining the utopian genre (but see Shelton 1993), for definitions are made on the basis of an already existing body of work on the basis of which one could then determine the common features (semantic and syntactical) of the genre. Instead, by analogy with the project of the Society of Utopian Studies, which links scholars and researchers working in such diverse fields as literary studies, political science, history, and architecture, I will propose a number of ways and perspectives by which scholars might begin to discuss the issue of utopian film. Without specifically invoking a utopian film genre, I will begin this examination with Lyman Sargent's "the three basic forms of utopianism": "utopian literature, communitarianism and utopian social theory" (Sargent 1988: 3). More specifically, the literary utopia, which seems the most fruitful for an investigation of the possibilities of utopian

1 This is a longer version of a paper read at the sixteenth annual meeting of the Society for Utopian Studies. I would like to thank Fred Jameson, Tom Moylan, Lyman Sargent, and Robert Shelton for their helpful comments and suggestions, as well as the many friends and colleagues who suggested films and possibilities for my taxonomy.

film (and with which I shall begin), is defined as a "non-existent society described in considerable detail" (Sargent 1988: 4).[2]

Utopias

There are of course utopian films, as everyone who has seen the H.G. Wells/Cameron Menzies/Alex Korda collaboration *Things to Come* (1936) would agree. However, there are not really any other similar examples of utopian film, except for those films which constitute what should be a distinct category: screen adaptions of utopian novels. The best known of these is Frank Capra's 1937 adaption of James Hilton's *Lost Horizon*. But this second category is also lacking in examples, for there are almost no films of the classics of the utopian tradition – with the exception of an obscure and apparently unsuccessful Soviet adaption of the classic Russian utopia, Efremov's *Andromeda*.[3]

Things to Come and *Lost Horizon* are emblematic of the ambiguous status of the utopian film for several reasons. The first lies in the visual nature of film and its differences from the literary; the second in the historical moment at which films were produced. In terms of the visual, it is significant that these two films devote relatively little space to the representation

2 Sargent also distinguishes between the positive and negative utopias – eutopia and dystopia – which were meant to be better or worse than the author's own society (Sargent 1988: 4–5).

3 Robert Rimmer's not-so-classic utopia *The Harrad Experiment* (1966) was filmed in 1973. There are as well several movies with the word "utopia" in the title, including Laurel and Hardy's *Utopia* (1950), a sad and depressing end to their career; and the very funny Bing Crosby/Bob Hope installment *The Road to Utopia* (1945), which relates their search for an Alaskan gold mine. David Butler's musical *Just Imagine* (1930) should perhaps be mentioned, if only because of its futuristic sets. In this sequel to the very successful *Sunnyside Up*, the hero is struck by lightning and awakes fifty years in the future. Lavish sums were spent on the futuristic sets of the New York of the future – which appeared as stock footage in later science fiction like *Buck Rogers* – but the film quickly degenerates into melodrama.

of the new society. While the spectator takes away strong visual impressions of these utopian communities, there are actually few details of what actually constitutes the future society, unlike what we usually learn from a written utopia. In *Things to Come* details about the society are replaced by a futuristic look which corresponds to the technological utopianism of the era, as manifested in modernist architecture (Frank Lloyd Wright's utopian city of Chandigarh)[4] and the "Streamline style." This vision was summed up in many of the buildings and exhibits of the 1939–1940 World's Fair. In *Lost Horizon*, on the other hand, a description of the utopia is replaced by a number of plot developments, beginning with the mysterious events leading up to the arrival in Shangri-la (followed by their attempts to leave), and most significantly, the presence in the narrative of a secret which sidetracks the viewer, namely the longevity which is granted the inhabitants of this valley.[5] Here the look of utopia owes more to the "lost civilization" tradition, like the many versions of H. Rider Haggard's *She* (1887), and most especially the many films which portray the lost continent of Atlantis (or the French versions of Atlantis-based on the Pierre Benoit novel *L'Atlantide* (1919) about a lost civilization in the Sahara).[6] While these films portray non-existent societies, I would tend to exclude them from the utopian category because the societies are not presented as alternatives, as somehow better or worse than contemporary society. But these evocations of lost worlds do call up other utopian possibilities to which I shall return in a moment.

4 See Chapter 19, "Urban Planning/Utopian Dreaming."

5 Sargent makes another distinction which is relevant here, between *body utopias*, simple "utopias of sensual gratification," more characteristic of Carnival and Cockaigne; and the *city utopia:* "the utopia of human contrivance" (1988: 6–7). Most literary utopias fall into the second category. But a society which, through some unknown geographical property, rather than through human endeavor or agency, grants longevity to its inhabitants suggests to me that Shangri-la is closer to the "body utopia."

6 Phil Hardy mentions seven versions of *She*, beginning with Georges Méliès's *La Dame du Feu* in 1899 (Hardy 1984: 87). The best known movies about Atlantis are *The Undersea Kingdom* (1936), *The Sirens of Atlantis* (1949), and *Atlantis, the Lost Continent* (1960).

The other clue to explaining the relative scarcity of utopian films follows from the realization that the two major utopian films were both made in the 1930s. As various critics have observed, this was a moment both of heightened utopian activity and of a strong belief in technology's ability to produce a better world. This conviction is perhaps most manifest, at one level, in the emerging genre of science fiction in the 1920s and 30s; and, on another level, in the monumental projects of the great modernist architects. Visually, as I've already mentioned, this technological utopianism is summed up in a "streamline" vision of the future common to both the covers of the SF magazines of the period and to many of the exhibits at the New York World's Fair. Thus, this historical moment was not only characterized by a certain utopian optimism, but by a distinctive style which summed up the gleaming promise of the future for decades to come.[7]

The most obvious way to expand the boundaries of utopian film is to look at negative or dystopian reworkings of the themes I have been discussing. There are, in fact, numerous versions of dystopian classics, from films of *Nineteen Eighty-Four* and *Brave New World* to the adaptations of Anthony Burgess's *A Clockwork Orange* and Margaret Atwood's *The Handmaid's Tale* (or of William Golding's *Lord of the Flies*); while under the heading of original dystopian films I would include such masterpieces as Fritz Lang's *Metropolis* (1926)[8] and Terry Gilliam's *Brazil* (1985). Such negative visions of future planned societies would also include the collapsing utopias of *Logan's Run* and *Zardoz*.

A slight enlargement of the utopian net would also accommodate a host of SF films which offer glimpses of a utopia, or which use a utopian

7 This look and its utopian planning assumptions are one of the factors which characterize the post-modern critique of high modernism in architecture. For an accessible collection of these magazine covers and the accompanying themes, see Paul Carter's *The Creation of Tomorrow* (New York: Columbia University Press, 1977). One of the best descriptions of this utopian optimism is Andrew Ross's chapter "Getting out of The Gernsback Continuum," in his *Strange Weather: Culture, Science and Technology in the Age of Limits* (London: Verso, 1991). See also Kihlstedt (1986), "Utopia Realized."

8 Although I called *Metropolis* an "original dystopian film," it was based on Thea von Harbou's novel. I include it nonetheless because von Harbou was Fritz Lang's wife, and they collaborated on the scripts of a number of his films including *Metropolis*.

or dystopian setting, although as might be expected, the dystopian setting predominates in many popular science fiction films of the past few decades, from *Soylent Green* and *Escape from New York* to the "Mad Max" films and the already classic *Blade Runner*.[9]

While so many of these dystopian visions are formulated as critiques of the utopian ideal of the planned society, the escape *from* that society, framed as a new beginning, is often an escape *to* some more "natural" existence. The tranquil valley of Shangri-la in *Lost Horizon* is a society whose origins are explained (and which was, thus, to some extent planned), but its primary appeal seems to lie in the evocation of a simpler and happier existence away from the struggles and turmoil of modern life.

The representation of other, older, simpler and happier communities as societal models or alternatives should include another subset, that of the ethnographic film, or at least those films which portray lost or vanishing cultures in positive terms. This could be seen as one of the organizing principles in the British "Disappearing World" television series, which has

9 Some of these dystopian films are discussed by John Erickson (1993) and Régine-Mihal Friedman (1993). In the latest edition of Hahn and Jansen's *Lexikon des science fiction films: 1000 Filme von 1902 bis 1987* (Munich: Heyne Verlag, 1987), the authors establish a thematic index (primaren Motiv) of SF films, of which the first list of 100 films is entitled "Positive und negative (Zukunfts-) Welten, Utopien/Anti-Utopien." The first three titles on the chronological list are *Things to Come, Lost Horizon* and *Metropolis*. The list quickly reaches the 1950s and SF films, almost all of which (apart from some film versions of dystopian classics like *Nineteen Eighty-Four* and a German television production of *We*) are films with dystopian backgrounds, from *Planet of the Apes* (and its various sequels), through *The Time Machine, Alphaville, Fahrenheit 451, Wild in the Streets, THX 1138, Westworld, Zardoz,* (Woody Allen's) *Sleeper, Escape from New York, Blade Runner* and the "Mad Max" films. Because of its science fiction perspective, the main lines of the utopian categories I am proposing have been overlooked or simply not taken into account. *Blade Runner* deserves a special place in a catalogue of utopian films as it has become a central reference point for cultural critics as well as architects for the reformation of visions of the future. For a representative selection of these views, see the collection of essays in *Retrofitting Blade Runner*, edited by Judith Kerman (Bowling Green, OH: Bowling Green University Press, 1991); as well as David Harvey's chapter "Time and Space in the Postmodern Cinema," in his *The Condition of Postmodernity* (London: Blackwell, 1989: 308–326).

produced more than fifty one-hour documentaries since 1970. Each film is made in collaboration with an anthropologist who specializes in the group being recorded, and documents the daily lives and folk ways of a specific community. This type of documentary was pioneered by Robert Flaherty in his celebrated *Nanook of the North* (1922).[10] As in the lost civilization films just mentioned, the satisfaction and contentment depicted often seem to follow from lives lived in harmony with the rhythms of the natural world rather than from the community's social arrangements; these communities appear (or are presented as) having evolved "naturally" rather than as the result of specific choices and decisions. Another version of this development lies in Hollywood's own revision of its portrayal of North America's native peoples, as in recent popular films like *Black Robe* and *Dances with Wolves*.

Once we have raised the possibility of the documentary as a category of the utopian film, there are several other types which immediately come to mind, including documentaries which look, not to a lost golden age, but to the glowing technological future evoked in *Things to Come*. One can certainly find such an explicitly technological utopianism in some of the more than 500 short films and documentaries which were shown at the New York World's Fair of 1939–1940. More modern examples of this

10 This vision can be seen as well in the recently released 1926 film of Cooper and Schoedsack *Chang*, which actually predates their well-known *King Kong*. Of course, there are several contradictions at work in Flaherty's project: firstly that between his desire to preserve a particular way of life and his awareness of his role in bringing about its destruction; as well as the apparent neutrality of the camera and the transparent recording of events, and his actual interventions: "[He had] a growing sense that he himself represented the cultural destruction that troubled him […] Yet as he entered the Eskimo world, he knew that he did so as the advance guard of industrial civilization […] What I want to show is the former majesty and character of these people while it is still possible – before the white man has destroyed not only their character, but the people as well. […]The urge to capture on film the nature of rapidly vanishing cultures has been pursued also by anthropologists, who have given it the name of 'salvage ethnography […] It has been called 'romantic' in that *Flaherty was not recording a current way of life but one filtered through memories of Nanook and his people*. Yet a people's self-image may be a crucial ingredient in its culture, and worth recording" (Barnouw 1983: 45; my italics)

type of utopian documentary would include many of the films shown at Disneyworld's Epcot.

Still with the documentary, there are of course filmic records of actual utopian experiments and communities, and many intentional communities have made films introducing their own communities.[11] As well, there are fictional films about real (and imaginary) utopian experiments like J.-L. Comolli's *La Cecilia* (1974) about an Italian anarchist commune established in Brazil in the late nineteenth century. (See Judd Ne'eman's [1999] discussion of "Zionist utopias.")

The appeal of some simpler time also characterizes nostalgic evocations of moments in our own historical past, which are then portrayed as a lost Golden Age. Such a nostalgia might be said to characterize some of Frank Capra's other films, or the many films set in Camelot (as well as the powerful resonance of the image as it came to be applied to the Kennedy years). But I think that the most familiar use of the past as a happier time can be seen in various television series from and about the 1950s, from *The Adventures of Ozzie and Harriett* through the nostalgic recreation of the decade in *Happy Days*. In these television series the atmosphere of peace and tranquility is achieved through the substitution of the family for society at large; by obscuring societal conflict and rewriting it in terms of the comforting image of a nuclear family in which "father knows best" – to name another of the more successful family series of the period (*My Three Sons*, *Leave it to Beaver*, etc.).

The image of the family as utopia has a more progressive dimension, however, in films which, particularly in the wake of the second wave of feminism, attempt to imagine new domestic arrangements other than the nuclear family, as well as alternatives to interpersonal relationships based on the subordination of women. I will return to the question of feminism and utopian film in a moment. Even if we limit the utopian to images of a community – as opposed to a couple or nuclear family[12] – there are films

11 The most recent example of such a utopian documentary is Monique Gauthier's videotape, *Follow the Dirt Road: An Introduction to Intentional Communities in the 1990s*, available from The Cinema Guild, 1697 Broadway, New York City, 10019.

12 Here is Sargent's definition of a utopian or "intentional community" which distinguishes it from some large or extended family: "a group of five or more adults and their children, if any, who come from more than one nuclear family and who have chosen to live together for a mutually agreed upon purpose" (Sargent 1990: 17).

which portray such alternatives, as in Alain Tanner's *Jonah who will be 20 in the year 2000*; and there are numerous glimpses of such alternatives, from the commune in *Easy Rider* to the entire community of *The Milagro Beanfield War*.

The Utopian Politics of the 1960s

> [There was a] widely shared feeling that in the 60s, for a time, everything was possible
>
> (Jameson 1984: 207)

Another approach to the question of identifying utopian films might be to draw a parallel with the revival of utopian writing in the 1970s. If this revival of utopianism is seen as an outgrowth of the social and political upheavals of the 1960s, it is then relevant to ask what films are associated with that moment. Posed this way, we think first of those films which depicted real or imaginary revolutions in ways which presented those moments as filled with hope for a new world which would emerge from the ruins of the old. The most celebrated example of these revolutionary films of the 1960s is Gillo Pontecorvo's *The Battle of Algiers* (1966). If we can call filmic depictions of a revolutionary moment *utopian*, this substantially widens the scope of possible utopias, for there are a number of important films which have depicted earlier moments of revolutionary upheaval in positive terms, like Eisenstein's 1928 *October/Ten Days That Shook the World*, Jean Renoir's 1937 *La Marseillaise*, or Paul Leduc's *Reed: Insurgent Mexico* (1971). (This category might also include strike movies: *Salt of the Earth*, *Harlan County*, and *Matewan*.) On the fictional level this category might also include some of the youth-rebellion movies of the late 1960s like Lindsay Anderson's *If* or Peter Watkins's *Privilege*. The 1960s also include more metaphorical or whimsical utopian rebellions which – following from the radical psychology movement – focused on schizophrenia and insanity as a form of revolt and escape, like *King of Hearts* or *Morgan*. The negative version of these revolutionary moments of transition refers us back to some dystopian films I mentioned above, bleak visions which portray an escape from the dystopia, as at the end of *Logan's Run, THX 1138* or *The Handmaid's Tale.*

The Political Film

The issue of the 1960s and the relationship to the utopian revival of the 1970s raises more generally the question of the utopian potential or dimension of the political film itself – a genre which seems more substantial than its literary equivalent. I have already mentioned films which portray moments of revolutionary upheaval, but in another way – for which there is not really an equivalent situation for written utopias (except of course in the utopian manifesto itself) – it might be said that *some* of these films were made as part of a larger project of utopian social transformation. This is evident, first of all, in various national cinemas where, following a revolution, we can see conscious attempts to develop a new collective vision, as in the Soviet Union of the 1920s and 1930s, China during the Cultural Revolution or in Cuba after 1959. Soviet examples would include many of the films of Eisenstein while the most accessible film about the Cultural Revolution in China is Joris Ivens's twelve-hour documentary *How Yukong moved mountains*. And there are a number of Cuban films from the 1960s which strive to develop an alternative vision of its past and future, from the political documentaries of Santiago Alvarez, to fiction films like Gutierrez Alea's *Memories of Underdevelopment*, Manuel Gomez's *First Charge of the Machete*, and Humberto Solas's *Lucia*. These films might be characterized as utopian for both extrinsic and intrinsic reasons: in terms of their function in some larger project of social transformation; and in terms of their portrayal, as with revolutionary films, of historical moments out of which a new society will *be* born.

At the same time, particularly in Latin and South America, the 1960s saw an outpouring of political and revolutionary films made to serve as weapons to challenge and overthrow existing governments. Perhaps the most famous of these was Fernando Solanas's *Hour of the Furnaces* (1967), a four-and-one-half-hour examination of the situation in Argentina which combines documentary with the techniques of agit prop theater. The best known of these directors was the Brazilian Glauber Rocha, and I will have more to say about both Solanas and Rocha in a moment. There were, of course, equivalent developments in African and Asian cinema and, more generally, in the emergence of what is sometimes called "Third Cinema."[13]

Because of film's visual power and its ability to reach a mass audience, governments often attempt to set and control film policies; and while I began by mentioning situations which followed a revolution in which there was – at least for a time – an attempt to imagine a different and better society, this category should perhaps include, as well, all attempts to move the spectator to support a government or political ideal, including the most infamous of such films – the Nazi propaganda of Leni Riefenstahl – *Triumph of the Will*.[14] This category might also include more straightforward films, which seek to portray a particular society in glowing positive terms, and one might mention as well the visual rhetoric of films made for political campaigns and the like, although this does take us far away from our starting point. Finally such a category might even include travel films, although the focus on the social would be a crucial factor in deciding whether it was utopian.

While it is hard to think of examples of an explicitly utopian cinema to match the revival of utopian fiction which followed the upheavals of the 1960s, there were numerous calls at the time for the cinema to realize its transformative and political potential as part of a larger revolutionary struggle. Solanas's *Hour of the Furnaces* moved beyond the representation of events to break with the conventions of cinema in ways which reflected developments in the political avant-garde in Europe and, more

13 The concept of "Third Cinema" was originally developed by Fernando Solanas and Octavio Getino, "Toward a Third Cinema," *Cineaste* 4 (Winter 1970–1971), 3–12. See the discussion in Roy Armes's *Third World Film Making and the West* (Berkeley: University of California Press, 1987), as well as the anthology edited by John Downing (New York: Praeger, 1987), and that edited by Jim Pines and Paul Willemen (London: British Film Institute, 1989).

14 For a discussion of the necessity of including right-wing and indeed fascist utopias under the general heading of *utopia*, see Chapter 4, "Utopia Beyond our Ideals."

importantly, which pointed back to the Russian avant-garde following the October revolution. While the challenging of the newly emerging dominance of representation can be seen in the expressionism of Eisenstein's first film, *Strike* (1925), it was Dziga Vertov's writing and most particularly his pathbreaking *The Man with a Movie Camera* (1929), which sums up and realizes this alternative aesthetic – an influence marked forty years later when the most important figure of the New Wave of European film makers – Jean Luc Godard – turned his back on a successful career and the institutions of cinema to set up (in 1969) the Dziga Vertov group to collectively make and distribute political films.

In the 1960s and 1970s, political film seemed to divide along such lines – realism versus challenges to the conventions of realistic film narrative – and this division, often described as an opposition between first and third world, was pictured in a famous sequence in the 1970 Godard/Dziga Vertov film *Vent d'est* in which the Brazilian director Glauber Rocha is shown at a crossroads. Here is James MacBean's description of that scene from his book *Film and Revolution*:

> As Rocha stands with arms outstretched at a dusty crossroads, a young woman with a movie camera comes up one of the paths [...] "Excuse me for interrupting your class struggle [she says] but could you please tell the way toward political cinema?"
>
> Rocha points first in front of him, then behind and to his left, and he says, "That way is the cinema of aesthetic adventure and philosophical inquiry, while this way is the Third World cinema – a dangerous cinema, divine and marvellous, where the questions are practical ones like production, distribution, training three hundred filmmakers to make six hundred films a year for Brazil alone, to supply one of the world's biggest markets." (MacBean 1975: 116)

Unlike political films whose utopian quality lay in the representation of historical events with which I began, this latter development raised formal issues apparently far removed from the depiction of an ideal society. But it is grounded, nonetheless, in the utopian ideal of the transformative power of art, and specifically of film and its ability to reach a mass audience. This radical break with traditional ideas about political cinema should be seen as a reprise of what was often called the Brecht-Lukacs debate, but which was certainly anticipated, as I've said, in Dziga Vertov's *Man with a*

Movie Camera.[15] In the late 1960s, in journals like *Tel Quel* and then *Screen*, critics and theoreticians argued that while the strategy of politicizing (or of analyzing in political terms) literature and film might have been a valid activity of the committed artist, such an approach overlooked the ideological function of the traditional forms and methods of the cinema (or of the novel, and so on).[16] Political art had been traditionally seen in terms of representation and realism (as epitomized by the literary criticism of Lukacs and in Socialist Realism itself), but now critics and artists argued that the dominant ideology reproduced itself through popular acquiescence, an acquiescence which was in many ways fostered by popular entertainment: not only through the representation of the values and ideals of that society, but through the forms and means of perception and knowing implicit in representation, and through the passive attitudes fostered in the audience through traditional realistic narratives. While filmic representations of a particular situation could still be seen as part of the struggle against a repressive regime in the United States – as in two political films set against the background of the police riot at the 1968 Democratic convention in Chicago and the subsequent show trial, Haskell Wexler's *Medium Cool* and Peter Watkins's *Punishment Park*, in France and in Britain these theoretical debates led much more to formal experimentation and to attempts to use film to deconstruct the medium's own ideological presuppositions – as can be seen in the Dziga Vertov group's own film of the Chicago Seven trial, *Vladimir and Rosa* (1970).

For a variety of reasons, however, including the ability of the dominant ideology to co-opt its opponents (through making fashionable currents which oppose it), and because of the resistance of a public accustomed to

15 Dziga Vertov's importance does not rest solely on *Man with a Movie Camera*. His career in film began immediately following the Bolshevik revolution with editing work for newsreels. In 1921 he published the first of a series of manifestos – Kino-Pravda – and began to make political documentaries, the most important of which is *One Sixth of the World* (1926; see Barnouw 1983: 51–75).

16 D.N. Rodowick's *The Crisis of Political Modernism: Criticism and Ideology in Contemporary Film Theory* (Urbana: University of Illinois Press, 1988) is an interesting examination of some of the positions associated with *Screen* and *Tel Quel*. See also Colin MacCabe's *Godard* (Bloomington: Indiana University Press, 1980).

entertainment as spectacle, these attempts, however progressive in their intentions, were increasingly confined to an avant-garde whose own political allegiances underwent important transformations in the 1970s and 1980s.

By the end of the 1970s Godard had returned to somewhat more traditional practices of film making. But as my earlier reference to Riefenstahl suggests, one important feature of this critique of traditional moviemaking is based on the realization that there is a troubling similarity between the rhetorical and performative mechanisms at work in *Triumph of the Will* and in political films like *The Battle of Algiers*. As MacBean puts it:

> These latter films are useful in stirring up emotional support and sympathy for the revolutionary cause, as well as in stirring up a healthy sense of revolutionary outrage at the paramilitary machinations the ruling class uses to maintain its power and privileges. But *The Battle of Algiers, Burn!* and *State of Siege* (to name only the best of such films) do not go very much beyond the emotional level; and we have seen from Leni Riefenstahl's *Triumph of the Will* just how frighteningly easy it is to use the emotional power of the cinema to arouse masses of people to support even the most unjust and ignominious causes. (MacBean 1975: 9)

Utopian Film and the Critics

Another way of approaching the question of utopian film is to look at the literature. There is no reference to "utopian film" in the various books on film genre I consulted. Nor do any of the standard works on SF film address the issue, although there are, of course, a number of discussions of the bleak futures portrayed in science fiction movies over the past few decades, as in Bruce Franklin's (1983) "Don't Look Where We're Going: Visions of the Future in Science Fiction Films, 1970 to 1982." Thus far, I have only been able to find two books on film with utopia in the title, both in Italian, and one special issue of a French journal. Paolo Bertetto's *Cinema dell'utopia* is an explication and adaption of the political ideas associated with the *Cahiers du Cinema* and *Tel Quel* and with the work of Godard. It is not concerned with the possibility of a filmic equivalent of the literary utopia, but with attempts to break away from the "bread and circuses" of the popular film. Similarly Guido Aristarco's *L'utopia cinematografica* is an examination of film's political potential from a Marxist and Brechtian perspective, with only marginal references to the utopian concerns with which we began.

On the other hand, the special issue of *CinémAction* "60–80: Vingt ans d'utopies au cinéma" comes closer to the utopian terms with which we are familiar for it includes short articles on a number of issues – from the promises of new media technology to the impact of feminism on the portrayal of the couple.[17]

Body Utopias

There is, however, another use of the term "utopia" in some recent writing about film which follows from Richard Dyer's seminal 1977 article "Entertainment and Utopia" in which he analyzes the movie musical.[18] He specifically addresses my starting point when he writes that "Entertainment does not [...] present models of utopian worlds [...] Rather the utopianism is contained in the feelings it embodies. It

17 There are some twenty-five relatively short articles and interviews dealing with four general areas of film-making since 1960: (1) "The impact of May '68: Changing Society and Changing the Cinema," which includes discussions of collectives and collective film-making; (2) "Changing Life and the Relations between People"; (3) "Socialisms, History and Utopia"; and (4) a catch-all section which includes articles on the myth of the noble savage, on Glauber Rocha, and a very brief look at science fiction film, "New York as the Atlantis of the Future," which describes NYC as a locus of utopian/dystopian visions. Although some 400 films are mentioned, there is no coherent or overall presentation; the general focus lies with film as a means or reflection of the utopian rather than with discussions of the thematic or pragmatic potential of film.

18 According to *The Chronicle of Higher Education*, Caryl Flinn's *Strains of Utopia: Gender, Nostalgia, and Hollywood Film Music* (Princeton, NJ: Princeton University Press, 1992) "analyzes aspects of romanticism in film scores that attempt to convey a sense of an idealized, lost past, and shows how the utopian impulse in such music was associated with the feminine" (July 15, 1992, p. A9).

presents, head-on as it were, what utopia would feel like rather than how it would be organized" (1977: 177).

Dyer sets out five "categories of entertainment's utopian sensibility" ("energy, abundance, intensity, transparency and community," 1977: 180–182) which respond to and offer imaginary solutions to "specific inadequacies in society" (1977: 183–184).[19] After explaining these aspects of utopian sensibility, Dyer proposes an example of a specifically utopian musical. In contrast to most musicals which segregate the musical numbers from the narrative, as in films about making a musical (e.g., *A Chorus Line*), in utopian films the musical numbers invade and transform the realistic space of the narrative. He illustrates this proposition through an analysis of the film version of the Broadway show *On The Town*. Unlike other musicals, which reverse the potential utopianism of what he calls the "integrated musical" by moving the events back or away from the present (like the turn-of-the-century setting of *Meet Me in St. Louis*), *On The Town* is set in an American city in the present. While in "most musicals, the narrative

19 Thus scarcity and the unequal distribution of wealth are the "inadequacy" for which "abundance" is the utopian solution; work as exhaustion and alienated labor are countered by "energy"; the dreariness and monotony of daily life is countered by the excitement of "intensity"; the manipulation of daily life, from advertising to sex roles are answered by visions of open and spontaneous modes of communication ("transparency"); while the fragmentation of daily life by visions of "community" (Dyer 1977: 183–184). There was another development of the concept of utopia as applied to cinema made at about the same time by Fredric Jameson in his seminal "Reification and Utopia in Mass Culture" (1979). From his early exposition of the Frankfurt School (in *Marxism and Form* [1971]), Jameson has shown how the mechanisms of popular culture are based on a dialectic between an ideological and utopian function: "their Utopian or transcendent potential [is] that dimension of even the most degraded type of mass culture which remains implicitly, and no matter how faintly, negative and critical of the social order from which, as a product and a commodity, it springs [...] [W]orks of mass culture cannot be ideological without at one and the same time being implicitly or explicitly Utopian as well" (1979: 29). While this formulation has led to a number of extremely fruitful analyses, it takes the discussion of utopian film in a completely different direction. For some of these developments, see the Bloch issue of *Utopian Studies* 1/2 (1990). For Jameson on utopian literature in the stricter sense of the term, see his (1977a) "Of Islands and Trenches: Neutralization and the Production of Utopian Discourse."

represents things as they are, to be escaped from [...] *On The Town* is about the transformation of New York into utopia [...] It shows people making utopia rather than just showing them from time to time finding themselves in it" (1977: 188).

Dyer's analysis, while quite brief, has inspired other critics to use his categories to look for utopian moments in other types of film, as can be seen perhaps most surprisingly in Linda Williams's (1989) *Hard Core: Power, Pleasure and the "Frenzy of the Visible,"* in which her chapter on Marilyn Chambers and what she calls the "Utopian Energy of Sex" (entitled "Hard-Core Utopias") is juxtaposed to a chapter on the "dystopian side of hard-core visual porn: violent sadomasochistic fantasies" (183). While the representation of Marilyn Chambers's quest for satisfaction may not seem to fulfill the essential utopian requirement of the depiction of a new society, Williamson goes on to describe some recent films of Femme productions, films made by a group of female porn stars who have attempted to make pornography for women. These films are important, as they seek to "educate desire" – for men and women – and they point to new forms of interpersonal and subjective relationships which follow from representations of sexual pleasure which are no longer based solely on the male gaze or on male pleasure and ejaculation.

While at first glance, a discussion of pornography (particularly as presented by a man) might seem to be a perverse betrayal of the feminist utopianism of the 1970s, this issue raises two dimensions of the utopian film: the question mentioned above of *representations of interpersonal relationships* which are no longer based on the patriarchal norms to which I alluded in my references to visions of the family in television series; and in a second way, to the potential for a *subversion of the dominant system* through the celebration of sexuality. Here is Amos Vogel's introduction to his discussion of the "Forbidden Subjects of the Cinema" from his book, *Film as a Subversive Art*: "The attack on the visual taboo and its elimination by open, unhindered display is profoundly subversive, for it strikes at prevailing morality and religion and thereby at law and order itself. It calls into question the concept of eternal values and rudely uncovers their historicity. It proclaims the validity of sensuality and lust as legitimate human prerogatives" (1974: 201).

In Vogel's subversive canon, the film which best combines this assault on taboos with revolutionary politics is Dusan Makavejev's (1971) *WR – Mysteries of the Organism*. Banned in Yugoslavia when it was made, this film presents the ideas of Wilhelm Reich, specifically the equation of sexual and political liberation, in an erotic political comedy whose high point is the juxtaposition of a Soviet propaganda film about Stalin with scenes of seduction as the heroine sets out to demonstrate that "FREE LOVE WAS WHERE THE OCTOBER REVOLUTION FAILED!" (Cited in Vogel 1974: 155). While the notion of "Sexual Revolution" has come to mean something decidedly unrevolutionary today, these ideas do point to a particular sea change to which I have only alluded – the relative decline of utopian politics in the 1980s, for almost all of the films mentioned thus far were made before 1980. But of course there is one fundamental exception to the previous statement, for utopian politics in the 1980s have been shaped by feminist politics, and feminist film-making (and feminist film criticism) over the past two decades has worked through many of the strategies and forms of political film which I have been describing.[20] Let me begin my discussion of feminist film and utopia by raising one last possible category of utopian film.

New Technologies

Like Dziga Vertov's original vision of the democratizing and liberating powers of the movie camera, some activists in the late 1960s turned to what they saw as the utopian potential of new television and film technologies to open up and democratize the political process. These new technologies included cable and community access television as well as the hand-held camera and the video recorder. While the progressive

20 I do not have space here to attempt an outline of recent developments in feminist film theory and feminist film-making, but the interested reader will find an excellent summary in Teresa de Lauretis's "Guerrilla in the Midst: Women's Cinema in the 80s," *Screen* 31/1 (1990), 6–25.

features of these developments have been documented by critics like Doug Kellner, and while interactive television, for instance, was an important feature of the utopian democracy of Ernest Callenbach's *Ecotopia* (1975), they seem perhaps less utopian today ten or twenty years later.[21] Yet political activists, and particularly feminists, continue to work within these alternative currents and there are many recent films and video projects which testify to these utopian hopes. My first example is a little-known Mexican documentary, *Weaving Sea and Wind* (1987), which is composed of three films. The first documents how some Zapotec women in a small village are given super-8 equipment and instructed in the techniques of moviemaking. The women are also shown an older documentary about the village, which romanticized and misrepresented their lives by focusing on the exotic rituals of the Day of the Dead. Finally, we are shown the results of this endeavor: a film made by the women of the village about a day in their lives. This film is emblematic of the utopian project of empowerment – of understanding how society controls and constructs us and how new technologies might allow one to take back that social control. But this is only a first step; any project of self-transformation soon comes up against larger constraints and forces, and this brings us to my second example, Lizzie Borden's *Born in Flames* (1983).

Born in Flames is set in New York City, ten years after a social-democratic "war of liberation." Despite the new government's promises and egalitarian principles, women's issues have been moved to the background and it is politics as usual. The suspicious death in prison of a member of the underground Women's Army acts as a catalyst, bringing together very diverse groups of women who have been marginalized by the straight, white ruling elite and who are outraged by the government's attempts to

21 For a discussion of the "Guerilla Television" in the 1970s as well as the interest in public access television in the 1980s, particularly the work of the Manhattan based Paper Tiger video production collective, see William Boddy, "Alternative Television in the United States," *Screen* 31/1 (1990), 91–101. For a brief account of the earlier moment and the hopes for new technology, see Richard DeCordova, "Cable Technology and the Utopian Subject," *On Film* 12 (1984), 23–27. The best recent account of the use of television by political activists is Doug Kellner's (1987) "Public Access Television: Alternative Views."

cover up this death. To emphasize and illustrate the full implications of egalitarian feminist goals, the women of the film are mostly those marginalized women who are denied standing in contemporary society and its image industry – lesbians and women of color, single mothers, and punk performers. My description does little to impart a sense of Borden's film and her technique, her use of cutting and non-traditional forms of narrative, or for that matter, her use of punk music. But this film is essential to my discussion because it focuses not only on the *images* of struggle, but on the issue of the power of representation and the control of images. Much of the film is set in two alternative feminist radio stations, which serve as rallying points for the struggle. At another point, a group of women break into a television network studio to broadcast a tape they have made, ironically interrupting a presidential address dealing with the crisis and promising wages for housework. To draw attention to the importance of the control of the means and forms of representation in the battle for an egalitarian society, *Born in Flames* ends with the destruction of a network television tower. This action has symbolic and real consequences, for it is meant to break the hold of the dominant media to define and control our lives – similar to the women's rejection of the documentary about their village in *Weaving Sea and Wind*.[22]

In its depiction of an increasingly militant struggle for a new society, the film returns us to my earlier discussion of revolutionary and political films. But there are some important differences. This uprising is set in the future, and it *follows* a successful socialist revolution. At a moment of deepening crisis, when progressive movements are confronted by a cacophony of claims that we have reached the end of history, of ideology, of utopia, this film is significant in its juxtaposition of the shortcomings of traditional left politics with the ongoing dream of a better future. Rather than despair, this film is charged with hope. As the title suggests, the new

22 This act becomes central in John Carpenter's SF film *They Live* (1988). Aliens secretly control the United States by means of powerful broadcast rays which make them look human – except to an intrepid few who develop sunglasses which reveal the aliens for what they are. The aliens are finally defeated when a small band of humans break into their headquarters, located in a television network building, and blow up the broadcast tower.

is struggling to be born out of the destruction of the present; in the portrayal of women of different races and classes working together, the film offers the viewer powerful images of an alternative to capitalist patriarchy. Thus, *Born in Flames* seems to confirm my earlier suggestion that the utopian potential of film lies in its ability to capture moments of revolutionary upheaval and the hopes for social change.

I conclude my attempt to lay out some of the possible categories of the utopian film with two films which are not utopian in any strict sense of the term insofar as they do not portray alternatives. The *first – Weaving Sea and Wind* – is from the "Third World" and stages the retaking of misdirected utopian images of a nostalgic disappearing world, as they are replaced by images of empowerment through technology. The *second – Born in Flames* – is set in our own "developed" world, in New York City which has its own utopian history, for if it began as serving as the focal point for technological optimism, today (in movies like *Escape from New York*, *Soylent Green* and *The Ultimate Warrior*) it has become par excellence the dystopian cityscape. While neither my categories nor my examples are meant as definitive, I hope that they have at least provided a starting point for a discussion of what has been a largely overlooked area of utopian scholarship.

Table 1 Films Discussed

Title	**Director, Year**
The Andromeda Nebula (Tumannost Andromedy)	Y. Sherstobitov 1968
The Battle of Algiers	Gillo Pontecorvo 1966
Black Robe	Bruce Beresford 1991
Blade Runner	Ridley Scott 1982
Born in Flames	Lizzie Borden 1983
Brave New World	B. Brinkerhoff 1980
Brazil	Terry Gilliam 1985
La Cecilia	J.-L. Comolli 1974
A Clockwork Orange	Stanley Kubrick 1971
Dances with Wolves	Kevin Costner 1990
Easy Rider	Dennis Hopper 1969
Escape from New York	John Carpenter 1981
First Charge of the Machete	Manuel Gomez 1969
The Handmaid's Tale	Volker Schlondorff 1990
Harlan County U.S.A.	Barbara Kopple 1977
Hour of the Furnaces	Fernando Solanas 1967
How Yukong moved mountains	Joris Ivens 1976
If	Lindsay Anderson 1969
Jonah who will be 20 in the year 2000	Alain Tanner 1976
King of Hearts	Philipe de Broca 1967
Logan's Run	Michael Anderson 1976
The Lord of the Flies	Peter Brook 1963
Lost Horizon	Frank Capra 1937
Lucia	Humberto Solas 1968
Mad Max: Beyond Thunderdome	George Miller 1985
The Man with a Movie Camera	Dziga Vertov 1929
La Marseillaise	Jean Renoir 1937

(*continued*)

Table 1 Continued

Title	**Director, Year**
Matewan	John Sayles 1987
Medium Cool	Haskell Wexler 1969
Memories of Underdevelopment	Gutierrez Alea 1968
Metropolis	Fritz Lang 1926
Mistress of Atlantis (L'Atlantide)	Georg Pabst 1932
The Milagro Beanfield War	Robert Redford 1988
Morgan	Karel Reisz 1966
Nanook of the North	Robert Flaherty 1922
1984	M. Anderson. 1956/M. Radford 1984
October/Ten Days That Shook the World	Sergei Eisenstein 1928
On the Town	Gene Kelly/Stanley Donen 1950
Privilege	Peter Watkins 1967
Punishment Park	Peter Watkins 1971
Reed: Insurgent Mexico	Paul Leduc 1971
Salt of the Earth	Herbert Biberman 1954
Soylent Green	Richard Fleischer 1973
Strike	Sergei Eisenstein 1925
Things to Come	William Cameron Menzies 1936
THX 1138	George Lucas 1971
Triumph of the Will	Leni Riefenstahl 1935
The Ultimate Warrior	Robert Clouse 1975
Vent d'est	J.L. Godard/Dziga Vertov group 1970
Vladimir and Rosa	Dziga Vertov group 1970
Weaving Sea and Wind	Luis L. Fasano 1987
WR – Mysteries of the Organism	Dusan Makavejev 1971
Zardoz	John Boorman 197

CHAPTER 16

The Second Alien

In the following discussion, I will attempt to set out the situation and functions of the film *Alien* as an ideological practice which reproduces in the spectator a particular understanding of the real and of his or her place in that reality. In other terms, analogous to the work of the dream (and its subsequent decoding and analysis), cultural artifacts seek to resolve in an imaginary way, through the work itself, real conflicts and contradictions. Like the unconscious, ideology conceals and obscures real conflicts; and art, like the dream, becomes the privileged place in which this unconscious expresses and manifests itself, albeit in a displaced and covert fashion which it is the critic's task to unravel and disclose. Popular narrative forms – here specifically the SF-horror film – function through the displacement of authentic fears and anxieties generated by the contradictions of contemporary life under capitalism onto the source of the terror and suspense proposed by the film. Like the images of a dream which disturb us without our understanding why, the monster becomes a coded figuration of what we imagine to be the source of our problems and anxieties.

The central conflict of *Alien*, the immediate source of the spectator's tension and anxiety, lies with the fate of the crew of the space-freighter *Nostromo* and the terror and death they undergo. The first threat to them is, of course, the alien monster which stalks and kills them after they have brought it on board. But there is a secondary threat in the betrayal of the machines – Ash, the android science officer and Mother, the computer – who are programmed to act in the unnamed Company's best interests, even at the expense of the crew.

Alien builds on and develops three of the major trends of the SF film. First it is an SF monster film, a genre which characterizes the SF film boom of the 1950s. Second, *Alien* uses the theme of robots and computers, which also has an important literary and filmic history, but which is most prevalent in the movies made in the late 1960s and early 1970s. Finally, *Alien* is very much a part of the most recent trend toward big-budget SF films in which special effects predominate.

The first wave of SF monster films begins with the "Creature Cycle" of the 1950s – with films in which the earlier monsters of folklore and fiction (werewolves, Frankenstein, etc.) and particularly the prehistoric monsters of various "lost worlds" (a title borrowed from the Conan Doyle novel and filmed at least twice – in 1925 and 1960; see also the first *King Kong* or the five versions of Jules Verne's *Mysterious Island*), are renewed and transformed through the impact of the atomic bomb. From primordial, chthonic creatures awakened from the depths (as in *The Beast from 20,000 Fathoms* [1953] and Honda's films in Japan, beginning with *Godzilla* [1955]) to the monstrous mutations produced by atomic tests (beginning with the giant ants of Douglas's *Them* [1954]), this genre degenerates into the low-budget formula films of the "giant insect cycle": *The Black Scorpion, Tarantula, Attack of the Giant Leeches, The Deadly Mantis, Earth vs. the Giant Spider*, etc.[1]

The 1950s also witnessed a wave of alien monster and alien invasion films which illustrate a number of themes suggestive for a reading of *Alien.*

1 Films followed by dates are SF films generally recognized as particularly important. In addition to my own trips to the movies I have relied on three works for the SF film: John Baxter, *Science Fiction in the Cinema* (New York: Warner Books, 1970); John Brosnan, *Future Tense: The Cinema of Science Fiction* (London: The Book Service Limited, 1978); and James Robert Parish and Michael R. Pitts, *The Great Science Fiction Pictures* (Metuchen, NJ: Scarecrow Press, 1977). These works generally confirm the three waves I describe, although the specific interpretations are my own. Based on the more than 145 SF films discussed, I established the following profile for the years 1950–1976: in the years 1950–1961 there were more than 130 SF films made, beginning with three in 1950 and ending with twelve in 1961, and peaking with twenty-three in 1958. The second wave begins in 1965 with thirteen films (there were twenty-one films in the three years 1962–1964) and thirteen films again in 1966; in the following years production did not rise above ten per year until 1971. And since 1972 there has been an average of only five SF films per year, including a number of SF films made for television.

Some films present a single alien: it is almost always hostile and frequently preys on humans, as in Nyby's *The Thing* (1951), one of the first and probably the best of the 1950s SF monster movies and the most evident antecedent for Ridley Scott's *Alien*.[2] In *The Thing*, a group of men is pitted against a vicious, predatory alien which, in a masterpiece of pacing and suspense, stalks and kills them within the enclosed space of a small military base. Like *Alien*, *The Thing* begins with the investigation of an alien spacecraft – a UFO which has crashed near the North Pole – and with the recovery of what is thought to be the corpse of an alien frozen in ice. The alien accidentally thaws out and escapes into the Arctic night, returning to attack and kill. As in *Alien*, the film's suspense and terror come from the monster's ability to hide and from the group's attempts to find and destroy it. As in *Alien*, there is a crucial scene in which the men watch a Geiger counter slowly come to life and begin to beep faster and faster as the unseen monster approaches and then bursts into the room where it is, at least in the first film, then burned and destroyed. Other significant resemblances include references in both films to the alien's amazing adaptability and ability to survive and reproduce, and the term "perfect organism" is used in both movies. In both also there are images of the monster's biological stages and each sets out to reproduce itself. There are also significant differences. The Thing, although it is described as a plant (actually a carrot!), is intelligent; the monster of *Alien* is not. Moreover, the defeat of the Thing is a victory for a familiar Hawksian practicality and tough-mindedness as well as the victory of a group over an attacking enemy. The crew of the *Nostromo*, on the other hand, is eliminated one by one, despite all their group efforts, until Ripley single-handedly defeats the monster.

The mutated insects and awakened monsters of the first group of 1950s movies may be seen as mirroring contemporary anxieties about, as Susan Sontag put it, living under the threat of "something almost insupportable psychologically – collective incineration and extinction which could come

2 This film is usually attributed to the film's producer, Howard Hawks. It is based on John W. Campbell, Jr.'s story, "Who Goes There?," *Astounding Science Fiction* (August 1938). Campbell, as the editor of *Astounding Science Fiction* magazine, is often considered the most influential force on U.S. SF in the 1940s and early 1950s.

at any time, virtually without warning" (Sontag 2001: 224).[3] The first type of alien film, on the other hand – with its vicious and predatory alien – seems to evoke a deeper and more archaic kind of terror which is similar to the fears and anxieties exploited by the contemporary horror film. In the horror film, in Robin Wood's Freudian formulation, the monster figures as the repressed psyche of late capitalism: first of all, the sexually repressed, the deviations from the norm of capitalist patriarchy; but also the excluded others of our society who are perceived as threatening – homosexuals and non-whites, workers and foreigners.[4]

In the SF film repression is itself a theme, particularly in terms of the supposed opposition between the human and animal sides of "human nature." This opposition may be seen in the SF film as early as 1932 in *The Island of Lost Souls* (from H.G. Wells's *The Island of Doctor Moreau*, remade in 1977). In the context of the SF film boom of the 1950s, the most striking and explicit reformulation of this dualistic legitimization of repression is the film *Forbidden Planet* (1956), in which, on the abandoned alien world of Altair IV, two marooned humans live among the still-functioning machines of the vanished Krel. Vast alien machines designed to transform and concretize wishes and desires allow Dr. Morbius, while he is asleep, to unknowingly summon a "monster from the Id" to attack the Earthmen who have arrived to rescue Morbius and his daughter. Morbius finally realizes what he is doing when the invisible monster attacks his own house to prevent Morbius's daughter from leaving with the ship and the commander with whom she has fallen in love.

Society's need for the control and repression of instinctual drives is represented through the filmic tradition of juxtaposing white European Civilization with the barbarism and savagery of the world's non-white peoples and cultures. It can be seen in the portrayals of our own native peoples in the U.S. Western or in the older accounts of different civilizing missions to Africa, Asia, and the Americas as well as in recent films which deal with the war in Vietnam and the innate savagery of the Vietnamese

3 See also Fredric Jameson's commentary in *Marxism and Form* (1971: 404–406).

4 Robin Wood, "An Introduction to the American Horror Film," in R. Wood et al., *American Nightmare* (Toronto, ON: Festival of Festivals, 1979).

people (including *The Deerhunter* and *Apocalypse Now*). In the SF film, this racist sub-text is an important part of the significance of aliens. They either resemble insects, animals, etc., so that their bestial nature is inscribed in their very appearance; or, in the case of humanoid aliens, they are frequently not white, as is the case for the popular Flash Gordon serials of the 1930s and 1940s, in which the blond, fair-skinned Flash is pitted against the Asiatic Ming the Merciless.

There is, then, an important distinction in the functioning and significance of the alien in the SF film, from the elemental or archaic biological terror which is invoked in the portrayal of the single alien to the more complex social fears inscribed in the alien as a group or collectivity. The model of this second type of SF film, which also flourished during the boom of the 1950s, is the *invasion* in its many manifestations. The best example of this type of film is perhaps the 1953 version of H.G. Wells's *The War of the Worlds*. Made during the Korean War, this film shows the Martian invasion of Southern California (as opposed to the tranquil English countryside of Wells's novel). Although the Martians themselves are only rarely glimpsed, the advance of their invulnerable war machines and the scenes of the evacuation of Los Angeles were understood by many in terms of the "yellow hordes" reportedly pouring into South Korea and in terms of the "Communist menace" in general – particularly because of a scene in which a news commentator reports on the many struggles going on throughout the world against the Martian invaders.

While many of the invasions from outer space were seen and understood in terms of the explicit political realities of the period, other SF films seemed to deal with an even more frightening aspect of the Communist threat – the insidious and seemingly undetectable presence among us of Communist agents. The classic instance of this fear was Don Siegel's *Invasion of the Body Snatchers* (1956; remade in 1978), where a small-town doctor in Northern California discovers that his patients and friends are being replaced by simulacra. Here the struggle against the invaders is almost secondary to the task of detecting the aliens. This film is an allegory for the McCarthy period and the difficulties encountered in uncovering the Communists at work in our midst – a difficulty which was summed up in the film *I Married a Monster from Outer Space* (1958), where the wife's horrifying discovery of the true identity of her husband parallels the wife's discovery in *I Married a Communist* (1949).

Thus far I have tried to situate the monster of *Alien* in terms of the portrayal of aliens in the SF movies of the 1950s. In these terms, the threat which the monster seemed to represent has both an individual and a social significance. Whereas the individual alien evoked an archaic, biological terror, this fear was further developed in the invasion films to suggest a political menace as well. Again the differences between *The Thing* and *Alien* are suggestive, for these are differences not only in the possible meanings of the alien, but in the groups themselves. In Hawkes's film, the group includes civilians and scientists, but it is primarily a military organization. The crew of the *Nostromo* is a smaller and more heterogeneous group, made up of employees of the Company which owns the ship. Unlike the white men who confront the Thing, this crew of seven includes two women and one black. And in this sense, the crew might be said to pose, in miniature, the model for an enlightened and progressive capitalism which has been able to integrate into it blacks and women – two groups whose struggles for emancipation and equality have intensified the internal crisis of bourgeois democracy. But there is also a difference in what binds the two groups together: in *The Thing* it is a common ideal – Science for the scientists, Patriotism for the soldiers; but the crew of *Nostromo* is there for the money, a topic which is discussed on several occasions in the film. Moreover, in distinction from the older stereotype of wage slavery, the *Nostromo* represents an advanced "participatory" capitalism where the workers share directly in the company's profits.

But if the crew of the *Nostromo* is seen as a microcosm of society, it must be remembered that the Alien is not the only threat. The android, Ash, and the computer, Mother, also menace the lives of the human crew insofar as these machines are programmed to effect the capture of the Alien, even at the cost of the humans on board. The presence and importance of these machines refer us to a second wave of SF films.

The SF films of the late 1960s and early 1970s deal less with aliens and alien invasions and are more explicitly preoccupied with visions of the future of the social order, a preoccupation which corresponds to the concerns and crises of the U.S. in the 1960s. The image of a future Earth in which computers manage global affairs while humans are free to work and grow was described positively in the concluding stories of Isaac Asimov's *I, Robot* (1950). But this technological optimism soon disappeared in the films of the 1960s. It was replaced by dire warnings about the future in which the individual's freedom has been subjected to the impersonal and inhuman reason of the computer. The most significant and best known of these films of oppressive, computer-run societies – whose sub-text is the stereotyped image of government control and regimentation in the socialist countries – include Godard's *Alphaville* (1965), *Colossus: The Forbin Project* (1970), *THX 1138* (1971), and *Logan's Run* (1976).[5]

The threat of the Alien takes, then, its meaning from the context of two filmic traditions: the monster in the horror film as the return and revenge of the repressed psyche, on the one hand; and on the other – from the filmic legitimizations of the imperialist exploitation and expropriation – the portrayal of the world's non-white peoples and cultures as ignorant and barbaric savages. In similar fashion, there is a contextual dimension for the threat represented by the thinking machines of *Alien*. For, apart from a brief moment when these themes symbolized progress through technology, the robot and the computer are generally associated today with an increasing sense of alienation and loss of freedoms. In this way, the actual commodification and alienating effects of late capitalism are obscured and given other explanations and causes. Capitalism presents itself as the political will of free individuals, in opposition to socialism and communism, under which, or so our civics textbooks tell us, the individual is subject and secondary to the needs and will of the state. The dystopias of twentieth-century Anglo-American SF are almost always written in terms of the suppression of the individual – a suppression which is frequently figured through the mechanization of life and, more recently, through the images of computers and of computer surveillance and control of human behavior.

5 Other important films from this period which deal specifically with the collapse of the existing social order and which portray the near future in pessimistic terms include: *Privilege* (1967), *Fahrenheit 451* (1966), *Wild in the Streets* (1968), *Punishment Park* (1970), *No Blade of Grass* (1970), *Clockwork Orange* (1971), *Soylent Green* (1973), and *Rollerball* (1975).

In these terms, the *Nostromo* and its crew suggest the U.S.'s own current self-image. The *Nostromo* is a threatened ship, an image reminiscent of the current vogue of the pseudo-scientific "Lifeboat Ethics" of Garrett Hardin. According to this theory, in a world faced with overpopulation, pollution, and the imminent exhaustion of our non-renewable resources, the industrialized capitalist world, and most particularly the U.S., must not make the mistake of trying to save the rest of the world. According to Hardin, the U.S. is like a lifeboat with only so much room and limited resources – a lifeboat which will itself be lost if we attempt to rescue any more of the world's dispossessed and starving peoples. (This argument, like the present indignation over the plight of the "boat people," conveniently overlooks the U.S. role in the creation of the problem.) In this way, the Alien of the film is able to stand in for and symbolize, in a displaced fashion, our fear of the Third World, whose suffering and poverty is an integral part of our own comfort and satisfaction. And if the biological and instinctive "animal" characteristics of the Alien were not enough to suggest such a reading, the term *alien* is itself indicative. For in everyday linguistic practice *alien* refers not to beings from outer space, but to "citizens of a foreign state." It does not refer to the European visitor, but as the most familiar contemporary use of the term indicates, to those other, undesirable foreigners – the "illegal aliens."

Ripley's triumph over the alien thus is a victory for some new and enlightened capitalism, as well as the resolution of the spectator's fears and anxieties by means of a redefinition of the problems which threaten it. Her single-handed victory reaffirms the individualistic ideology of capitalism while positing the successful integration into capitalism of a powerful force for social change – feminism – which today threatens its continued smooth functioning. But this filmic displacement and resolution of the spectator's confused and mystified anxieties is an illusory one. For the real victor is the nameless company which owns the ship and which is directly responsible for all the threats and dangers that the crew must face. This responsibility belies the harmonious resolution of a triumphant and progressive capitalism and leads us back to the very contradictions the film, as ideological practice, sought to dispel. In sum, both the ravages of the monster and the betrayal of human lives by the machines were the result of simple business decisions. The film's resolution – the defeat of the monster – which apparently reaffirms capitalism's defense of the *human*, as it has been defined in opposition to the savage voraciousness of the Third World and to the "suppression of the individual" under a Socialist alternative, is in fact incidental, an accidental by-product of the production of profit. Nor does the film criticize the Company. It ends, rather, on a note of calm resolution: the spectator's emotions at that point would seem to be keyed to Ripley's own relief and calm and to her dutiful preparation of a report for the Company. Normality has been threatened and has emerged triumphant; the spectator's authentic anxieties about the existing social order have been dispelled through the fantasy identification and resolution of the problem – a fantasy solution in which the victims of U.S. imperialism are identified, in this displaced and coded fashion, as themselves the source of our problems.

Thus far I have attempted to read *Alien* as an example of the popular film which uses the fascination and appeal of two film subgenres – SF and horror – to manage and resolve collective fears and anxieties. This is done by situating the alien monster of this film within the context of the SF film and within the filmic tradition of the racist coding of non-white characters and cultures and by distinguishing between the more fundamental and primal biological terror of the horror film (which seems to envision more specifically "psychological" forms and areas of repression – particularly sex and sexual norms) and the SF film's preoccupation with more explicit fears about threats to the social order itself. In this way, I have argued that the crew of the *Nostromo* might be seen as the model for a renewed and enlightened capitalism, while the Alien suggests the threats which an increasingly militant Third World is seen as posing. The secondary threat of the *Nostromo*'s machines – Ash and Mother – are then images of the stereotyped fears of the inhuman subjection and control of a socialist world.

What remains to be explained in any such reading of a film is the spectator's own repeated need for such imaginary resolutions. If popular movies simply manipulate their audience, reiterating again and again variations of a single message – the experience of capitalism as both desirable and able to defeat its enemies – why do we need to keep on hearing that message repeated?[6] These films surely correspond to real needs, and the repetition has to do with their simultaneous promise of an end to and a resolution of our anxieties and sense of alienation, and with their inability to do so. We return to these types of movies because capitalism is in crisis, because we are frustrated and repressed and very often exploited and oppressed. These films attract us because in their very defense and reaffirmation of capitalism they lure and entice us with glimpses of alternatives which are subsequently denied and repudiated, but which remain the portents of a world of freedom in which the conflicts and exploitation of class society will no longer exist.

If the hopes for a different and more humane future implied in the composition and profit-sharing arrangements of the crew of the *Nostromo* are in effect contradicted by the film's ending, there is another, even more crucial utopian theme which is raised and then denied in *Alien*. The utopian possibilities of advanced technology and the deliberate foreclosing of those possibilities are perhaps what best characterizes the last and most recent wave of SF films. For the big-budget spectaculars, with those special effects by which they conspicuously consume useless technology (a characteristic also of the James Bond films), reject and repudiate one of SF's original starting points – the linking of technology and technological advance with the possibility of social transformation.

Star Wars (1977), to begin with the most famous and most successful of these films, is in reality anti-SF. Made with all the features of SF – spaceships, other worlds, robots and aliens, and an awesome array of advanced technology, the film uses these elements to efface and deny the utopian possibilities inherent in such impressive technical and technological developments. There is instead a blocking off of any alternatives. First, stated right from the film's opening, the story is set "a long, long time ago in a galaxy far, far away." Second, the film attempts to avoid any specific comparison with or reference to contemporary reality by omitting all of the

6 Charles Grivel, *Production de l'intérêt romanesque* (The Hague: Mouton, 1973). See also the articles by Stanley Aronowitz, John Brenkman and Fredric Jameson on these matters in the first issue of *Social Text*, and Fredric Jameson's review of Will Wright's *Sixguns and Society* and John Cawelti's *Adventure, Mystery and Romance* in *Theory and Society* 4 (1977), 543–559.

principal actors in today's struggles: although there is war and even the destruction of an entire inhabited world, there are no peoples struggling for liberation, no working people, no blacks (although there are a variety of aliens in various supporting and minor roles), no homosexuals, and no women outside the most stereotyped and sexist roles. Foregoing even the most simplistic "psychological" explanations of the sources of human behavior and conflict, in a way very similar to the recent film of Tolkien's *Lord of the Rings* (the first half of the trilogy was released as an animated feature in 1978), *Star Wars* mystifies real conflicts and their causes by presenting the film's conflicts as part of a universal and eternal struggle between the forces of Good and the forces of Evil.

Close Encounters of the Third Kind (1978), the other major big-budget/special effects SF film of the late 1970s,[7] takes as its model not Tolkien but Arthur C. Clarke (and von Daniken) and Kubrick's *2001: A Space Odyssey* (1968). This earlier film, which began the trend toward big budgets and lavish special effects, presents a three-step account of human history: a prehuman phase, the human epoch, and a third, post-human (spiritual) transfiguration. But this evolution is not presented as the gradual emergence and growth of the human; it is rather a transformation effected by an outside agency.[8] According to this Christian accommodation to evolutionary theory, humans have indeed evolved physically from "lower" forms; however, their intelligence, their Soul, is the result of a specific, extrinsic intervention (which is depicted in the film by the appearance of the "slab"). *Close Encounters* renews this metaphysical rewriting of human history by focusing on our contemporary sense of anxiety and alienation and then offering a religious solution. The answers to our current troubles and dilemmas do not lie in human activity or understanding, the film tells us, but outside and beyond us, in the heavens. The possibility or desirability of social transformation is eschewed in favor of sentimental and teary-eyed scenes of religious expectation and enlightenment.

7 The special effects of *Close Encounters* – particularly the "mother ship" of the film's ending – were considered so successful commercially that the film has been withdrawn from circulation while additional special effects scenes are shot.

8 See also Clarke's original story, "The Sentinel" (1954), as well as his novel, *Childhood's End* (1953).

The deflection of *Close Encounters'* implicit critique of consumer society, from the liberating potential of the visitors' advanced technology to a mystical solution from above, is a disheartening return to irrationalism and ignorance. Yet despite the obscurantism of real alternatives in these films, there is nonetheless a utopian dimension which can be detected through the application of a device similar to the electronic scanner which the crew of the *Nostromo* uses to locate the monster. The scanner I am thinking of is Greimas's semantic rectangle,[9] which permits a mapping of the possibilities and permutations of the original opposition I have noted in *Alien* between the animal and the human. In addition to the human crew of the *Nostromo*, we have noted the presence of at least one animal – the cat – as well as the various machines and mechanical devices which, at least in the case of the android Ash, constitute another life form. And there are alien life-forms as well, which range from the plant-like eggs in the hold of the alien ship to the monster's vaguely human adult form. Using Greimas's rectangle, these differing forms can be represented in a first schema (where expresses opposition and contradiction):

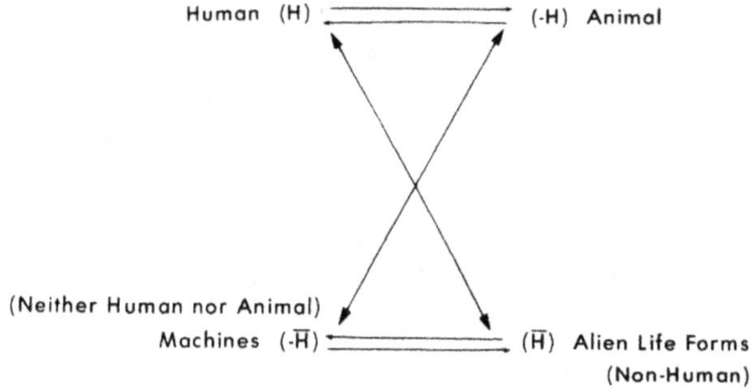

Figure 2 *Alien's* Semantic Field – First Schema

This first elementary semantic field becomes suggestive as the basic terms generate syntheses which lead to the three principal actors in the

9 A. J. Greimas, "Elements d'une grammaire narrative," in *Du Sens* (Paris, 1970), 160–161. For an application to SF see Fredric Jameson, "After Armageddon: Character Systems in *Dr Bloodmoney*;" *Science Fiction Studies* 5 (1975), 31–41.

film. Ripley, the film's final victor, represents the synthesis of the human and the animal: not only in her designation as the owner of the cat and in the familiar (sexist) coding of female sexuality in terms of the feline and more generally in terms of the instinctive, but more importantly, in terms of her single-handed victory as the return to an earlier Social-Darwinist model of the survival of the fittest. In our discussion of the alien monster we have frequently referred to the monster's instinctive drive, which stood in opposition to the hesitation and larger considerations and emotions of the human crew. In this sense, the alien monster represents the synthesis of the animal and the non-human. And the synthesis of the human and the machine would be the android, Ash, who was the Alien's principal ally as well as Ripley's chief antagonist among the crew members.

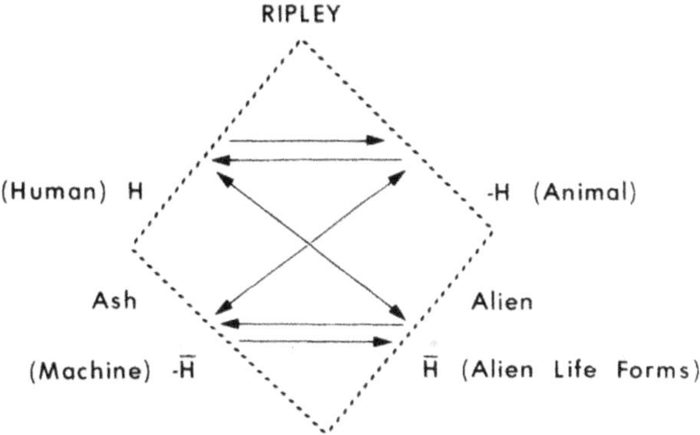

Figure 3 *Alien's* Semantic Field – Second Schema

The fourth term, the synthesis of the machine and the non-human, is missing. Like the utopian dimension itself in *Alien*, it has been suppressed and concealed. The discovery and exploration of the derelict spaceship reveals an important fact which is never again mentioned in the film: that there are in fact *two* alien races. There is, of course, the race of instinctive monsters whose eggs have stood waiting in the hold for some new host. There is also the race which built the spaceship – a race whose appearance we can only guess at based on the fossilized remains seated at something resembling a telescope (or an anti-aircraft gun), with a gaping hole in its thorax, like the hole the monster makes when it bursts from Kane's chest later in the film. Unlike the alien monsters, this race is intelligent, and even compassionate, for they have set up a beacon to warn other spacecraft away (a fact which Ripley discovers too late when she decodes what Ash had said was an SOS). But this suppressed fourth term is not simply the *other* alien, for what is most impressive about the other alien is its absence. This absence marks the place of the missing fourth term – the synthesis of the machine and the non-human – in a very precise way. For the alien ship is clearly an artifact, a machine, and yet it appears to be somehow organic. Its organic qualities are even more evident in the book of stills and artists' conceptions and drawings which has just been published (*Alien*, 1979) and in the novelization of the film by Alan Dean Foster. As Dallas, Kane, and Lambert approach the colossal, horseshoe-shaped craft, it seemed to them as if the spaceship had been grown rather than manufactured.

The film recounts, then, the passage from the instinctive to the "human" and the devastating effects of this repressive transformation of the life instincts under capitalism. But *Alien* is also a reflection on the theme of collectivity and what binds differing interests and competing individuals together in a system of social relations based on inequality and exploitation, particularly when that system is threatened and under attack. The older "glue" was exemplified in *The Thing*, in which the collective struggle against the Thing typified an older sense of common values and goals – the ideology of Americanism – which today has lost its cohesive, moral force and has been replaced by the ideology of consumerism. The new capitalism implicit in the motives and actions of the crew of the *Nostromo* holds these men and women together by direct material incentives – a share in the profits. Nor are there any personal human relations in evidence among the members of the crew (no love interest as in *The Thing*). The bond of material incentives is already under strain early in the film as Parker and Brett grumble about the size of their shares. And the film's conclusion, as I have pointed out, seems to contradict the ideal of group effort in favor of an older, more ruthless struggle for survival.

The suppressed fourth term, then, is the utopian impulse itself, as figured in a displaced and deformed way in the wonder and awe which the alien ship invokes. It is non-human, a negation of everything about the *Nostromo:*

the corporate system, the reduction of human beings to tools which can be switched on and off (they are awakened only when necessary for the ship's operation), the subjection of humans to the rule of machines, and the latter's ability to sacrifice the lives of the former. Moreover the alien ship transcends the utilitarian: it has an aesthetic dimension which, as Marcuse never tired of repeating, is the "eternal protest against the organization of life by the logic of domination, the critique of the performance principle" (1955: 130). And finally, the concept of the organic which characterizes the ship refers to the unspoken hope for a radically transformed reality, one held together and given force by life-giving and commonly held goals and aspirations, like the ship itself. This organic ship, then, returns SF to its utopian origins, to the dream of a humanized and liberating technology which will be the means of our freedom, "a science and technology released from their service to destruction and exploitation, and thus free for the liberating exigencies of the imagination" (Marcuse 1969: 38).

CHAPTER 17

Futurecop: The Neutralization of Revolt in *Blade Runner*[1]

My grand theme – who is human and who only appears (masquerades) as human?
– Philip K. Dick, Comment on "Second Variety" (1976)

Is it still necessary to state that not technology, not technique, not the machine are the engineers of repression, but the presence, in them, of the masters who determine their number, their life span, their power, their place in life, and the need for them? Is it still necessary to repeat that science and technology are the great vehicles of liberation, and that it is only their use and restriction in the repressive society which makes them into vehicles of domination?
– Herbert Marcuse, An Essay on Liberation (1969)

1. The look of the future in *Blade Runner* (1982) is what strikes us first of all about the film – a look unlike the high-tech visions of so much SF in its more realistic mix of technological advance and continuing decay. Indeed, the visual power and integrity of this glimpse of the future has been the focus of much of the critical writing about the film.[2] In the following remarks, I would like to focus on the actual putting into images

1 This article is an expanded and revised version of a paper read at an international conference (July 1986) on "Philip K. Dick et la Science Fiction Moderne," cosponsored by the Université de Paris IV (Sorbonne), Le Centre franco-americain Universitaire (Paris), and the University of California at Riverside.

2 The look of the film has interested critics in two ways: (a) for its portrayal of the near future "the densest, most arresting futuristic society in screen history" (Dempsey 1983: 34); "a future city which perpetuates corporate capitalism's distinguishing features – urban decay, commodification, overcrowding, highly skewed disparities of wealth and poverty, and authoritarian policing. The film's urban images present a world where advanced capitalism's worst features have coalesced to produce a polluted, overpopulated city in a society controlled by giant corporations" (Kellner

of Philip K. Dick's *Do Androids Dream of Electric Sheep?* (1968), for this recoding, from novel to film, distorts the novel's ethical message while foregrounding the tracking and "retirement" of the escaped replicants. I am not criticizing the film for what it omits from the novel per se, but for its conversion of a moral dilemma into a cynical legitimization of the status quo.

Without going into a full discussion here, the novel's ethical dimension lies not only in Dick's "grand theme" – "who is human and who only appears (masquerades) as human?" – but in the empathic spiritual experience of "Mercerism" which is dropped from the film.[3] The adherent grasps handles attached to an "empathy box" and then experiences Mercer's climb up a hill as he is pelted by stones, thereby joining in the struggle against entropy and the "tomb world" (1969: 140–141):

> [He] gradually experienced a waning of the living room in which he stood [...]. He found himself, instead, as always before, entering into the landscape of drab hill, drab sky. And at the same time he no longer witnessed the climb of the elderly man. His own feet now scraped, sought purchase, among the familiar loose stones [...].
>
> He had crossed over in the usual perplexing fashion; physical merging – accompanied by mental and spiritual identification – with Wilbur Mercer had reoccurred. As it did for everyone who at this moment clutched the handles, either here on Earth or

---

et al.: 6); and (b) as a blending of the conventions of SF and "film noir" (see Doll and Faller 1986; Dresser 1985).

3 Although many of the critiques of the film mention the novel, there is little extended comparison. The one exception is Wingrove's brief entry in his *Film Source Book* (London: Longman, 1985). On the other hand, Dick's critics have paid even less attention to the novel, accepting Suvin's judgment that it is one of the author's "outright failures" (1983: 93). *Androids* is discussed in Robinson (1983: 90–93) and in Warrick (1980: 223–228; 1983: 205–209). Despite my assertion that moral issues in the novel have been pushed to the background in the film, some critics do call attention to philosophical issues, particularly Dresser's "Science Fiction and Transcendence" – to which I shall return – and Telotte's "Human Artifice and the Science Fiction Film," in which he studies a "number of recent films which take as their major concern or as an important motive the potential doubling of the human body and thus the literal creation of a human artifice" (1982: 44). The development of Mercerism is an opening to the increasing use of transcendental themes by Dick in his late novels.

> on one of the colony planets. He experienced them, the others, incorporated the babble of their thoughts, heard in his own brain the noise of their many individual existences. They – and he – cared about one thing; this fusion of their mentalities oriented their attention on the hill, the climb, the need to ascend. (1969: 21–22)

Empathy, as we shall see in a moment, is the key to the novel.

Most movie-goers are familiar with the story of the "blade runner" Rick Deckard, who is forced out of retirement for one last job – to find and "terminate" four advanced androids ("replicants") who have rebelled and returned illegally to Earth. In Los Angeles in the year 2019, in a world in which pollution and radiation have apparently caused the death of many of the other living creatures on the planet, human technology has made it possible to copy the nearly extinct animals of the recent past. A similar technology makes it possible to build near-perfect copies of human beings. ("More human than Human" is the motto of the replicants' builder, the Tyrell Corporation.)

These androids were apparently developed to replace men and women in space under conditions in which humans could not function – in a vacuum, for instance, or in extreme cold or heat. While animals and other "lower" life-forms on Earth are presumably duplicated out of nostalgia and guilt, because the original terrestrial animals are almost extinct, there are few reasons given why anyone would go to the expense and trouble of developing a robot which could pass for a human being – especially since this resemblance is the source of considerable anxiety about androids passing as human, an anxiety which generates the plot in both the novel and the film. There is some explanation in the novel, as we learn when Deckard objects to the builder about the development of androids which are almost indistinguishable from humans. Eldon Rosen (renamed Tyrell in the film) replies in strict business terms: "We produced what the colonists wanted […] We followed the time-honored principle underlying every commercial venture. If our firm hadn't made these progressively more human types, other firms in the field would have" (1969: 41).[4] Whatever the

4 As opposed to this profit-motive explanation, Telotte argues in terms of the subjective motives of the replicants' creators: "Tyrell, it seems, is moved solely by his fascination with creating ever more perfect copies, replicants which can defy those tests for humanity which have developed in this future world […] Sebastian has

explanation, the robot and its ancestors and relatives have been used – at least since Mary Shelley's *Frankenstein* – as a figure for collective anxieties about the dangers of science and technology. At the same time, the robot has often been taken positively, as a figure of the labor-saving possibilities of technology (as summed up in the fiction of Isaac Asimov).[5]

---

turned his engineering skills to no less subjective end [sic], the task of filling his lonely life with manufactured 'friends'" (1982: 48). The important point – central to Telotte's article – lies in his attempt to analyze the fascination with "doubling": "As Arendt noted [in *The Human Condition*] – and as our accomplishments in genetic engineering every day point up – we already possess the potential which science fiction films have so frequently described, that for crafting artificial versions of man. What these films hope to forestall is the dark obverse of this capacity, that for making human nature artificial as well" (1982: 51). Corporate interests and machines which pass as humans are also an important element in Ridley Scott's earlier SF film, *Alien* (1979), where the science officer of the *Nostromo* is discovered to be an android and to have been acting against the interests of the humans on board. See, on this matter, Chapter 16, "The Second Alien," and Thomas Byers, "Commodity Futures: Corporate State and Personal Style in Three Recent Science-Fiction Movies," *Science Fiction Studies* 14/3 (1987), 326–339.

5 Without conducting a full review of the history of robots and androids (and their cousin, the computer), several points should be made. Even as the figure of the robot may point to actual technological developments, it is clear that it means much more. In general, one could speak of an opposition between *positive* images of the robot as the visible sign of the triumph of reason, the Enlightenment dream of human progress, as well as a more immediate symbol of the liberation from drudgery; and *negative* visions, which, at least since *Frankenstein* (1818), have paralleled those same beliefs and hopes in technological progress. While genealogies are always difficult (and there will always be someone with an earlier example), for many SF readers the theme of a robot "passing" for a human was introduced in Isaac Asimov's *I, Robot* (1950), and in particular in the story "Evidence" (1946). Set in the twenty-first century in the context of the anxieties of those who distrusted the increasing use of ever more sophisticated robots and computers, the story revolves around a politician who is accused of being a robot. In the larger context of *I, Robot,* this story is significant for its discussion of the moral dimension of the "Three Laws of Robotics" when juxtaposed to human morality. Asimov's own positive attitudes about the liberating potential of technology are summed up in the final story ("Evitable Conflict"), which depicts a utopian future where the world is run by the "Machines" – the extensions of the "positronic brains" of the robots. (Note that in the early 1940s, there was still no commonly accepted word for the

2. As is well known, Philip K. Dick used the figure of the robot, and more precisely that of the android, to raise a number of issues, including that of the original and the copy in the age of mechanical reproduction. *Do Androids Dream of Electric Sheep?* deals with what could be labelled the "blurring of the human and the machine." Here Dick walks a very fine line between attempting to elicit sympathy for the androids (the robot as metaphor of the oppressed and the exploited) and using the android to remind us of the growing risks to our humanity in an increasingly mechanized society.

---

computer. It is usually associated with the work of Eckert and Mauchly and the development of the ENIAC [Electronic Numerical Integrator and Calculator] in 1946, followed by the UNIVAC [Universal Automatic Computer] in 1951. Asimov saw that the upper limit to the development of sophisticated robots lay in the area of what is now referred to as "artificial intelligence," so he posited the development of a "positronic brain" for his robots.) Asimov's optimism is important in light of the shift in attitudes toward computers over the next decades. Along with a general distrust of technology following the use of the atomic bomb against the Japanese, the computer came to be one of our most powerful images of government control (Fitting 1979, 1980). And now, in the 1980s, there has been again a reversal in attitudes toward the computer, whose potentiality for control is increasingly subverted: in films like *Tron* (1982), *War Games* (1983), and the British television series *Max Headroom;* and of course in the writing of the so-called cyberpunks, beginning with Vernor Vinge's *True Names* (1984) and reaching its apogee in the writing of William Gibson (*Neuromancer* [1985], *Count Zero* [1986], and the anthology *Burning Chrome* [1986]). This is the subject of a book in itself. For a discussion of the first two periods, see for instance, Patricia Warrick's (1980) book. In the context of the robot as a figure for the liberation from drudgery, the rebellion of the machines in *Androids* should remind us that there is also another side to the meaning of the robot: as a figure of the increasing roboticization of the work process, not only in the increasing use of robots in the work place, but in the development of work processes – as epitomized by the assembly line – which rob the worker of individual choice by transforming him/her into a cog in the machine – as in Chaplin's classic film *Modern Times* (1936). The standard analysis of this transformation of the work process in the twentieth century and the alienation of the worker is Harry Braverman's *Labor and Monopoly Capital: The Degradation of Work in the Twentieth Century* (New York: Monthly Review Press, 1974). For an application of this issue to the robots of Asimov, see Portelli (1980). In their article on *Blade Runner*, Kellner et al. (1984) briefly raise this issue.

In the novel, the androids are not so much *not*-human as *in*human. As we have seen, the crucial difference is the ability to feel empathy:

> He had wondered […] precisely why an android bounced helplessly about when confronted by an empathy-measuring test. Empathy, evidently, existed only within the human community, whereas intelligence to some degree could be found throughout every phylum and order including the arachnida. (1969: 27)

Empathy is not only the key to distinguishing the human from the non-human (by measuring the ability to feel empathy for other living creatures – the "Voigt-Kampf Empathy Test"), but also, as already noted, the basis for "Mercerism," the inexplicable empathic mystical experience which is omitted from the film. The androids lack empathy; they cannot participate in the Mercer experience, and in the novel they are eager to expose it as a fraud (1969: 136). But their inhumanity is especially apparent in the manifestations of the replicants' cruelty and indifference, as summed up in a crucial scene – absent from the film – in which John Isidore (the model for JF) watches in horror as the androids torture and kill a spider (1969: 135–140).[6]

Nor is this the only instance in the novel of a rejection of the androids and what they represent, as can most explicitly be seen in the changes to the character of Rachel. The relationship between Rachel and Deckard reflects and increases his growing empathy for the androids he is expected to "retire," but in the novel Rachael (sic) explains that she has gone to bed with him so as to make it impossible for him to retire any more androids, a strategy which she has already used with nine bounty hunters before him (1969: 131–133).[7] In the film, Rachel does not set out to seduce Deckard.

6 "The android, which is the unauthentic human, the mere reflex machinery, is unable to experience empathy": Dick's 1978 comments (quoted in Dick [1987]: 389) on his "The Little Black Box" (1964), a story which deals with Mercerism. For a further discussion of these themes, see Dick's Vancouver speech, "The Android and the Human" (1972); see also the anthology of many of Dick's robot stories edited by Warrick and Greenberg (1984).

7 I do not have the space here to discuss the increasing appearance of misogynist themes in Dick's writing – a theme which his critics, myself included, have avoided for too long. For a novel which also mixes a "predatory" female and a sympathetic

On the contrary, he is the sexual aggressor, while she is frightened and vulnerable. She did not know that she was not human until Deckard gave her the empathy test and now she is afraid, confused, and lost. She does not ally herself with the other androids – as does Rachael in the novel – but with the one human who tells her the truth. (She in fact saves his life by killing the replicant Leon.) In the novel Pris and Rachael are identical models, made from the same "prototype" – a characteristic which again underlines that the androids are not human. Although Deckard cannot "kill" Rachael, he does kill her "duplicate," Pris, even as "it" attempts to use its resemblance to Rachael to kill him (1969: 145–146).

Despite Deckard's – and the reader's – hesitations and growing sympathy for the androids, then, a number of incidents, including their torture of the spider, their attempts to undermine Mercerism, and their inability to participate in that empathic experience, as well as the calculatedness of Rachael's seductive behavior, all make clear in the novel that the androids are meant to be understood as evil and inhuman. Yet the novel ends on an ambiguous note, with Deckard's continuing doubts about what he has done. The film, on the other hand, eliminates the ambiguity and doubts underlying Deckard's position through the happy ending, even as it blurs the reasons why the androids must be retired.

Although the replicants occasionally demonstrate superhuman physical abilities, there are few suggestions in the film of their underlying nonhuman nature. Instead they are obsessed with becoming human. To counteract attempts to return to Earth and live as humans, the replicants of the film have been built with a "fail-safe" – a four-year lifespan.[8] For this reason, they have come to Earth to learn how to control the aging process. More interestingly, and in ways which are not present in the novel, they are

---

humanoid robot, see his *We Can Build You* (1972). For a discussion of this issue in *Blade Runner*, see Barr (1991).

8 The expression "fail-safe" is used during the briefing on the escaped replicants by Deckard's boss. The "andys" of the novel also have a four-year lifespan, but it is presented as a by-product of their manufacture rather than as an intentional limitation, and as such, it plays no part in the androids' motivations in the novel. There is some confusion in the film on this subject, for although Tyrell tells Roy that he cannot reverse the process, Rachel has been built with "no termination date."

preoccupied with overcoming their non-humanity – witness their attempts to construct for themselves an individual human past, as summed up in the packs of family photographs which they collect and treasure. Roy, in appearance the coldest and least human of the four replicants, is also the one who thinks the most about his incomplete humanity. The last of Deckard's "assignments," Roy will die not because the bounty-hunter is able to retire him, but because his own brief lifespan has run out. Moreover, when he could kill Deckard, Roy instead lets him live, as a gesture toward the life he has only begun to know. As Deckard says in the voice-over:

> I don't know why he saved my life. Maybe in those last moments he loved life more than he ever had before. Not just his life – anybody's life. My life.
>
> All he'd wanted were the same answers the rest of us want. Where do I come from? Where am I going? How long have I got?

Seen from this perspective, there is a fundamental contradiction at the core of the film; for in the novel, even if it is not completely successful, there was an ethical juxtaposition of the human and the mechanical, a valorization of life and the living and a rejection of the machine; and this polarization between good and evil legitimized and explained the necessity of "retiring" runaway robots. Thus when Deckard consults Mercer, he is told that although all life deserves respect, he must continue to hunt and terminate the escaped androids: "What you are doing has to be done" (1969: 145). The film, on the other hand, wants it both ways, and at times the narrative of the replicants' struggle to survive threatens to overwhelm the viewers' sympathy with Deckard. There are, for instance, several long scenes in the film which focus entirely on the replicants; and there is, of course, Roy's death, to which I shall return. Indeed, according to Dick, the changes in the presentation of the androids constituted the principal difference between his novel and the film:

> [In the novel] the replicants are deplorable [...] cruel, cold and heartless. They have no empathy [...] and don't care what happens to other creatures. They are essentially *less* than human.
>
> [Ridley] Scott regarded them as supermen without wings.[9]

9 Quoted in Sammon (1982: 26). So far as I am aware, this particular difference is dealt with in only one of the articles on *Blade Runner*, David Wingrove's entry in

Interestingly enough, there is an even more surprising and revealing analogy that the film momentarily brings up to describe the status and meaning of the replicants. Early on, *Blade Runner* explicitly draws a similarity between the androids and another group of Americans who attempted to escape from their enslavement and "pass" for human: when Deckard says (in the voice-over narration) that his boss, because he calls the replicants "skin jobs," is the kind of person who in an earlier day "would have called black men niggers." Although the film does not return to this comparison (however, before he dies, Roy says to Deckard: "quite an experience to live in fear; that's what it is to be a slave"), it clearly points to the contradictory treatment of the androids in the film. This contradiction becomes sharper if we attempt to pursue the analogy between robots and slaves, for it would be difficult for any but the most racist viewer to continue to sympathize with Deckard if the hunting and killing of the replicants were transformed into the tracking of runaway blacks. In that case, sympathy would clearly and unequivocally lie with the escaped slaves from the beginning. But, as it is, the film retains its ambiguity: the replicants both draw our sympathy and yet, somehow deserve to be killed; or rather, it is only when they are dead that they no longer deserve to be killed! This contradiction suggests that the meaning of the film, unlike the novel, no longer lies with an interpretation of the ethical opposition between the androids and "living" creatures.

3. Instead, the narrative of the escaped androids, it seems to me, provided Scott with an opportunity to display once again filmic images of death and killing. Psychologists write about the effects of media violence on the spectator, but they address less frequently the causes of that violence,

---

his *Source Book*: "the main difference, and the one that subverts the central theme of the novel, is in the treatment of the androids. Dick makes it clear that his androids, no matter how sympathetic some of them appear, are radically *evil* because they lack souls. The movie, ironically, takes a more *humanistic* approach to the androids, or Replicants, and presents them as victims of human evil. The Replicants are capable of murder but even so they emerge, by the end of the film, as *morally* as well as physically superior to their human hunters" (1985: 40). In his brief account, Wingrove goes no further in his explanation or interpretation, but it is interesting that in such a short account he would stress a point which most of the other critics simply overlooked. I shall return to this in my conclusion.

the needs that it satisfies and that propel it.[10] I mention this, although I disagree with much of that research, because in the case of the most developed domain of the psychological study of effects, apart from advertising – namely, the effects of pornography – one can immediately identify, in however direct or indirect a fashion, the origins of this "need" with sexual drives. But violence? Many of you reading this may have explanations for the increasing need for pictorial and filmic representations of violence, but its origins are not as evident as with pornography, however much you may think of pornography as a debased or distorted form of human sexuality. What, we might ask, is the need for the portrayal of violence a distortion or debasement of? Without attempting to answer that question yet, I am arguing that in *Blade Runner* the actual hunting and "termination" of the replicants is but another version of the myriad contemporary depictions of hunting and killing other humans. Here the excuse for that display of killing is to be found in an SF device: the representations of violence with which we are already familiar, as seen in the narratives of cops, sheriffs, and soldiers who are only "doing their duty," is here justified as the hunting down and "termination" of rebellious machines who also happen to look like real men and women. This is but an aspect of what I consider one of the fundamental differences between SF writing and SF film, a difference

10 For an accurate sample of recent psychological studies of the effects of representations of violence, see the essays collected in Bryant and Zillman (1986). For a critique of this research, see Thelma McCormak's "Making Sense of the Research on Pornography" (in Burstyn 1985: 181–205). For a sensible discussion of the entire question, see Fraser's *Violence in the Arts* (1974). Finally, for discussions of the question of how film moves the spectator, see the articles by Dyer and Mulvey. My own approach is based on the work of Fredric Jameson, most specifically his "Reification and Utopia in Mass Culture," *Social Text* 1 (1979), 130–148; and on the discussion of 1950s monster movies at the end of his *Marxism and Form* (1971: 404–406). There, in a gloss on Susan Sontag's (2001) "Imagination of Disaster," he argues that the viewer's relationship to these films was caught up in contradictory feelings of anger and anticipation – anger at the society in which she or he was imprisoned and exploited, an anger which vented itself in the monsters' rampages. At the same time, glimpses of a repressed alternative could be seen both in the collective struggle against the monsters and in the figure of the scientist as an image of a non-alienated kind of work.

having to do with the increasing popularity of special effects since the success of *2001* (1968): namely, the foregrounding of visual pyrotechnics for their own sake, as opposed to SF's long claim – however restricted the number of works which actually achieved such a goal – to be a literature of ideas. This should not be taken as either a definition of what SF should be or a condemnation of the specular vocation of film. I may enjoy such spectacles; but liking is not enough, and it cannot be a substitute for an explanation. Without going into a discussion of such recent SF films as *Road Warrior* (1981) or *The Terminator* (1985), I would point out that films such as those are much more straightforward in their justification for the violence portrayed. *Blade Runner*, on the other hand, pretends that it is not really stimulating the desire for representations of violence since, after all, these are only machines. Moreover, as we shall see in a moment, some critics argue that violence and selfishness are transcended by the film's ending. Nonetheless, I am arguing that the foregrounding of violence and the change in the nature of the androids subtly and cynically distorts the major themes of Dick's novel by catering to violent escapist fantasies.

4. Let us return, then, to the question of what produces the need for these representations of violence and to the link between that need and the figure of the android. The robot, as I have already pointed out, has long been understood as our symbolic alter ego – a manifestation of the desire for liberation from toil and drudgery and from human frailty and imperfection, and also as the expression of an increasing awareness of our diminished status in the technological society we have built. The androids of *Blade Runner* suggest both of these contradictory possibilities: they offer a glimpse of a liberated and empowered humanity, which could be realized thanks to the wonderful possibilities of technology; but so too, they indicate the terrible price of that seductive empowerment in the substitution for our humanity of the qualities and characteristics of the machine.

Expressed this way, the film's theme seems faithful to Dick's novel, but this does not explain Scott's use of violence. Although Deckard carries out the retirements with increasing reluctance, the film presents those moments in much more vivid and graphic detail than does the novel. Indeed, through the lingering depiction of the termination of the four androids – particularly the two female replicants – the film substantially changes the initial

Dickian theme. In the transfer from book to film, then, a new element is introduced which can only be dealt with through the spectacle of violence.

Nonetheless, the scene in which Roy lets Deckard live has led some critics to argue for the "transcendence" of both characters at the end, through their "renunciation of violence" (Kellner et al. 1984: 7):

> Deckard must put aside his distrust of women, must transcend his emotional aloofness, must finally make the ultimate commitment – to give of himself and his humanity. To his credit, *Blade Runner* resolves its issues with the specific science fiction context it creates. Man merges with his creation. This new Adam and his genetically engineered Eve will become first father and mother of a new species. And they – we – have an ambiguous, ambivalent, violent rebel angel to thank for it.
>
> If Roy Batty is Satan, Adam, and Christ all rolled into one, and Deckard is the human recipient of the replicant's redemptive/heroic mission, what are we left to conclude? Mainly that the allusions to *Paradise Lost*, to *Frankenstein*, and to other works similarly concerned with the question of what it means to be a person, allow *Blade Runner* itself to participate in the redemptive process [...]. The replicants are products of technology and imagination [...] works of art made in our human image. Art, we may understand, can take on a life of its own beyond what its maker intended, but such a life can be positive. Such a work can possess innate qualities that improve our lives and make us whole. Art, whether it is the creation of "replicants" or the creation of *Blade Runner*, holds out the possibility of transcendence. (Dresser 1985: 178)

In opposition to such a reading, I am arguing that despite the scene in question, the film's meaning is a profoundly cynical and reactionary one. The hero's distaste for his job of killing escaped androids is contradicted by the film's sensuous and prolonged fascination with the depiction of those killings, even as his doubts are simplistically resolved in the happy ending. Three characters supposedly transcend their condition: the two "machines" – Rachel and Roy – and the human bounty-hunter, Deckard.

What Roy tells Deckard he has seen during his brief life does not completely confirm the renunciation of violence:

> I've seen things you people wouldn't believe. Attack ships on fire off the shoulder of Orion. I watched sea beams glitter in the dark near the Tannhauser Gate. All those moments will be lost in time, like tears in rain.
>
> Time to die.

Roy spares Deckard in a recognition of life, and the above words point to his sense of beauty; but his first example – an expression of Scott's own aesthetics of violence – is a scene from the battlefield. How does this beauty differ from the slow-motion death of Zhora as she crashes through a series of plate glass windows after Deckard shoots her in the back?[11]

More importantly, this argument for redemption would be more convincing if Roy's death were the final scene, but it is followed by the flight of Deckard and Rachel into the sunset. It is interesting to see how the critics explain this final resolution: Dresser, above, writes that Deckard has "transcended his emotional aloofness [... making] the ultimate commitment" (1985: 178); while for Kellner et al. this "symbiosis of humans and machines" is an indication that the film is not technophobic (1984: 7): "The flight to an empathetic and romantic interior space away from the external realm of public callousness suggests a general human aversion to capitalist market values" (1984: 8). I read the significance of the final scene very differently. Deckard is rewarded by the system he serves for his successful suppression of an armed revolt; while Rachel transcends her machine status by becoming a "real" woman – something which it is increasingly difficult for flesh and blood women to accept – namely, a submissive sex object, subject to her man's wishes and desires. Farfetched? The one exception to the absence of reasons why these machines should be built to resemble humans in the film lies in the replicant Pris's status as "a basic pleasure model" – an advanced sex doll. The importance of this latter theme in SF, as epitomized in Jeff

11 There is little depiction of the actual killing or "retirement" of the androids in the novel (Polkov, 65; Luft, 91; the Battys, 147; and Rachel, 145). The increase in violence from novel to film cannot be explained by arguing that film, by its visual nature, emphasizes violence in the way a novel does not. Compare the violence in Mickey Spillane's *I, the Jury* with the 1953 film version, where the situation is almost reversed: the protracted brutality of the novel is almost completely missing from that film. Moreover, not all violent films "aestheticize" violence in the way *Bonnie and Clyde*, *Clockwork Orange*, or *The Wild Bunch* do. A test case might be Pasolini's version of De Sade's *120 Days of Sodom* (Salo, 1975). For a sympathetic overview of low budget "gore (violence) and sexploitation" films, see the special issue of *Re/Search*, "Incredibly Strange Films" (Vale and Juno 1986). For a powerful analysis of the progressive political dimension of horror films, see Robin Wood's "An Introduction to the American Horror Film" (1979).

Renner's "The Shortest Science Fiction Love Story Ever Written" ("Boy Meets Girl/Boy Loses Girl/Boy Builds Girl") as well as the fact that the other replicants have been built with specific functions, allow us to ask what other functions Rachel has been given.

The happy ending as well as the resolution which is identified by Dresser as "transcendence" have in this regard another meaning. In both film and novel Deckard carries on until all of the escaped replicants are dead. In the novel, these retirements were the source of the novel's ethical concerns:

> "Don't you see? *There is no salvation.*"
>
> "Then what's this for?" Rick demanded. "What are you for?"
>
> "To show you," Wilbur Mercer said, "that you aren't alone. I am here with you and always will be. Go and do your task, even though you know it's wrong [...]. You will be required to do wrong no matter where you go. It is the basic condition of life, to be required to violate your own identity. At some time, every creature which lives must do so. It is the ultimate shadow, the defeat of creation; this is the curse at work, the curse that feeds on all life. Everywhere in the universe." (1969: 119; italics in original. See also 158)

In the film, however, in opposition to the somber ending of the novel, Deckard is not only rewarded for the risks he has undergone and for his reluctant exercise of violence in the maintenance of the status quo; the happy ending also absolves him of his doubts.

Finally, the possible redemption of the characters – human or machine – is made possible only by Roy's convenient death: he transcends his machine nature not by letting Deckard live, but by dying. The argument for transcendence (based on the renunciation of violence) falls apart if we ask what would have happened if Roy had not died (whether he spared Deckard's life or not). Deckard – or someone else – would have had to kill him. If Deckard had refused, he would not have been rewarded with the convenient overlooking of Rachel's continuing existence. She, too, would have been terminated.

Roy's renunciation and transcendence resemble the death of the villain in other narratives who repents as he lies dying. But as the comparison with black slaves suggests, Roy is not a villain. Although the replicants/escaped slaves analogy is made early in the film, the viewers' reactions toward them are carefully orchestrated so that we only fully sympathize with them once they are all dead! Roy's acquiescence and death remind us of the necessity of choosing between acceptance and rejection of the world as it is. Critics like Dresser speak of Roy's redemption insofar as it conforms to Christian salvation, which involves renunciation of attempts to change a flawed and oppressive world in return for a promised reward in the hereafter. The dove which Roy releases is a symbol of his soul, which ascends to heaven even as his body "dies." The character who represents an active threat to the status quo cannot be allowed to live, but in exchange for his voluntary death, Roy is offered a reward "greater than life itself": forgiveness for his mistaken rebellion and the promise of salvation in another life. On one level, critics like Dresser are right about Roy's transcendence in the film, but they have avoided spelling out its full meaning as an acceptance of the world as it is, and they have overlooked its violation of Dick's life and work.

Thus the question of our fascination with representations of violence is, in a sense, a false problem which points to a more profound deformation of the novel's original moral dilemma. In displaying at length the termination of the rebellious slaves, the film legitimizes the use of violence in defense of the status quo, even if that world is repressive and unjust. The film's violence can be seen, at least at the beginning, as the displaced expression and release of the spectator's anger at the abuses and waste of the present system. But this anger is gradually transferred in the film, from the wealthy – like Tyrell – to the exploited victims who dare to rebel. The robot workers who revolt against a system which exploits them and even denies them the status of "human" are hunted and killed with the complicity of the spectator. Yet somehow, because the most vicious of them, in his own death, still aches with the pain of all that is denied him, the film is read as the expression of a generalized human transcendence.

This is the story, then, of the trajectory from book to film, a trajectory whose implications Dick himself resisted. The film's producers offered him $400,000 if he would agree to suppress the novel *Do Androids Dream of Electric Sheep?* and allow it to be replaced by the screenplay of *Blade Runner*. Dick refused.[12]

5. Much popular art serves to maintain the status quo by stimulating our repressed hopes and fears; and then, rather than permitting those awakened feelings to become knowledge or praxis, it sets out to defuse this nascent recognition of social contradiction by redirecting and draining off those threatening emotions. These representations of violence provide incomplete satisfaction for the anger and frustration we feel when confronted with a world of plenty in which science and technology and the fruits of human labor are squandered in the intensifying race for new forms of destruction. Blade Runner co-opts and redirects our rage from the political and economic structures responsible for this exploitation and waste to its victims. The film does this by merging in a single figure – that of the escaped replicants – both the machines which are used to exploit us and all those who would refuse and rebel against that system of exploitation. For although the androids are the target of that anger in the film, they are not its real cause. Our frustration and alienation stem not from the increasing presence of machines in our daily lives, but from the imperatives of production and consumption which those machines serve and from the human misuse and misapplication of technology. This can be seen in the fact that the characters – whether human or android – are not in control of their lives in the film. Deckard is forced out of retirement to hunt and retire replicants against his will, while the androids themselves are nothing more than slaves; and Rachel is the product of a cynical psycho-technological experiment. Paradoxically, the film identifies and nourishes our fantasies of refusal and revolt against a system which

12 Sammon (1982: 26) quotes Dick as follows: "I was offered a great deal of money, and a cut in the merchandizing rights, if I would do a novelization of the screenplay, or if I would let someone like Alan Dean Foster come in and do it […] My Agent figured that I would make about $400,000 from this deal. But part of this package required the suppression of my original novel, and I said no […] They got nasty again. They began to threaten to withdraw the logo rights – we wouldn't be able to say that my book was the novel on which *Blade Runner* was based […] We remained adamant, though, and stuck to our guns, and they eventually caved in. In re-releasing the original novel I only made about $12,500. But I kept my integrity. And my book."

uses and manipulates us, by allowing us to empathize for a time with the four androids and their desperate rebellion. But as they are retired one by one, the film forcibly reminds us of the futility of struggle. Our frustration and resentment toward an order which increasingly turns to machines to exploit and control us is then displaced, from the human and societal source of that exploitation, to its victims, who are punished for their refusal of the impossible conditions of their existence. As opposed to the novel, which ends on a note of resignation with Deckard's acceptance of personal responsibility for human suffering, the film is a cynical denial of that message and of the major themes of Dick's book. Resistance to the status quo, however unjust the existing system is, will be punished, the film tells us, while the willingness to participate in the forcible maintenance of inequality and exploitation will be amply rewarded. The film ends with our first look at the world outside the dark, rainy city, as Deckard and his reward – his very own personal android, a grateful and subservient – and ageless – sex doll, fly off into a Playboy sunset.

CHAPTER 18

You're History, Buddy:

Postapocalyptic Visions in Recent Science Fiction Film[1]

A number of people who don't ordinarily go to science fiction movies have nonetheless seen Paul Verhoeven's *RoboCop*. Here a Dutch director, with no background in SF, consciously attempted to both use and critique some of the forms of popular American film so that it would attract two rather different audiences. On the one hand, through its mix of humor and violence it appealed to mass market tastes; at the same time, because of its political framing – particularly through the TV spots – it was able to satirically depict a Reaganite near future, a stance that drew more politically conscious viewers and introduced them to this subgenre of violence-oriented SF. In the following I will offer four overlapping and rather politicized readings of the violence portrayed in several recent films from within this tradition which are without the ostensible political stance of *RoboCop:* James Cameron's *The Terminator* (1984) and George Miller's three Mad Max films (*Mad Max* [1979], *Road Warrior* [1981], and *Beyond Thunderdome* [1985]).[2]

1 I thank David Galbraith for his many comments and suggestions.

2 Of course, the director of the Mad Max films – George Miller – is an Australian, but while Verhoeven's status as an "outsider" is apparent, I think, in the peculiar mix of violence and political satire, there is no such perception of an outsider's hand at work in the North American reception of the Mad Max films (although the first of the series could perhaps be called an Australian film). Updating this in 1992, I should add that in the interim, Paul Verhoeven has become the preeminent

The pleasure we take from films that are seemingly without aesthetic value or any progressive political content poses a dilemma for me, one whose workings and components provide the focus of this paper. If the following can be considered a form of analysis of the "social unconscious," an attempt to "deconceal" the repressed fears and hopes of the popular imagination, it must also be understood as an attempt at understanding the ways society shapes my own desires and perceptions. There is no "out there," no impersonal and objective stance from which to observe and comment.

In one way, these films might best be compared to so-called sexploitation movies, except that here it is not prurience that overlays the original SF premise (e.g., *Flesh Gordon* [1974]) but an apparent pandering to the audience's taste for violence. Narrative and generic conventions are used as the vehicle for *special moments*, like the nudity or couplings in sex film, which are held together rather than generated by the plot. The organizing principle of such films lies in the frequency and spacing of these moments rather than in the unfolding and outcome of the narrative. Moreover, in the case of the SF film itself, there are also special moments specific to the genre. The SF film reached a first peak in the 1950s with the various creature and invasion movies, which were related to the larger social and political climate of the period (the cold war, the bomb).[3] In addition to these popular hybrids of the SF and horror film, there is a second, "ideas," current in SF, perhaps best illustrated by the long success of the television series *Star Trek* (seventy-nine programs from 1966 to 1969, and in reruns a regular feature of non-prime time television). With the Arthur C. Clarke-Stanley Kubrick collaboration on *2001: A Space Odyssey* (1968), which was also the culmination of the "ideas" SF film, special effects became SF's main

---

Hollywood director specializing in cinematic violence: *Total Recall* (1990) and *Basic Instinct* (1992).

3 Among the many books on SF and film, the most recent is Vivian Sobchack's *Screening Space: The American Science Fiction Film* (New York: Ungar, 1987). For more encyclopedic reference works, see Phil Hardy, ed., *Science Fiction* (New York: Morrow, 1986); and David Wingrove, *The Science Fiction Film Source Book* (London: Longman, 1985). For a brief history, see also Chapter 16, "The Second Alien." For an attempt to situate the films of the 1950s in their social context, see Peter Biskind, *Seeing Is Believing: How Hollywood Taught Us to Stop Worrying and Love the Fifties* (New York: Pantheon, 1983).

attraction.[4] Although our ability to be dazzled by special effects has begun to wane (primarily because of their now repetitive character), SF films have been firmly established as money-makers since 1977 and the phenomenal success of *Star Wars* and *Close Encounters of the Third Kind*; the studios' earlier reservations have been replaced by wholehearted enthusiasm.

This intensification of particular moments could be written just as easily, for instance, using the history of the car chase scene, which is not without some relevance to the Mad Max films: from *Bullitt* to the spectacular chase in William Friedkin's *The French Connection* (which subsequent films have continually tried to outdo, as in his own *To Live and Die in LA*), such a study would go on to consider the development of the "car movies" (*Smokey and the Bandit* or the TV spin-off, *Dukes of Hazard*), "trucker" films (*Convoy*), and again, the overlap into SF (*Death Race*, *Damnation Alley*, *Battle Truck*).

What makes the films under study interesting to me is not the moments of violence themselves but their location in a future in ruins following World War III. This setting is made most explicit in the opening sequences of *Road Warrior*, which tell of the final clash of "two great warrior tribes" and the resulting chaos and destruction. *Mad Max*, on the other hand, is set in the context of a worsening energy crisis and the fight for gasoline to power people's cars, but the larger nuclear war-post-apocalypse background that interests me is hardly mentioned.[5] In *Road Warrior* the city is

4 For the question of special effects, see Michael Stern, "Making Culture into Nature; or, Who Put the 'special' into 'special Effects'?," *Science Fiction Studies* 7 (1980), 263–269; and Manfred Nagl, "The Science Fiction Film in Historical Perspective," *Science Fiction Studies* II (1983), 262–277; as well as the final chapter of Sobchack's *Screening Space*. The shift to special effects also explains the relative failure of the Star Trek films, for the original appeal lay in their situations and ideas. The films work only in reference to the TV series, for what is primarily a public of loyal fans. Although SF films are now acknowledged as money-makers, popular wisdom is that SF will not work on television, a mistaken idea that will only be confirmed by the new TV "Star Trek."

5 Because *Mad Max* addresses the energy crisis without really addressing the issue of nuclear war or a larger conflict, I confine my remarks to *Road Warrior* and *Beyond Thunderdome*. *Mad Max* feels like a film that is still finding its way. In this discussion I also exclude films like *Aliens* (1986), which certainly shares the violence of the others but does not share the postapocalyptic setting.

gone and we are in the "Wasteland," where Max plays out a western scenario: helping a group of decent people besieged by a gang of sadistic bikers. *Beyond Thunderdome* follows Max into two further models of emerging post-holocaust communities (although neither future seems to be the outcome of the escaped settlers in *Road Warrior*): the first, "Bartertown," is a social Darwinist view of life after the apocalypse in which only the toughest survive; and the second provides a glimpse of a utopian new beginning.

The first future is that of the myth of the origin of the state: the frontier town before the arrival of families, churches, or morality; one based, moreover, on a premoney economy, where we see not only the "superstructure" (Auntie Entity [Tina Turner] and her cronies, or the various items and services for sale) but also at least an aspect of the "base": the production of methane gas from pig shit. Nor does the pertinence of this economic model stop there, for the film also embodies the geopolitical reality of the late twentieth century, in which the base is increasingly centered in the cheap labor and natural resources of the Third World. This geopolitical reference is made explicit through the "embargo" when Master turns off the power, reminding everyone where political power ultimately lies. In the context of the film, the embargo forcefully demonstrates what an exploitative superstructure needs Max for – to control through violence the rebelliousness of the masses, in this case to kill Master's protector (Blaster). At the same time the embargo also reminds the film's First World audience of their dependence on the continuing ability of the developed countries to exploit Third World energy. Like the oil crisis of the mid-1970s, the image of Bartertown grinding to a halt resonates far beyond its immediate diegetic function through its indirect evocation of the lines at the gasoline pumps during the crisis. As in *Road Warrior*, then, there is an overemphasis on energy and the energy crisis, which, paradoxically, leads to a vision of the future in which there is an excess of available energy at the same time that many of the other features of advanced technological civilization have disappeared. There are few books, no television or household appliances, and little technology apart from that involved in keeping the cars running.

If Bartertown is the future of the attempt to reconstruct technology, the second future of *Beyond Thunderdome* is that of the no-longer-understood traces of technology. Max is expelled from Bartertown and abandoned in the desert when he refuses to kill Blaster. There he is rescued by a group of children who live in a pastoral Eden, awaiting the return of the savior – Max – who will lead them out of the wilderness, back to the wonders of civilization. But as Max tries to tell them, all this has been destroyed. Yet, as the film ends, we see some of the children now living in the abandoned buildings of a great city where they camp like nomads among the ruins of a technology whose meaning and functions will be lost within another generation.

The vision of the collapse of civilization, where people move among the ruins of a technology they no longer understand, is an important subset of the post-holocaust future in written and film SF, and it begins with evocations of the ruins of *other* (nonterrestrial) collapsed civilizations – most familiar to us in the remains of the civilization of the Krull in the film *Forbidden Planet* or in the many films and novels that depict Mars as an older dying planet, one on which, by extension, civilization has blossomed and died, as in the Martian novels of Edgar Rice Burroughs. This thematic current may be juxtaposed to visions of a future Earth where our descendants wander in the rubble, no longer understanding the remnants of technological civilization, from H.G. Wells's *Time Machine* (1895, film version 1960) through Jack Vance's *Dying Earth* (1950) and Russell Hoban's *Riddley Walker* (1980). (This category might also include the "lost civilizations" of A.A. Merritt and H. Rider Haggard, and by extension "sword and sorcery" of the Conan type, although such works are increasingly distant from the vision of a lost *technological* civilization, which is my starting point.) Images of collapsed terrestrial civilizations are not so popular in film – except as the result of nuclear war – although the ruined Statue of Liberty in *Planet of the Apes* is a striking visual representation of that theme.[6]

Finally, the theme of world destruction and world rebuilding *after* nuclear destruction is a staple of SF writing. (This theme is exhaustively cataloged in Paul Brians's recent *Nuclear Holocausts: Atomic War*

6 *No Blade of Grass* (1970) is perhaps the best-known postdisaster film in which the disaster was not caused by war. Based on the John Christopher novel, *The Death of Grass*, the film portrays the moment of collapse after a virus destroys most of the world's crops. In tone and mood, the disaster is, as I argue for *Road Warrior*, more of a pretext than a serious look at a post-holocaust world.

in Fiction, 1895–1984 [Kent, OH: Kent State University Press, 1987].) Films that deal with these themes range from more "serious" treatments, such as *Dr. Strangelove*, *The War Game*, *The Day After*, *On the Beach*, and *Fail-Safe*, through films closer to the mood of *Road Warrior*, such as *A Boy and His Dog*, *Panic in the Year Zero*, *Damnation Alley*, and *The Ultimate Warrior*, and include some particularly awful Italian Mad Max imitations: *Exterminators of the Year 3000*, *The New Barbarians* [*I nuovi barbari*], and *Stryker*.[7]

The Terminator is set primarily in the present. A few years into the future, nuclear war has broken out and the "defense network computers" have taken over and decided to exterminate humans. Against overwhelming odds, human resistance to the rebellious machines is nonetheless on the verge of success. In a last-ditch attempt to change their imminent defeat into victory, the machines send an android killer into the past to kill the mother of the leader of the resistance as a way of altering their present! In turn, the resistance sends a man back to protect her and to kill the "terminator." This is the background to the film's focus on the terminator and its mission, although we are given glimpses of the future in which the battle still rages, as gigantic war machines fly overhead blasting everything that moves, while a ragged guerrilla band of humans fights on.

7 See the special issue of *Science Fiction Studies* (July 13, 1986) edited by Bruce Franklin on "Nuclear War and Science Fiction." For a discussion of many of these themes in written SF, see Eric Rabkin, Martin Green, and Joseph Olander, eds., *The End of the World* (Carbondale: Southern Illinois University Press, 1983), particularly Gary Wolfe's "The Remaking of Zero" (1–19), in which he proposes a five-stage "narrative formula" in fictional end-of-the-world stories: "(1) the experience or discovery of the cataclysm; (2) the journey through the wasteland created by the cataclysm; (3) settlement and establishment of a new community; (4) the reemergence of the wilderness as antagonist; and (5) a final decisive battle or struggle to determine which values shall prevail in the new world" (1983: 8). Particular stories may pass through all of these phases or be limited to one or more moments. I cannot deal here with the differences between his model and my own, particularly since I am dealing with only a few films while he is attempting to generalize about a large body of works.

"Vehicles of liberation"

> Is it still necessary to state that not technology, not technique, not the machine are the engineers of repression, but the presence, in them, of the masters who determine their number, their life span, their power, their place in life, and the need for them? Is it still necessary to repeat that science and technology are the great vehicles of liberation, and that it is only their use and restriction in the repressive society which makes them into vehicles of domination?
>
> (Marcuse 1969: 21)

The aspect of these films that raises the ire of many of the critics of popular culture is the large place given to violence. On one level, the question of violence is a sociological or anthropological one: these representations may be designed to produce an effect, although probably not the "incitement to violence" sometimes described by sociologists.[8] Our society is permeated with images, games, and rituals of violence, from comic books and TV cartoons through the sham brutality of wrestling and the ambiguous ferocity of our supposedly non-violent sports, as well as the increasing bloodiness and gore of contemporary cinema and television. Arguments that attempt to blame the omnipresent spectacles and representations of violence for an increasing level of violence in "reality" do little to explain either the causes of social violence or our fascination with its repeated representation. To the contrary, it seems more reasonable to see these representations as symptoms of something else, and I am particularly interested in explanations of this "imaginary" violence which see it as an attempt to "manage" socially produced angers and frustrations, although sometimes such displaced imaginary resolutions are – in terms of the status quo – unsuccessful, and the rage and frustration erupt into the real.[9]

8 For a critique of this research see Thelma McCormak's "Making Sense of the Research on Pornography," in *Women Against Censorship*, ed. Varda Burstyn (Toronto, ON: Douglas and McIntyre, 1985), 181–205.

9 My approach is based on the work of Fredric Jameson, most specifically on his "Reification and Utopia in Mass Culture" (1979), and on the discussion of 1950s SF-monster movies at the end of his *Marxism and Form* (1971: 404–406). There – in a gloss on Susan Sontag's "Imagination of Disaster" – he argues that the viewer of

Much popular art serves to maintain the status quo by stimulating our repressed hopes and fears; then, rather than permitting those awakened feelings to become knowledge or praxis, it sets out to defuse this nascent recognition of social contradiction by redirecting and draining off those threatening emotions. These representations of violence provide only an incomplete satisfaction for the anger and frustration we feel when confronted with a world of plenty in which science and technology and the fruits of human labor are squandered in the intensifying race for new forms of destruction.

In the Mad Max films, that rage is fixed on the automobile itself, for the automobile embodies many of the basic contradictions of contemporary capitalism. Automobile production is the essential industry of the most developed capitalist countries. It was here that the techniques of the advanced capitalist mode of production – the assembly line – were developed and perfected. When it became a consumer good – the *private* automobile – this development intensified and hastened the growth of the U.S. economy for half a century. Today, as a result of competition from abroad, the North American economy's dependence on the automobile industry has been a primary cause of the recession of the last fifteen years. It is the "commodification" of the automobile, the conversion of the U.S. public away from a reliance on public transportation to a "need" for private automobiles, which, since World War II, has had a greater impact on our daily lives than that of any other technological development. The car is the quintessential totem of American (and one supposes of Australian) culture. Moreover, this conversion from public transit was based on the selling of a "preference" for private transportation which encapsulates our resistance to *collective* answers to social problems, an ideological blindness to certain kinds of solutions directly attributable to and orchestrated by corporate interests. (The classic case of this "impact" is the motorization of

---

these films is caught up in contradictory feelings of anger and anticipation. The anger is directed at the society in which he or she was imprisoned and exploited, an anger that vented itself in the monsters' rampages; while, at the same time, glimpses of a repressed utopian alternative may be seen in the collective struggle against the monsters, and in the figure of the scientist, as an image of a nonalienated kind of work.

public transport in the United States, of which the most famous example is General Motors's purchase of various municipal trolley and railway systems – most notoriously in Los Angeles – which were then converted to motor buses manufactured by GM.)[10]

Our relationship to our cars is at the core of the Mad Max movies, for what is more important in the first two films than keeping the cars running? And what is more important or pleasurable to the spectator than watching those cars be destroyed? Behind the appeal of violence is a secret fascination with representations of the destruction of that which best sums up our "lifestyle" for the rest of the world. For viewers in the developed countries, these films speak to the underlying recognition of the contradiction between a society of abundance in which so much is wasted and squandered, and the daily experience for many of increasing immiseration. The spectator's anger and resentment are here *displaced* from an identification of the systemic causes of inequality and exploitation, and from a recognition that alienation and suffering are the result of corporate decisions based on profit calculations, to the objects that incarnate that wasteful lifestyle.[11]

This redirection of the spectator's rage, away from the people who profit from this "preference" for private cars and toward the machines that have been used to exploit and enslave us, is made explicit in *Terminator*, in which the machines have become the enemies of humanity, bent on eradicating the human species from the planet. If the raison d'être of the

10 For an interesting discussion of the decline in public transportation in the United States as the result of a "preference" for the private automobile, see David St. Clair, *The Motorization of American Cities* (New York: Praeger, 1986), particularly his discussion of the "conspiracy theory" of Bradford Snell, according to which General Motors "purposefully sought to destroy electric public transportation in the United States by forcing an inferior technology on them – that is, the motor bus" (16).

11 There are numerous instances in art of the celebration of the car, and of its destruction. This has been one of the major preoccupations of video artists like "Ant Farm," as in their *Cadillac Ranch*, a film that "documents the creation of the Cadillac Ranch in Amarillo, Texas, where ten Cadillacs were buried in a wheat field on Route 66 as a monument to the rise and fall of the Cadillac tailfin" (*Art Metropole Videotape Catalogue* [Toronto, ON: Art Metropole, 1982.]. p. u). One could also peak of the popularity of various entertainments that feature exaggerated features of the automobile and their destruction, as in the various "monster" cars and trucks.

Mad Max films might be said to be the cars or their destruction, here the figure of the "terminator" itself is the film's center. The objectified physique body-builder Arnold Schwarzenegger itself becomes a gleaming machine, which is gradually disassembled and reduced to a metal skeleton before it is finally destroyed.[12] His weak acting and his notorious woodenness here become assets insofar as they work to suggest a machine trying to pass as human (best summed up in the scene in which his computer-brain searches for and then finds the appropriate reply to the landlord of the sleazy hotel where he is hiding: "Fuck you, asshole").

From the explanation of representations of violence as a way of managing resentment and anger which might otherwise threaten the status quo, I now argue that these films also raise questions about violence and the state. For the post-holocaust setting gives us a world without a state, and thus without the dilemma posed by state violence outside the boundaries of the law, as epitomized in the justifications presented by some of the witnesses during the Iran-contra hearings. This extralegal violence stems not from a psychological "need" for violence but from the structural contradiction between the capitalist state's "need" to protect free enterprise (at home or abroad) and its ostensible commitment to democracy. On another level, the frustration of the partisans of free enterprise when confronted with legislative attempts to protect consumers is figured in film in the frustrations of the policeman trying to preserve a society in which criminals have too many rights (Clint Eastwood in the *Dirty Harry* movies).

Road Warrior is a classic western in which "real" values only emerge when the veneer of society and its rules falls away. But like Shane and similar western heroes, Max disappears at the end; society must try to

12 There is, of course, a filmic subset that combines these themes, namely film about cars coming alive, from Walt Disney's *The Love Bug* to the more sinister car of *Killdozer*, Spielberg's *Duel*, or Stephen King's *Christine* (dir. John Carpenter). The specific prototype of the android that hunts a human who tries to run and must eventually turn and fight is, of course, the cowboy robot (played by Yul Brynner) in *Westworld* (1973). In the earlier film, the chase is the result of a malfunction; in the sequel *Futureworld*, the robot has been programmed to hunt and kill.

maintain itself without recourse to violence.[13] In this vein, *Terminator* offers two visions of violence beyond the law which are then sanctioned by the principle of self-defense: in the future setting, when the state has collapsed, through the depiction of armed resistance to the machines; and in the present setting, when the police are unable to protect Sarah, through the celebration of individual courage and force akin to the visions of Clint Eastwood or Oliver North. *Beyond Thunderdome* also demonstrates attitudes toward the state and violence, for with Bartertown it tries to imagine the reemergence of the state in social Darwinist terms, one based not on any innate or learned system of morals or laws but functioning solely on economic conventions. The economic system of Bartertown, however, as I have already tried to show, is itself riven by the contradiction between an emergent state apparatus and the actual "producers" of power – many of whom, by the way, are indentured slaves or prisoners, a rather brutal description of what a free-enterprise society might look like without even the veneer of bourgeois legal rights and freedoms.

After World War III

> The fall of outdated social systems, and of great empires based on them, makes some people imagine that the world is coming to a catastrophic end, and their terrified visions often take the form of art.
>
> (Franklin 1972)

Since at least World War II there has been a decline in positive, utopian visions of the future and an increase – particularly in science fiction – of

13 These themes are raised in a similar way through the setting of many of the Japanese samurai movies of Akira Kurosawa during the "time of troubles" of a collapsing feudal system. These more problematic moral dilemmas are vastly simplified in Western borrowings from Kurosawa, from the moral simplicity of *Star Wars (Hidden Fortress)* to the more cynical and nihilistic rip-offs of *The Seven Samurai* or Sergio Leone's reworking of *Yojimbo.*

visions of imminent decline and disaster. Fictional and filmic images of mass destruction have been a staple of the popular imagination, and critical strategies for "reading" such visions have often lain with demonstrating and understanding their relationship to the historical moment that produced them. In dealing with works that take the bomb or its aftermath as a theme, there are certain conventions that determine the critics' reactions. Visions of a post-holocaust landscape are deemed acceptable insofar as they are used as warnings about the dangers of nuclear war, for instance, while works that simply use such settings as a pretext for something else are not.

Indeed, one of the principal objections made against "trash" – whether in the name of high art or in terms of the "politically correct" – follows from the absence of an implicit moral standard which, in the case of the thematics of nuclear disaster, either depends on a work's mobilizing force as a warning or, by extension, on the realism of the portrayal of the disaster ("this is how it could happen," as in Peter Watkin's *The War Game*); or even at a further remove, by the use of this theme as a contextualization for other legitimate themes and stories that illustrate the eternal qualities of the human condition. What critics criticize in such films as *Terminator* or *Road Warrior* is their trivialization of this magisterial theme – their too-obvious utilization of this setting as a pretext for the scenes of excessive and stereotyped violence at their core. Although *Road Warrior* and *Terminator* do attempt to explain how this predicament came about and do portray a stereotyped struggle between good and evil, they are not perceived as really dealing with such moral issues, and certainly not as serious statements about the near future or the aftermath of World War III.[14]

14 There is little sense of how people actually live in the future in the films under discussion. Some more modest post-holocaust movies have paid more attention to images of how people in the post-holocaust future live, as in *The Ultimate Warrior* (1975) or *Escape from New York* (1981) – both set in New York – or *A Boy and His Dog* (1975). These three films give us more worked out visions of how people's lives are organized around daily survival, although all of them fall into the "exploitation" category as well. For a reading of the Mad Max films that argues their "serious" nature – in contradistinction to movies like *Damnation Alley* "where the nuclear aftermath is only a pretext for the adventure" – see Hall and Erlich (1987: 322). By attempting to apply Northrop Frye's "mythic patterns," the authors empty these

An illustrative example of this critical expectation about the correct treatment of apocalyptic themes can be seen in the reversal of the conventional treatment of a closely related theme in J.G. Ballard's "worlds" trilogy (*The Drowned World* [1962], *The Drought* [U.S.: *Burning World* (1964)], *The Crystal World* [1966]). There in each case the familiar scenario of a worldwide disaster is distorted in a troubling and "unacceptable" fashion. The workings of this theme – a cousin to that of the aftermath of a nuclear war – are familiar to us through many of the SF films of the 1950s, beginning with the awakened monsters in the films of Inoshiro Honda in Japan (*Godzilla;* and in the United States, *The Beast from 20,000 Fathoms*), through various U.S. "creature" and invasion films. In many of those films, the world – or some important part of it – is threatened and the film recounts the collective struggle against the marauding invader. Without going into a detailed description of the historical significance of these threats, what interests me here is the almost universal narrative trajectory of these films: from threat to collective struggle to the defeat of that threat. (There are, of course, exceptions which prove the rule: films in which the threat is not defeated, and this failure is used to intensify the film's warning quality, as in the original *Invasion of the Body Snatchers* [1956].)

In his novels Ballard portrays the human community in the context of worldwide cataclysms (e.g., an increase in temperature followed by the melting of the polar ice caps and a subsequent flooding) in *Drowned World* where, in opposition to the official struggle against the disaster, the main character turns against that effort and embraces the destructive force. Although there have been attempts to read Ballard's novels in some "positive" way (e.g., as elaborate Jungian metaphors of transformation), many of his readers within the science fiction community are extremely hostile to these works, even as they trigger new enthusiasms in other readers (and have led in part to the "new wave" in science fiction). Readers react to the inherently "wrong" ethical treatment of the theme, although Ballard

---

works of their historical specificity while falling into the trap of accepting the categories and values of the established canon and then trying to show how some films rise above the dross to meet these standards.

continues to go about his heretical rewriting of terminal landscapes in a very different vein than in the films under discussion.[15]

Returning, then to Mad Max and *The Terminator*, they share both the post-cataclysmic setting and an "unacceptable" treatment of this context. Rather than using the disaster as a warning, or even presenting it "realistically," these works use this setting as a pretext for the spectacle of violence.

Yet I would like now to reverse my position. For between the ethically acceptable treatment of a future post-holocaust setting, based on a work's attempts to warn us, and the unacceptable trivialization of the theme of the all-too-possible destruction of our world, there is another, third, way of reading those terminal landscapes. This reading situates the blasted, ruined settings not in a possible or probable future – the usual terrain for most discussions of these films – but *in the present*: as the scandalous images of a disaster that has already happened and in whose ruins we can already walk, although only if we are prepared to actually visit the collapsing inner cities of the great metropolises of the United States (Watts or the south Bronx). Like the light from Shelton's nova, an explosion that happened thousands of years ago and whose light is only reaching us now, these films give us temporally dislocated images of a present of which we are only dimly aware. In both cases there is a crucial misperception, so that we misinterpret temporally what we are seeing: as we gaze at the stars, we think that faraway explosion has just happened, and as we watch these films, we think they are referring to a collapse yet to come. Yet such positivistic thinking, which limits itself to the evidence of the senses and which resists more complex modes of thought, is a form of willed ignorance, a deliberate flight from the reality of the present, a temporal blindness that can be compared with that of the central figure in Philip K. Dick's novel *Time Out of Joint* (1959), in

15 The work of J.G. Ballard is in the process of being rediscovered, thanks to the success of his "mainstream" novel *Empire of the Sun* (1984) and Stephen Spielberg's recent film version. When that novel was short-listed for the Booker Prize in Britain, his portrayal of the British in the Japanese internment camps in Shanghai provoked the same sort of negative comments I have been talking about: instead of showing the heroism or noble suffering of the internees, he instead used this harsh setting as a pretext for his own aesthetics. For an overview of his work close to my own perspective, see the special issue of *Re/Search* on J.G. Ballard (Juno 1984: 8–9).

which, in a neurotic escape from the present, the main character carefully constructs a world from his past, a happier time from which the tensions and disorders of the present are banished. Like the manifest content of our dreams, which emerge only in heavily censored and coded representations, these filmic images of the future are displaced signals from the social unconscious. Distorted so as to be unrecognizable, these indications of major troubles in our present, signs of its fractures and contradictions, work their way to the surface more easily in these less-censored popular films, while the catastrophes of which they speak are not to be talked or thought of in polite society – nor in the great art of the canon, I might add, from which the "ideological" and the "political" are banned in the name of an art that stands outside time, and, when it does depict moments of social upset and strife, can only show the "eternal" values of the human race.

Conclusion

> The avant-garde is always a way of celebrating the death of the bourgeoisie, for its own death still belongs to the bourgeoisie; but further than this the avant-garde cannot go; it cannot conceive the funerary term it expressed as a moment of germination, as the transition from a closed society to an open one; it is impotent by nature to infuse its protest with the hope of a new assent to the world: it wants to die, to say so, and it wants everything to die with it.
>
> (Roland Barthes 1972: 69)

Let us return now to *RoboCop* and to the ways the films I discuss above image the future. Through its deliberate choice of political satire, *RoboCop* places itself outside the "unconscious" framework I have been using. Moreover, its attempt to consciously critique the SF genre leaves the film without an implicit alternative vision of the future. We are left instead with the image of a decaying inner city where the only apparent solution is an increased and more heavily armed police force – albeit one that will apply the law more equitably. The society of *RoboCop* is indistinguishable from the present, or from the media portrayal of the inner cities; the film depicts a society on the verge of collapse. The actual moment of collapse is, as we have seen, the setting of *Mad Max* and *The Terminator*. From this first moment, one can posit a historical narrative underlying these films which moves from the moment of collapse to the efforts to set out and rebuild in *Road Warrior* – an effort that is partially realized in the social Darwinist frontier of Bartertown. Collapse and rebuilding are then followed by a third moment – the radically different future glimpsed at the end of *Beyond Thunderdome*.[16]

Another version of this "narrative" can be seen by working back through the issues I discussed above. I began by arguing that we need to ask what the violence in these films is directed against. I answered that it is the automobile, and in a larger sense the machines of *The Terminator*, which have become the displaced targets for the anger and frustration of the spectator. Rather than take that reading further, however, I turned to the social context of this violence and discussed the films as reflections on the question of violence and the state at a time when the Right is increasingly dissatisfied with the too-liberal legal rights and restraints of capitalist bourgeois democracy. These concerns find expression in a narrative that again attempts to "manage" the spectator's repressed anger by identifying social problems with the myth of an overly lenient justice system and the concomitant feeling that if we could take the law into our own hands, we could somehow deal with those problems (e.g., Clint Eastwood in the

16 An important precursor for the theme of collapse and rebuilding after a (non-nuclear) war is the 1936 Menzies-Wells collaboration, *Things to Come*. Part 2, set in 1967–1970, depicts the emergence of a small, authoritarian society based on harsh social Darwinist principles analogous to those of Bartertown, although here the "chief" has consolidated his position through his strict enforcement of a decision to kill all victims of the highly contagious "wandering sickness" rather than through the physical might-energy production dialectic of Bartertown. There is, however, a major contradiction at the core of this portrayal of the shining technological future of 2036, which is built on the ruins of the "old world," although it is rarely mentioned by critics. While the film explains the familiar transition from war to the ruined Everytown of 1970, no explanation is given of how the highly advanced, enlightened "free-masonry of science" – made up of "the old engineers and mechanics" – which has "pledged [itself] to salvage the world," has managed to emerge from the war years without the destruction and barbarism shown in the depiction of Everytown.

Dirty Harry films, or better, Charles Bronson in *Death Wish*). The violence in the SF movies under discussion is, I argued, a manipulation of the spectator's anger by turning the viewer's attention away from the *final* causes of frustration and exploitation and focusing it instead on their *instrumental* or material causes.

The world of the children in *Beyond Thunderdome* is, on the other hand, a glimpse of a society beyond the violence and exploitation offered us in the Reaganomics of Bartertown. It is now time to link utopia and violence, time to turn my argument around again and say that these films are not so much fantasies in which violence is used as a solution beyond the boundaries of what is sanctioned by the state, but fantasies of the destruction of the state itself – the recognition of the necessity of overthrowing our present social forms in order to build an egalitarian future. And the final, shocking step in such a reading is to suggest that here the representation of global disaster, in its most terrible, appalling form – nuclear destruction itself – may be seen as figuring our mixed feelings, our real hopes and fears for a radically different future. Let me hasten to add that such a reading is not meant to downplay the real threat of nuclear destruction or the urgency of combating exterminism. I am attempting, rather, to articulate the repressed, irrational side of those visions. As these films suggest, a different society will not grow "naturally" out of the present, just as a better public transportation system could not grow out of decisions based on corporate profit. That new future, as glimpsed at the end of *Beyond Thunderdome*, can only follow from the destruction of capitalism. And the narratives I have outlined, from collapse through rebuilding efforts to the brief glimpse of a utopian society, make clear how painful that struggle will be; without, moreover, any definite idea of what that other future would be like. As the Beatles put it in their reworked version of "Revolution" (the "white album"), "When you talk about destruction, you know you can count me out/in." There is a fundamental ambivalence toward violence in these films. I share it. In a happier society of the future (*Beyond Thunderdome?*), I would hope that violence will have disappeared. But for the present violence seems, in some situations, unavoidable, if only in the face of the brutal suppression of peaceful strategies for social change: from within (in South Africa) or from without (in Nicaragua).

My analysis cannot stop here. The destruction of this society guarantees nothing. My point is not to argue that these films are somehow "progressive," that seeing them will shake capitalism to its roots. To the contrary, I have tried to show that even as – in a vision somewhere between dream and nightmare – these popular works nourish utopian hopes for what R.E.M. calls an "end to our world as we know it," even as they raise the possibility of a qualitatively different future, they also disarm and contradict such hopes by draining off the spectator's anxieties and energy into imaginary solutions and violent satisfactions. In describing these works I have tried to bring out their contradictory functioning as both ideology and utopia. I would like to be able to conclude by referring again to the utopian moments in these works, by pointing to their endings as signs of a better society which will rise from the rubble. But they stop on the threshold, as it were, with the destruction of this world. This is so even in *Beyond Thunderdome*, where, in the final scene, we see the children who went to live in the city, years later, huddled in a cavernous building lit only by candles, as Savannah repeats the now-ritual telling of "history back" and how they came to be there. But the film's final shot is of Max – like Toshiro Mifune at the end of so many samurai movies – standing alone, his back to us, with a sword over his shoulder.

Moreover, Savannah's importance at the end serves to remind us that until *Beyond Thunderdome*, the Mad Max films reflected an older cinema in which women were relegated to fairly minor and stereotyped roles; and certainly Tina Turner's character (like that of Grace Jones in the second Conan film) can hardly be seen as a breakthrough. It is in *The Terminator* that we see the "new" woman of the eighties (although not perhaps as "new" and tough as Ripley, Sigourney Weaver's character in the two Alien films). After a fairly conventional beginning in which Sarah is portrayed as fearful and indecisive (huddled behind a desk in the police station, for instance), her character is transformed, and at the end she becomes an independent, self-sufficient woman who heads south into the desert to hone her survival skills in preparation for the "coming storm."

Like *Beyond Thunderdome*, *The Terminator* also ends with the voice of a woman, as Sarah speaks into a tape recorder, giving advice and information to her not-yet-born son (who, remember, will grow up to lead the resistance against the machines). This moment of transition, this vision of a present pregnant with the future, is a potentially powerful image of a new beginning whose full implications are avoided in these films. As my conclusion, then, I would have liked to have been able to compare Sarah with those women who are prepared to fight for an alternative future, as in Lizzie Borden's feminist utopian film *Born in Flames;* or to the warrior women of recent feminist utopian novels (like Joanna Russ's *The Female Man* or Marge Piercy's *Woman on the Edge of Time*), works that not only speak of the need to destroy this society but go on to imagine an egalitarian future beyond the distortions and exploitation of capitalist patriarchy.[17] But I cannot offer such a conclusion. Sarah's role is only an instrumental one, and a modest one at that, because she will not so much give birth to the future as to the preservation of the past: for she serves as an intermediary between two men, the father and the son, both of whom, in a paradoxical rejection of the utopian politics of feminism, leave her to the present, while they are, if only in the regressive terms of this film, the men of the future.

It is this temporal paradox that perhaps best sums up the ideological limits of these films; for, in attempting to imagine the future, they must keep returning to the past. Sarah's son will be born, fight, and die; and on the verge of military defeat, the machines will send the terminator into the past to kill her. But she will be saved by a man from the future who will also father that son who will lead the resistance against the machines and then die again. Unlike this despairing, cyclical narrative of a perpetual return to barbarism, I have tried to sketch another narrative, of the unfolding of a different future, one that will not happen automatically but must be fought for and won. These films will certainly not change the outcome of

17 Contemporary utopian fiction represents a range of attitudes toward violence, particularly in the transition to the new society, from the peaceful strategies of Sally Gearhart's *Wanderground* (1978), to attempts to displace inherent violent tendencies through ritualized violence (Ernest Callenbach's *Ecotopia* [1976]), to more brutal assessments of the continuing presence of some violence in our lives: Joanna Russ's *Female Man* (1975), or Marge Piercy's *Woman on the Edge of Time* (1976). For a further discussion of these novels, see Chapter 9, "So We All Became Mothers."

that struggle, but a critical attention to the repressed hopes for an escape from that temporal loop, with its social Darwinist explanations of the immutability of human nature or the limits of our human future, may serve as the first step in the call for an art which, like the feminist utopias to which I just referred, speaks more explicitly of the contradictions of the present and of the possibility of a future of our own choosing.

CHAPTER 19

Urban Planning/Utopian Dreaming: Le Corbusier's Chandigarh Today[1]

> On the day when contemporary society, at present so sick, has become properly aware that only architecture and city planning can provide the exact prescription for its ills, then the time will have come for the great machine to be put in motion and begin its functions [...] The house that can be built for modern man (and the city too), a magnificently disciplined machine, can bring back the liberty of the individual – at present crushed out of existence – to each and every member of society.
>
> (Le Corbusier 1967: 143)

1 I wish to thank my travelling companion and guide to Brasilia and Chandigarh, Fredric Jameson, for all his observations at the time and for his comments and suggestions on this paper. I also wish to thank the architect Marie France Chatenet for giving me a tour of the "unité d'habitation" in Marseilles. I would like to thank as well the anonymous referees whose comments helped in my revisions. As I was correcting the final version of this chapter, I received the proofs of Vikramditya Prakash's Chandigarh's *Le Corbusier: The Struggle for Modernity in Postcolonial India* (Seattle: University of Washington Press, 2002). The author brings a unique perspective to this study of Le Corbusier at Chandigarh, for he is the son of one of the members of Le Corbusier's architectural team at Chandigarh and an architect and professor of architecture himself. The book's focus is on the intersections of Le Corbusier's architectural vision with Nehru's convictions about the importance of modernization for the new nation: "for Nehru, the repudiation of the colonizer did not also entail the repudiation of the promises of the colonial enterprise" (Prakash 2002: 11). In his account of these two visions and especially in their fruition in the Capitol Complex of Chandigarh, Prakash's reading attempts "to reinstate some of the losing voices in Chandigarh's history, those that are not heard so often or at least not so well. I would count Nehru's opposition to foreign architects and to the 'Anglo-Saxon' predilections of the bureaucrats, as well as Le Corbusier's poignant identification with the rural peasant as amongst those" (2002: 151). It includes an account of the genesis of Chandigarh, an attempt to make sense of Le Corbusier's "naive and somewhat troubled" ideas, as well as a close examination of some aspects of the Capitol Complex, in particular the history and legacy of the monument of the Open Hand.

> The critique of the utopian view of modernism, its imperialistic vision, and the manner in which it has been implemented in our cities and landscapes, has caused many to retreat from any discussion of utopianism. Indeed, the critique of the modernist version of daily life is well deserved as can be seen in the use of Le Corbusier's "Radiant City" as a model for many public housing projects, or Howard's "Garden City" as played out in the needless tracks of suburbs. There is an appropriately critical perspective in the recognition that the imposition of one "man's" utopian vision on a culture results in destructive imperialism. It is understandable that the design fields have largely retreated from an explicitly utopian project, seeking instead to "fit into" what is perceived as the mainstream culture.
>
> (Schneekloth 1998: 1)

Since the earliest utopias, the link between town planning – the arrangement of dwellings and work-places, malls, and public spaces – and its impact on the inhabitants of utopia has been crucial; indeed the organization of space is understood not just as a reflection or symbol of the new ideals, but as a decisive component in the production of the new man or woman, to the extent that some planners thought that planning itself could bring about larger social transformation. As Robert Fishman states in his presentation of the utopian visions of perhaps the three most important such planners – Ebenezer Howard, Frank Lloyd Wright and Le Corbusier:

> Many people dream of a better world; Howard, Wright and Le Corbusier went a step further and planned one. Their social consciences took this rare and remarkable step because they believed that, more than any other goal, their societies needed new kinds of cities. They were deeply fearful of the consequences for civilization if the old cities, with all the social conflicts and miseries they embodied, were allowed to persist. They were also inspired by the prospect that a radical reconstruction of the cities would solve not only the urban crisis of their time, but the social crisis as well. (Fishman 1977: 3–4)[2]

2 For a more general overview of urbanism and utopia, see Francoise Choay's introduction "L'urbanisme en question" to her anthology *L'Urbanisme: Utopies et réalités* (1965: 7–83). For an "intellectual history of urban planning and design in the twentieth century," see Peter Hall (1988), *Cities of Tomorrow*. In his study of Brasilia, James Holston explains that Oscar Niemeyer's plan was based on two premises: "The first premise is that the plan for a new city can create a social order

Architectural and social engineering are two interrelated aspects of city planning in the twentieth-century sense of the term "urbanism," forms of planning which grow directly out of the urban crises of European cities in the early nineteenth century.[3] Responses to the crisis generated by industrialization can be seen in the critiques of the capitalist city, epitomized in Engels's *Situation of the English Working Class* (1845), and in the reforms of Robert Owen and Charles Fourier, with their models for alternatives. The first of these urban utopias was the "Garden City" of Ebenezer Howard (1902) which revives a familiar utopian dichotomy between urban and anti-urban, between industrial progress and nostalgic visions of the past; or, remembering that Howard was reacting to *Looking Backwards*, between the

---

in its image; that is, one based on the values that motivate its design. The second premise projects the first as a blueprint for change in the context of national development. It proposes that the new city should be a model of radically different social practices. It argues that if this model could serve as an exemplar of progress for the rest of the nation, then it would be possible not only to generalize its innovations, but also to propel the country as a whole into the planned future it embodies. [...] The key point of modernist internationalism – often linked in the minds of both modernists and their critics with Soviet internationalism – was that the theory and technology of the modernist city provided an already developed means of saving the underdeveloped world from the chaos and inequities of Europe's Industrial Revolution. Salvation required implementing a national policy of urban development in which modernist cities would serve as the models and nodes of regional development. If the governments of third-world countries could exercise their authority to impose this policy, they would bring their nations into the machine age in an orderly and rational fashion. The construction of new cities, especially capitals, would stimulate technology, establish networks of communications, integrate vast and backward regions of untapped resources, and organize social relations collectively to maximize the potential benefits of the machine" (Holston 1969: 4, 82)

3 By the mid-nineteenth century, Barcelona had the highest population density in Europe (Lopez de Aberasturi 1979: 14). Following the first general strike of 1854, the city ramparts were demolished and the city government called for proposals for an expansion of the city. The successful extension of Barcelona was the work of the engineer and architect Ildefonso Cerdá (1815–1876) who is usually credited with coining the term "urbanization" in his *General Theory of Urbanization* (1859), which laid out his plan for the expansion of Barcelona. For a full description of the urban crisis of the nineteenth century, see Hall, Chapter 2, "The City of Dreadful Night" (1988: 13–46).

visions of Bellamy and Morris, or between those of St. Simon and Fourier; and more generally, between pastoral and urban utopias.[4]

In terms of the technological, planned city, the most influential and visionary architect of the twentieth century was Charles Edouard Jeanneret (1887–1965), better known as Le Corbusier, whose early projects played a major role in the emergence of "Modern Architecture" and the

4 Francoise Choay labels these two groups of planners the "progressives" and the "culturalists" (1965: 16–26). By "nostalgic" I am thinking of the "Afterword" to *Communitas*, where Percival Goodman describes a utopian future of 2020 in which the only remaining large cities are "museum cities" like Venice, while the principles of town planning derive not from Le Corbusier, Kenzo Tange, "nor even a Frank Lloyd Wright [...] but [from] a Victorian, John Ruskin" (240). Unlike Fishman, who opposes Howard's "moderate decentralization" to Le Corbusier's "great metropolis," Jane Jacobs (following Percival and Paul Goodman) rejects such a dichotomy, seeing Howard and Le Corbusier as two sides of the same authoritarian utopian-planning coin: "The most important thread of influence starts [...] with Ebenezer Howard, [who] looked at the living conditions of the poor in late-nineteenth-century London, and justifiably did not like what he smelled or saw or heard. He not only hated the wrongs and mistakes of the city, he hated the city and thought it an outright evil and an affront to nature that so many people should get themselves into an agglomeration. His prescription for saving the people was to do the city in. The program he proposed, in 1898, was to halt the growth of London and also repopulate the countryside, where villages were declining, by building a new kind of town – the Garden City, where the city poor might again live close to nature. So they might earn their livings, industry was to be set up in the Garden City, for while Howard was not planning cities, he was not planning dormitory suburbs either. His aim was the creation of self-sufficient small towns, really very nice towns if you were docile and had no plans of your own and did not mind spending your life among others with no plans of their own. As in all Utopias, the right to have plans of any significance belonged only to the planners in charge" (Jacobs 1961: 17). "The man with the most dramatic idea of how to get all this anti-city planning right into the citadels of iniquity themselves was the European architect Le Corbusier. He devised in the 1920s a dream city which he called the Radiant City, composed not of the low buildings beloved of the Decentrists, but instead mainly of skyscrapers within a park. [...] In Le Corbusier's vertical city the common run of mankind was to be housed at 1,200 inhabitants to the acre, a fantastically high city density indeed, but because of building up so high, 95 percent of the ground could remain open. The skyscrapers would occupy only five percent of the ground. [...] Le Corbusier was planning not only a physical environment. He was planning for a social Utopia too. Le Corbusier's Utopia was a condition of what

"International Style" in the 1920s and 1930s.[5] Late in life, Le Corbusier was responsible for two of the most important utopian cities of the twentieth century: the new capital city of Chandigarh in the 1950s; and then, a few

he called maximum individual liberty, by which he seems to have meant not liberty to do anything much, but liberty from ordinary responsibility. In his Radiant City nobody, presumably, was going to have to be his brother's keeper any more. Nobody was going to have to struggle with plans of his own. Nobody was going to be tied down. The Decentrists and other loyal advocates of the Garden City were aghast at Le Corbusier's city of towers in the park, and still are. Their reaction to it was, and remains, much like that of progressive nursery school teachers confronting an utterly institutional orphanage. And yet, ironically, the Radiant City comes directly out of the Garden City. Le Corbusier accepted the Garden City's fundamental image, superficially at least, and worked to make it practical for high densities. He described his creation as the Garden City made attainable" (Jacobs 1961: 21–22). John Gold posits two "Grand Narratives" or ways of interpreting the Modernist Movement: the first (from the 1920s), explained modern architecture as arising from "deep social commitment [and] the rational application of technology to building and construction. As such it was regarded as the only authentic contemporary architecture in that it employed the materials and constructional methods specific to that age and matched built forms to the functions that they served" (1997: 2). The second, the reaction to this first interpretation, "traced chains of causation that linked the *deficiencies* of recently designed urban environments back to the flawed visions of pioneering modern architects" (1997: 4).

5 There are several versions of Le Corbusier's ideal city, including his "Contemporary City for Three Million People" (1922), the "Plan Voisin" for Paris (which involved razing the Marais district and building eighteen skyscrapers in its place; see Fishman 1977: 206), and the "Radiant City" (1925). In addition to these utopian projects, Le Corbusier's role in Modern Architecture lies in the founding of the International Congress of Modern Architects (CIAM) in 1928, and his drafting of its manifesto, the "Charter of Athens" (1941). For a brief history of CIAM before World War II which stresses the differences within the group as well as Le Corbusier's rewriting of what was to become the "Athens Charter," see Gold (1997: 56–77); he continues with CIAM in the post-war period later in *The experience of modernism*. These visions formed the basis for the utopian future city in films like David Butler's *Just Imagine* (1930) and William Cameron Menzies's version of H.G. Wells's *Things to Come* (1936): "[His was] an exciting and compelling vision of the manner in which the industrial-age city could be transformed, not by escape into small garden cities, but by accepting the fact of urban concentration and high density and exploiting to the utmost the possibilities of modern technology in creating a new urban

years later, the new capital of Brazil, Brasilia, designed by his student Oscar Niemeyer (with whom he had worked in Brazil in the 1930s).[6]

This is not an essay about city planning per se: the literature on the subject would take years to even read and, in any case, I am in no position to provide definitive answers or even to adequately summarize all of the debates. Rather this is an essay about the impact of a visit to Le Corbusier's Chandigarh on someone who writes and thinks about the continuing validity and usefulness of utopianism today. Here then I will try to untangle and describe some key questions about social planning and utopia.

The first complication lies in the different types of criticisms of Le Corbusier's urban visions, criticisms which range from critiques of any

---

environment. The use of high-rise structures would permit the accommodation of an urban populace, yet leave large areas of the ground free for park and recreational use [...]. The plan [as laid out in his 1922 "City for Three Million People" embodied four basic principles: (1) decongestion of the centers of cities; (2) increase of density; (3) enlargement of the means of circulation; and (4) enlargement of the landscaped areas" (Evenson 1966: 29). In addition to the utopian socialists (Fourier, Owen, Saint-Simon), Le Corbusier was influenced by the visionary utopianism of Tony Garnier (1869–1948) whose detailed drawings and illustrations for an ideal city were published in 1917 as *Une cité industrielle, étude pour la construction des villes*. Although Garnier was never given the opportunity to build his ideal city, he designed and built a number of buildings in Lyon (where he lived and practiced), most especially a section of the city, "le quartier des Etats-unis," which was begun in the early 1930s and which was never completed. For a brief history of early twentieth-century "visionary ideas about the urban future," see Gold's first chapter, "Anticipations" (1997: 19–47).

6 Lucio Costa and Oscar Niemeyer's Brasilia is the supreme example of the "modernist city," a concept which is thoroughly defined in James Holston's *The Modernist City: An Anthropological Critique of Brasilia* (Chicago: University of Chicago Press, 1969). Holston studies Brasilia as the realization of modernist ideas and principles, as outlined in the manifesto of the International Congress of Modern Architecture – the "Athens Charter" – written by Le Corbusier in 1941. From Lucio Costa's original plan and Brazilian President Juscelino Kubitschek's choice of Oscar Niemeyer to design it, through its actual construction, it followed these ideals, unlike Chandigarh which, as I shall explain, was designed by a follower of Ebenezer Howard and which was then modified by Le Corbusier; and who then turned over the design of the residential sectors to his partners and concentrated on the capitol complex.

form of planning "from above" and those who recoil from Le Corbusier's emphasis on technology or from his vision of "skyscrapers in a park," or those who would flee the city altogether; while at the other end of the spectrum are those who simply think that this "Corbu" design or that building doesn't work. In addition to this distinction between Le Corbusier as an architect and as a utopian planner, it is also important to recognize and untangle some of the more ideologically based criticisms of Le Corbusier, beginning with those who (explicitly or not) reject utopianism itself with its dreams or plans for a better society (particularly as it assumes collective rather than individual solutions), as opposed to those who accept the need for some overall plan or pattern for the city but who argue that such plans should come from the citizens themselves and not "from above" (Bookchin, the Goodmans, etc.).

In his history of city planning in the twentieth century, Peter Hall describes and discusses what he considers the "key approaches" to city planning. Although his analysis goes well beyond the basic dichotomies I offered above (e.g., pastoral vs. urban), Hall deems all of these approaches "reactions to the evils of the nineteenth-century city" (1988: 7). The first basic attitude is Ebenezer Howard's "garden-city," one which generates its logical extension, regional planning: "the answer to the sordid congestion of the giant city is a vast programme of regional planning, within which each subregional part would be harmoniously developed on the basis of its own natural resources, with total respect for the principles of ecological balance and resource renewal. Cities, in this scheme, become subordinate to the region" (Hall 1988: 8).

These regional ideas begin with Patrick Geddes and come to North America in the 1920s via Lewis Mumford and the Regional Planning Association of America. In contrast to these developments, there is what Hall labels the "monumental tradition of city planning" which he associates with the Baron Haussmann in Paris and Ildefonso Cerdá in Barcelona. Le Corbusier's approach, in Hall's account, is different, borrowing elements from both the garden city and monumental traditions: he was an "all powerful master planner [who] would demolish the entire existing city and replace it by a city of high-rise towers in a park" (1988: 9).

The "line of planning thought" for which Hall has the most sympathy, however, and which flows from Geddes and the anarchist tradition, is grounded in the conviction that "the built forms of cities should, as generally they now do not, come from the hands of their citizens; that we should reject the tradition whereby large organisations, private or public, build for people, and instead embrace the notion that people should build for themselves" (9).

I will return to the discussion of anarchist planning in my conclusion. Let me now turn to the design and construction of Le Corbusier's Chandigarh, as a way of illustrating some questions about social planning and utopia, questions alluded to in my epigraphs and which – following visits to both Brasilia and Chandigarh – have been raised afresh for me.

How Did Chandigarh Come About?

With independence in 1947 came the partition of India into two countries, India and Pakistan (which were established along communal lines, Hindus and Muslims). The state of Punjab was itself divided, and Lahore, the former provincial capital, found itself in Pakistan, leaving the Indian state of Punjab without a capital. Rather than establish a new capital in an already existing town, the decision was made to start afresh, with an entirely new city, as Prime Minister Jawaharlal Nehru explained, "free from existing encumbrances of old towns and old traditions" (cited in Nilsson 1973: 89); "Let this be a new town, [he declared] symbolic of the past [...] an expression of the nation's faith in the future" (cited in Evenson 1966: 6).[7]

7 For a discussion of Nehru's role in the project see von Moos. Nehru's view of the importance of Chandigarh is summed up by Evenson: "The colonial yoke had been thrown off, and the moment had arrived for India to show the world that she could stand alone, that she could command her own destiny and govern her own house, and that against the brutality of nature and the vastness of her continent she could impress an ordered yet viable pattern of human life – proof that Indian civilization, though ancient, was still vigorous and creative" (1966: 6).

There were of course practical as well as symbolic considerations for the decision to build a completely new capital city. None of the existing towns could house the new capital, for none of them seemed capable of supporting the expansion necessary to provide for government functions, particularly insofar as the population of the state had actually increased with the migration of displaced persons from Pakistan. Once the decision was made to establish a new capital, there was the question of finding an appropriate city planner. Since the British colonial government had not encouraged or supported the training of Indian architects, it was necessary to look abroad.[8] Consequently in August 1948, the Indian government began to search for a foreign architect to build "an administrative center accommodating half a million people and expandable to one million" (Evenson 1966: 8). This

8 Although there was a Hindu tradition of city planning, in the twentieth-century cities had grown by accretion around the cantonments of the British. Bombay, Madras, and Calcutta were trading centers which spread out from the ports like any commercial city in the West; and although New Delhi had been laid out by the British architect Edwin Lutyens, next to the old city, population influx, particularly following partition, quickly overflowed the densities and boundaries of that plan. Le Corbusier will look to Lutyens and his plan in the design of Chandigarh (von Moos 1977: 426 and passim), while critics of Modern Architecture, like Peter Blake, dislike Lutyens's New Delhi as well: "Much scarier are certain single-use patterns that have literally demolished the cities upon which they were imposed. One of the most interesting examples of this abuse is New Delhi, whose incredible, bombastic central avenue – the Raj Path – was designed by Sir Edwin Lutyens, the great architect of the declining years of the British Empire [... A]bout ten minutes away, by car, is the main street of *old* Delhi, Chandni-Chawk. It wasn't designed by anybody in particular. It just happened [...] It is a totally disorganized and frenetic mess [...] Nothing works on Chandni-Chawk, that is, except life itself. For this is precisely the heart of the city, this is the place where all the action is! [...] Chandni-Chawk is the very essence of urban life itself: it is everything that people come to cities to experience, everything that suburbanites miss in their splendid isolation" (Blake 1977: 118–119). Sten Nilsson's *The New Capitals of India, Pakistan and Bangladesh* includes a chapter on the British decision to make Delhi the capital of India. As with Le Corbusier and the Mayer plan, the architect Edwin Luytens substantially modified the consultant adviser, Henry Vaughn Lancaster's original plan for New Delhi, a plan which was very much influenced by Patrick Geddes – just as Mayer's plan for Chandigarh was influenced by Ebenezer Howard. Peter Hall also discusses Luytens and New Delhi in his chapter on "Monumental Planning" (1988: 183–192).

process led to the selection of the New York architect Albert Mayer, who had been a lieutenant colonel in India during World War II. Mayer's experience in town planning followed to some degree the English Garden City Movement and "its reaction against [...] the sterility and monotony of the classical-geometric approach to planning" (Evenson 1966: 13–14), an approach which can be seen in his 1941 Baldwin Hills project near Los Angeles. For Chandigarh, Mayer envisioned:

> a fan-shaped outline, spreading gently to fill the site between the two river beds. The provincial government buildings [would be] located beyond the upper edge of the city within a fork in one of the rivers, while the central business district [would occupy] an area near the center. A curving network of main roads [would surround] the residential superblocks, each of which [would contain] a central area of parkland. (Evenson 1966: 13–14)

Mayer worked with Matthew Nowicki, who was put in charge of on-site architectural control, but Nowicki's death in an airplane crash in 1950 threw the project into disarray. After various consultations (and the need to find architects from a soft currency area), a new team was found to supervise the realization of the Mayer plan: from England, the architect couple, Jane Drew and Maxwell Fry; and from France, Le Corbusier and his cousin Pierre Jeanneret. Le Corbusier would be the "architectural advisor" and the other three, the senior architects (the original contract stipulated that Le Corbusier be there "four weeks twice a year" during its construction, von Moos 1977: 420). As they settled down to work, "Le Corbusier took charge of developing the master plan, designing the capitol complex, and establishing architectural control. Jeanneret and the Frys concerned themselves with directing the actual construction of the city and designing the remainder of the city's buildings" (Evenson 1966: 27).[9]

9 In New York, Mayer soon realized that Le Corbusier was substantially revising his plan; after a series of detailed letters to Fry, he went to India to meet with the new team (in June 1951), but it was too late. For the story of the abandoning of the Mayer plan, see Evenson (1966: 26–27). *The Open Hand*, the collection of essays edited by Russell Walden, includes the recollections of both Jane Drew ("Le Corbusier as I Knew Him") and Maxwell Fry ("Le Corbusier at Chandigarh"). In the same collection, Stanislaus von Moos gives an interesting account which states that Le

Construction lasted several years, but by the end of 1952, most government departments had moved from the city of Shimla to Chandigarh, and by September 1953 the move was complete. The differences between the two plans are summed up by Norma Evenson:

> It is in the emphasis on a monumental axial composition that the second plan of Chandigarh differs most noticeably from the initial scheme. Although in both designs the capitol area was planned to stand against the mountains, only in Le Corbusier's plan was there an effort to provide a single monumental approach linking the body of the city to its symbolic head and relating along a single axis the two main public areas of the city, the capitol complex and the civic center. (Evenson 1966: 32)

While considerations of Le Corbusier's Chandigarh tend to focus on the monumental Capitol Complex, it is important to include as well the 240 acres of the city itself, as a place to live and work. The basic residential feature in the Mayer plan was the superblock (which has been renamed sector and which are connected by Le Corbusier's seven types of roads (les "sept Voies").[10]

Corbusier's modifications to the Mayer plan are limited to decisions about the "size of the neighbourhood units" and most especially the replacement of curved roadways with Le Corbusier's "beloved" rectilinear axes (von Moos 1977: 422). One can also consult the notebooks ("carnets") that Le Corbusier kept during his trips to India and which include his drawings and notes and which allow us to follow the development of his ideas.

10 "Each rectangular sector of Chandigarh measured about 4,000 by 2,600 feet and was to be regarded as a largely self-contained urban community. Sectors were linked – and separated – by a grid of different-sized roads varying in size from small bridle (or rather bicycle) paths within the sectors, to residential arteries, throughways, and finally the grandiose Jan Marg running up the centre of the city towards the Capitol. In all seven main types of circulation were worked out […] Evidently Le Corbusier was anticipating a time when motor traffic might become a major force in India. In other respects too the plan followed old Corbusian prescriptions: the separate zoning of living, working, circulation and leisure; the fusion of country and city through the planting and provision of trees and parks; rigid geometrical control and delight in grand vistas and processional axes; a sense of openness rather than enclosure; a lingering hope that urban order might bring social regeneration in its wake" (Curtis 1986: 190).

The northern zone serves the functions of the civic administration while the southern zone houses the activities of the district administration. It is connected to the Capitol Complex, to the university, and to the industrial area by fast traffic roads. At the heart of the City Center is a central chowk or "piazza," marking the crossing of two' wide pedestrian ways running northeast to southwest and northwest to southeast in the form of a cross. Around the Hall, the Central Library, the Post and Telegraph offices, cinemas, shops, restaurants, banks, and so forth. A slow-traffic road encircles the chowk with large areas set aside for car parking. The chowk itself is free from any vehicular traffic […] and is ideally suited for religious activities and other festive congregations that are so important to the Indian way of life. The chowk is connected to other spaces of the City Center by a network of pedestrian ways. (Kalia 1994: 111)

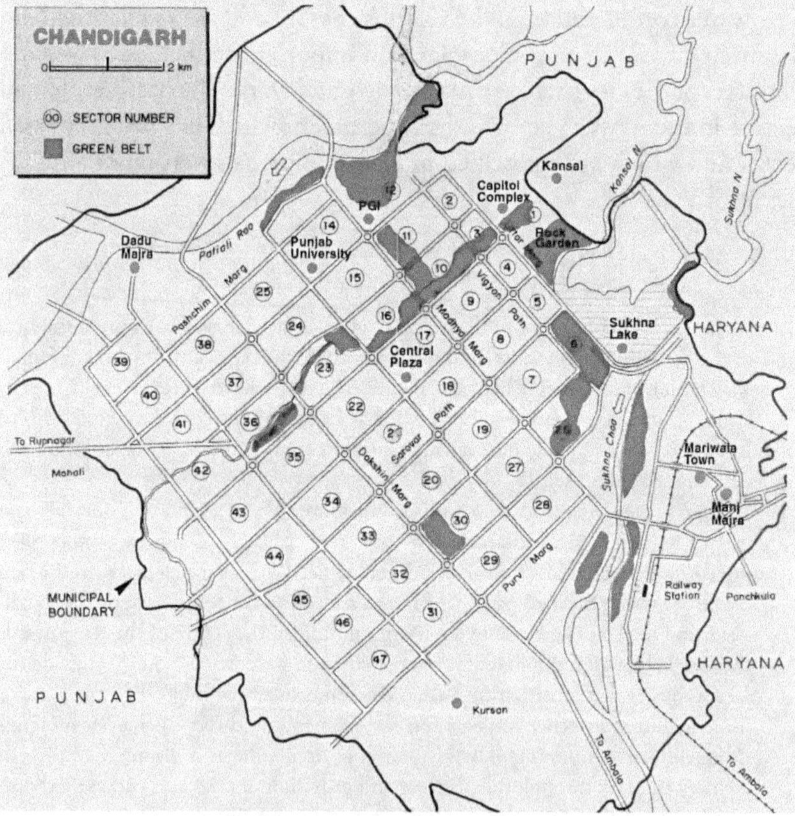

Figure 4 Map of Chandigarh, downloaded from Chandigarh public information site: <http://chandigarh.nic.in>

What Are the Problems?

As is implicit in the distinction I made between pastoral and urban utopias, Le Corbusier's vision of the city was grounded in the new industrial civilization (outlined first in 1923 in *Vers une architecture*, often mistranslated as "Toward a new architecture"), a vision hotly opposed by architectural critics like Lewis Mumford who (in the more organic tradition of William Morris) looked for inspiration in the work of Patrick Geddes and Ebenezer Howard. Mumford was horrified by Le Corbusier's "worship of science and technology," declaring "from the time I read the first edition of his *Vers une architecture* [...] I knew we were [...] predestined enemies" (cited in Fishman 1977: 258). Later Mumford reviewed his single most important building – the Marseilles "unité d'habitation" – in a 1957 article in *The New Yorker* entitled "The Marseilles Folly"; and as Fishman points out, today "Mumford's view of Le Corbusier has become almost standard":[11] "His Le Corbusier is an elitist technocrat, an authoritarian classicist, a sociologically naïve formalist with his grand design, his Cartesian elegance but also – alas! – with his Baroque insensitiveness to time, change, organic adaptation, functional fitness, ecological complexity' (Fishman 1977: 259).

These criticisms of Le Corbusier had already been made by Percival and Paul Goodman (1947); but the contemporary critique of Modern Architecture began with "the most influential book on planning in recent years" (Fishman 1977: 268), Jane Jacobs's 1961 *The Death and Life of Great American Cities*, and continues with books like Peter Blake's 1977 *Form Follows Fiasco: Why Modern Architecture Hasn't Worked*. These criticisms, with frequent reference to Le Corbusier, alternate between describing the alienating effects of high rises and planned cities, and the practical consequences of some of the principles of Modern Architecture, which – in its ideal of purity – has led to the construction of overly expensive, highly impractical buildings which cannot withstand the "real world of ice and

11 See in particular Mumford's "The Case Against *Modern Architecture*" (Miller 73–84) and "Yesterday's City of Tomorrow" (Miller 176–183).

snow and hail and rain and broiling sun and soot and otherwise polluted air" (Blake 1977: 40). At the level of daily life, these critics argue that such "sacred" planning concepts as zoning and single-use neighborhoods (e.g., residential separate from work space or business etc.), produce buildings and living spaces which are profoundly alienating, particularly because of the absence of street life.[12] Some of these criticisms can be found in Ravi Kalia's ambivalent characterization of Chandigarh, as safe and yet boring, unIndian and yet an inspiration for Indian architects:[13]

> The sectors, which make up the residential section, are marked by a sameness that leaves a visitor lost, without landmarks. Each sector is self-contained, providing essential services within walking distance of every dwelling. The most positive aspect of the sectors is that they provide a safety area for children. They can play, walk to school, and to shopping areas, usually without crossing a street.
>
> Chandigarh was meant to be something beyond a new state capital. But it lacks a culture. It lacks the excitement of Indian streets. It lacks bustling, colorful bazaars. It lacks the noise and din of Lahore. It lacks the intimacy of Delhi. It is a stay-at-home city. It is not Indian. It is the anti-city.
>
> But with all its shortcomings, Chandigarh provokes the interest of people far beyond the borders of India. Neighbouring Pakistan wanted to consult Le Corbusier and the Chandigarh administration as it got ready to build its new

12 "Le Corbusier's idealism [...] was indeed touching: he proposed beaming towers scattered among groves of trees, lawns, lakes, and streams in almost lyrical terms, speaking of man's yearning for greenery, sunlight, fresh air, and space. All very true; but man's primary yearning, it seems, is not for great expanses of open space, *but for other men* (and women and children) [...] What is missing from these well-intentioned diagrams for Ideal Cities is something so obvious that it has escaped the eyes of most critical observers. What is missing is *the street*, that most vibrant, exciting, irritating, and yet most stimulating of all outdoor spaces" (Blake 1977: 88; emphasis in original). This reproach can be found as well in the critiques of Brasilia, as for instance in James Holston's explanation of "modernism's doctrine of salvation [as] the elimination of the figural street" (1969: 133), and the resulting failure on the attempt to "stimulate new forms of public gathering" (1969: 310). The classic defense of street life is to be found in Jane Jacobs and particularly in the chapters devoted to "The Uses of Sidewalks" (1961: 29–88).

13 "Safe and boring": Depending on one's perspective, this description might be seen as either what is right or wrong with the model towns of the New Urbanism. See discussion below.

> capital at Islamabad. Burma, wanting to profit from the experience of Le Corbusier, sent him prepaid return ticket to visit Rangoon. The rest of the world closely watched the development of a planned city and the results it would bring. In India the city became an educating experience for India architects and planners, who rushed to other parts of the country to duplicate the features of Chandigarh. (Kalia 1994: 152)

Whatever the failings or triumphs of Chandigarh as a symbol of a transformed culture, its existence as an actual city where people live and work has been complicated by two sets of external problems, stemming from the explosive growth of the city over the past forty years, and from the political problems of the region. While the original plan called for "an administrative center accommodating half a million people and expandable to one million" (Evenson 1966: 8), the population today stands at just under seven million, and this does not include the numerous, unplanned satellite cities which have sprung up around Chandigarh. To make matters worse, in 1966 communal tensions led to the creation of two unilingual states, Punjab and Haryana, out of the previously bilingual state. Chandigarh was caught between Haryana and Punjab, each state demanding the city as its own capital. To resolve this predicament, Chandigarh was made into a "union territory" (like the District of Columbia), except that it was to serve as the joint capital of Punjab and Haryana, and the two chambers of Le Corbusier's bicameral Assembly building each became the legislature for a different state! This has also fueled the growth of the Chandigarh region as the two states have encouraged the development of adjacent satellite cities and industrial sectors as a way of increasing their competing claims to the capital. These new cities are completely unplanned, with no urban infrastructure, so that they depend on Chandigarh for medical services, education and other social services, even as they have sprung up in what were to be greenbelt in the original plan.

The architecture of Le Corbusier at Chandigarh will be remembered primarily for his capitol complex, which is composed of three monumental buildings: the Secretariat, the Assembly, and the High Court.

Here Le Corbusier uses much of the technology and ideas that he had developed for the sunny Mediterranean climate and his Marseilles apartment block (under construction at the time), particularly its utilization of rough concrete. The High Court was the first building to be completed and was put into use in March 1956; by the end of its first decade it was already too small.[14]

The Secretariat is a long, glass-walled office building with a central pavilion for the ministers. It resembles the Marseilles "unité d'habitation" and is based on the office project he had designed for Algiers in 1938–1942. Le Corbusier had wanted to build a high-rise office building but the project director was adamant that there would be no high-rise buildings in Chandigarh, so he came up with this "massive wall" (254 m long, 42 m high), composed of six 8-story blocks. (In his 1958 visit, Mayer found it "crude and chunky" [Evenson 1966: 80]).

Like the High Court building, it quickly proved too small, and the open balconies on each floor have been converted into additional offices. The most striking of the three buildings is the Legislative Assembly, which faces the High Court across the expansive plaza.

Finally, in the vast space between the High Court and the Assembly, there is the monument of the open hand: a giant hand, some 85 ft from an excavated plaza, which turns in the wind (and which was not completed until 1985).

As Norma Evenson sums up the general effect:

> It is this monumental aspect of the city which obviously attracted Le Corbusier's primary interest, and his efforts were directed toward the immediate development of a powerful capitol complex and toward giving the whole urban fabric the imprint of a monumental symbolism, drawing certain of its dimensions from the large-scale ordering of Paris. [...] The scale of the design may perhaps be justified [...] if it is remembered that Chandigarh was intended not merely to house a provincial government but to stand as a symbol of the creativity and vigor of the new Republic of India. [...]
>
> Perhaps the most praiseworthy aspect of the present master plan of Chandigarh, however, is that it provides for the integration of two orderings and two scales: first, a large geometric framework linking the monumental elements of the city, providing for rapid traffic, and defining the residential sectors; and second, within these sectors, opportunity for the establishment of more varied, informal elements appropriated for a pedestrian-dominated domestic environment. (Evenson 1966: 39)

14 When Mayer visited in 1958, he was impressed, calling it "a great evocative work of sculpture, not in fact architecture" (cited in Evenson 1966: 78).

The limits or failings of Chandigarh stem not only from its explosive, unplanned growth, but also from the design decision that separated the capitol complex from the city. This act rendered the monumental dimension of Le Corbusier's vision remote and distant from the citizens of Chandigarh. The sad irony of Le Corbusier's monument of the Open Hand – a symbol of "peace and reconciliation"[15] – is rendered even more distant and remote by the difficulties one encounters in trying to visit Le Corbusier's buildings, for the Secretariat and the Legislative Assembly, following the assassination of the chief minister of Punjab by Sikh militants in 1995, are now guarded by the army, leaving only the Courts open to the public.

As stated earlier, the criticisms of Le Corbusier and Chandigarh vary widely. Some objections lie at a practical level of architectural design who point to things that don't work in the grand designs of architects like Le Corbusier (e.g., Peter Blake). There were some problems with the High Court's "functional efficiency," for instance, beginning with the sound in the court-rooms – which Le Corbusier attempted to solve through the use of tapestries which he designed himself (and when some judges objected to them as "aesthetically unacceptable," Nehru insisted that they be kept [von Moos 1977: 437]). To deal with the summer heat, Le Corbusier developed sun breakers ("brises soleil"), although today the High Court is completely dependent on air-conditioners.

There are others, like Percival and Paul Goodman, Lewis Mumford, Jane Jacobs, and Peter Hall, who reject his ideas of city planning as based on a profound misunderstanding of human nature. These critiques, shared with most condemnations of Modern Architecture, focus on the alienating effects of life in such planned cities, and particularly on the absence of street life, stemming from Le Corbusier's notion of "vertical density" (a vision denounced most explicitly in Percival and Paul Goodman and in Jane Jacobs). In Chandigarh, however, this concept was not put into effect, primarily because of the opposition of the P.L. Varma, the chief engineer, who accepted all of Le Corbusier's changes to the Mayer-Nowicki plan, but who also insisted that there be no high rises. In any case, as we have seen,

15 In a letter to Nehru, Le Corbusier wrote that "the Open Hand will assert that the second era of the Machine Age has begun: the Era of Harmony" (cited in von Moos 1977: 447).

Le Corbusier quickly turned over responsibility for the residential part of the city and concentrated on the Capitol Complex (Fry 1977: 361–362).

There is some validity in the critiques of modern architecture. Yet it should be pointed out that some of the architects and urbanists who find fault with Le Corbusier's designs or buildings are not necessarily convinced of the free market's ability to produce alternatives.[16] More generally, market-driven alternatives to urban planning have little to offer our contemporary cities beyond a continuing flight to the suburbs and the gated communities of the rich. The first denunciations of the conditions of working-class life in London early in the nineteenth century still seem appropriate as descriptions of life in many of today's metropolises. Our cities, left to the laws of the market, can only reflect contemporary economic and class divisions. In the attempt to contrast planning from above and individual choice, the attacks on urban planning feed into contemporary criticism of any kind of planning, indeed of government itself, and these criticisms have become part of the rhetorical arsenal of those who are dismantling the welfare state. Meanwhile, attempts to (re)produce the unalienated city

16 See for instance Peter Blake's more autobiographical reflections in *No Place Like Utopia*: "Although I was not aware of it at the time, I now realize that something rather unfortunate had been happening to architecture in the U.S. during the years following World War II. While the Modern Movement, in the twenty years between the two wars, had been totally committed to the improvement of the human condition in a world that was becoming very rapidly urbanized and even more rapidly overpopulated, modern architecture in the wealthiest country on earth became increasingly the earmark of the very rich. The best modern buildings constructed in the U.S. after 1945 were almost invariably such glistening corporate headquarters as Gordon Bunshaft's Lever House in Manhattan and his equally splendid headquarters for the Manufacturers Trust Bank, for Pepsi Cola, for Union Carbide, and for countless other corporate giants […] More and more frequently, as time went on and downtown became associated with danger, these sumptuous headquarters were located in suburban Gardens of Eden far removed and carefully insulated from our problem cities and their poverty, crime, and physical decay. The Modern Movement – once dedicated to the ideals of an egalitarian democracy – had suddenly become the symbol of American capitalism at its most exploitative; and virtually no modern architect of any reputation was involved in such mundane problems as housing for the poor or even for those of low-to-middle income" (Blake 1993: 306–307).

of Jane Jacob's 1950s lower west side (now called the West Village) seemed to be based on the assumption that livable communities somehow develop organically, from within, and that people will be able to maintain and preserve their neighborhoods, while holding developers and land speculators at bay, without government intervention.[17]

Recently, in the United States, this impasse has produced the "New Urbanism," a nostalgic return to a vision of small-town America, whose most well-known exemplars are to found in Florida: Seaside – where *The Truman Show* was filmed – and Disney's Celebration, although many commentators have dismissed such experiments as artificial "theme parks."[18]

17 "Yet for all her enthusiasm for the cities, Jacob's message is an essentially negative one. Her faith in individual action is more than counterbalanced by an overwhelming scepticism about what people can accomplish together [...] For Jacobs, the cities are already built. They can be renovated but never transformed. To expect citizens to agree on a better kind of city and unite together for its construction is either a delusion or the self-serving illusion of the 'new aristocracy of altruistic planning experts.' Nor does her very real concern for the urban poor imply a commitment to any economic or social reforms. Indeed, the logic of her argument calls for even greater freedom for the capitalist entrepreneur" (Fishman 1977: 271). Fishman is not alone in pointing out some of the flaws in the belief that livable urban communities develop naturally. After a description and defense of the "richness" and importance of Jacob's "remarkable book," Marshall Berman turns to the failings of this "pastoral" vision of her New York City neighborhood, "for it is the city before the blacks got there [... before] the 1960s [when] millions of black and hispanic people would converge on America's cities – at precisely the moment when the jobs they sought, and the opportunities that earlier poor immigrants had found, were departing or disappearing" (Berman 1982: 324–325). On the other hand, John Dyckman accuses Jacobs of "editing the factory out of the city [...] neighbourhoods in which the monster of industrialization never intrudes" (cited in Ellin 1996: 135).

18 This expression is from Jane Jacobs, quoted in Robert Shibley (1988: 88). Jacobs is of course interested in preserving existing city neighborhoods; her book is as much an attack on the "decentrists" (e.g., Geddes and Mumford) and their rejection of the city in favor of "the ideal of cozy town life" (Jacobs 23) as it is on the city planning of Le Corbusier. While the New Urbanism cannot be reduced to the idea of building isolated new towns (like Celebration and Seaside), they are frequently cited as such and constitute a very different response to the crisis of the city today in North America. Although I am not really able to discuss at any length the New

While I certainly can't resolve these issues, or even summarize the vast literature on urban planning and renewal, let me make some points following from what might be seen as three general planning attitudes toward the city, namely (1) those who would flee the city in one way or another (and in this context the New Urbanism often seems like a new version of that attitude); (2) those "monumental planners" who would build entirely new cities (like Le Corbusier at Chandigarh); and (3) those who seek to work to improve and enhance existing cities.

In contrast to the apparent escapism of the New Urbanism (which, at least judging by the examples of Seaside and Celebration, seem little different from existing gated cities), Murray Bookchin's *From Urbanization to Cities* offers a much more interesting set of proposals for the renewal of city planning "from the bottom up," in his outline for a "new municipal agenda," (not unlike the "Municipal Charter" movement championed by Jane Jacobs).[19] The question that has preoccupied thinkers like Jane Jacobs

---

Urbanism here, and although I do not agree with all of his conclusions, Shibley's "The Complete New Urbanism and the Partial Practices of Placemaking" is an excellent introduction to the subject. He also quotes Herbert Muschamp, who called such projects "Potemkin villages for dysfunctional families" (88). For a critique of the New Urbanism that objects to it as a failed form of "social engineering" that has produced communities little different from other suburban communities and that fails to address the central "metropolitan problems," see Gordon and Richardson (1998). For a discussion of Celebration in the context of the New Urbanism, see Andrew Ross, *The Celebration Chronicles* (1999). For a cranky denunciation of Le Corbusier's pernicious influence on urban development and planning in the United States along with an endorsement of Seaside and the New Urbanism, see James Kunstler, *The Geography of Nowhere* (1993: 78–81 and 253–260), and his reprise of many of these ideas in *Home From Nowhere* (1996). The best known popularization of these attacks on Le Corbusier and modern architecture is Tom Wolfe's *From Bauhaus to Our House* (1981).

19 The aims and principles of the Municipal Charter movement can be found on their web site, <www.localselfgovt.org;> or in the collection of essays edited by Mary W. Rowe, *Toronto: Considering Self-Government* (Toronto, ON: Ginger Press, 2000). Peter Hall describes the anarchist planning tradition, which stretches from Geddes through Percival and Paul Goodman to Murray Bookchin, as starting from the conviction that "citizens make cities." This is how Hall's book begins: "For me, however unrealistic or incoherent, the anarchist fathers had a magnificent vision of

and Murray Bookchin is how to preserve and enhance the cities we already have. Bookchin goes well beyond the view that livable cities simply happen, arguing forcibly that "our chances for a natural and ecological society are much better in this [local and citizen-oriented] approach than in those that ride on centralized entities and bureaucratic apparatuses" (1995: 263).

---

the possibilities of urban civilization, which deserves to be remembered and celebrated; Le Corbusier, the Rasputin of this tale, in contrast represents the countertradition of authoritarian planning, the evil consequences of which are ever with us" (1988: 5). It is important to mention Percival and Paul Goodman's *Communitas* here for its early [1947] influence on a number of thinkers. The Goodmans focus on regional solutions and present three "community paradigms." The first, "A City of Efficient Consumption," is "founded on the premises of the official economics" (1947: 124): a metropolis of five million people organized in a series of concentric circles (with a total radius of five miles) with the core reserved for light manufacture and commerce, markets and restaurants, followed by a zone for universities and the arts, and finally the domestic sphere, and all this surrounded by open fields (and some heavy manufacture). The second model (which they prefer) is one which has reduced production and consumption (or in their terms which has "eliminated the difference between production and consumption"), so that work itself has become meaningful. (Lyman Sargent has assured me that this is the model for some of Ursula K. Le Guin's better known utopian societies, in *The Dispossessed*.) This results in smaller urban centers (200,000) with nearby farms and factories; and individuals are able to change activities over the course of the year ("a well rounded schedule of jobs for each man" [1947: 158]). The third alternative is labeled "Planned Security with Minimum Regulation," although this is not some libertarian world, but one of "assured minimum subsistence," a model which "has obvious applications to regions that are poorly industrialized but densely populated." The difficulty with these paradigms, at least in the context of my discussion, lies in the fact that these are all models of new cities: the first is an alternate New York, the second, very attractive utopia "is easiest to think of [...] as growing in virgin territory with new people" (1947: 220); and the third is a model for developing countries (although "in advanced countries too this scheme is not irrelevant" [1947: 220]). Since there no longer seems to be much chance for an entirely new city, I am interested in proposals for dealing with existing cities. Of course the Goodmans's utopian proposals for new cities are very different than those of Le Corbusier (whom they dismiss as "a poor social critic and a bad prophet," [1947: 48]. For a discussion of his ideas see Goodman and Goodman 1947: 42–49, and passim): "for in the end, the great machine of the Ville Radieuse, with all its constructivist beauty, is not a city at all" (1947: 49).

While I certainly agree with Bookchin's prescription for a politics which moves up rather than down, from the neighborhood to the municipal level (and beyond), I am still uncomfortable with abandoning existing "centralized entities and bureaucratic apparatuses." Despite his very persuasive arguments, in the context of the neoliberal dismantling of social programs and of the attacks on a number of hard-won legal protections (e.g., from the U.S. Food and Drug Administration to the U.S. Environmental Protection Agency, passing by labor and anti-trust legislation, patients' rights, etc.), I am unwilling to restrict my energies to the local level. Instead these protections and legal safeguards – with all the accompanying rules and regulations – are worth defending. As long as we live in developed nation states (however much we despise them in principle), local initiatives are inadequate to stand up to the unchecked free market.[20] At one point, Bookchin complains that one of his critics has argued that his "decentralist" vision would not prevent "Troy, New York from dumping its untreated wastes into the Hudson River, from which downstream cities like Perth Amboy draw their drinking water" (1995: 247). Bookchin gives two answers to this very pertinent objection. He first attacks the assumption that centralized government is "necessary to prevent one locality from afflicting another ecologically," calling such an assumption "an unconscious acceptance of the economic status quo" (1995: 247–248); and then, even less convincingly, I think, he writes, "that in a society that was radically veering toward a decentralistic, participatory democracy, guided by communalistic and ecological principles, *it is only reasonable to suppose* that people would not choose such an irresponsible social dispensation as would allow the waters of the Hudson to be so polluted" (1995: 249, my italics). I'm afraid that I am too conscious of the realities of the "economic status quo" to accept such a supposition as a sufficient guarantee of the safety of my

20 John Brunner's *Shockwave Rider* (New York: Harper and Row, 1975) is another example of a utopian "enclave" whose citizens drop out, but they retain a number of defenses which they must use when the inevitable attack on them eventually comes. The military threats to the new society of "Ecotopia" (in Ernest Callenbach's novel of the same name, 1975) must similarly be answered. The image of a small society forced to defend itself against its more powerful neighbors, because of the threat it poses as an alternative reminds us of the situation of Cuba.

drinking water. People may be reasonable, but the profit motive provides a different sort of reason which often overrides individual good intentions. Any further relaxing of government controls will only further endanger us, as can be seen in the Ontario government's cutbacks to its Environmental Safety branch and the resulting breakdown of local water testing services which led to seven deaths in the summer of 2000 after an *E. coli* outbreak in the town of Walkerton. Not only are such disasters occurring elsewhere, but the growing acknowledgment of the problems associated with global warming, for instance, forcibly remind us that we can no longer escape (by moving to the country or even to some other region of the globe) the effects of environmental pollution. This unfortunately suggests not the need for less government (as the free marketers would have it), but for some sort of overarching world agency with the authority to enforce limitations on planet-warming gases.[21]

Although I have drastically simplified Bookchin's arguments, as well as his replies to such objections, the above constitutes a first argument for the need for planning and government intervention. The second argument against these visions of a municipal agenda lies in a danger which Jacobs almost seems to welcome and which Bookchin warns against – while saying that there are no guarantees that this won't happen – namely the appearance of "parochial city-states" (1995: 236), of privileged enclaves which will seek to preserve their own advantages by cutting themselves off from the outside world in what would be another version of the gated city.[22]

21 A recent newspaper report states that "in a surprising result," an "Environics International poll of 9,000 people from the G-8 countries" found that four out of ten people supported what the pollsters referred to as the "radical, but hypothetical option" of "giving the United Nations the power to impose legally binding actions on national governments to protect the Earth's climates" (*The Globe and Mail* [Toronto], Friday July 20, 2001, p. A5).

22 See, for instance, Edward Blakeley, and M.G. Snyder, *Fortress America* (1999). Perhaps the best fictional depiction of such a gated city is Larry Niven and Jerry Pournelle's 1981 novel, *Oath of Fealty* (New York: Timescape Books), which begins with the familiar specter of urban unrest and stepped-up crime rates, in order to make a concrete utopian proposal: the "arcology" of Todos Santos, an armed and insulated retreat for 250,000 affluent Americans built in the ruins of Los Angeles

While there is certainly a risk that such communities would turn their backs on the outside world, such projects and neighborhoods might also be seen as playing a utopian role, if their impact and influence were to spread outward from the neighborhood to the city and to the region.[23] As Lynda Schneekloth points out, while the majority of architectural design is for building and projects that are meant to be implemented or built, there is also a type of architectural work whose "intention is to give visual form to a critique of current conditions, or to create an imaginary world of as if" (1985: 19), and it is on this note that I would like to conclude.

Chandigarh was built not only to stand as a symbol of the "new India," but to contribute "to the creation of an ideal society that would provide all the prerequisites of complete happiness and fulfilment" (Sutcliffe 1977: 218). Chandigarh – or Brasilia for that matter – do work. The three buildings of Le Corbusier's capitol complex and, in particular, the structure of the Open Hand, stand as monuments to a transformed, utopian

---

and surrounded by the crumbling city. The plot involves the unsuccessful attempts of the "American Ecology Army" to sabotage and discredit the utopian experiment.

23 This is the basic argument of Fredric Jameson's "Architecture and the Critique of Ideology," in an extended dialogue with Manfredo Tafuri's *Architecture and Utopia* (Cambridge, MA: MIT Press, 1976). Jameson distinguishes two positions within a properly Marxist and Gramscian framework for architectural critics. The first, represented by Tafuri, is that "there can be no qualitative change in any element of the older capitalist system – for instance, in architecture or urbanism – without beforehand a total revolutionary and systemic transformation" (Jameson 1985: 68). In the second position, (central to those of us interested in the role of utopian images), he calls for a critical architecture practice, "according to which the emergent future, the new and still nascent social relations that announce a mode of production that will ultimately displace and subsume the as yet still dominant one, is theorized in terms of small yet strategic pockets or beachheads within the older system" (1985: 70). Without repeating his entire complex argument, Jameson argues that both Tafuri and the post-modernists (with their rejection of the utopianism of Modern Architecture and their embrace of a "new free play of ideas") are fundamentally pessimistic recognitions of the fact that "nothing new can be done," a position which he rejects in favor of a continuing search for alternatives: a project which "proposes itself, as we have already suggested, as a radically different, revolutionary, or subversive enclave from which little by little the whole surrounding fabric of fallen social relations is to be regenerated and transformed" (Jameson 1985: 83).

world, one which has not yet been realized; a monumental reminder, then, of those dreams and of the understanding that the utopian city can only be achieved in the context of a larger social transformation.

Epilogue

During the revision of this text I had the opportunity to visit Le Corbusier's most famous building, the "unité d'habitation" in Marseilles (often called "la cité radieuse") that was completed in 1952, while he was working on the Chandigarh project. By chance it was the residents' semi-annual garage sale and the lobby was filled with tables, with residents and outsiders, children with their pets and toys as they examined the items for sale. Despite all the criticisms of this building (most famously Lewis Mumford's 1957 denunciation in *The New Yorker*) it is, with its nine floors and almost 350 apartments and more than 500 inhabitants, a rather remarkable success story – an apartment building which is functioning well fifty years after it was built with no major modifications or changes, and where the residents speak of the building with pride and affection. The success of the building as a place to live can be measured, too, in the absence of any available apartments, although there are a few empty shops on the third floor as stores and supermarkets have been built nearby – for as Marseilles has grown the building is no longer located on the outskirts of the city. But this is an accomplishment of a slightly different kind than Le Corbusier and his government sponsors originally intended since it was designed as the prototype for low-income housing; while today, the apartments are all owned by the residents who are often professionals (and the resident who took me around was herself an architect).

Le Corbusier saw his prototype for a new type of attractive and inexpensive housing (hence the use of concrete instead of steel), a "vertical garden city," a "horizontal skyscraper" to be set on pillars and standing in a park, with a pool and health club as well as a nursery school on the roof, with a commercial sector on the third floor, including shops and a hotel (which is still in operation), not to mention the beautiful vistas: of the Mediterranean on the one side and the rocky hills on the other, and each of the twenty-three types of apartment Le Corbusier designed includes both views. All of this was part of Le Corbusier's design and is an integral part of the building today. Moreover, there has been an increasing concern on the part of the residents to respect his plans and designs, for he designed much of the interior of the building: not only the layout of the apartments, as well as the wide halls and elevators, but the furniture, the mail boxes and so on. Whatever the reasons for the building's success (the beauty of the site, the deliberate commitment of the residents, etc.), it is hardly the cold, alienating building described by his critics, none of whom has ever designed an apartment building which is still standing and loved by its inhabitants fifty years later.

Needless to say, this building is very different from the monumental government complex at Chandigarh, just as it is very different form the many depressing apartment blocks whose design – whether deliberate or not – is blamed on Le Corbusier.[24] This is not India, nor is it anything approaching a planned city, but it works and was seen as a building block in his larger vision.

24 This building was explicitly intended as a prototype. In addition to a number of other housing projects which were never built (Bordeaux, Dijon, Annecy, Villacoublay, Brétigny, Tours, etc.), four other *unités* were built, which for a variety of reasons, usually having to do with financial considerations during construction, are considered less successful: three in France, at Rezé-lès-Nantes (1955), Briey-en-Forêt (1963), Firminy (1967), and one in Berlin (1957). For an extensive discussion of these projects, see Gilles Ragot, and Mathilde Dion, *Le Corbusier en France* (Paris: Le Moniteur, 1997).

CHAPTER 20

Beyond This Horizon: Utopian Visions and Utopian Practice

In the following essay, I want to explain how I came to the study of Utopia as well as to outline the theoretical and methodological framework of my work. Simply put, my interest in Utopia (the literary utopia as well as utopianism) grows out of some crucial friendships and out of the merging of my interest in science fiction (sf) with my own political evolution – developments which have shaped my academic career even as they have led me to the study of utopianism. My utopian method and approach have evolved, following from my discovery of utopian fiction, in terms of what I understand it to be and the role I see it playing in the world. To describe this method, I will outline three overlapping moments in my study of Utopia, before concluding with some thoughts about the place of the utopian today.

To begin at the beginning, I do not come from a politically active background, but from a solid middle-class family. Until graduate school, I attended private Catholic schools in California, first with the Carmelite nuns, and then with the Jesuits in high school, and with the Christian Brothers in college. While I retain little of the religious part of that Catholic education, and while there was little in the way of explicit politics in the California schools of the 1950s, or at home, for that matter, I somehow became aware of the social message contained in a certain Catholic tradition – certainly against the grain of Catholic orthodoxy of the time.[1] But in terms of politics, or utopianism, there was certainly none of that until

1 Although Vatican II and the espousal of socially progressive ideas did not take place until 1962–1965, Tom Moylan has pointed out to me how much was already happening in the time leading up to Pope John XXIII's momentous redirection of the Church, "including existentialist work; and what became the theology

I reached graduate school – the University of Minnesota, first of all (and it is serendipity that Lyman Tower Sargent and I were there at the same time at the beginning of the 1960s, although we did not meet until almost twenty years later!). Of course, the early 1960s were marked by the civil rights movement and then by the increasing opposition to the U.S. intervention in Vietnam, and by feminism. This context was undoubtedly the background to my growing social awareness. And I use the word "social" deliberately, since this awareness was not yet political – my response to the war and to existing social inequities were determined by ethical considerations rather than by an analysis or understanding of how they had come about. That would come later, during the 1970s.

I began my teaching career at the University of Toronto in 1966, as a professor of French language and literature, where I soon became involved in anti-war actions. But still, I had not made any real connections between the war and my academic work. I was, however, an avid reader of sf; and it was a meeting with the sf writer and critic Judith Merril that led me to start thinking about what I was doing.[2] Judy had just moved to Toronto (in

influenced by Bloch and the Marxist-Christian dialogue begun in France" (personal communication).

2 Merril (1923–1997) was the author of a number of sf stories and novels, including her first sf story, "That Only a Mother," in 1948, which is seen as an important pre-feminist story that brought a woman's perspective to the genre. Other important works include *Daughters of Earth* and two collections of her stories, *Survival Ship and Other Stories* and *The Best of Judith Merril*. Her biggest impact on the genre, however, was as a critic and especially as an editor. She edited numerous sf anthologies beginning in 1950, notably Dell's series of *Year's Best SF* from 1956–1967; and she was the "Books" columnist for *The Magazine of Fantasy and Science Fiction* from 1965–1969. She became interested in and a proponent of the "New Wave" in sf during her trips to London in the mid-1960s, leading to the anthology *England Swings SF*. When she moved to Rochdale College in Toronto (a housing cooperative which was at the same time a free university and the center of Toronto's counter-culture), she established its library, based largely on her own private collection. When Rochdale closed, she donated the collection to the Toronto Public Library, creating the Spaced Out Library, now called The Merril Collection. During the 1980s she did much to encourage Canadian sf, founding Hydra North in 1984 (Canada's first association of sf professionals) and, in 1985, editing *Tesseracts*, an anthology of Canadian sf that has now become a series.

1968) to express her opposition to the Vietnam War, and we would meet to talk about sf and politics. We started a "speculative fiction" reading group, and then, in 1970, I was able to offer an sf course at the university – in what was then called "interdisciplinary studies," since the English department was not yet interested in sf. Through our conversations, she made me realize that it might be possible to take the critical tools and methodological approach I had been given for the study of French literature and apply them to sf; and she helped me to realize that there was a connection between contemporary sf and what was happening in the world.

As a French professor, I was aware of the French tradition of Left cultural theory and practice, particularly under the impetus of the French Communist Party and the upsurge in left political activity during the late 1950s in opposition to France's continuing colonialist rule in Indochina and (after the fall of Dien Bien Phu in 1954) in Algeria. In the early 1960s, under the influence of Russian Formalism, some literary critics had begun to consider the question of the politics of form itself; turning the debates about politics and literature from questions of the artist's political commitment (Sartrean *engagement*, etc.) and about the *contents* of art (as in "socialist realism") to questions about the role that the very forms of literature – as well as its teaching and consumption – played in maintaining the status quo. (All of this is epitomized in the work of Louis Althusser and his rethinking of the concept of ideology.)[3]

3 For a brief synopsis of these issues as they appeared at the time, see Eagleton's *Marxism and Literary Criticism*. Althusser's "Ideology and Ideological State Apparatuses" was published in 1970. While I can hardly do justice to Althusser and the ideology debates here, let me briefly sum up the issues that concerned me. Before Althusser, the Marxist concept of ideology was usually considered as a form of false consciousness, an illusory view of reality that could be dispelled through education and the disclosure of the true reality of class struggle and capitalist exploitation. Under the influence of Jacques Lacan and psychoanalysis (and in reaction to the growing popularity of the recently published "humanist" texts of the early Marx), Althusser made some substantial revisions and additions to this concept, beginning with the emphasis that "ideology has a material existence"; ideology is not just false ideas or misunderstandings, but the ways that we live and experience the world we live in, through our daily activities, rituals, and the like. Moreover, Althusser insists, there will always be ideology; reality will always be mediated (and constructed)

With this background in mind, I would like to call this first political moment *pre-utopian:* the moment of sf and of Marxism, but without any real understanding or awareness of Utopia and its possibilities. There were three components to my reading and political work at this time that then led me toward the study of Utopia.

First of all, my interest in sf as political was influenced by a particular French variant of Marxism: the *Tel quel* group – which, in the United Kingdom, was a tendency that manifested itself in film studies around the journal *Screen* and the work of Colin McCabe and Stephen Heath – while in terms of literary studies, this position was summed up by Rosalind Coward and John Ellis in their book *Language and Materialism* (1977).[4] In short, this was the attack on representation and realism and an argument for a subversive potential to be found in certain kinds of non-representational and avant-garde writing, a literary direction exemplified for the *Tel quel* group by James Joyce's *Finnegans Wake*. (I tried to apply this method to sf, as can be seen in my article on Philip K. Dick's *Ubik* (Fitting 1975); while *Tel quel*'s own turn to the right in the 1980s suggests the obvious political limits in such a position.)[5]

through the various "positions" which constitute our subjectivity – our race, class, gender, nationality, religion, and so on. In his *Ideology: An Introduction*, Eagleton defines the Althusserian moment as the passage "from a *cognitive* to an *affective* theory of ideology": "For Althusser one can speak of description or representations of the world as being either true or false; but ideology is not for him at root a matter of such descriptions at all, and criteria of truth and falsehood are thus largely irrelevant to it. Ideology for Althusser does indeed represent – but what it represents is the way I 'live' my relations to society as a whole, which cannot be said to be a question of truth or falsehood. Ideology for Althusser is a particular organization of signifying practices which goes to constitute human beings as social subjects, and which produces the lived relations by which such subjects are connected to the dominant relations of production in a society" (2007: 18).

4 There have been some recent accounts of *Tel quel* in English: see, ffrench (Oxford: Clarendon Press, 1995); Marx-Scouras (University Park: Pennsylvania State University Press, 1996); and ffrench and Lack (London: Routledge, 1998). For a less sympathetic view that uses the analytical approach of Pierre Bourdieu to demystify *Tel quel*, see Kauppi (Berlin: Mouton de Gruyter, 1994).

5 For a presentation and critical analysis of the structuralist moment, see Jameson (1974), as well as Jameson (1975–1976).

At the same time, in North America, the mid-1970s saw the founding of the Marxist Literary Group (MLG). Many college and university teachers were trying to integrate Marxism into their teaching, particularly Marxist aesthetic theory, as a way of doing political work. Leaving aside for a moment the question of how political this was anyway, it is important to point out that such an approach was primarily analytical, and consisted of the (ideological) analysis of the works of the past and of the present, and of the canon and the profession; but also that there was often little sense of what political writing should be – apart from the subversive option I have just mentioned.

Third, I was dissatisfied with what could be done at the university, and I tried to do politics by going "outside," to a "socialist school" (the Toronto Marxist Institute) where we gave courses open to the public on a range of topics; and where I taught a series of courses on Marxism and culture as a way of trying to understand what I was reading.

Meanwhile, on the sf front, in the aftermath of World War II, U.S. sf was ostensibly no more political than U.S. society in general. But as Merril and others have pointed out, during the McCarthy era "science fiction became, for a time, virtually the only vehicle of political dissent" (Merril 1971: 74); this developed as a form of critique epitomized by Frederick Pohl and C.M. Kornbluth's novel, *The Space Merchants* (1953). Of course, as the 1960s unfolded, sf reflected both the larger fractures in U.S. society and the sense that another world was possible. In her reviews of sf, in the *Magazine of Fantasy and Science Fiction*, Merril wrote about the work of some younger sf writers in terms of the search for a "new mythology," a term which might best be understood as her own word for ideology. Shaken by the civil rights and later the women's movements, and especially by the mounting opposition to the U.S. intervention in Vietnam, the tranquility and harmony, and the apparently shared values of U.S. society in the 1950s collapsed, a narrative which is summarized in the events of the film *Pleasantville*. In writing about a new mythology, Merril was calling for sf to play a role in imagining and developing new values for a society in transition.

Here it is important to acknowledge sf's special ability to deal with reality – a position which would soon become codified in Darko Suvin's definition of the genre as "cognitive estrangement":

> sf is, then, a literary genre whose necessary and sufficient conditions are the presence and interaction of estrangement and cognition, and whose main formal device is an imaginative framework alternative to the author's empirical environment. (1979: 7–8)

Thus, in the 1960s and 1970s, sf offered writers a means of thinking critically about the present and the possibility of alternatives in a way that mainstream "realist" fiction could not. The classic illustration of this can be found in Ursula K. Le Guin's novel, *The Left Hand of Darkness* in 1969, in which she takes an issue very much on the feminist agenda of the day and uses sf to pose it in a way which was (and remains) impossible for realist fiction to do: could sex and gender be separated?[6] The utopian moment of the early 1970s was the moment in which writers began to go beyond Le Guin's speculative separation of sex and gender to imagine utopian worlds in which the whole panoply of feminist demands have been realized, as in Le Guin's own extraordinary *The Dispossessed*. As we can see from this example, if an estranged critique of the present could be seen as a first element of political awareness, this critique soon led to attempts to imagine *alternatives* to the present. Already, in the late 1950s and early 1960s we can see the genre's interest in alternatives, from alternatives to the technological worldview of earlier sf, as in Arthur C. Clarke's *Childhood's End*, the telepathic collectivity of Theodore Sturgeon's *More than Human*, Robert Heinlein's Michael Valentine Smith in *Stranger in a Strange Land*, or a few years later, Samuel R. Delany's questing hero in *The Einstein Intersection*. This was followed, in the 1970s, then, with a series of feminist influenced utopias which include (all from the period 1974–1980): Le Guin's *The Dispossessed*, Delany's *Triton*, Marge Piercy's *Woman on the Edge of Time*, and Joanna Russ's *The Female Man*. Along with these, one should mention a more traditional utopia, Ernest Callenbach's *Ecotopia*, as well as Suzy McKee

6 On the world of Gethen, in Le Guin's novel, people have no sexual characteristics nor sexual drive most of the time. But then, for a few days a month, like animals in heat, their lives are given over entirely to the sexual drives. They take on female or male sexual characteristics in a more or less arbitrary fashion. See *The Left Hand of Darkness*, Chapter 7.

Charnas's "science fantasy" *Motherlines*, and one important instance of a feminist utopian fantasy, Sally M. Gearhart's *The Wanderground*.[7]

One of the features of second-wave feminism was a renewed interest in what a world without sexual exploitation and domination would actually look and feel like and how men and women might live together according to new social and sexual relationships. While many feminists concentrated on the analysis of the forms and nature of capitalist patriarchy, and many more women (and men) were involved in struggling against the institutions and practices of patriarchy, some writers set out to imagine non-patriarchal societies. In the 1970s, then, there was a revival in the literary depiction of alternate societies based on new social and sexual relationships, as writers attempted to portray non-hierarchical and non-oppressive social and sexual relationships and patterns of behavior, to imagine the society which would be created by these new patterns and structures of behavior as much as it would enable them.

For me, this newer sf seemed to present the ideal fusion of art and politics: sf was not only a genre which was outside the mainstream (and thus perhaps less corrupted by it, with a credibility that the works of the canon did not have); but it was also a type of fiction which many people read for pleasure, and which seemed to be dealing with the very political questions which concerned me – questions which seemed further and further from the aesthetic preoccupations of university critical practice. This was the moment when I began to realize that what was important about this new kind of sf was its ability to go beyond some estranged representation of the present, to actually imagine a different future.

This then was the Utopian Moment. In this way, our awareness and interest in utopian writing grew out of developments in sf in the early 1970s, especially under the impact of feminism. In terms of a *utopian method*, I was increasingly convinced that what these works were doing – why they were needed, why they were important – had to do with their ability to give us a glimpse of what an alternative might actually look and feel like; and in that sense the "critical utopia," under the influence of feminism, focused

7 I tried to tell this story in Chapter 1, "The Modern Anglo-American SF Novel." See also Chapter 3, "Ideological Foreclosure and Utopian Discourse."

not so much on alternative structures, constitutions, and governing bodies, but on daily life in a different world, with new values and structures of feeling, gender relations, and so on. Such visions seemed essential to the struggle for human emancipation because they helped us to articulate what we understood by a qualitatively *different* society, something we often lost sight of in the midst of our day-to-day lives. These alternate visions were important because they reached beyond the restricted public of the already politicized and spoke to a wider audience which often seemed to no longer believe in the possibility of desirable or feasible alternatives to the fundamental insufficiency of the present.[8]

Here, I would like quickly to point to a few historical circumstances which might help to understand the specificity of this particular utopian development. For however predominant U.S. sf has been since the 1930s, there are other significant sf traditions: in Britain, France, Germany, Russia, and Japan. But this is not the case for the utopian revival of the 1970s which is almost exclusively a U.S. phenomenon.[9] Why is this so? The first part of an answer may lie in what is often called "American exceptionalism," a concept which refers to the fact, often noted by social scientists and historians, that unlike Canada, where I live, or most European countries, there is virtually no Left tradition in the U.S., no socialist or communist or even social-democratic parties, at least not in the sense that they play any significant electoral or extra-parliamentary role.[10] While I do not think that this is the only or even the principle reason for the upsurge in utopian writing in the U.S. in the 1970s, I think that it is a factor that should be looked at in trying to understand why utopian writing emerged so strongly at this moment in American sf. In this way, it might be argued that it is the absence

8 This certainly influenced my teaching and critical writing in the 1980s, as summed up in Chapter 9, "So We All Became Mothers."

9 The best-known exception – Monique Wittig's *Les Guerilleres* – was written in France by an author who was soon to move to the U.S. While this experimental utopian fiction was little-known in the sf community, it was widely embraced by U.S. feminists – and much less so by feminists in France. See Anderson (1991).

10 "American exceptionalism refers to the curious situation in which the United States is the only major industrial country of the twentieth century without the presence of a significant socialist/social democratic and/or communist party in its polity" (Markovits and Hellerman 2001: 7).

of a Left tradition which has made that utopian revival possible. Although Marxism can certainly be seen as a utopian philosophy of hope, it is important to remember that classical Marxist thought has often juxtaposed utopian thinking and writing to "true" political practice, as if the utopian was the impractical and unrealistic, a juxtaposition explicit in the title of Friedrich Engels's *Socialism Utopian and Scientific*. In these terms, Utopia is seen as a distraction from the urgent task of organizing the working class and of making a revolution. The absence, then, of a Left tradition, along with the vitality of sf and its ability to refract the present through the lens of the future may have contributed to the ability to think of alternatives without focusing very much on the transition, and on such practical questions as how we are to actually get to this new society.[11]

In today's bleak times, it is also important to remember that in the late 1960s and early 1970s there was a strong sense that things were changing for the better, hopes that were summed up in the title of Tom Moylan's book, *Demand the Impossible*, a title which was the second half of a slogan, "Be realistic, demand the impossible," taken from May 1968 in Paris, the most intense manifestation (in the developed countries at least) of that belief that the world was changing.[12]

These unleashed utopian energies and hopes obviously had a lot to do with the upsurge in utopian writing at the time.

My discovery of the literary utopia and its importance and potential role in political action was hardly an isolated event: across North America, other students and scholars were making the same connection, and this led to some academics, with Sargent playing a leading role, to organize a scholarly association devoted to the study of Utopia, one that would investigate

11 In a complete study of this issue, one would also have to discuss the specificity of this utopian moment in terms of the particular nature of U.S. feminism. One should also mention in this context, the absence of historical thinking or awareness more generally, made worse or seemingly sanctioned by structuralism and postmodernism.

12 For an overview of this moment, see Jameson, "Periodizing the 1960s." There he reminds us of a number of other utopian developments in the "third" world, beginning with the Bandung Conference, the Cuban and Algerian revolutions, and so on.

all of the various and many strands of the utopian tradition: not just the literary, but the political and historical, as well as the revival of utopian experiments in various communes and small communities in the 1960s.[13] The founding of the Society for Utopian Studies, in 1975, was followed by Sargent's launching of the journal *Utopian Studies*, which he edited from its inception in 1988 to 2004. I started attending the meetings of the Society in the early 1980s, and under Lyman's sometimes not-so-gentle prodding, I started to learn that there was already a significant utopian tradition, and that these recent literary utopias were not a completely new development.[14]

So what was my utopian method in all this? As I started to explain, it was posited on the conviction that these utopian novels had a role to play in political work, precisely as visions of an alternative and "alternative" was for many of us a code word for socialism. That is to say, these novels provided us with a way of showing people that there *were* alternatives, as well as what those alternatives would look and feel like – as opposed to the perceived abstractions and tired slogans of much traditional Left discourse. In fact, they could even serve as a place for outlining and debating the forms and structures of the new society we were interested in building. Thus, despite my own supposed theoretical sophistication, I and many others looked at these novels "literally," at least in the sense of how they analyzed and dealt with the contemporary situation, how they imagined the new society would emerge, and what that society would look like. The

13 For an explanation and description of the many strands of utopianism, see Sargent 1994.

14 The Society for Utopian Studies has always been an interdisciplinary organization – following Sargent's three interests – as well as a place where there seemed to be less competition than in the academy generally, and where there has always been support and encouragement. Like the women's movement that gave it a kick start in the 1970s, the Society tries to live out its utopian ideals in its practice as a scholarly group. This is also the place to mention the importance of the role of Moylan in the development and promotion of utopian ideas. I first met Moylan through sf and then shortly afterwards at the MLG's summer institute (in St. Cloud, MN); and *Demand the Impossible* (Moylan 1986) stands as the most important articulation of these positions – of what I saw as the union of a Marxist politics and of an involvement in sf, along with the realization that feminism had introduced a new, utopian dimension into sf.

literal-mindedness of some critics – myself included – often went further than that of the authors themselves; and in this context, one could perhaps map the principal authors of the utopian revival on a spectrum, from "literalists," like Callenbach, to the more "critical" utopians – those writers who, in their awareness of the utopian tradition, distanced themselves from it as a way of trying to moderate and qualify this tendency toward reading the work as a literal representation of an alternative – and I am thinking especially of Le Guin's *The Dispossessed* and Delany's *Triton*.

The literal approach involved not only the discussion of the structure and forms of the new society, but the question of the "transition" as well: of how we go from here to there. The classic example of the question of the transition in the literary utopia can be seen in William Morris's *News from Nowhere*, which constitutes a critique of the peaceful transition to socialism portrayed in Edward Bellamy's *Looking Backward*, a changeover which is unrealistic and naïve since it implies that those in power would voluntarily give up their privileges. This is an important component of the Marxist critique of utopianism which often dismisses utopian visions as the "imaginary resolution" of real problems, a wish-fulfillment that diverts our energies from working for change to dreaming about it. In sf terms, this critique could also be seen as referring to the familiar trope of the "frontier" of so much U.S. cultural production – visions of an empty and "untamed" American West, or of an uninhabited planet, just waiting to be discovered and developed.[15] At the other end of the spectrum of critiques of the transition, the fervor of the 1960s also produced those who argued that such a transformation could come from within, through a change in consciousness, as summed up in Charles Reich's best seller, *The Greening of America*.[16]

15 On this subject, see Mogen (1994).

16 This is also relevant to the critique of *Tel quel* which believed (at least for a while) that changing our perceptions would change the world. The best sf novel on this theme is Ian Watson's *The Embedding* (London: Gollancz, 2018). I tend to side with Marx's reply to these positions, in the Preface to *The Critique of Political Economy*: "It is not the consciousness of men that determines their being, but, on the contrary, their social being that determines their consciousness" (Marx and Engels 1968: 182).

To sum up this utopian moment, then, if we see writing, or any artistic production, more generally as what Fredric Jameson has called – in his Sartrean mode – a "verbal thrust," a response and reaction to historical events as much as to the writing of others, we can appreciate more fully the remarkable exchange of utopian ideas and visions throughout the 1970s among a number of writers and readers. Obviously (and in hindsight, predictably) this writing did not and could not in itself produce those new societies we so longed for; but they did stir up reactions and responses, as did the calls for equity and the larger advances of feminist and movement politics more generally throughout the decade. Positive responses as well as negative ones, the latter in the form of a backlash – one that is still with us today. This is without doubt the case in the larger, historical sphere: as marked by the elections of Margaret Thatcher and Ronald Reagan, the rise of neo-liberalism, and the attacks on the many gains in the areas of equity and equal opportunity (all of which are chronicled, for example, by Susan Faludi in her book *Backlash*). Within sf, there was as well a reaction against some of this writing, and a decline in the writing of utopias.[17]

Thus, we come to a third *moment*, that of a retreat or, at least of a re-thinking of the utopian optimism I have been describing. This has produced several different reactions or ways of negotiating this shift (one that is the focus of Moylan's *Scraps of the Untainted Sky*). I will attempt to address these differing, but not contradictory, positions on Utopia and utopian methodology by introducing the work of my next interlocutor, one who has been there since the beginning but whose ideas about Utopia it has taken me longer to understand and incorporate into my own practice. (As you may have gathered, these interlocutors have all been or become friends, and this particular friendship is the oldest of them all, going back forty years.) Jameson and I have been talking about Marxism, sf, and Utopia for some time; and while our positions and focus may seem somewhat different, his work has been essential to my own approach and development.[18]

17 For the impact of this backlash on sf, see Chapter 10, "The Turn from Utopia."

18 I am not sure I can claim to have introduced him to sf and utopia, since he had a student in the early 1970s who went on to become one of the most important contemporary sf/utopian writers – Kim Stanley Robinson. Jameson's influence on Robinson is also crucial since Robinson began his Ph.D. thesis on Dick with Jameson before he moved to Yale. See Fitting (1998).

While there have been other, more sophisticated applications and descriptions of Jameson's theory of Utopia, I will only mention briefly three ideas I have taken from his work and which definitely do not exhaust his writing on Utopia.[19] Jameson's most fruitful and troubling intervention lies in his proposal that the literary utopia should not be seen as the representation of an ideal society, but as a reflection on "our own incapacity to conceive [utopia] in the first place" (1975: 230); or, as he wrote a few years later, our "constitutional inability to imagine Utopia itself, [is not due] to any individual failure of imagination but is the result of the systemic, cultural, and ideological closure of which we are all in one way or another prisoners" (1982: 153). I take this point in what I consider its classical Marxist sense, as a gentle reminder of the illusion or trap of Utopia:

> the utopian text [...] hold[s] out for us the vivid lesson of what we cannot imagine [...] our own incapacity to see beyond [our] epoch and its ideological closures. This is the correlative, the obverse and the negative side, of Marx's great dictum [...] namely that the world has long since dreamed of something of which it needs only to become conscious for it to possess it in reality. (1996: 75)

One way to attempt to summarize Jameson's argument is to say that the imagined utopia in the literary work is limited to a kind of reformism since we can only conceive of what is already there, making the utopia what Phil Wegner (following Ernst Bloch) has called a *repairing* of the present rather than its transformation. In this same vein, I should mention that, in other places, Jameson has stressed that rather than seeing them as representations of a future society, one should read these literary utopias as calling attention to and identifying what in our society needs to be changed.

The second point I take from Jameson comes from his interest in popular culture and the observation that there is always a utopian dimension or core in the most degraded popular works as well as in even the most oppressive and hateful forms of consciousness. In *The Political Unconscious*, like Bloch before him, Jameson extended the concept of Utopia, explaining that the deepest appeal of even the most reprehensible forms of class

19 See Fitting (1998) and Moylan (1998).

consciousness lay in a buried utopian vision of "a specific historical and class form of collective unity" (1981: 291):

> all class consciousness – or in other words, all ideology in the strongest sense, including the most exclusive forms of ruling-class consciousness just as much as that of oppositional or oppressed classes – is in its very nature Utopian (1981: 289).

Here I think that he is reminding us that while these anticipatory utopian instances are to be found in some unlikely places, these utopian yearnings are not necessarily positive or (even) transformative; and it is up to critics to explain and draw these distinctions, as well as to detect and describe the utopian mechanisms to be found in the cultural productions which surround us. It is up to us to recognize and foster utopian desire, and to develop and encourage its critical edge. This dialectic of "ideology and utopia" at work in cultural texts has long influenced my own readings of sf. At the same time, the concern for tracking the utopian has led me beyond the literary utopias of the 1970s in a variety of directions, to the utopian tradition of the eighteenth and nineteenth centuries, to the generic possibility of right-wing utopias, to the question of the reading pleasure of utopia, and especially to film – in the question of what a utopian film would be as well as to asking how this dialectic works in popular film.

The third suggestion that I have taken from the work of Jameson is his presentation of "dialectical thinking" in *Marxism and Form*, where he argued (as Althusser did for ideology) that Utopia has a history and that its function changes and evolves. This stress on the historicity of concepts and strategies informs all of his subsequent work and is essential for understanding and tracking the dialectic of "ideology and utopia" I mentioned above:

> for where in the older society (as in Marx's classic analysis) Utopian thought represented a diversion of revolutionary energy into idle wish-fulfilments and imaginary satisfactions, in our own time the very nature of the utopian concept has undergone a dialectical reversal. Now it is practical thinking which everywhere represents a capitulation to the system itself, and stands as a testimony to the power of that system to transform even its adversaries into its own mirror image. The Utopian idea, on the contrary, keeps alive the possibility of a world qualitatively distinct from this one and takes the form of a stubborn negation of all that is. (1971: 110–111)

Those words were written in 1971, even before the utopian revival which was only just beginning; and I shall return to the question of the timeliness of Utopia in a moment.

Each of the points I have taken from Jameson and described brings us back, I think, to a paradoxical reaffirmation of the need for utopian imagining, even as these visions and descriptions are not meant to be taken literally, but – to put it crudely – to remind us of all that we lack and are denied by the crushing mechanisms of capital. Where does this leave us? What place is there for utopian studies or Utopia itself in these increasingly dark times? I think that my own evolution – from a more *positive* view of Utopia (as models or visions) to a more (Jameson influenced) dialectical and *negative* view (Utopia as a reminder of what we do not have) – is but one way of reacting to the present situation. To conclude, then, I want to review what I see as some of the different ways of negotiating the present.

First of all, it is important to emphasize that utopian writing did not end with the elections of Thatcher and Reagan, that however powerful the backlash, inside the sf community and in the outside world, some writers continued, and continue today, to use the utopian form. There are, however, differences in post-1980 utopian fiction that acknowledge these changed times. This change is demonstrated for me by two novels by Piercy. In the first, *Woman on the Edge of Time*, we can see a classic 1970s utopia, one in which there is still a struggle going on to ensure and defend the utopian future, but one in which, nonetheless, most of our planet constitutes a utopian society, while the corporate forces which are attacking the utopia are mostly confined to a satellite from which they launch their attacks. This situation is reversed in her 1991 novel, *He, She and It* (U.K. title, *Body of Glass*), in which the earth is a bleak, corporate dystopia, a wasted and plundered planet, and where the events of the novel are centered around a small utopian enclave which is threatened on all sides.[20]

20 In Chapter 15 of *Woman on the Edge of Time*, Piercy describes an alternative to the utopia of Mattapoisett: a terrible, bleak future in which sexism and capitalism have flourished. In *Woman*, that brief nightmarish chapter was limited to Gildina's windowless 126th floor apartment. A surgically "built-up contracty [...] [Gildina was born] with brain deficiencies from protein scarcity in foetus and early childhood" (1976: 299). It is from this sex-slave that we learn of life in a toxic, polluted future,

Another form of utopian writing can be seen in the *Mars* trilogy of Kim Stanley Robinson (*Red Mars*, *Green Mars*, and *Blue Mars*). If Piercy's later utopia was characterized by a change from the depiction of a utopian world under attack (and struggling to come into being) to a utopian enclave in the midst of a larger dystopian world, Robinson's Martian novels focus on the transition itself – hundreds of pages of meetings, debate, and discussions about what the new world of Mars should be: discussions involving the various stakeholders, investors, corporations, states, as well as those who are attempting to transfer an ideology or a world-view, or to build a better world, or to guarantee a profit, or to bring about the triumph of or more simply the survival of their way of life, or to protect some "original" Mars, or to avoid the mistakes made on Earth, and so on. In this way, we are given some two-hundred years of Martian history – as expressed in the progression of the three titles: beginning with the adventures of the first men and women to arrive, through the gradual transformation of the red desert planet into a world closer to our own, with green fields and forests and then dotted with blue lakes and seas. In the beginning Mars is not yet a utopia, and humans can only live there with great difficulty. It is only in the third novel, *Blue Mars*, that this flash of recognition must vary for different readers, when one realizes, in the midst of the description of one activity or another, someone hang-gliding or a shared meal, that this is in fact a utopia and that Utopia is a process rather than a realized goal.[21]

When coming to terms with this apparent retreat from the utopian optimism of the 1960s and 1970s, it is also important to remember that, however inhospitable the present moment is to Utopia, it is essential to defend and maintain what we have accomplished in the past few decades,

---

where the rich live segregated from the diseased and undernourished masses who to survive were often forced to sell their bodies, or their organs. This dystopian vision is the basis for the future of 2059 in *He, She and It*.

21 In fact, this pause on the threshold of utopia, as it were, is typical of a number of 1980s utopias, or at least of their titles, and they might be summed up as "liminal" utopias, societies on the verge of becoming utopia, with titles like: Pamela Sargent's *The Shore of Women;* Joan Slonczewski's *A Door into Ocean*; and Sherri Tepper's *The Gate to Women's Country*. See also Wegner (2002), as well as Jameson's (2000) reading of the *Mars* trilogy, "If I find one good city I will spare the man."

and to continue that scholarly and critical work. This is exemplified in Sargent's ongoing scholarly projects: his bibliography, his studies of national character and Utopia, as well as his questions about the existence of non-western utopias, his work for the *Society for Utopian Studies*, the journal, and so on: all this in preparation for better times.[22]

Another way of negotiating the present can be found in the work of Raffaella Baccolini and Moylan on the "critical dystopia" – research which, in these terms, can be seen as a means of recovering the utopian dimension from what has perhaps too quickly been seen as the abandonment of Utopia. This involves distinguishing those works which simply assume and use a dystopian background as a setting for their adventures (most famously this is a critique often made of cyberpunk) from the militant pessimism of other works which reject resignation even as they attempt to confront the present. However dystopian the worlds they portray, these latter dystopias display some critical awareness of the present, as they attempt to explain how this dystopia came about rather than simply taking it for granted; and these works, too, also hold out some utopian hope. The model of the critical dystopia in this sense is Margaret Atwood's 1985 *The Handmaid's Tale*, for it holds out the prospect of hope (Offred's escape, and the novel's Epilogue, in a distant future in which Gilead is nothing more than the subject of historical research.[23]

These attempts to track the utopian in dystopian times point more generally to the question of refocusing the discussion of Utopia, beginning with questions about Utopia and national identity and whether utopianism is limited to the Western tradition. But I think, too, that it may be that new utopian struggles and the seeds of change are emerging from outside the developed countries of the west. This concern has taken me

22 This basic scholarly position is essential, for without it we are doomed to begin over, like the people of the planet Lagash in Isaac Asimov's story "Nightfall," or Walter Miller Jr.'s *A Canticle for Leibowitz* (New York: Bantam, 1959).

23 For a discussion of *The Handmaid's Tale*, see Chapter 10, "The Turn from Utopia." In recent work, I have tried to find such positive dimensions in contemporary dystopian film, by juxtaposing the "false" escapes of the heroes of *Dark City* and *The Truman Show* to the more complex situations in *The Matrix* and especially *Pleasantville*. See Fitting (2003c).

most recently to the World Social Forum (WSF) in Porto Alegre (whose slogan is "Another World Is Possible"). With all its flaws and limitations, the WSF is an alternative utopian vision, one which not only gives voice and hope to the voiceless, to groups like that of landless workers (MST) or the Via Campesina network of peasant organizations from around the world; indeed, the WSF has developed into a global association working alongside existing state forms, but without seeking to reproduce or replace them. I do not have time here to describe the range and activities of this convening of extra-governmental groups opposed to neo-liberalism and committed to an alternative globalization, but it too constitutes a significant utopian vision which has taken an extra-literary form.

At the same time, this looking outside the developed countries in the context of the formulation of an alternative globalization is a promising new way of considering world events, one which is summed up for me in Michael Hardt and Tony Negri's political treatise *Empire* from which I draw, perhaps too simplistically, some important lines of reasoning. Rather than simply denouncing or attacking globalization – in the name of a threatened nation-state, for instance – Hardt and Negri's book develops some very relevant themes, beginning with the vision of a global utopia. Summarizing quickly, I take their concept of the *multitude*, as reminding us that social transformation may come from actors from outside the developed world and/or from outside the proletariat as traditionally defined.[24] Significantly, in these utopian terms their book concludes with three demands which not only reiterate many of the visions of the utopias of the 1970s, but which – in true utopian fashion – are impossible under a market economy: the demand for the realization of these all too reasonable and necessary goals would spell the end of capitalism. These three demands are: global citizenship, a social wage, and the "the right of reappropriation," a broadening of the familiar call for the seizing of the means of production, which now includes a full range of human activities and potential.

In the above, I have tried to outline some avenues of research and of struggle for utopian scholars and for those committed to those new

24 This concept was expanded in their subsequent (2004) book, *Multitude* (New York: Penguin Books, 2005).

visions in what may seem like especially discouraging times. In this context, Jameson – more than thirty years ago – gave some very good reasons for the continuing relevance of Utopia:

> [There is] not a crisis in Marxist science [but] in Marxist ideology. If ideology [...] is a vision of the future that grips the masses, we have to admit that, save in a few ongoing collective experiments [...] no Marxist or Socialist party or movement anywhere has the slightest conception of what socialism or communism as a social system ought to be and can be expected to look like. That vision will not be purely economic. [...] It is, as well, supremely social and cultural, involving the task of trying to imagine how a society without hierarchy, a society of free people, a society that has at once repudiated the economic mechanisms of the market, can possibly cohere. (1988a: 355)

Whereas, in the earlier quotation (from *Marxism and Form*) it was the appeal to "practical thinking" that represented the closing down of thinking about a better world, today the rejection of alternatives is even more insidious and dangerous, as it masquerades under the very banner of socialism, under which, we are told, we must be prepared to accommodate and accept capitalism. With the fall of the Soviet Union and the apparent triumph of a single mighty world power, progressives are told that there is only one alternative, the so-called third way, in which the market economy can somehow be disconnected from the social sphere. Utopia stands, in Jameson's terms, as a fierce rejection of this bogus option along with the reminder that there still are alternatives.

Bibliography

2001: A Space Odyssey, Stanley Kubrick, dir. (Metro-Goldwyn-Meyer, 1968) [film].

Adams, Frederick Upham, *President John Smith* (Chicago: Charles H. Kerr, 1897).

Adams, Percy G., *Travel Literature and the Evolution of the Novel* (Lexington: University Press of Kentucky, 1983).

Adorno, Theodore, "Aldous Huxley and Utopia," in *Prisms*, trans. S. Weber and S. Weber. (Cambridge, MA: MIT Press, 1981), 97–117.

Adorno, Theodore W., and Max Horkheimer, *The Dialectic of Enlightenment*, trans. John Cumming (New York: Herder & Herder, 1972).

Aldiss, Brian, *Billion Year Spree: The True History of Science Fiction* (New York: Schocken, 1974).

Aldridge, Alexandra, *The Scientific World View in Dystopia* (Ann Arbor, MI: UMI Research Press, 1984).

Aliens, James Cameron, dir. (Twentieth Century Fox, 1986) [film].

Althusser, Louis, "Idéologie et appareils idéologiques d'État," 4 *La Pensée* (mai-juin 1970), 3–38.

Altman, Rick, ed., *Genre, The Musical: A Reader* (London: Routledge & Kegan Paul, 1981).

Amis, Kingsley, *New Maps of Hell: A Survey of Science Fiction* (New York: Harcourt, 1960).

Andermahr, Sonya, "The Politics of Separatism and Lesbian Utopian Fiction," in Munt (1992), 133–152.

Anderson, Kristine, "Encyclopedic Dictionary as Utopian Genre: Two Feminist Ventures," *Utopian Studies* 2/1&2 (1991), 124–130.

Angenot, Marc, "Le Discours Social: Problématique d'ensemble," *Cahiers de Recherche Sociologique* 2/1 (1984), 19–45.

———, "Science Fiction in France before Verne," *Science Fiction Studies* 5/1 (1978), 58–66.

———, "The Emergence of the Anti-Utopian Genre in France," *Science Fiction Studies* 12 (1985), 129–135.

Annas, Pamela J., "New Worlds, New Words: Androgyny in Feminist Science Fiction," *Science Fiction Studies* 5 (1978), 143–156.

Appel, Benjamin, *The Funhouse* (New York: Ballantine, 1959).

Armes, Roy, *Third World Film Making and the West* (Berkeley: University of California Press, 1987).

Aronowitz, Stanley, "Film: The Art Form of Late Capitalism," *Social Text* 1 (1979), 110–129.

Ash, Brian, *Faces of the Future* (London: Unwin, 1975).

Ashley, Michael, *The Illustrated Book of Science Fiction Lists* (New York: Cornerstone Library, 1982).

Asimov, Isaac, *I, Robot* (New York: Signet, 1950).

Asimov, Isaac. "Nightfall," *Astounding Science Fiction* (September 1941), 9–34.

Atwood, Margaret, "Interview," *New York Times* 17 (1986).

———, *The Handmaid's Tale* (Toronto, ON: McClelland and Stewart, 1985).

Baccolini, Raffaella, and Tom Moylan, eds., *Dark Horizons: Science Fiction and the Dystopian Imagination* (New York: Routledge, 2003).

Badami, Mary Kenny, "A Feminist Critique of Science Fiction," *Extrapolation* 18/1 (1976), 6–19.

Baggesen, Søren, "Utopian and Dystopian Pessimism: Le Guin's *The Word for World Is Forest* and Tiptree's 'We Who Stole the Dream,'" *Science Fiction Studies* 14/1 (1987), 34–43.

Ballard, J.G., *Empire of the Sun* (New York: Simon & Schuster Paperbacks, 2005).

———, *The Crystal World, Crash, Concrete Island* (New York: Quality Paperback Book Club, 1991).

Barnard, Ian, "Macho Sluts: Genre-Fuck, S/M Fantasy, and the Reconfiguration of Political Action," in Kibbey et al. (1994), 265–291.

Barnouw, Erik, *Documentary: A History of the Non-Fiction Film* (New York: Oxford University Press, 1983).

Barr, Marleen S., "Metahuman 'Kipple'; Or, Do Male Movie Makers Dream of Electric Women?: Specieism and Sexism in Blade Runner," in Kerman (1991), 25–31.

———, ed., *Future Females: A Critical Anthology* (Bowling Green, OH: Bowling Green Popular Press, 1981).

———, "*He, She and It* [review]," *American Book Review* (June–July 1992), 11–13.

Barr, Marleen S., and Nicholas D. Smith, eds., *Women and Utopia: Critical Interpretations* (Lanham, MD: University Press of America, 1983).

Barrett, Michèle, and Mary McIntosh, *The Anti-Social Family* (London: NLB, 1982).

Barthes, Roland, *Critical Essays* (Evanston: Northwestern University Press, 1972).

———, *S/Z* (Paris: Editions du Seuil, 1976).

Barthes, Roland, Patrick ffrench, and Roland-François Lack, *The "Tel Quel" Reader* (London and New York: Routledge, 1998).

Basic Instinct, Paul Verhoeven, dir. (Carolco Pictures, 1992) [film].

Baxter, John, *Science Fiction in the Cinema* (New York: Warner Books, 1970).

Beauchamp, Gorman, "Jack London's Utopian Dystopia and Dystopian Utopia," in Roemer (1981), 91–107.

Berger, Harold L., *Science Fiction and the New Dark Age* (Bowling Green, OH: Popular Press, 1976).

Berman, Marshall, *All That Is Solid Melts into Air: The Experience of Modernity* (New York: Simon and Schuster, 1982).

Bertetto, Paolo, *Il cinema dell'utopia* (Salerno: Rumma, 1970).

Betrayed, Costa-Gravas, dir. (United Artists, 1988) [film].

Biskind, Peter, *Seeing Is Believing: How Hollywood Taught Us to Stop Worrying and Love the Fifties* (New York: Pantheon, 1983).

Blake, Peter, *Form Follows Fiasco: Why Modern Architecture Hasn't Worked* (Boston, MA/Toronto, ON: Little, Brown, 1977).

———, *No Place Like Utopia: Modern Architecture and the Company We Kept* (New York: Alfred A. Knopf, 1993).

Blakeley, Edward J., and Mary Gail Snyder, *Fortress America: Gated Communities in the United States* (Washington, DC: Brookings Institution Press, 1999).

Bloch, Ernst, *Philosophy of the Future* (New York: Herder & Herder, 1970).

———, *The Principle of Hope*, trans. Neville Plaice, Stephen Plaice, and Paul Knight. 3 vols. (Oxford: Blackwell, 1986).

Boddy, William, "Alternative Television in the United States," *Screen* 31/1 (1990), 91–101.

Bookchin, Murray, *From Urbanization to Cities: Towards a New Politics of Citizenship* (London: Cassell, 1995).

Born in Flames, Lizzie Borden, dir. (The Jerome Foundation, 1983) [film].

Bouchard, Guy, Laurent Giroux, and Gilbert Leclerc, *L'utopie aujourd'hui* (Montréal: Les Presses de l'Université de Montréal, 1985).

Bova, Ben, ed., *The Science Fiction Hall of Fame: The Greatest Science Fiction Novellas of All Time* (London: Gollancz, 1973).

A Boy and His Dog, L.Q. Jones, dir. (LQ/JAF, 1975) [film].

Bozzetto, Roger, *L'obscur Objet d'un Savoir: Fantastique et Science-Fiction: Deux Littératures de l'imaginaire* (Aix-en-Provence: Université de Provence, 1992).

Bradley, Wendy, "[Review of *He, She and It*]," *Interzone* (September 1992), 64–65.

Braverman, Harry, *Labor and Monopoly Capital: The Degradation of Work in the Twentieth Century* (New York: Monthly Review Press, 1974).

Bray, Mary Kay, "The Naming of Things: Men and Women, Language and Reality in Suzette Haden Elgin's *Native Tongue*," *Extrapolation* 27/2 (1986), 49–61.

Brecht, Bertolt, and John Willett, *Brecht on Theatre: The Development of an Aesthetic* (London: Methuen, 1988).

Brenkman, John. "Mass Media: From Collective Experience to the Culture of Privatization," *Social Text* 1 (1979), 94–109.

Brians, Paul, *Nuclear Holocausts: Atomic War in Fiction, 1895–1984* (Kent, OH: Kent State University Press, 1987).

Britton, Andrew, Richard Lippe, Tony Williams, and Robin Wood, eds., *American Nightmare: Essays on the Horror Film* (Toronto, ON: Festival of Festivals, 1979).
Brosnan, John, *Future Tense: The Cinema of Science Fiction* (London: The Book Service Limited, 1978).
Browder, Earl, *What Is Communism?* (New York: Vanguard Press, 1936).
Brownmiller, Susan, *Against Our Will: Men, Women, and Rape* (New York: Simon and Schuster, 1975).
Brunner, John, *The Shockwave Rider* (New York: Harper and Row, 1975).
Brunsdon, Charlotte, ed., *Films for Women* (London: British Film Institute, 1986).
Bryant, Dorothy, *The Kin of Ata Are Waiting for You* (New York: Moon Books, 1976).
Bryant, Jennings, and Dolf Zillman, *Perspectives on Media Effects* (Hillsdale, NJ: Lawrence Erlbaum Associates, 1986).
Burnet, Thomas, *The Sacred Theory of the Earth* (London: Centaur Press, 1965).
Burstyn, Varda, ed., *Women Against Censorship* (Toronto, ON: Douglas & McIntyre, 1985).
Byers, Thomas, "Commodity Futures: Corporate State and Personal Style in Three Recent Science-Fiction Movies," *Science Fiction Studies* 14/3 (1987), 326–339.
"*Cadillac Ranch*," *Art Metropole Videotape Catalogue* (Toronto, ON: ArtMetropole, 1982).
Cadillac Ranch/Media Burn, [n. dir.] (Ant Farm, 1975) [VHS].
Califia, Pat, *Doc and Fluff: The Dystopian Tale of a Girl and Her Biker* (Boston, MA: Alyson, 1990).
———, "Feminism and Sadomasochism," *Heresies* 3/4 (No. 12, 1981), 30–34.
———, *Macho Sluts* (Boston, MA: Alyson, 1988).
———, *Melting Point* (Boston, MA: Alyson, 1993).
———, *Public Sex: The Culture of Radical Sex* (Pittsburgh, PA: Cleis, 1994).
Callenbach, Ernest, *Ecotopia: The Notebooks and Reports of William Weston* (Toronto, ON: Bantam Books, 1982).
Campbell, John W., Jr. "Who Goes There?," *Astounding Science Fiction* (August 1938), 60–98.
Carter, Angela, *The Sadean Woman* (London: Virago, 1979).
Carter, Paul Allen, *The Creation of Tomorrow: Fifty Years of Magazine Science Fiction* (New York: Columbia University Press, 1977).
Caute, David, *The Great Fear: The Anti-Communist Purge Under Truman and Eisenhower* (New York: Simon and Schuster, 1978).
Cawelti, John, "Adventure, Mystery and Romance," *Theory and Society* 4 (1977), 543–559.
Cerdá, Ildefonso, *La Théorie générale de l'urbanisation. Présentée et adaptée par Antonio Lopez de Aberasturi* (Paris: Seuil, 1979).
Chandigarh public information site. <http://chandigahr.nic.in>.

Chapman, Robert S., "Science Fiction of the 1950s: Billy Graham, McCarthy and the Bomb," *Foundation* 7/8 (1975), 38–53.
Charnas, Suzy McKee, "A Woman Appeared," in Barr (1981), 103–108.
———, *Motherlines* (New York: Berkeley Books, 1979).
Chevrier, Yves, "Blade Runner; or, The Sociology of Anticipation," *Science Fiction Studies* 11 (1984), 50–60.
Choay, Francoise, *L'Urbanisme: Utopies et réalités* (Paris: Seuil, 1965).
Christine, John Carpenter, dir. (Columbia Pictures, 1983) [film].
Christopher, John, *The Death of Grass* (London: Penguin, 1958).
Clarke, Arthur C., *Against the Fall of Night* (New York: Gnome Press, 1953)
———, *Childhood's End* (Orlando, FL: Harcourt, Brace & World, 1953).
———, *City and the Stars* (London: Frederick Muller, 1956).
———, *Rendezvous With Rama* (London: Gollancz, 1973).
———, "The Sentinel," *New Worlds Science Fiction* 22 (1954), 47–55.
Close Encounters of the Third Kind, Steven Spielberg, dir. (Julia Phillips and Michael Phillips Productions, 1977) [film].
Clute, John, "*He, She and It* [review]," *The New York Review of Science Fiction* 43 (March 1992), 6–7.
Clute, John, and Peter Nicholls, eds., *The Encyclopedia of Science Fiction* (London: Orbit, 1993).
Coates, James, *Armed and Dangerous: The Rise of the Survivalist Right* (New York: Hill and Wang, 1987).
Comfort, Alex, "The Warrior and the Suffragette: Notes on the Science Fiction of John Norman," *Paunch* 48/49 (1977), 48–89.
Comfort, Alex, et al. *The Joy of Sex: A Gourmet Guide to Love Making* (New York: Simon and Schuster, 1972).
Corn, Joseph, *Imagining Tomorrow: History, Technology, and the American Future* (Cambridge: MIT, 1986).
Coward, Rosalind, and John Ellis, *Language and Materialism: Development in Semiology and the Theory of the Subject* (London: Routledge, 1977).
Creet, Julia, "Daughters of the Movement: The Psychodynamics of Lesbian S/M Fantasy," *Differences: A Journal of Feminist Cultural Studies* 3/2 (1991), 135–159.
Curtis, William, *Le Corbusier: Ideas and Forms* (New York: Rizzoli, 1986).
Damnation Alley, Jack Smight, dir. (Zeitman-Landers-Roberts Productions, 1977) [film].
The Day After, Nicholas Meyer, dir. (ABC Circle Films, 1983) [film].
de Lauretis, Teresa, "Aesthetic and Feminist Theory: Rethinking Women's Cinema," *New German Critique* 34 (1985), 154–175.
———, *Alice Doesn't: Feminism, Semiotics, Cinema* (Bloomington: Indiana University Press, 1984).

———, "Guerrilla in the Midst: Women's Cinema in the 80s," *Screen* 31/1 (1990), 6–25.

de Quincy, Thomas, and Niels Klim, *Niels Klim, Being an Incomplete Translation from the Danish of Ludvig Holberg, Now Edited from the Manuscript by S. Musgrove* (Auckland: Auckland University College, 1953).

DeCordova, Richard, "Cable Technology and the Utopian Subject," *On Film* 12 (1984), 23–27.

Deery, June, "Ectopic and Utopic Reproduction: *He, She and It*," *Utopian Studies* 5/2 (1994), 36–49.

Del Rey, Lester, "Helen O'Loy," *Astounding Science Fiction* (December 1938), 118–125.

Delany, Samuel R., *Flight from Nevèrÿon* (Toronto, ON: Bantam, 1985).

———, *Stars in My Pocket Like Grains of Sand* (New York: Bantam, 1984).

———, *Triton* (New York: Bantam, 1976).

D'Emilio, John, "Capitalism and Gay Identity," in Snitow et al. (1983), 100–113.

Dempsey, Michael, "*Blade Runner*," *Film Quarterly* 36/2 (1982), 33–38.

Der Golem, Henrik Galeen and Paul Wegener, dirs. (Deutsche Bioscop GmbH, 1915) [film].

Der Golem: Wie Er in die Welt Kam, Carl Boese and Paul Wegener, dirs. (Projektions-AG Union, 1920) [film].

Dick, Philip K., *Do Androids Dream of Electric Sheep?* 1968 (Toronto, ON: Signet, 1969).

———, "Man, Android, and Machine," in Peter Nicholls, ed., *Science Fiction at Large* (London: Gollancz, 1976), 199–224.

———, "The Android and the Human," *SF Commentary* 31 (1972), 4–26.

———, *The Collected Stories of Philip K. Dick*, 5 vols (Los Angeles, CA: Underwood/Miller, 1987).

———, *The Three Stigmata of Palmer Eldritch* (Boston, MA: Mariner Books, 2011).

Dick, Philip K., *Do Androids Dream of Electric Sheep?* (Toronto, ON: Signet, 1969).

Diderot, Denis, *Supplément au Voyage de Bougainville*, ed. Julie Cuvillier (Paris: Belin-Gallimard, 2011).

Dietz, Frank, "*He, She and It* [review]," *The New York Review of Science Fiction* (September 1992), 13–14.

Dimen, Muriel, "Seven Notes for the Reconstruction of Sexuality," *Social Text* 6 (1982), 22–30.

Disch, Thomas M., *On Wings of Song* (New York: St. Martin's Press, 1979).

———, *The Genocides* (New York: Berkeley Books, 1965)

Doll, Susan, and Greg Faller, "*Blade Runner* and Genre: Film Noir and Science Fiction," *Literature Film Quarterly* 14/2 (1986), 89–100.

Donaldson, Stephen, *The Chronicles of Thomas Covenant The Unbeliever* (New York: Harper-Collins, 1993).
Donawerth, Jane L., and Carol A. Kolmerten, eds., *Science Fiction by Women: Worlds of Difference* (Syracuse, NY: Syracuse University Press, 1994).
Downing, John, ed., *Film and Politics in the Third World* (New York: Praeger, 1987).
Dr. Strangelove or: How I Learned to Stop Worrying and Love the Bomb, Stanley Kubrick, dir. (Columbia Pictures, 1964) [film].
Dresser, David, "*Blade Runner*: Science Fiction and Transcendence," *Literature Film Quarterly* 1/3 (1985), 172–179.
Drew, Elizabeth, "Le Corbusier as I Knew Him," in Walden (1977), 364–373.
Dryden, John. *A Discourse Concerning the Original and Progress of Satire* (Boston, MA: Houghton Mifflin, 1908).
Duel, Steven Spielberg, dir. (Universal Television, 1971) [film].
Dunlop, John Colin, *The History of Fiction* (Edinburgh: James Ballantyne, 1814).
Dunn, Sara, "Voyages of the Valkyries: Recent Lesbian Pornographic Writing," *Feminist Review* 34 (1990), 161–170.
Dyer, Richard, "Entertainment and Utopia," *Movie* 24 (1977), 2–13.
Eagleton, Terry, *Ideology: An Introduction* (London: Verso, 2007).
———, *Marxism and Literary Criticism* (London: Methuen, 1983).
Echols, Alice, "The New Feminism of Yin and Yang," in Snitow et al. (1983), 439–459.
Eddy, William, *Gulliver's Travels: A Critical Study* (Princeton, NJ: Princeton University Press, 1923).
Elgin, Suzette Haden, *Native Tongue* (New York: Daw Books, 1984).
———, *The Judas Rose* (New York: Daw Books, 1987).
Elkins, Charles, "An Approach to the Social Functions of American Science Fiction," *Science Fiction Studies* 4 (1977), 223–227.
———, "Isaac Asimov's *Foundation* Novels," *Science Fiction Studies* 3 (1976), 26–36.
Ellin, Nan, *Postmodern Urbanism* (Oxford: Blackwell, 1996).
Elliott, Robert C., *The Shape of Utopia: Studies in a Literary Genre* (Chicago: University of Chicago Press, 1970).
Elshtain, Jean Bethke, "Against Androgyny," in Phillips (1987), 139–159.
Empire of the Sun, Steven Spielberg, dir. (Amblin Entertainment, 1987) [film].
Engels, Friedrich, *Socialism Utopian and Scientific* (New York: International Publishers, 1998).
———, *The Origin of the Family, Private Property and the State* (London: Lawrence and Wishart, 1972).
Erickson, John, "The Ghost in the Machine: Gilliam's Postmodern Response in *Brazil* to the Orwellian Dystopia of *Nineteen Eighty-Four*," *Utopian Studies* 4/2 (1993), 26–34.

Ernst, Morris Leopold, *Utopia, 1976* (New York: Greenwood Press, 1969).

Escape from New York, John Carpenter, dir. (Embassy Pictures, 1981) [film].

Estivals, R., "L'avant-garde culturelle, le gauchisme et la societe de consummation," in *Actes du VIe Congrès de l'Association Internationale de Littérature Comparée* (Stuttgart, 1975).

An Evaluation of Our American Heritage (Rochester, WA: Sovereign Press, 1982).

Evans, Arthur B., "The Origins of Science Fiction Criticism: From Kepler to Wells," *Science Fiction Studies* 26/2 (1999), 163–186.

Evenson, Norma, *Chandigarh* (Berkeley: University of California Press, 1966).

The Exterminators of the Year 3000, Giuliano Carnimeo, dir. (2T Produzione Film, 1983) [film].

Fackenheim, Emil, *To Mend the World: Foundations of Future Jewish Thought* (New York: Schocken, 1982).

Fail-Safe, Sidney Lumet, dir. (Columbia Pictures, 1964) [film].

Fairbairns, Zoë, *Benefits* (London: Virago, 1979).

Faludi, Susan. *Backlash: The Undeclared War Against American Women* (New York: Anchor, 1992).

Feenberg, Andrew, "Science Fiction of the Nuclear Age," *Johns Hopkins Magazine* (1977), 12–22.

ffrench, Patrick, *The Time of Theory a History of Tel Quel (1960–1983)* (Oxford: Clarendon Press, 1995).

Fishman, Robert, *Urban Utopias in the Twentieth Century: Ebenezer Howard, Frank Lloyd Wright, and Le Corbusier* (New York: Basic Books, 1977).

Fitting, Peter, "A Virtue of Necessity: Financial Limitations and the Emergence of the Video Fringe," in Gary Westfahl, George Slusser, and Eric Rabkin, eds, *Science Fiction and Market Realities* (Athens: University of Georgia Press, 1996), 171–183.

———, "Anticipazione e negazione: la politica della fantascienza," in Luigi Russo, ed., *La fantascienza e la critica* (Rome: Feltrinelli, 1980), 252–259.

———, "Beyond the Wasteland: A Feminist in Cyberspace," *Utopian Studies* 5/2 (1994), 4–15.

———, "Beyond This Horizon: Utopian Visions and Utopian Practice," in Baccolini and Moylan (2007), 245–266.

———, "Buried Treasures: Reconsidering Holberg's Niels Klim in the World Underground," *Utopian Studies* 7/2 (1996), 93–112.

———, "Constructing Our Future: Men, Women, and Feminist Utopian Fiction," in Michael Kauffman, ed., *Beyond Patriarchy: Essays by Men on Pleasure, Power, and Change* (Toronto, ON: Oxford University Press, 1987), 298–317.

———, "Count Me Out/In: Post-Apocalyptic Vision in Recent Science Fiction Film," *Cineaction* 11 (1987), 42–51.

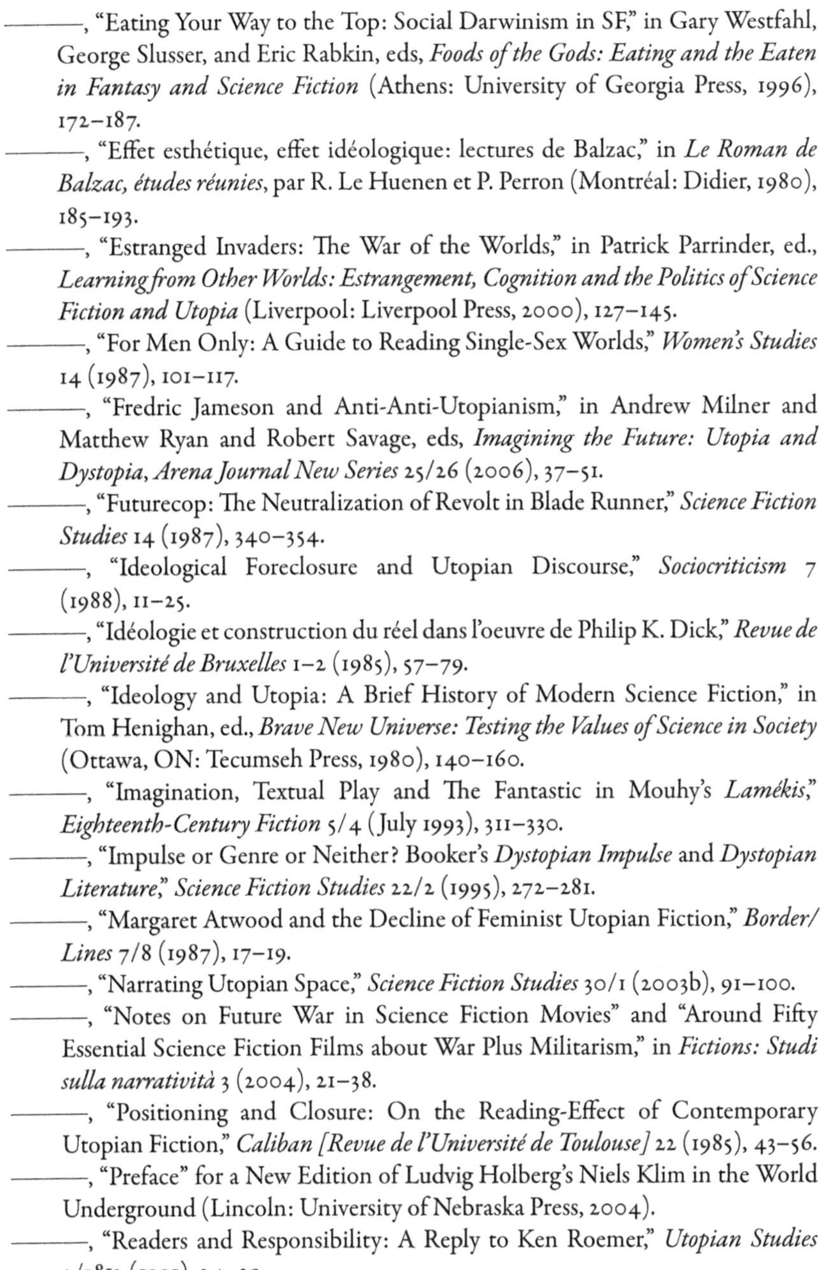

———, "Eating Your Way to the Top: Social Darwinism in SF," in Gary Westfahl, George Slusser, and Eric Rabkin, eds, *Foods of the Gods: Eating and the Eaten in Fantasy and Science Fiction* (Athens: University of Georgia Press, 1996), 172–187.

———, "Effet esthétique, effet idéologique: lectures de Balzac," in *Le Roman de Balzac, études réunies*, par R. Le Huenen et P. Perron (Montréal: Didier, 1980), 185–193.

———, "Estranged Invaders: The War of the Worlds," in Patrick Parrinder, ed., *Learning from Other Worlds: Estrangement, Cognition and the Politics of Science Fiction and Utopia* (Liverpool: Liverpool Press, 2000), 127–145.

———, "For Men Only: A Guide to Reading Single-Sex Worlds," *Women's Studies* 14 (1987), 101–117.

———, "Fredric Jameson and Anti-Anti-Utopianism," in Andrew Milner and Matthew Ryan and Robert Savage, eds, *Imagining the Future: Utopia and Dystopia, Arena Journal New Series* 25/26 (2006), 37–51.

———, "Futurecop: The Neutralization of Revolt in Blade Runner," *Science Fiction Studies* 14 (1987), 340–354.

———, "Ideological Foreclosure and Utopian Discourse," *Sociocriticism* 7 (1988), 11–25.

———, "Idéologie et construction du réel dans l'oeuvre de Philip K. Dick," *Revue de l'Université de Bruxelles* 1–2 (1985), 57–79.

———, "Ideology and Utopia: A Brief History of Modern Science Fiction," in Tom Henighan, ed., *Brave New Universe: Testing the Values of Science in Society* (Ottawa, ON: Tecumseh Press, 1980), 140–160.

———, "Imagination, Textual Play and The Fantastic in Mouhy's *Lamékis*," *Eighteenth-Century Fiction* 5/4 (July 1993), 311–330.

———, "Impulse or Genre or Neither? Booker's *Dystopian Impulse* and *Dystopian Literature*," *Science Fiction Studies* 22/2 (1995), 272–281.

———, "Margaret Atwood and the Decline of Feminist Utopian Fiction," *Border/Lines* 7/8 (1987), 17–19.

———, "Narrating Utopian Space," *Science Fiction Studies* 30/1 (2003b), 91–100.

———, "Notes on Future War in Science Fiction Movies" and "Around Fifty Essential Science Fiction Films about War Plus Militarism," in *Fictions: Studi sulla narratività* 3 (2004), 21–38.

———, "Positioning and Closure: On the Reading-Effect of Contemporary Utopian Fiction," *Caliban [Revue de l'Université de Toulouse]* 22 (1985), 43–56.

———, "Preface" for a New Edition of Ludvig Holberg's Niels Klim in the World Underground (Lincoln: University of Nebraska Press, 2004).

———, "Readers and Responsibility: A Reply to Ken Roemer," *Utopian Studies* 2/1&2 (1991), 24–29.

———, "Reality as Ideological Construct: A Reading of Five Novels by P. K. Dick," *Science Fiction Studies* 10/2 (1983), 219–236.

———, "Recent Feminist Utopias: World Building and Strategies for Social Change," in George E. Slusser and Eric S. Rabkin, eds, *Mindscapes: Selected Proceedings of the Ninth Eaton Conference* (Carbondale, IL: Southern, 1989), 155–163.

———, "Reconsiderations of the Separatist Paradigm in Recent Feminist Science Fiction." Science-Fiction Studies 19.1 (56) (March 1992): 32–48.

———, "Representing Utopia," *Utopian Studies* 12/1 (2001), 108–132.

———, "Science Fiction Criticism in France," *Science Fiction Studies* I. 3&4 (1974), 276–279.

———, "SF, Fantasy and the Elaboration of Imaginary Worlds," *Actes du Premier colloque international de Science-Fiction de Nice, Métaphore 9/10* (Centre d'étude de la métaphore, Faculté des Lettres, Université de Nice, 1984), 139–144.

———, "'So We All Became Mothers': New Roles for Men in Recent Utopian Fiction," *Science Fiction Studies* 12 (1985), 156–183.

———, *Subterranean Worlds: A Critical Anthology* (Middleton, CT: Wesleyan University Press, 2004).

———, "Sun Ra at The Diamond," *Border/Lines* 11 (1988), 10–11.

———, "The Concept of Utopia in the Work of Fredric Jameson," *Utopian Studies* 9/2 (1998), 8–17.

———, "The Lessons of Cyberpunk," in Constance Penley and Andrew Ross, eds, *Technoculture* (Minneapolis: University of Minnesota Press, 1991), 295–315.

———, "The Modem Anglo-American SF Novel: Utopian Longing and Capitalist Cooptation," *Science Fiction Studies* 6 (1979), 59–76.

———, "The Second Alien," *Science Fiction Studies* 7/3 (1980), 285–293; 302–303.

———, "The Turn from Utopia in Recent Feminist Fiction," in Libby Falk Jones and Sarah Webster Goodwin, eds, *Feminism and Utopian Narrative* (Knoxville: University of Tennessee Press, 1990), 141–158.

———, "To Read the World: Barthes' Mythologies Thirty Years Later," *Queen's Quarterly* 95 (1988), 857–871.

———, "*Ubik*: The Deconstruction of Bourgeois SF," *Science Fiction Studies* 2 (1975), 47–54.

———, "Unmasking the Real? Critique and Utopia in Recent SF Films," in Raffaella Baccolini and Tom Moylan, eds., *Dark Horizons: Science Fiction and the Dystopian Imagination*, (London: Routledge, 2003c), 155–166.

———, "Urban Planning/Utopian Dreaming: Chandigarh Today," *Utopian Studies* 13/1 (2002), 69–93.

———, "Utopia Beyond Our Ideals: The Dilemma of the Right-Wing Utopia," *Utopian Studies* 2/1&2 (1991), 95–109.

———, "Violence and Utopia: John Norman and Pat Califia," *Utopian Studies* 11/1 (2000), 91–108.

———, "What is Utopian Film?: An Introductory Taxonomy," *Utopian Studies* 4/2 (Fall 1993), 1–17.

Fitting, Peter, and Lise Leibacher-Ouvrard, "L'Imaginaire utopique: paradigme, formes et fonctions," Introduction to a special issue of *L'esprit Créateur* 34/4 (1994), 5–17.

Flesh Gordon, Michael Benveniste and Howard Ziehm, dirs. (Graffiti Productions, 1974) [film].

Flinn, Caryl, *Strains of Utopia: Gender, Nostalgia, and Hollywood Film Music* (Princeton, NJ: Princeton University Press, 1992).

Flynn, Kevin, and Gary Gerhardt, *The Silent Brotherhood: Inside America's Racist Underground* (New York: Free Press, 1989).

Follow the Dirt Road: An Introduction to Intentional Communities in the 1990's, Monique Gauthier, dir. (The Cinema Guild, 1992) [VHS].

Forbidden Planet, Fred M. Wilcox, dir. (Metro-Goldwyn-Meyer, 1958) [film].

Fortunati, Vita, and Raymond Trousson, eds., *Dictionary of Literary Utopias* (Paris: Honoré Champion, 2000).

Foucault, Michel, *Les mots et les choses* (Paris: Gallimard, 1966).

———, ed., *Théorie d'ensemble: choix* (Paris: Editions du Seuil, 1980).

Foulkes, A.P., *Literature and Propaganda* (London: Methuen, 1983).

Franklin, H. Bruce, "Chic Bleak in Fantasy Fiction," *Saturday Review* (July 15, 1972), 42–45.

———, "Don't Look Where We're Going: Visions of the Future in Science Fiction Films, 1970 to 1982," *Science Fiction Studies* 10/1 (1983), 70–80.

———, ed., "Special Issue on Nuclear War and SF," *Science Fiction Studies* (July 13, 1986).

Fraser, John, *Violence in the Arts* (Cambridge, UK: Cambridge University Press, 1974).

Friedman, Régine-Mihal, "'Capitals of Sorrow': From *Metropolis* to *Brazil*," *Utopian Studies* 4/2 (1993), 35–43.

Friend, Beverly, "Virgin Territory: Women and Sex in Science Fiction," *Extrapolation* 14/1 (December 1972), 49–58.

Fry, Maxwell, "Le Corbusier at Chandigarh," in Walden (1977), 350–363.

Frye, Northrop, "Varieties of Literary Utopias," in Frank E. Manuel, ed., *Utopias and Utopian Thought* (Boston, MA: Houghton Mifflin, 1966), 25–49.

Futureworld, Richard T. Heffron, dir. (American International Pictures, 1976) [film].

Garnier, Charles-Georges-Thomas, ed., "Voyages imaginaires, Songes, Visions et Romans cabalistiques. 36 vols," Amsterdam, n.p., 1787–1789.

Garnier, Tony, *Une cité industrielle: étude pour la construction des villes* (Paris: Sers, 1988).

Gearhart, Sally Miller, “Future Visions: Today's Politics: Feminist Utopias,” in Rohrlich & Baruch (1984), 296–309.

———, *The Wanderground: Tales of the Hill Women* (Watertown, MA: Persephone Press, 1978).

Gerber, Richard, *Utopian Fantasy: A Study of English Utopian Fiction since the End of the Nineteenth Century* (New York: McGraw-Hill, 1973).

Gershuny, H. Lee, “The Linguistic Transformation of Womanhood,” in Rohrlich & Baruch (1984), 189–199.

Gillette, King Camp, *The Human Drift* (Boston, MA: New Era Publishing, 1894).

Gold, John R., *The Experience of Modernism: Modern Architects and the Future City, 1928–1953* (London: E & FN Spon, 1997).

Goldmann, Lucien, *Towards a Sociology of the Novel* (London: Tavistock Publications, 1975).

Goldsmith, Arnold, *The Golem Remembered, 1909–1980: Variations of a Jewish Legend* (Detroit, MI: Wayne State University Press, 1981).

Goodman, Percival, and Paul Goodman, *Communitas: Means of Livelihood and Ways of Life* (Chicago: University of Chicago Press, 1947).

Goodwin, Barbara, and Keith Taylor, *The Politics of Utopia: A Study in Theory and Practice* (London: Hutchinson, 1982).

Gordon, Peter, and Harry Richardson, “A Critique of New Urbanism,” Paper presented at the Meeting of the American Collegiate Schools of Planning, 1998. <http://www-rcf.usc.edu/~pgordon/urbanism.html>.

Gorz, André, and Michael Sonenscher, *Farewell to the Working Class: An Essay on Post-Industrial Socialism* (Boston, MA: South End Press, 1987).

Gove, Philip Babcock, *The Imaginary Voyage in Prose Fiction: A History of Its Criticism and a Guide for Its Study, with an Annotated Check List of 215 Imaginary Voyages from 1700 to 1800* (New York: Columbia University Press, 1941).

Grahn, Judy, *Mundane's World* (Freedom, CA: The Crossing Press, 1988).

Grant, Barry Keith, ed., *Film Genre Reader* (Austin: University of Texas Press, 1986).

Greene, Gayle, “Choice of Evils,” *Women's Review of Books* 3/10 (1986), 14–15.

Greimas, A.J., *Du sense* (Paris: Seuil, 1970).

Greven-Borde, Hélène, *Formes du roman utopique en Grande-Bretagne, 1918–1970. Dialogue du rationnel et de l'irrationnel* (Gif sur Yvette: Université de Rouen et du Havre, 1995).

Grivel, Charles, *Production de l'intérêt romanesque* (The Hague: Mouton, 1973).

Hahn, Ronald, and Volker Jansen, *Lexikon Des Science Fiction Films: 1000 Filme von 1902 Bis 1987* (Munich: Heyne Verlag, 1987).

Hall, Peter, *Cities of Tomorrow: An Intellectual History of Urban Planning and Design in The Twentieth Century* (London: Basil Blackwell, 1988).

Hall, Peter C., and Erlich, Richard D., "Beyond Topeka and Thunderdome: Variations on the Comic-Romance Pattern in Recent SF Film," *Science Fiction Studies* 14 (1987), 316–325.

Hammer, Simon C., *Ludvig Holberg: The Founder of Norwegian Literature and an Oxford Student* (Blackwell: Oxford, 1920).

Haraway, Donna, "A Manifesto for Cyborgs: Science, Technology, and Socialist Feminism in the 1980s," in Linda J. Nicholson, ed. *Feminism/ Postmodernism* (New York: Routledge, 1985), 190–233.

Hardt, Michael, and Antonio Negri, *Empire* (Cambridge, MA: Harvard University Press, 2000).

———, *Multitude: War and Democracy in In Age of Empire* (New York: Penguin, 2004).

Hardy, Phil, ed., *Science Fiction: The Complete Film Sourcebook* (New York: Morrow, 1984).

Harvey, David, *The Condition of Postmodernity* (London: Blackwell, 1989).

Healey, Emma, *The Lesbian Sex Wars* (London: Virago, 1996).

Heer, Jeet, "Marxist Literary Critics Are Following Me! How Philip K. Dick betrayed his academic admirers to the FBI," *Lingua Franca* 11/4 (May/June 2001). <http://linguafranca.mirror.theinfo.org/print/0105/cover.html>.

Heinlein, Robert, *Beyond This Horizon* (New York: Signet, 1948).

Henderson, Lisa, "Lesbian Pornography: Cultural Transgression and Sexual Demystification," in Munt (1992), 173–191.

Henriques, Julian, Wendy Hollway, Cathy Urwin, Couze Venn, and Valerie Walkerdine, *Changing the Subject: Psychology, Social Regulation, and Subjectivity* (New York: Methuen, 1984).

Herbert, Frank, *Dune* (New York: Ace, 1965).

Hertzler, Joyce, *The History of Utopian Thought* (New York: Cooper Square, 1965).

Hillegas, Mark, *The Future as Nightmare: H.G. Wells and the Anti-Utopians* (New York: Oxford University Press, 1967).

Hoban, Russell, *Riddley Walker* (London: Cape, 1985).

Hodgson, Godfrey, *America in Our Time* (Garden City, NY: Doubleday, 1976).

Holberg, Ludvig, *The Journey of Niels Klim to the World Underground*, ed. James Ignatius McNelis, Bison Frontiers of Imagination (Lincoln: University of Nebraska Press, 2004).

Holberg, Ludvig *Holberg's Memoirs: An Eighteenth Century Danish Contribution to International Understanding*, ed. Stewart Fraser (Leiden: Brill, 1970).

Hollway, Wendy, "Gender Difference and the Production of Subjectivity," in Henriques et al. (1984), 227–263.

Hölscher, Lucian, "Utopie," trans. Kirsten Petrak, *Utopian Studies* 7/2 (1996), 1–65.

Holston, James, *The Modernist City: An Anthropological Critique of Brasilia* (Chicago: University of Chicago Press, 1969).

Hougaard, Jens Ludvig, *Holberg: The Playwright and His Age up to 1730* (Odense: Odense University Press, 1993).

Huet, Marie-Helene, *Monstrous Imagination* (Cambridge, MA: Harvard University Press, 1993).

Hughes, David, "The Ghost in the Machine: The Theme of Player Piano," in Roemer (1981), 108–114.

Hunt, H.L., *Alpaca Revisited* (Dallas, TX: H.L. Products, 1967).

Huntington, John, "Utopian and Anti-Utopian Logic: H.G. Wells and his Successors," *Science Fiction Studies* 9 (1982), 122–146.

Hurst, L.J., "John Nonnan: The Literature of Difference," *Foundation* 33 (1985), 36–55.

I Nuovi Barbari, Enzo G. Castellari, dir., (Deaf International, 1983) [film].

Jacobs, Jane, *The Death and Life of Great American Cities* (New York: Random House, 1961).

Jameson, Fredric, *Archaeologies of the Future: The Desire Called Utopia and Other Science Fictions* (London: Verso, 2005).

———, "Architecture and the Critique of Ideology," in Ockman (1985), 51–87.

———, "After Armageddon: Character Systems in *Dr. Bloodmoney*," *Science Fiction Studies* 2/1 (1975), 31–42.

———, "Cognitive Mapping," in Cary Nelson and Lawrence Grossberg, eds., *Marxism and the Interpretation of Culture* (Urbana: University of Illinois Press, 1988a), 347–360.

———, "Forward," A.J. Greimas, *On Meaning: Selected Writings in Semiotic Theory* (Minneapolis: University of Minnesota Press, 1987).

———, " 'If I find one good city I will spare the man': Realism and Utopia in Kim Stanley Robinson's *Mars Trilogy*," in Parrinder (2000), 208–232.

———, *Marxism and Form: Twentieth Century Dialectical Theories of Literature* (Princeton, NJ: Princeton University Press, 1971).

———, "Marxism and Science Fiction," (Unpublished paper, 1973).

———, "Of Islands and Trenches: Naturalization and the Production of Utopian Discourse," *Diacritics* 7/2 (1977a), 2–21.

———, "Periodizing the 60s," in Sohnya Sayers, Anders Stephanson, et al. *The 60s without Apology* (Minneapolis: University of Minnesota Press, 1984), 178–209.

———, "Pleasure: A Political Issue," in Fredric Jameson, Terry Eagleton, Cora Kaplan, Laura Mulvey, *Formations of Pleasure* (London: Routledge, 1983), 1–14.

———, *Postmodernism, or, The Cultural Logic of Late Capitalism* (Durham, NC: Duke University Press, 1991).

———, "Progress versus Utopia: Or, Can We Imagine the Future?," *Science-Fiction Studies* 9/2 (July 1982), 147–158.

———, "Reification and Utopia in Mass Culture," *Social Text* 1 (1979), 130–148.

———, "Review of Will Wright's *Sixguns and Society* and John Cawelti's *Adventure, Mystery and Romance*," *Theory and Society* 4 (1977b), 543–559.

———, "The Ideology of the Text," *Salmagundi* 31/32 (1975), 204–246.

———, "The Ideology of the Text," in *The Ideologies of Theory* (Minneapolis: Minnesota University Press, 1988b), 17- 71.

———, *The Political Unconscious: Narrative as a Socially Symbolic Act* (Ithaca, NY: Cornell University Press, 1981).

———, *The Prison-House of Language: A Critical Account of Structuralism and Russian Formalism* (Princeton, NJ: Princeton University Press, 1974).

———, *The Seeds of Time* (New York: Columbia University Press, 1996).

———, "World Reduction in Le Guin: The Emergence of Utopian Narrative," *Science Fiction Studies* 2 (1975), 221–230.

Jansen, F.J. Billeskov, *Ludvig Holberg* (New York: Twayne, 1974).

Jauss, Hans Robert, *Aesthetic Experience and Literary Hermeneutics* (Minneapolis: University of Minnesota Press, 1982).

Jeffreys, Sheila, "Sadomasochism: The Erotic Cult of Fascism," in *The Lesbian Heresy: A Feminist Perspective on the Lesbian Sexual Revolution* (London: The Women's Press, 1994), 220–226.

Jensen, Jane, "Representations of Difference: The Varieties of French Feminism," *New Left Review* 180 (1990), 127–160.

Jhirad, David, Marian Lowe, and Paolo Strigini, "The Limits to Capitalist Growth," *Science for the People* 7 (1975), 14–19; 34–37.

Jill, von Konen, *Camp 38* (Rochester, WA: Sovereign Press, 1984).

Jones, James F., "Adventures in a Strange Paradise – Utopia in *Nicolai Klimii Iter subterraneum*," *Orbis Litterarum* 35 (1980), 193–205.

Jones, Libby Falk, and Sarah Webster Goodwin, eds., *Feminism, Utopia, and Narrative* (Knoxville: University of Tennessee Press, 1990).

Juno, Andrea, and V. Vale, *J.G. Ballard* (San Francisco, CA: V/Search, 1984).

Just Imagine, David Butler, dir. (Fox Film Corp., 1930) [film].

Kafton-Minkel, Walter, *Subterranean Worlds: 100,000 Years of Dragons, Dwarfs, the Dead, Lost Races & UFOs from Inside the Earth* (Port Townsend, WA: Loompanics Unlimited, 1989).

Kalia, Ravi, *Chandigarh in Search of an Identity* (Carbondale: Southern Illinois University Press, 1994).

Kaplan, Alice Yaeger, *Reproductions of Banality: Fascism, Literature, and French Intellectual Life* (Minneapolis: University of Minnesota Press, 1986).

Kateb, George, *Utopia and Its Enemies* (New York: Schocken, 1972).

Kaufman, Michael, ed., *Beyond Patriarchy: Essays by Men on Pleasure, Power, and Change* (Toronto, ON and New York: Oxford University Press, 1987).

Kauppi, Niilo, *The Making of an Avant-Garde: Tel Quel* (Berlin: Mouton de Gruyter, 1994).

Kellner, Doug, "Public Access Television: Alternative Views," in Lazere (1987), 610–618.

Kellner, Doug, Flo Leibowitz, and Michael Ryan, "*Blade Runner*: A Diagnostic Critique," *Jump Cut* 29 (1984), 6–8.

Kepler, Johannes, *Somnium: The Dream, or Posthumous Work on Lunar Astronomy*, trans. Edward Rosen (Madison: University of Wisconsin Press, 1967).

Kerman, Judith, ed., *Retrofitting Blade Runner* (Bowling Green, OH: Bowling Green University Popular Press, 1991).

Kessel, John, "Letter," *New York Review of Science Fiction* 96 (August 1996), 23.

Kessler, Carol Farley, "Bibliography of Utopian Fiction by United States Women, 1836–1988," *Utopian Studies* 1/1 (1990), 1–58.

———, ed., *Daring to Dream: Utopian Fiction by United States Women, 1836–1919* (Boston, MA: Pandora Press, 1984).

Kibbey, Anne, Kayann Short, and Abouali Farmanfarmaian, eds., *Sexual Artifice: Persons, Images, Politics* (New York: New York University Press, 1994).

Kihlstedt, Folke, "Utopia Realized: The World's Fairs of the 1930s," in Corn (1986), 97–118.

Killdozer, Jerry London, dir. (Universal Television, 1974) [TV movie].

King, Betty, *Women of the Future: The Female Main Character in Science Fiction* (Metuchen, NJ: Scarecrow Press, 1984).

Kipnis, Laura, *Bound, and Gagged: Pornography and the Politics of Fantasy in America* (New York: Grove Press, 1996).

Klein, Gerard, "Discontent in American Science Fiction," *Science Fiction Studies* 4 (1977), 3–13.

Krappe, Alexander, "The Subterraneous Voyage," *Philological Quarterly* (1941), 119–130.

Krutch, Joseph Wood, *The Measure of Man: On Freedom, Human Values, Survival, and the Modern Temper* (New York: Grosset & Dunlap, 1954).

Kuhn, Annette, ed., *Alien Zone: Cultural Theory and Contemporary Science Fiction Cinema* (London: Verso, 1990).

———, *Women's Pictures: Feminism and Cinema* (London: Routledge & Kegan Paul, 1982).

Kumar, Krishan, *Utopia and Anti-Utopia in Modem Times* (Oxford: Blackwell, 1987).

Kunstler, James Howard, *Home from Nowhere* (New York: Simon and Schuster, 1996).

———, *The Geography of Nowhere: The Rise and Decline of America's Man-Made Landscape* (New York: Simon and Schuster, 1993).

Lazere, Donald, ed., *American Media and Mass Culture* (Berkeley: University of California Press, 1987).

Le Corbusier, *Carnets*, vol. 2, 1950–1954 (Paris: Herscher/Dessain et Tora, 1981).

———, *Carnets*, vol. 3, 1954–1957 (Paris: Herscher/Dessain et Tora, 1982).

———, *Photographs of Chandigarh*, courtesy of la Foundation Le Corbusier (Paris).

———, *The Radiant City* [1933], trans. Pamela Knight, Eleanor Levieux, and Derek Coltman (New York: Orion, 1967).

Le Guin, Ursula K., *Always Coming Home* (New York: Harper and Row, 1985).

———, *The Dispossessed* (New York: Avon, 1975).

———, *The Left Hand of Darkness* (New York: Ace, 1969).

———, *The Word for World Is Forest* (New York: Berkley Books, 1972).

Leenhardt, Jacques, and Pierre Jozsa, *Lire la lecture: essai de sociologie de la lecture* (Paris: L'Harmattan, 1982).

Leith, Linda, "Marion Zimmer Bradley and Darkover," *Science Fiction Studies* 7 (1980), 28–35.

Lesser, Simon, *Fiction and the Unconscious* (New York: Vintage, 1962).

Levitas, Ruth, *The Concept of Utopia* (Syracuse, NY: Syracuse University Press, 1990).

Lew, Roland, and Hubert Galle, "Sous les pavés de l'enfer utopique," *Science Fiction* (Paris 1984), 50–72.

Lewicki, Steff, "Feminism and Science Fiction," *Foundation* 32 (1984), 45–59.

Lopez de Aberasturi, Antonio, "Pour une lecture de Cerdá: Introduction à La Théorie générale de l'urbanisation," in Cerdá (1979), 13–65.

Lord, M.G., "Pornutopia: How Feminists Learned to Love Dirty Pictures," *Lingua Franca* 7/4 (1997), 40–48.

The Love Bug, Robert Stevenson, dir. (Walt Disney Productions, 1968) [film]

Lukacs, Georg, *The Theory of the Novel* (Boston, MA: MIT Press, 1971).

Tim Luke, "Culture and Politics in the Age of Artificial Negativity," *Telos* 35 (Spring 1978), 56–72.

Lynn, Elizabeth, *Dancers of Arun (The Chronicles of Tornor Book 2)* (New York: Ace, 1979).

———, *The Northern Girl (The Chronicles of Tornor Book 3)* (New York: Ace, 1980).

MacBean, James Roy, *Film and Revolution* (Bloomington: Indiana University Press, 1975).

MacCabe, Colin, *Godard: Images, Sounds, Politics* (Bloomington: Indiana University Press, 1980).

Macdonald, Andrew (pseud. William Pierce), *The Turner Diaries* (Arlington, VA: National Vanguard Books, 1987).

Mad Max, George Miller, dir. (MGM Studios, 1979) [film].

Mad Max Beyond Thunderdome, George Miller, dir. (Warner Brothers, 1985) [film].

Mailloux, Steven, *Interpretive Conventions* (Ithaca, NY: Cornell University Press, 1982).

Manuel, Frank E., "Toward a Psychological History of Utopia," in Manuel (1996), 69–98.

———, *Utopias and Utopian Thought* (Boston, MA: Houghton Mifflin, 1966).

Marcuse, Herbert, *An Essay on Liberation* (Boston, MA: Beacon Press, 1969).

———, *Eros and Civilization* (Boston, MA: Beacon Press, 1955).

———, *One-Dimensional Man* (Boston, MA: Beacon Press, 1964).

Markovits, Andrei S., and Steven L. Hellerman, *Offside: Soccer and American Exceptionalism* (Princeton, NJ: Princeton University Press, 2001).

Maroney, Heather Jon, "Embracing Motherhood: New Feminist Theory," *Canadian Journal of Political and Social Theory* 9 (1985), 40–64.

Marx, Karl, and Friedrich Engels, "Manifesto of the Communist Party," in Lewis Feuer, ed., *Basic Writings of Marx and Engels* (New York: Anchor, 1959).

———, *Selected Works* (Moscow: Progress, 1968).

———, *The German Ideology*, ed. C.J. Arthur (New York: International Publishers, 1970).

Marx-Scouras, Danielle, *The Cultural Politics of Tel Quel: Literature and the Left in the Wake of Engagement* (University Park: Pennsylvania State University Press, 1996).

Massé, Michelle, "'All You Have to Do Is Know What You Want': Individual Expectations in *Triton*," in Slusser et al. (1983), 49–64.

McCaffrey, Larry, ed., *Storming the Reality Studio: A Casebook of Cyberpunk and Postmodern Science Fiction* (Durham, NC: Duke University Press, 1991).

McCormak, Thelma, "Making Sense of the Research on Pornography," in Burstyn (1985), 181–205.

McKillip, Patricia, *Riddle-Master: The Complete Trilogy* (New York: Ace Books, 1999).

McNelis, James I., "Introduction," in *Ludvig Holberg, the Journey of Niels Klim to the World Underground* (Lincoln: University of Nebraska Press, 2004), vii–xxvii.

McQuarie, Donald, "Utopia and Transcendence: An Analysis of Their Decline in Contemporary Science Fiction," *Journal of Popular Culture* 14 (1980), 242–250.

Merril, Judith, *Daughters of Earth: Three Novels* (Garden City, NY: Doubleday, 1969).

———, *Survival Ship and Other Stories* (Toronto, ON: Kakabeka, 1973).

———, "That Only a Mother," *Astounding Science Fiction* (June 1948), 88–95.

———, *The Best of Judith Merril* (New York: Warner Books, 1976).

———, "What Do You Mean: Science? Fiction?," in Thomas Clareson, ed., *SF: The Other Side of Realism* (Bowling Green, OH: Bowling Green University Press, 1971), 53–95.

Messac, Regis, "Voyages modernes au centre de la terre," *Revue de Littérature comparée* (1929), 74–104.

Miller, Casey, and Kate Swift, *The Handbook of Non-Sexist Writing* (London: Women's Press, 1981).

Miller, Donald, *Lewis Mumford Reader* (Athens: University of Georgia Press, 1995).

Miller, Douglas T., and Marion Nowak, *The Fifties: The Way We Really Were* (Garden City, NY: Doubleday, 1977).

Miller, Mark Crispin, "The Crushing Power of Big Publishing," *The Nation* 264/10 (March 17, 1997).

Miller, Walter M., Jr., *A Canticle for Liebowitz* (New York: Bantam, 1959).

Mogen, David, *Wilderness Visions: The Western Theme in Science Fiction Literature* (San Bernardino, CA: Borgo, 1994).

More, Thomas, *Utopia*, ed., intro. and trans. Paul Turner (London: Penguin, 1984).

Morris, William, *Three Works*, ed. A.L. Morton (London: Lawrence & Wishart, 1977).

Moylan, Tom, *Demand the Impossible: Science Fiction and the Utopian Imagination* (New York: Methuen, 1986).

———, "Ideological Contradiction in Clarke's *The City and the Stars*," *Science Fiction Studies* 4/2 (1977), 150–157.

———, "Introduction: Jameson and Utopia," *Utopian Studies* 9/2 (1998), 1–8.

———, *Scraps of the Untainted Sky: Science Fiction, Utopia, Dystopia* (Boulder, CO: Westview, 2000).

———, "The Locus of Hope: Utopia Versus Ideology," *Science Fiction Studies* 9/2 (1982), 159–167.

Mullen, R.D., and Darko Suvin, ed., *Science-Fiction Studies, Second Series: Selected Articles on Science Fiction 1976–1977* (Boston, MA: Gregg Press, 1978).

Mulvey, Laura, "Visual Pleasures and Narrative Cinema," *Screen* 16/3 (1975), 6–18.

Munt, Sally, ed., *New Lesbian Criticism: Literary and Cultural Readings* (Toronto, ON: Harvester/Wheatsheaf, 1992).

Nagl, Manfred, "The Science Fiction Film in Historical Perspective," *Science Fiction Studies* 31 (1983), 262–277.

Ne'eman, Judd. "The Death Mask of the Moderns: A Genealogy of 'New Sensibility' Cinema in Israel," *Israel Studies* 4/1 (Spring 1999), 100–128.

Negley, Glenn, and J. Max Patrick, eds., *The Quest for Utopia: An Anthology of Imaginary Societies* (New York: Henry Schumann, 1952).

Nilsson, Sten, *The New Capitals of India, Pakistan and Bangladesh*, Scandinavian Institute of Asian Studies Monograph 12 (London: Curzon, 1973).

Niven, Larry, and Jerry Pournelle, *Oath of Fealty* (New York: Pocket, 1982).

No Blade of Grass, Cornel Wilde, dir. (Theodora Productions, 1970) [film].

Norman, John, *Hunters of Gor* (New York: Daw, 1974).

———, "How Far Is Too Far? An Open Letter from John Norman," *The New York Review of Science Fiction* 83 (July 1995), 1, 10–15.

———, *Imaginative Sex* (New York: Daw, 1974).

Ockman, Joan, ed., *Architecture, Criticism, Ideology* (Princeton, NJ: Princeton Architectural Press, 1985).

Olander, Joseph, and Martin Harry Greenberg, eds., *Philip K. Dick* (New York: Taplinger, 1983).

On the Beach, Stanley Kramer, dir. (Stanley Kramer Productions, 1959) [film].

Orth, Michael, "Reefs on the Right: Fascist Politics in Contemporary American Libertarian Utopias," *Extrapolation* 31 (1990), 293–316.

Paludan, Julius, *Om Holbergs Niels Klim, med sæligt hensyn til tidligere satirer i Form af opdigtede og vidunderlige reiser* (Copenhagen: Wilhelm Priors, 1878).

Panic in Year Zero!, Roger Corman, dir. (Roger Corman Productions, 1962) [film].

Parish, James Robert, and Michael R. Pitts, eds., *The Great Science Fiction Pictures* (Metuchen, NJ: Scarecrow Press, 1977).

Parrinder, Patrick, ed., *Learning from Other Worlds: Estrangement, Cognition, and the Politics of Science Fiction and Utopia* (Liverpool: Liverpool: University Press, 2000).

———, ed., *Science Fiction: A Critical Guide* (New York: Longman, 1979).

Pearson, Carol, "Coming Home: Four Feminist Utopias and Patriarchal Experience," in Barr (1981), 63–70.

Pearson, Wendy, "After the (Homo)Sexual: A Queer Analysis of Anti-Sexuality in Sheri S. Tepper's *The Gate to Woman's Country*," *Science-Fiction Studies* 69 (1996), 199–226.

Pells, Richard H., *The Liberal Mind in a Conservative Age: American Intellectuals in the 1940s and 1950s* (New York: Harper & Row, 1985).

Peters, Sigrid Ludvig, *Holbergs Menippeische Satire: Das 'Iter subterraneum' und seine Beziehungen zur antiken Literatur* (Frankfurt: Peter Lang, 1987).

Petras, James, "Europe's Counterfeit Reformists," *New Left Review* 146 (July–August 1984), 37–52.

Pfaelzer, Jean, "The Impact of Political Theory on Narrative Structures," in Roemer (1981), 117–132.

———, *The Utopian Novel in America, 1886–1896* (Pittsburgh, PA: University of Pittsburgh, 1984).

———, "What Happened to History?," in Jones & Goodwin (1990), 191–200.

Phillips, Anne, ed., *Feminism and Equality* (New York: New York University Press, 1987).

Piccone, Paul, "The Crisis of One Dimensionality," *Telos* 35 (Spring 1978), 43–54.

Piercy, Marge, *Dance the Eagle to Sleep* (Garden City, NY: Doubleday, 1970).

———, *He, She and It* (New York: Knopf, 1991).

———, *Woman on the Edge of Time* (New York: Fawcett Crest: Books, 1976).

Pines, Jim, and Paul Willemen, eds., *Questions of Third Cinema* (London: British Film Institute, 1989).

Planet of the Apes, Franklin J. Schaffner, dir. (APJAC Productions, 1968) [film].

Plank, Robert, "The Modern Shrunken Utopia," in Roemer (1981), 206–230.

Platt, Charles, "Two Kinds of Censorship," *Interzone* 25 (1988), 49–50.

Poe, Edgar Allan, *The Complete Tales and Poems of Edgar Allan Poe* (New York: Modern Library, 1938).

Pohl, Frederik, and C. M Kornbluth, *The Space Merchants* (New York: Ballantine Books, 1953).

Pordzik, Ralph, *The Quest for Postcolonial Utopia: A Comparative Introduction to the Utopian Novel in the New English Literatures* (New York: Peter Lang, 2001).

Portelli, Alessandro, "The Three Laws of Robotics," *Science Fiction Studies* 7 (1980), 150–156.

Prakash, Vikramditya, *Chandigarh's Le Corbusier: The Struggle for Modernity in Postcolonial India* (Seattle: University of Washington Press, 2002).

Rabkin, Eric S., "Science Fiction Women Before Liberation," in Barr (1981), 9–25.

Rabkin, Eric S., Martin Harry Greenberg, and Joseph D. Olander, eds., *The End of the World*, (Carbondale: Southern Illinois University Press, 1983).

Ragot, Gilles, and Mathilde Dion, *Le Corbusier en France. Projets et réalisations* (Paris: Le Moniteur, 1997).

Rand, Ayn, *Atlas Shrugged* (New York: Random House, 1957).

Raspail, Jean, *The Camp of the Saints* (New York: Scribner, 1975).

Reich, Wilhelm, *Sex-Pol: Essays, 1929–1934* (New York: Vintage Books, 1972).

"Review of Caryl Flinn, *Strains of Utopia*," *The Chronicle of Higher Education* (July 15, 1992), A9.

"Review of Jost Hermand's *Der Alte Traum Vom Neuen Reich: Volkische Utopien Und Nationalsozialismus*," *Utopian Studies* 1/1 (1990), 137–140.

Rhodes, Jewell Parker, "Ursula Le Guin's *Left Hand of Darkness*: Androgyny and the Feminist Utopia," in Barr & Smith (1983), 108–120.

Rich, Adrienne, "Compulsory Heterosexuality and Lesbian Experience," in Snitow et al. (1983), 177–205.

———, *Of Woman Born: Motherhood as Experience and Institution* (New York: W.W. Norton, 1976).

Richards, Jeffrey, *Visions of Yesterday* (London: RKP, 1973).

The Road Warrior, George Miller, dir. (Kennedy Miller Productions, 1981) [film].

Roberge, Gaston, *Another Cinema for Another Society* (Calcutta, India: Seagull, 1985).

Robert, Heinlein, *The Moon Is a Harsh Mistress* (New York: Berkeley, 1968).

Robinson, Christopher, *Lucian and His Influence in Europe* (London: Duckworth, 1979).

Robinson, Kim Stanley, *Blue Mars* (New York: Harper Collins, 1996).
———, *Green Mars* (New York: Harper Collins, 1993).
———, *Red Mars* (New York: Harper Collins, 1992).
———, *The Novels of Philip K. Dick* (Ann Arbor, MI: UMI Research Press, 1983).
RoboCop, Paul Verhoeven, dir. (Orion Pictures, 1987) [film].
Rodowick, D.N., *The Crisis of Political Modernism: Criticism and Ideology in Contemporary Film Theory* (Urbana: University of Illinois Press, 1988).
Roemer, Kenneth, ed., *America as Utopia* (New York: Burt Franklin, 1981).
———, "Petition for an MLA Discussion Group in Science Fiction, Utopian, and Fantastic Literature," Internal document, Modern Language Association, 20 February 1997.
Rohrlich, Ruby, and Elaine Hoffman Baruch, eds., *Women in Search of Utopia: Mavericks and Mythmakers* (New York: Schocken, 1984).
Ross, Andrew, *No Respect: Intellectuals and Popular Culture* (New York: Routledge, 1989).
———, *Strange Weather: Culture, Science, and Technology in the Age of Limits* (London: Verso, 1996).
———, *The Celebration Chronicles: Life, Liberty, and the Pursuit of Property Value in Disney's New Town* (New York: Ballantine, 1999).
Ross, Ellen, and Rayna Rapp, "Sex and Society: A Research Note from Social History and Anthropology," in Snitow et al. (1983), 51–73.
Rossel, Sven Hakon, *Holberg: A European Writer* (Amsterdam: Rodopi, 1994).
Rowe, Mary W., *Toronto: Considering Self-Government* (Toronto, ON: Ginger Press, 2000).
Ruppert, Peter, *Reader in a Strange Land: The Activity of Reading Literary Utopias* (Athens: University of Georgia Press, 1986).
Russ, Joanna, "Amor Vincit Foeminam: The Battle of the Sexes in SF," *Science Fiction Studies* 7 (1980), 2–15.
———, *How to Suppress Women's Writing* (Austin: University of Texas Press, 1983).
———, "Recent Feminist Utopias," in Barr (1981), 71–85.
———, "Reflections on Science Fiction: An Interview with Joanna Russ," *Quest* 2 (1975), 40–49.
———, "SF and Technology and Mystification," *Science Fiction Studies* 5 (1978), 250–260.
———, "*The Dispossessed*," *The Magazine of Fantasy and Science Fiction* (1975b), 41–44.
———, *The Female Man* (New York: Bantam, 1975a).
———, "The Image of Women in Science Fiction," in Susan Koppelman Cornillon, ed., *Images of Women in Fiction: Feminist Perspectives* (Bowling Green, OH: Bowling Green University Press, 1972), 79–94.

———, *We Who Are About To …* (New York: Dell, 1977).

Ruthven, Kenneth K., *Feminist Literary Studies: An Introduction* (Cambridge: Cambridge University Press, 1986).

Salmonson, Jessica Amanda, "Letter," *New York Review of Science Fiction* 96 (1996), 20–22.

Sammon, Paul, "The Making of *Blade Runner*," *Cinefantastique* 12/5&6 (1982), 20–47.

Sargent, Lyman Tower, "Australian Utopian Literature: An Annotated, Chronological Bibliography, 1667–1999," *Utopian Studies* 10/2 (1999), 138–173.

———, *British and American Utopian Literature, 1516–1985: An Annotated, Chronological Bibliography*, Garland Reference Library of the Humanities, vol. 831 (New York: Garland, 1988).

———, "Capitalist Eutopias in America," in Roemer (1981), 192–205.

———, "Eutopias and Dystopias in Science Fiction: 1950–75," in Roemer (1981), 347–366.

———, "Political Dimensions of Utopianism, with Special Reference to American Communitarianism" (Unpublished paper, 1990).

———, "The Three Faces of Utopianism," *Minnesota Review* 7/4 (1967), 222–231.

———, "The Three Faces of Utopianism Revisited," *Utopian Studies* 5/1 (1994), 1–37.

———, "Utopian Literature and Communitarian Experiments before Bellamy," *American Transcendental Quarterly* 3/1 (1989), 135–146.

———, "Utopian Literature in English Canada: An Annotated, Chronological Bibliography, 1852–1999," *Utopian Studies* 10/2 (1999b), 174–206.

———, "Utopianism and the Creation of New Zealand National Identity," *Utopian Studies* 12/1 (2001), 1–18.

Sargent, Pamela, ed., *More Women of Wonder: Science Fiction Novelettes by Women about Women* (New York: Vintage Books, 1976).

———, *The Shore of Women* (New York: Bantam, 1986).

———, ed., *Women of Wonder: Science Fiction Stories by Women about Women* (New York: Vintage Books, 1974).

Sartre, Jean-Paul, *What Is Literature?*, trans. Bernard Frechtman (London: Methuen, 1983).

Sayers, Sohnya, Anders Stephanson, Stanley Aronowitz, and Fredric Jameson, eds., *The Sixties, Without Apology* (Minneapolis: University of Minnesota Press, 1984).

Schaer, Roland, Gregory Claeys, and Lyman Tower Sargent, eds., *Utopia: The Search for the Ideal Society in the Western World* (New York: New York Public Library/ Oxford University Press, 2000).

Schneekloth, Lynda, "Unredeemably Utopian: Architecture and Making/Unmaking the World," *Utopian Studies* 9/1 (1998), 1–25.

Scholes, Robert, and Eric S. Rabkin, *Science Fiction: History, Science, Vision* (New York: Oxford University Press, 1977).

"Science Fiction by Women [Special Issue]," intro. Veronica Hollinger, *Science Fiction Studies* 51 (1990).

Sedgewick, Cristina, "The Fork in the Road: Can Science Fiction Survive in Postmodern, Megacorporate America?," *Science Fiction Studies* 53 (1991), 11–52.

Segal, Howard P., "Utopia Diversified: 1900–1949," in Roemer (1981), 333–346.

Serceau, Michel, ed., "60–80: Vingt ans d'utopies au cinéma," *CinémAction* 25 (1983).

Shelton, Robert, "The Utopian Film Genre: Putting Shadows on the Silver Screen," *Utopian Studies* 4/2 (1993), 18–25.

Shibley, Robert, "The Complete New Urbanism and the Partial Practices of Placemaking," *Utopian Studies* 9/1 (1998), 80–103.

Shippey, T.A., "The Cold War in Science Fiction, 1940–1960," in Parrinder (1979), 90–109.

Shklar, Judith, "The Political Theory of Utopia: From Melancholy to Nostalgia," in Manuel (1996), 101–115.

Silverberg, Robert, ed., *The Science Fiction Hall of Fame, Volume One, 1929–1964* (New York: Avon Books, 1971).

Simak, Clifford D., *City* (New York: Gnome Press, 1952).

Skinner, B.F., "Utopia as an Experimental Culture," in Roemer (1981), 28–42.

———, *Walden Two* (Indianapolis: Hackett Publishing, 1948).

Slonczewski, Joan, *The Door into Ocean* (New York: Avon, 1986).

Slusser, George E., Eric S. Rabkin, and Robert Scholes, eds., *Coordinates: Placing Science Fiction and Fantasy* (Carbondale: Southern Illinois University Press, 1983).

Smith, Curtis C., "The Books of Olaf Stapledon," *Science Fiction Studies* 1 (1974), 297–299.

Smith, David Alexander, "No More Gor: A Conversation with John Norman," *New York Review of Science Fiction* 92 (1996), 1, 4–7.

Smith, L. Neil, *The Probability Broach* (New York: Ballantine, 1980).

Snitow, Ann, Christine Stansell, and Sharon Thompson, eds., *Powers of Desire: The Politics of Sexuality* (New York: Monthly Review Press, 1983).

Sobchack, Vivian, *Screening Space: The American Science Fiction Film* (New York: Ungar, 1987); 2nd, enl. ed. (New Brunswick, NJ: Rutgers University Press, 1997).

Sobel, Alan, *Pornography: Marxism, Feminism, and the Future of Sexuality* (New Haven, CT: Yale University Press, 1986).

Solanas, Fernando, and Octavio Getino, "Toward a Third Cinema," *Cineaste* 4 (Winter 1970–1971), 3–12.

Sontag, Susan, "The Imagination of Disaster," in *Against Interpretation, and Other Essays* (New York: Picador U.S.A, 2001), 209–225.
St. Clair, David James, *The Motorization of American Cities* (New York: Praeger, 1986).
Stanton, William, *The Great United States Exploring Expedition of 1838–1842* (Berkeley: University of California Press, 1975).
Stapledon, Olaf, *Last and First Men* (London: Gollancz, 1999).
———, *Sirius* (United Kingdom: Methuen, 1944).
———, *Star Maker and First Men* (New York: Dover, 1937).
Stapleford, Brian, "Notes towards a sociology of Science Fiction," *Foundation* 15 (January 1979), 28–41.
Star Trek, Gene Roddenberry, creator (Desilu Productions, 1966–1969) [TV series].
Star Wars, George Lucas, dir. (Lucasfilm, 1977) [film].
Staton, Mary, *From the Legend of Biel* (New York: Ace Books, 1976).
Stern, Michael, "Making Culture into Nature; or, Who Put the 'special' into 'special Effects'?," *Science Fiction Studies* 7 (1980), 263–269.
Stillman, Peter G., "Recent Studies in the History of Utopian Thought: A Review Essay," *Utopian Studies* 1/1 (1990), 103–110.
Strick, Philip, "The Age of the Replicant," *Sight and Sound* 51 (1982), 168–172.
Stryker, Cirio H. Santiago, dir. (Cinema Vehicle Services, 1983) [film].
Sturgeon, Theodore, *Venus Plus X* (New York: Blue Jay, 1984).
Sutcliffe, Anthony, "A Vision of Utopia: Optimistic Foundations of Le Corbusier's Doctrine d'urbanisme," in Walden (1977), 216–243.
Suvin, Darko, "Artifice as Refuge and World View: Philip K. Dick's Foci," in Greenberg & Olander (1983), 73–95.
———, *Metamorphoses of Science Fiction: On the Poetics and History of a Literary Genre* (New Haven, CT: Yale University Press, 1979).
———, "On the Poetics of the Science Fiction Genre," *College English* 34 (1972), 372–383.
———, "Radical Rhapsody and Romantic Recoil in the Age of Anticipation," *Science Fiction Studies* 1/4 (1974) 255–269.
———, "Victorian Science Fiction, 1871–85: The Rise of the Alternative History Sub-Genre," *Science Fiction Studies* 10/2 (1983), 148–169.
Swift, Jonathan, *Gulliver's Travels. Norton Critical Edition*, ed. Robert Greenberg (New York: Norton, 1970).
Talk Radio, Oliver Stone, dir. (Cineplex Odeon Films, 1988) [film].
Tan, Cecilia, ed., *S/M Futures: Erotica on the Edge* (Boston, MA: Circlet Press, 1995).
———, *Forged Bonds: Erotic Tales of High Fantasy* (Boston, MA: Circlet Press, 1993).
———, *Selling Venus: Futuristic Tales of the Age Old Tradition of Exchanging Sex for Money* (Boston, MA: Circlet Press, 1997).
———, *TechnoSex: Cyber Age Erotica* (Boston, MA: Circlet Press, 1993).

———, *Telepaths Don't Need Safewords* (Boston, MA: Circlet Press, 1992).

———, *Wired Hard: Erotica for a Gay Universe* (Boston, MA: Circlet Press, 1994).

———, *Worlds of Women: Sapphic Science Fiction Erotica* (Boston, MA: Circlet Press, 1993).

Telotte, J.P., "Human Artifice and the Science Fiction Film," *Film Quarterly* 36 (1982), 44–51.

Tepper, Sheri, *The Gate to Women's Country* (New York: Bantam, 1989).

Terminator, James Cameron, dir. (Hemdale, 1984) [film].

Thelma McCormak, "Making Sense of the Research on Pornography," in Burstyn (1985), 181–205.

Things to Come, William Cameron Menzies, dir. (London Film Productions, 1936) [film].

Thorne, Barrie, Cheris Kramarae, and Nancy Henley, "Imagining a Different World of Talk," in Rohrlich & Baruch (1984), 180–188.

Tiptree, James, Jr., *Houston, Houston, Do You Read?* [1976], *The Science Fiction Book Club Collection* (Garden City, NY: Doubleday Book & Music Clubs, 1996).

The Time Machine, George Pal, dir. (George Pal Productions, 1960) [film].

Total Recall, Paul Verhoeven, dir. (Carolco Pictures, 1990) [film].

Trousson, Raymond, *Voyages aux pays de nulle part: Histoire littéraire de la pensée utopique* (Brussells: Editions de l'Université de Bruxelles, 1975).

Ullam, Adam, "Socialism and Utopia," in Manuel (1996), 116–134.

The Ultimate Warrior, Robert Clouse, dir. (Warner Brothers, 1975) [film].

Urwin, Cathy, "Power Relations and the Emergence of Language," in Henriques et al. (1984), 264–311.

Vaihinger, Hans, *The Philosophy of "As If": A System of the Theoretical, Practical and Religious Fictions of Mankind* (Mansfiend Center, CT: Martino, 2009).

Vairasse, Denis, *Histoire des Sévarambes* (Amiens, France: Encrage, 1994).

Vale, V., and Andrea Juno, eds., "Incredibly Strange Films," *Re/Search* 10 (San Francisco, CA: Re/Search Publications, 1986).

Vance, Carole S., ed., *Pleasure and Danger: Exploring Female Sexuality* (Boston, MA: Routledge and Kegan Paul, 1984).

Vance, Jack, *The Dying Earth* (New York: Pocket Books, 1977).

Vandermeer, John, "Hardin's Lifeboat Adrift," *Science for the People* 8/1 (1976), 16–19.

Verne, Jules, *Voyage au centre de la terre. Avec une Introduction de Simone Vierne*, intro. Simone Vierne (Paris: Garnier-Flarnmarion, 1977).

Versins, Pierre, *Encyclopédie de l'utopie et de la science fiction* (Lausanne, Switzerland: L'Age d'Homme, 1972).

Vogel, Amos, *Film as a Subversive Art* (New York: Random House, 1974).

Von Moos, Stanislaus, "The Politics of The Open Hand: Notes on Le Corbusier and Nehru at Chandigarh," in Walden (1977), 412–457.

Vonarburg, Élisabeth, "Letter," *New York Review of Science Fiction* 85 (September 1995), 22–23.
Wagar, Warren, "Utopian Studies and Utopian Thought: Definitions and Horizons," *Extrapolation* 19 (1977), 4–12.
Walden, Russell, ed., *The Open Hand: Essays on Le Corbusier* (Cambridge, MA: MIT Press, 1977).
Walsh, Chad, *From Utopia to Nightmare* (New York: Harper & Row, 1962).
Walter, William Grey, *The Curve of the Snowflake* (New York: W.W. Norton, 1956).
The War Game, Peter Watkins, dir. (BBC, 1966) [film].
Warrick, Patricia, *The Cybernetic Imagination in Science Fiction* (Cambridge, MA: MIT Press, 1980).
Warrick, Patricia, and Martin Greenberg, eds., *Robots, Androids, and Mechanical Oddities: The Science Fiction of Philip K. Dick [Stories]* (Carbondale: Southern Illinois University Press, 1984).
Watson, Ian, *The Embedding* (London: Orion, 2018).
Wegner, Phil, *Imaginary Communities: Utopia, the Nation, and the Spatial Histories of Modernity* (Berkeley: University of California Press, 2002).
Welcher, Jeanne K., ed., *Gulliveriana VIII: An Annotated List of Gulliveriana, 1721–1800*, (Gainesville, FL: Scholars' Facsimiles and Reprints, 1988).
Westfahl, Gary, "The Popular Tradition of Science Fiction Criticism, 1926–1980," *Science Fiction Studies* 26/2 (1999), 187–212.
Westworld, Michael Crichton, dir. (Metro-Goldwyn-Meyer, 1973) [film].
Whitaker, Reg, "Fighting the Cold War on the Home Front: America, Britain, Australia and Canada," in Ralph Miliband, John Savile, and Marcel Liebman, eds., *The Socialist Register* (London: Merlin Press, 1984), 23–67.
White, T.H., *The Once and Future King* (New York: Ace Books, 2008).
Widdicombe, Richard Toby, "Early Histories of Utopian Thought (to 1950)," *Utopian Studies*, 3/1 (1992), 1–38.
Williams, Linda, *Hard Core: Power, Pleasure and the "Frenzy of the Visible,"* (Berkeley: University of California Press, 1989).
Williams, Raymond, "Utopia and Science Fiction," in *Problems in Materialism and Culture* (London: Verso, 1980), 196–212.
Wingrove, David, ed., *The Science Fiction Film Source Book* (Harlow, Essex: Longman, 1985).
Wittig, Monique, *Les guérillères* (Paris: Les Éditions de Minuit, 2003).
Wolfe, Gary, "*He, She and It*, Marge Piercy [review]," *Locus* (January 1992), 29–30.
———, "The Remaking of Zero: Beginning at the End," in Rabkin et al. (1983), 1–19.
Wolfe, Tom, *From Bauhaus to Our House* (New York: Farrar Straus Giroux, 1981).
Wood, Robin, "An Introduction to the American Horror Film," in R. Wood et al., eds., *American Nightmare* (Toronto, ON: Festival of Festivals, 1979), 7–28.
Zamyatin, Yevgeny, *We*, trans. Gregory Zilboorg (New York: E. P. Dutton, 1924).

Index

Ralahine Utopian Studies

Ralahine Utopian Studies is the publishing project of the Ralahine Centre for Utopian Studies at the University of Limerick in association with the University of Bologna, the University of Cyprus, the University of Florida and the University of Maine.

The series publishes high-quality scholarship that addresses the theory and practice of utopianism (including Anglophone, continental European and indigenous and postcolonial traditions, and contemporary and historical periods). Publications (in English and other European languages) include original monographs and essay collections (including theoretical, textual and ethnographic/institutional research), English-language translations of utopian scholarship in other national languages, reissues of classic scholarly works that are out of print and annotated editions of original utopian literary and other texts (including translations).

While the series editors seek work that engages with the current scholarship and debates in the field of utopian studies, they will not privilege any particular critical or theoretical orientation. They welcome submissions by established or emerging scholars working within or outside the academy. Given the multilingual and interdisciplinary remit of the series, the editors especially welcome comparative studies in any disciplinary or transdisciplinary framework.

Those interested in contributing to the series are invited to submit a detailed project outline to one of the series editors listed below.

Email queries can also be sent to ireland@peterlang.com.

Series editors:
Raffaella Baccolini (University of Bologna)
Antonis Balasopoulos (University of Cyprus)
Joachim Fischer (University of Limerick)
Michael J. Griffin (University of Limerick)
Naomi Jacobs (University of Maine)
Michael G. Kelly (University of Limerick)
Tom Moylan (University of Limerick)
Phillip E. Wegner (University of Florida)

Ralahine Centre for Utopian Studies, University of Limerick
http://www3.ul.ie/ralahinecentre/

Volume 1 **Tom Moylan and Raffaella Baccolini (eds): Utopia Method Vision. The Use Value of Social Dreaming. 343 pages. 2007. ISBN 978-3-03910-912-8**

Volume 2 Michael J. Griffin and Tom Moylan (eds):
Exploring the Utopian Impulse. Essays on Utopian Thought and Practice.
434 pages. 2007. 408 pages. 2015. ISBN 978-3-03910-913-5

Volume 3 Ruth Levitas:
The Concept of Utopia. (Ralahine Classic)
280 pages. 2010. ISBN 978-3-03911-366-8

Volume 4 Vincent Geoghegan:
Utopianism and Marxism. (Ralahine Classic)
189 pages. 2008. ISBN 978-3-03910-137-5

Volume 5 Barbara Goodwin and Keith Taylor:
The Politics of Utopia. A Study in Theory and Practice. (Ralahine Classic)
341 pages. 2009. ISBN 978-3-03911-080-3

Volume 6 Darko Suvin:
Defined by a Hollow. Essays on Utopia, Science Fiction and Political Epistemology. (Ralahine Reader)
616 pages. 2010. ISBN 978-3-03911-403-0

Volume 7 Andrew Milner (ed.):
Tenses of Imagination. Raymond Williams on Science Fiction, Utopia and Dystopia. (Ralahine Reader)
253 pages. 2010. ISBN 978-3-03911-826-7

Volume 8 Nathaniel Coleman (ed.):
Imagining and Making the World. Reconsidering Architecture and Utopia.
393 pages. 2011. ISBN 978-3-0343-0120-6

Volume 9 Henry Near:
Where Community Happens. The Kibbutz and the Philosophy of Communalism.
256 pages. 2011. ISBN 978-3-0343-0133-6

Volume 10 Robert C. Elliott:
The Shape of Utopia. Studies in a Literary Genre.
Edited with an Introduction by Phillip E. Wegner. (Ralahine Classic)
170 pages. 2013. ISBN 978-3-0343-0772-7

Volume 11 Michael E. Gardiner:
Weak Messianism. Essays in Everyday Utopianism.
284 pages. 2013. ISBN 978-3-0343-0716-1

Volume 12 Matthew Beaumont:
The Spectre of Utopia. Utopian and Science Fictions at the *Fin de Siècle*.
319 pages. 2012. ISBN 978-3-0343–0725-3

Volume 13 Artur Blaim:
Gazing in Useless Wonder. English Utopian Fictions, 1516–1800.
366 pages. 2013. ISBN 978-3-0343-0899-1

Volume 14 Tom Moylan:
Demand the Impossible. Science Fiction and the Utopian Imagination.
Edited by Raffaella Baccolini. (Ralahine Classic)
358 pages. 2014. ISBN 978-3-0343-0752-9

Volume 15 Phillip E. Wegner:
Shockwaves of Possibility. Essays on Science Fiction, Globalization, and Utopia.
328 pages. 2014. ISBN 978-3-0343-0741-3

Volume 16 Angelika Bammer:
Partial Visions. Feminism and Utopianism in the 1970s.
(Ralahine Classic)
408 pages. 2015. ISBN 978-3-0343-0897-7

Volume 17 Edward K. Chan:
The Racial Horizon of Utopia. Unthinking the Future of Race in Late Twentieth-Century American Utopian Novels.
226 pages. 2016. ISBN 978-3-0343-1916-4

Volume 18 Darko Suvin:
Metamorphoses of Science Fiction. On the Poetics and History of a Literary Genre.
Edited by Gerry Canavan. (Ralahine Classic)
515 pages. 2016. ISBN 978-3-0343-1948-5

Volume 19 Michael S. Cummings:
Children's Voices in Politics.
536 pages. 2020. ISBN 978-3-0343-1943-0

Volume 20 Maïté Maskens and Ruy Blanes (eds):
Utopian Encounters. Anthropologies of Empirical Utopias. 248 pages. 2018. ISBN 978-1-78707-247-3

Volume 21 Peter Fitting (edited by Brian Greenspan, introduction by Fredric Jameson):
Utopian Effects, Dystopian Pleasures.
458 pages. 2021. ISBN 978-1-78874-353-2

www.ingramcontent.com/pod-product-compliance
Lightning Source LLC
Chambersburg PA
CBHW071732110726
47908CB00006B/1571

9781788743532